GLACIER
NATIONAL PARK

BECKY LOMAX

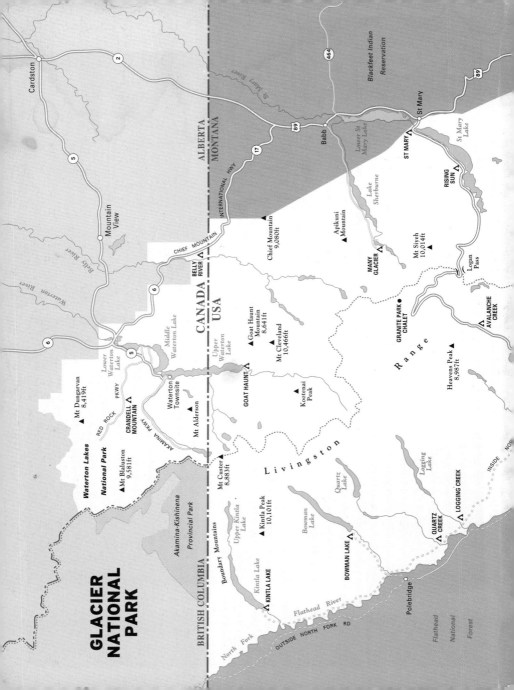

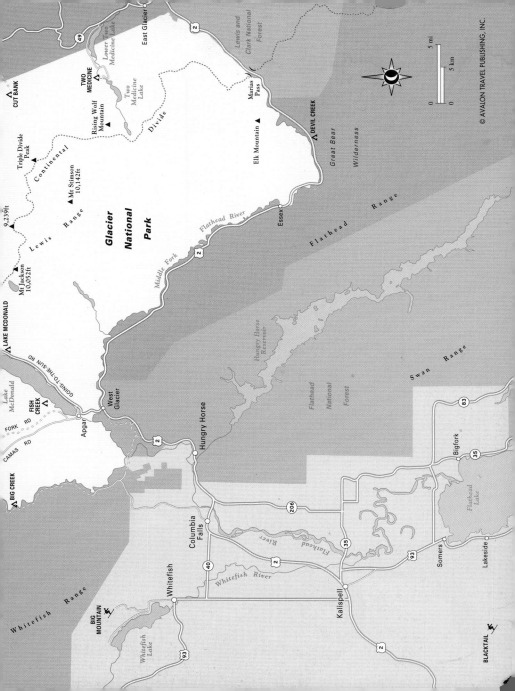

DISCOVER GLACIER NATIONAL PARK

Glacier National Park is the undisputed "Crown of the Continent." Its glaciers, tarns, and high meadowlands accent steep arêtes where mountain goats prance. Acres of parklands plunge down the Continental Divide's jagged pinnacles, exposing some of the world's oldest rock. Feeding North America's largest watersheds, winter snowfalls melt into rivers raging toward distant seas.

In this rugged country, grizzly bears and wolves make their homes in a rare intact ecosystem. Wolverines romp in high glacial cirques while bighorn sheep browse in alpine meadows. Columbian ground squirrels, pikas, and marmots shriek warning calls as golden eagles swoop low. Moose browse on pond weeds. Black bears forage for huckleberries. Mountain lions prowl for deer. Only two inhabitants present in Lewis and Clark's day are missing: woodland caribou and bison.

Hidden Lake Trail below Clements Peak at Logan Pass

Glacier National Park's one million acres (nearly 1,600 square miles) span the Continental Divide, the highest mountain range dividing Pacific from Atlantic waters. Giant watersheds here fuel major rivers: the Columbia, Missouri, and Saskatchewan. Nowhere is this watershed phenomenon more significant than Triple Divide Peak. Joining an elite few worldwide peaks, its summit, a hydrological apex, divides waters three ways, sending them into Hudson Bay, the Gulf of Mexico, and the Pacific Ocean.

At its lowest point, Glacier touches down at 3,150 feet on the Flathead River's confluence of the Middle and North Forks. From there, it soars over 7,000 feet to Mount Cleveland's 10,466-foot summit. Glacier's broad range of elevations is never so evident as when gazing on Cleveland's north face – one of the tallest vertical faces in the United States. Glacier's cliffs, arêtes, pinnacles, and horns shoot skyward with six peaks topping 10,000 feet.

Bisecting the park, historic Going-to-the-Sun Road climbs the Continental Divide. Along the Garden Wall, exploding with colorful wildflowers, the engineering marvel provides access to

heartleaf arnica

the high country for everyone. Tunnels, arches, and bridges lead visitors through precipices where no road seemingly could go. Every curve hears another intake of breath at the sights: Broad, glacially scooped valleys cascade rivers into mammoth lakes; even in August, snow clings to serrated peaks. Ice scouring abraded this world into a place where "wow" is never enough.

When summer rolls around, Going-to-the-Sun Road and Logan Pass all but burst their seams. Nearly two million visitors annually foray into the park, but surprisingly few leave the confines of the roads. For those who do, more than 700 trail miles snake up long valleys, shimmy beneath icy waterfalls, and crawl over high passes. Known as a hiker's park, Glacier sprinkles its mountains with paths for everyone, from wee toddlers to backpackers ready to pound down the miles. Setting foot in the backcountry unlocks the intricacies of glacial handiwork: moraines to moving ice, turquoise tarns to rock-strewn cirques.

On Glacier's western boundary, the North Fork of the Flathead River churns through a floodplain, rich with animal, plant, and bird

mountain goats, prominent alpine mammals at Gunsight Pass

life. The park's southern border roils with the Flathead River's Middle Fork. Both Wild and Scenic Rivers, their waters enrich habitat for wildlife and fish along with recreation.

On Glacier's east flank, the park shares a boundary line with Blackfeet Nation tribal lands. While Glacier served as a spiritual refuge for the Blackfeet — for sacred ceremonies, vision quests, and dances — tribal members left their cultural footprints on its face. Peaks, rivers, waterfalls, and lakes bear the stories of the Blackfeet in their names.

The 49th parallel dividing the U.S. from Canada marks Glacier's northern border, but this line hardly separates the 202-square-mile Waterton Lakes National Park from Glacier. With nary a thought to human-set boundaries, wildlife roams across the line, as do weather, geology, and flora. Humans, too; to access Glacier's remote northern sections, hikers cross through Canada's Waterton Lakes National Park. The separately managed parks protect one ecosystem larger than Delaware.

In 1931, Alberta and Montana Rotarians pioneered the world's

west side of Glacier's Continental Divide along the Garden Wall

© BECKY LOMAX

first peace park. In spite of the arbitrary international boundary, they recommended establishing Waterton-Glacier International Peace Park. A year later, both the U.S. Congress and Canada's Parliament designated the parks to serve as an example of peace. The International Peace Park celebrates the world's longest unde-fended border — 5,000 miles. Welcome to what is truly the "Crown of the Continent."

Scenic Point Trail at Two Medicine on Glacier's east side

© BECKY LOMAX

Contents

MAP CONTENTS

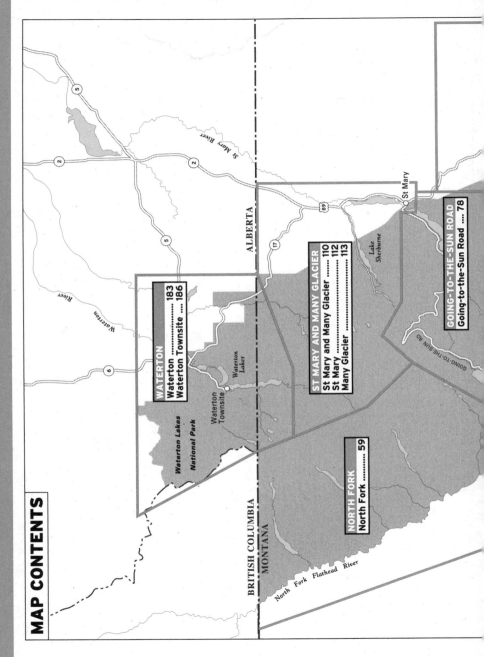

12

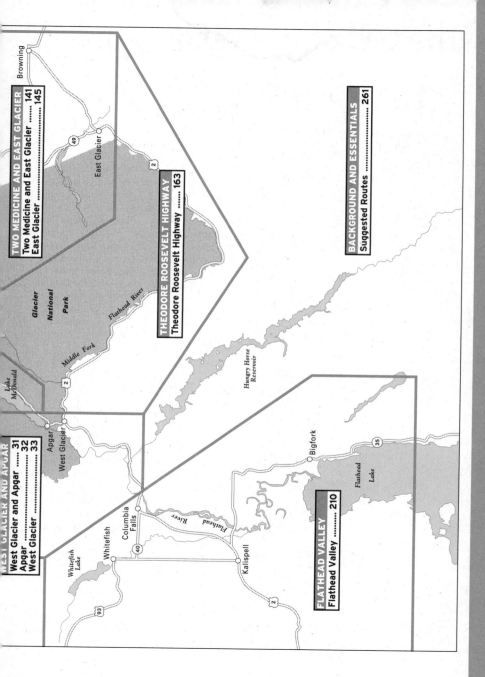

Browning

East Glacier

Glacier
National
Park

Lake
McDonald

Apgar
West Glacier

Middle Fork

Flathead River

Hungry Horse
Reservoir

Columbia
Falls

Flathead River

Whitefish
Lake

Whitefish

Kalispell

Bigfork

Flathead
Lake

The Lay of the Land

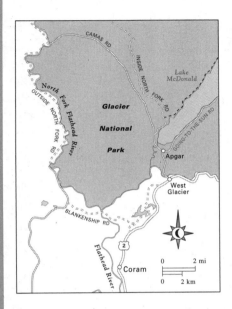

WEST GLACIER AND APGAR

Together, West Glacier and Apgar form the western portal to Glacier National Park. Two miles apart, divided by the Middle Fork of the Flathead River, the towns stir with activity in early June like a sleepy bear waking up from its winter nap. But by midsummer, a frenzy takes over as the pair serve as launch pads for river rafting, trail riding, fishing, kayaking, boating, hiking, backpacking, driving the historic **Going-to-the-Sun Road,** and going remote into the **North Fork.** Jointly, the towns have not only the largest campgrounds, but the most campgrounds of anywhere else in the park's vicinity. At the lowest elevations in the park, the area's beauty hangs in deep birch, hemlock, and cedar forests surrounding its Wild and Scenic Rivers and the largest of the park's waters—**Lake McDonald.**

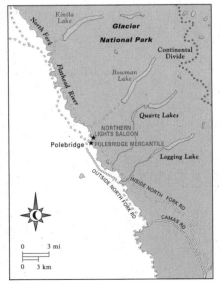

NORTH FORK

For those looking to escape the masses, the North Fork Valley is it. Remote, rugged, and, by modern standards, somewhat backwards, the North Fork is a haven for nighttime solitude serenaded by wolf howls in one of the park's most diverse animal habitats. Without electricity, **Polebridge Mercantile** and **Northern Lights Saloon** here function as welcome anachronisms in a technological world. Access is via dirt roads that some would deem too bad to travel but others relish for their sheer roughness. Definitely not for everyone, the North Fork kindles a spark in those who enjoy real rusticity rather than just the look of it. At Glacier's isolated northwest corner, **Bowman** and **Kintla Lakes** never feel crowded, even in high summer. And the trails that lead beyond venture into wild backcountry.

406
224 9392

GOING-TO-THE-SUN ROAD

By far the biggest attraction in the park, the 52-mile Going-to-the-Sun Road leads visitors into Glacier's rugged alpine country. Crossing the Continental Divide at **Logan Pass,** the road passes through thick cedar rainforests and subalpine wildflower meadows with the most diversity in its length than any other national park road. Glaciers, waterfalls, and mountain goats cling to its cliff faces. And in its ascending and descending miles, sometimes weather mutates from sun-laden summer to frigid winter and back again. It passes the park's two largest lakes—**St. Mary** and **McDonald,** the latter with historic **Lake McDonald Lodge** gracing its shore. A National Historic Landmark, Going-to-the-Sun Road stands peerless in America's scenic highways, but you'd better leave your fear of heights behind.

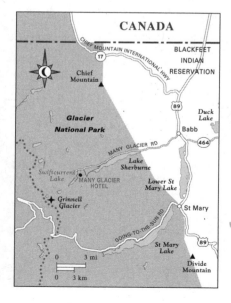

ST. MARY AND MANY GLACIER

The eastern gateways to Glacier, St. Mary and Many Glacier bridge national park lands and Blackfeet Nation tribal lands. A small seasonal enclave of campgrounds, lodges, cabins, groceries, cafes, and shops, St. Mary bustles in summer as a hub connecting East Glacier, Many Glacier, and Waterton and functioning as Going-to-the-Sun Road's eastern portal. Set in the heart of dense bear country, Many Glacier glimmers with lakes and glaciers. Hiking trails venture off toward all compass points, filled during the day with amblers, but left to the bears at night. The newly renovated historic Many Glacier Hotel roosts on the shore of Swiftcurrent Lake, with a backdrop of forbidding Mount Wilbur. When the sun drops below Ptarmigan Wall, watch for bats to emerge and possibly the northern lights.

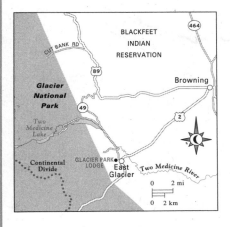

TWO MEDICINE AND EAST GLACIER

Historically the headliner hotel for the park, **Glacier Park Lodge** greeted arriving train travelers with a flowered walkway and a backdrop of the Rocky Mountains, much like it does today. Located on Blackfeet tribal land, rather than inside park boundaries, the hotel and the town of East Glacier spin with resort activities: golf, swimming, hiking, and trail rides. But just up the road, Two Medicine, with the highest drive-to lake in the park—**Two Medicine Lake**—is a quiet contrast. Hiking, boating, fishing, wildlife-watching, and camping all take place at the base of Rising Wolf peak, imposing and stunning in shades of red. Removed from the frenzy of Going-to-the-Sun Road, Two Medicine offers unique places to hike with fewer people and a rich legacy of Native American legend stamped across its features.

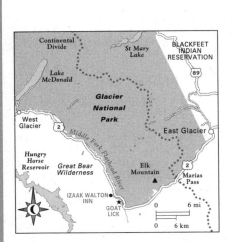

THEODORE ROOSEVELT HIGHWAY

While the Theodore Roosevelt Highway, otherwise known as U.S. Highway 2, pales in comparison to Going-to-the-Sun Road's drama, it connects West and East Glacier via the fastest route over the Continental Divide. Some locals even argue that on busy summer days you can drive it faster from St. Mary to West Glacier than over Going-to-the-Sun Road. Tucked between millions of roadless acres of Glacier Park and the **Bob Marshall Wilderness Complex,** the 57-mile drive tours around the park's southern border as it passes the **Goat Lick,** historic **Izaak Walton Inn,** and the Wild and Scenic **Middle Fork of the Flathead River.** It climbs to mile-high Marias Pass on the Continental Divide, where the terrain looks more like a big, broad valley than a mountain pass. Too bad Lewis and Clark missed this easy one!

WATERTON

In Canada, Waterton Lakes National Park is tiny compared to its northern sister parks, but alpine scenery, prairie grasslands, and wetlands cram within its boundaries. It feeds diverse wildlife with its varied habitats, and rare plants grow prolifically here. Via **Waterton Lake,** the park also stands as a portal to enter Glacier's isolated northern backcountry. Presided over by the historic **Prince of Wales Hotel,** Waterton Townsite embodies the essence of Canadian mountain towns, what Banff once was before booming commercialism. Facing uplake toward Glacier's highest rampart—Mount Cleveland—the town stares at the precipitous crags of Citadel Spires, which look like fingers raking the sky. Together with Glacier, the park is recognized as the world's first peace park, a Biosphere Reserve, and a World Heritage Site.

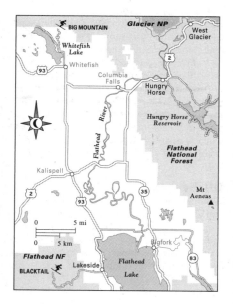

FLATHEAD VALLEY

More than a gateway to Glacier National Park, Flathead Valley is also an attraction in itself with boating, fishing, rafting, camping, bicycling, golfing, swimming, hiking, skiing, and snowmobiling. You'll have trouble deciding between the many options of what to do as well as where to stay. The four main towns—**Kalispell, Whitefish, Bigfork,** and **Columbia Falls**—each draw visitors for their unique small-town personalities. Bordered by Flathead National Forest and Flathead Lake—the largest freshwater lake west of the Mississippi—the valley prides itself on diversity from summer and winter resorts to artist communities, theaters to rodeos, small organic farms to world-recognized businesses. Regardless of where you are, outdoor recreation is the lifestyle here and it's only minutes from your doorstep.

Planning Your Trip

Planning a trip to Glacier National Park is not easy. It's out of the way, subject to snow in August, and riddled with grizzly bears with a nasty reputation. While you cannot drag the kitchen sink along with you, preparedness is your best assurance for a successful adventure. Once you get to Glacier, your time can be spent enjoying its mountain meadows rather than scouting around for supplies. As for the grizzly bears, a little preparation there too will enhance your safety.

Bar none, the most visited site in Glacier is its 52-mile historic scenic highway: Going-to-the-Sun Road. While many visitors consider driving the road as "seeing the park," Glacier is much more than the road that bisects it. Its 743 miles of trails crisscross its valleys and high passes, and only a small percentage of Glacier's nearly two million annual visitors step onto those trails. Although you can taste-test what the park offers in a whirlwind three-day tour, most visitors find that a week is still not sufficient to savor all the delicacies Glacier places on its menu. So, if you can, give yourself that full week or two. Then, plan your next trip back at a different time of the season.

Plan ahead. Make reservations early, for in high season, lodges book up. Gas up and stock up before entering the park: No vehicle services are anywhere within park boundaries, nor up the North Fork Valley. Because limited food services offer little opportunity to grab a cup of coffee or a candy bar, keep snacks, a small cooler, and lunch makings with you in the car for easier traveling.

In Glacier, guided tours abound: by historic red bus, historic wooden boat, horseback, and on foot. Professional guides direct your eyes to lesser-seen park gems. Travel details can be left to someone else, and you always have an expert along—one with a little grizzly bear savvy. Glacier's naturalist rangers guide free hikes in many locations, and the park's concessionaires cover touring, boating, trail riding, hiking, and backpacking.

WHEN TO GO

High Season

Summer—when Going-to-the-Sun Road, all hotels and lodges, campgrounds, and trails open—attracts hordes. Peak visitation crowds into four weeks—from mid-July to mid-August. Cars cluster in pullouts on Going-to-the-Sun Road; Logan Pass's daily parking lot maxes out early. Shoulder seasons offer less hectic times to visit.

In early summer, deep drifts, spring snowstorms, and avalanches may preclude driving Going-to-the-Sun Road's upper reaches. May 30 marks its most common opening date, but depending on snows, plows punch the road open any time from mid-May to June's end.

After June rains, July and August escort in more moderate weather, but occasional summer snowstorms transform the park to winter within hours. If you dream of hiking over high passes, be aware that snows often bury the alpine country in early summer. Instead, wait for high traverses to melt around mid-July; even then snow patches linger into August.

Bugs and mosquitoes descend with a vengeance in June and July. Wildflowers peak from mid-July through early August. Huckleberries ripen from late July through early September, when warm, bug-free days and cool nights usher in peak-top snows by the month's end.

Off-Seasons

Although saddled with unpredictable weather and closed commercial services, spring and fall are gorgeous: early spring glacier lilies juxtapose snow-laden peaks, and autumn smears golden leaves across the slopes. Some campgrounds open for primitive camping, and lower trails are hikable.

Going-to-the-Sun Road usually closes for winter on October's third Monday. Although closed to vehicles from Avalanche or The Loop to Rising Sun, newly plowed or snow-free sections allow hikers and bicyclists in spring and fall. In

winter, when snows bury the road, snowshoers and cross-country skiers tour its lower stretches.

Winter smothers Glacier in snow with only a few roads regularly plowed: Going-to-the-Sun Road's west side to Lake McDonald Lodge, Apgar Road, North Fork Road, U.S. Highway 2, and Highway 89. Snowmobiles are banned, guaranteeing a quiet heard few places.

WHAT TO TAKE

Northwest Montanans have a saying: "Wait five minutes, the weather will change." You may begin an August hike in shorts, but by afternoon high winds and wintry conditions can force you to bury them beneath long pants and rain gear. For that reason, layers make the most sense. Layers, layers, and more layers—lightweight wicking synthetics and fleeces combined with breathable waterproof or water-resistant fabrics. Bring gloves and a warm hat along with rain gear to add wind, rain, and snow protection. Guard against the beet-red look of acute sunburns from high elevations, snow, ice, and water with a sun hat or ball cap, sunscreen, and sunglasses. Don't forget to pack a sturdy pair of walking shoes or hiking boots.

Dressing for dinner here means putting on a clean T-shirt. Even in fine-dining restaurants around Glacier, casual attire is the norm, as are hiking boots. Although the Wild West heritage dug deep roots here, cowboy hats and boots garb only wranglers; most folks around the park wear comfortable shorts or hiking pants with river sandals running a close second to hiking shoes. Cool weather brings out the fleece rather than cashmere, and function always wins over fashion.

For hiking, bring a pack and a water bottle. Also include a compass or GPS device, flashlight, knife, bug spray, and first-aid kit. Although some supplies are available locally, like pepper spray to deter bears, stores are few and far between and brands are limited.

Nothing beats spying a grizzly bear rototilling for glacier lily bulbs, but you can't watch up close! Bring your binoculars and spotting scopes to maintain safety. And don't forget the camera, for Glacier's scenery creates foolproof photo opportunities. For safer wildlife photography, haul along telephoto lenses.

Researching your trip converts into more time spent enjoying the park and less planning once you are here. Guidebooks on fishing, human and natural history, geology, flora, fauna, and hiking and topographical maps—both USGS and Trails Illustrated—can be ordered either by phone or online from Glacier Natural History Association.

ENTRANCE FEES

For admittance to Glacier National Park, staffed entrance stations sell multiple types of park passes. Covering all passengers in the vehicle, a seven-day pass costs $20 (as of May 1, 2006, a seven-day pass will be $25). No single-day passes are sold. For single-person entry on foot, bicycle, motorcycle, or as part of a tour, the seven-day pass is $10 (as of May 1, 2006, the cost will be $12). If you plan on spending more than seven days in Glacier National Park, a one-year pass at $30 (good for all passengers in the vehicle) is more economical. If you plan to visit more than one U.S. national park in a year, consider purchasing the annual National Park Pass for $50. In general, only cash and local checks may be used at entrance stations; credit cards are not accepted. Special passes for seniors and travelers with disabilities are also available. For more information, check the National Park Service website: www.nps.gov.

For travelers heading into Waterton, a Parks Canada pass is needed. The U.S. National Park Pass is not valid, and yes, Americans ask the park entrance staff about using their U.S. park passes all the time! Even though Waterton and Glacier function together as an International Peace Park, no combined park pass is sold to date.

Explore Glacier National Park

ONE DAY IN GLACIER

One day in Glacier will leave you wanting more. But if that's all the time you have, cut straight for the heart of the park. Pack the day full with driving Going-to-the-Sun Road from West Glacier. (The route can also be driven in reverse from St. Mary.) Stock up on film, maps, and snacks before you go. For more flexibility, pack a lunch. Then you won't find yourself bypassing scenic stops because the stomach rumbles.

WEST GLACIER

Grab your favorite caffeinated hot beverage at the espresso stand in West Glacier; stock up on lunch, snacks, and water at the Mercantile; pick up film at the camera shop; and pop in the T-shirt shop for some laughs. Cross the Wild and Scenic Middle Fork of the Flathead River into the park on Going-to-the-Sun Road and head up Lake McDonald. Stop to suck in the view at one of the pullouts accessing the beach, especially if it's one of those rare glassy days with the water reflecting Stanton Peak.

LAKE MCDONALD

Pop in the National Landmark Lake McDonald Lodge 11 miles into your adventure for a taste of the park's history. To see the old entrance from the lake, walk through the hunting lodge lobby and out the back door. Snoop up close at the detail on the historic red jammer buses lining up to convey tourists to Logan Pass.

AVALANCHE CREEK

Farther up the road, several pullouts sneak peeks of McDonald Creek's striking blue-green pools against red argillite rock. Stretch the legs on Trail of the Cedars, an easy 0.7-mile loop walk through a rainforest whose canopy is held aloft by monstrous western red cedars.

THE WEST CLIMB

Continue driving to the West Side Tunnel, stopping here or just a bit farther at The Loop for striking views of Heavens Peak. The Loop also offers a glimpse into the 2003 Trapper Fire: Black charred timbers stand amid a rash of new greenery. Pull off frequently between The Loop and Logan Pass. Most notably, Haystack and Bird Woman Falls are worth a stop, as is Big Bend for its views of the Weeping Wall and often snow piles – avalanche debris – lasting well into August. Without a place to stop, Triple Arches zooms past in the upper stretches, and the road rounds into Oberlin Bend, the world of mountain goats.

LOGAN PASS

Grab up your lunch and tour the small Logan Pass Visitor Center, looking for the grizzly paw print. Hike up the boardwalk through fields of paintbrush and monkey flower toward Hidden Lake Overlook. Dodge mountain goats and bighorn sheep en route along with marmots. At the overlook, enjoy your scenic lunch spot, but watch for pesky ground squirrels who are accustomed to nabbing scraps of food when they can.

THE EAST SIDE

When you drive down the Continental Divide's eastern side, stop to see a glacier at Jackson

Glacier Overlook; binoculars are helpful here due to the distance. For photographs that even a point-and-shoot camera can make calendar-worthy, walk out to the bluff at Sun Point and pop in at Wild Goose Island Overlook. Turn toward the boat dock at Rising Sun, and hop aboard for a tour of St. Mary Lake on *Little Chief,* one of Glacier Park Boat Company's historic wooden boats.

ST. MARY

Upon reaching St. Mary, cool down with some berry pie à la mode at Park Café. Stroll a bit through the shops to locate something to send your mom.

Then, make a decision. You must either drive back 52 miles over Going-to-the-Sun Road, which is an entirely different experience coming from the opposite direction, or loop 90 miles down through East Glacier and Highway 2 back to your starting point. With heavy traffic on the slow, narrow, and curvy Sun Road versus better pavement and higher speed limits on Highway 2, driving times can be the same. For many, weather is the deciding factor, but those who return on Going-to-the-Sun Road can pick up missed sights or catch the alpenglow cast across the Garden Wall from the setting sun.

THE GLACIER SMORGASBORD

If you don't have an entire summer to explore Glacier, you still can taste a bite of its many flavors. Sightseeing, trail riding, boating, rafting, bicycling, and hiking all pack into eight days while seeing highlights from one end of the park to the other. By connecting Going-to-the-Sun Road and Highway 2, you make a large loop, taking spurs off to explore adjacent areas.

DAY 1

Begin on Glacier's west side, camping or lodging in West Glacier, Apgar, at Lake Mc-Donald Lodge, or Avalanche Campground for two nights. On your arrival day, head for a trail to unwind after your travels. Those with gumption should tackle Apgar Lookout for panoramic views of the park's rugged skyline and a bird's-eye view of Lake McDonald and West Glacier, but be prepared on a hot August day for a baker of a hike. A cooler and much less strenuous walk, Avalanche Lake is the most accessible subalpine lake in the park. For those looking for just a short stroll, head for Point of Rocks from Fish Creek. Rent a boat to enjoy the rest of the day lounging or fishing on Lake McDonald or hop a boat tour, which leaves frequently from the Lake McDonald Lodge dock. If you haven't already, make reservations for river rafting on your

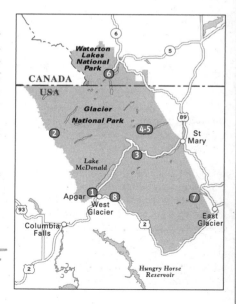

last day in the park. In the evening, take in the naturalist ranger talk to learn about Glacier.

DAY 2

Spend your second day exploring the remote North Fork, opting for whatever route suits your fancy and vehicle limitations. Stop at Polebridge Mercantile for a baked goodie en route to Bowman or Kintla Lake for a picnic. Scenic day-hike options include Quartz Lakes loop or Numa Lookout, and both lakes offer good fishing and strolls along the lakeshore trails. Return to Polebridge for a local microbrew at Northern Lights Saloon followed by the nightly specialty on the menu. At dusk, drive back to your lodging via the North Fork and Camas Roads for the most promising wildlife-watching.

DAY 3

Pack up and get an early start up Going-to-the-Sun Road. If you didn't stay in Lake McDonald Lodge, at least drop in to see the historic building. Then, blow off film as you stop at scenic pullouts on the National Landmark highway. Plan on at least one hike or short walk along its corridor: Trail of the Cedars, Hidden Lake Overlook, or St. Mary and Virginia Falls. And stroll around Logan Pass. With no food services at the pass, be sure to pack a lunch, snacks, and water. For a postcard picture upvalley, walk out to Sun Point. When you reach St. Mary, no matter what time of day, do as the locals do and hit Park Café for freshly baked pie before camping or lodging in Many Glacier or St. Mary for two nights.

DAY 4

Begin your day with a morning boat ride in Many Glacier across Swiftcurrent and Josephine Lakes, followed by a short walk to turquoise Grinnell Lake. In the afternoon, saddle up for a trail ride to Cracker Flats. While in Many Glacier, be sure to waltz through the historic Many Glacier Hotel if you're not staying there. Bask on the hotel's deck with

binoculars in hand to spot grizzly and black bears foraging on Altyn Peak's hillside.

DAY 5

In Many Glacier, hit the nine-mile round-trip Iceberg Lake trail early to avoid the crowds or, for something shorter, saunter up to Red Rocks Lake (two miles round-trip). Carry binoculars to watch for bear, mountain goats, and sheep. When you return, drive to Waterton for two nights, keeping the binoculars and camera handy for views of Chief Mountain en route and osprey and moose around Maskinonge Lake as you enter the park.

DAY 6

Rent a bike to tootle around Waterton: Ride by Cameron Falls and enjoy the beach at Cameron Bay, or tackle one of Waterton's biking trails with a mountain bike. For a scenic drive instead, head out Akamina Parkway to Cameron Lake. Book an early afternoon cruise on the historic MV *International* to Goat Haunt, U.S.A. On your return, be sure to pop into the Prince of Wales Hotel for a look-see if you haven't already.

DAY 7

Drive to Two Medicine. For a striking view out across the plains, hike the six-mile round-trip Scenic Point trail. From here, boats in the lake below look like ants while the hulk of Rising Wolf Mountain lives up to its reputation as the peak with the biggest mass. For a shorter hike, catch a boat uplake to walk to Twin Falls (two miles round-trip) before camping in Two Medicine or staying in East Glacier.

DAY 8

For your last day in Glacier, drive the Theodore Roosevelt Highway (U.S. Hwy. 2) over Marias Pass, stopping at the Goat Lick to catch sight of the white beasts and possibly elk high on the hillside above. The highway leads you back to West Glacier for river rafting, where the adventures started a week ago.

WILDFLOWER WANDERS

When Glacier's spring hits Lake McDonald and St. Mary, Logan Pass still cowers under winter snows. Lower-elevation flowers bloom first, and as summer progresses, like a mist lifting, buds pop open in higher and higher habitats. Wildflowers do not bloom parkwide all at once, but forests, prairies, aspen parklands, subalpine meadows, and alpine tundra peak at different times. To catch flowers in all locations, plan a trip in the last two weeks of July. To help identify wildflowers and the park's 1,200 documented plants (not all of them flowering, however), pick up a field guide from one of the Glacier Natural History Association bookstores.

FORESTS

Forest wildflowers, often tiny and in pale cream colors, choose habitats under deep fir, hemlock, and cedar trees for their shade-producing canopies. Thick branches protect fragile plants from the sun's drying rays and drop needles to the forest floor, creating a rich, organic duff. Queen's cup, fairybell, twinflower, wood nymph, bunchberry, foamflower, and pipsissewa scatter no more than boot-high across the duff. Most trails in the McDonald and North Fork valleys bloom with these gems. For an easily accessible trail, try Trail of the Cedars at Avalanche.

Keep your eye out for orchids, too. Not the big showy tropical type, but diminutive ones whose flowers are often smaller than a child's finger tip. Look for spotted coralroot, yellow lady's slipper, and bog orchids. Pink calypso or fairy slipper orchids grow along the beginning of Quartz Lakes loop. Like orchids, saprophytes lacking chlorophyll (such as pinesap, Indian pipe, and pine drops) huddle in forests in need of the organic soil.

PRAIRIES

Prairie wildflowers grow below timberline in grasslands, replete with over 100 species of grasses. With the exception of the North Fork Valley's prairies, most grasslands amass on the park's east side, especially in Waterton where a 13-square-mile of prairie is preserved. Without trees for shade, wild-flowers here adapt to dry conditions: high temperatures, wind, and less rain. Look for striking yellows of the arrowleaf balsamroot and pale pinks of the prairie smoke.

ASPEN PARKLANDS

In a rich interface habitat mixing meadows and aspen groves, many flowers proliferate. Mountain death camas, paintbrush, pasque flower, lupine, stonecrop, and horse mint span the color array here. Along Two Medicine Road, blue camas blooms hardily. Beside Many Glacier Road, pink sticky geranium makes a show. And between cattle-trodden paths along Chief Mountain International Highway, wild roses and tiger lilies line the road to Waterton, which is home to 35 rare plants found only in its borders.

SUBALPINE

A drive to Logan Pass on Going-to-the-Sun Road climbs into the subalpine zone – a rough place to be a wildflower. Long winters, high winds, little shade, and a short growing season mean that wildflowers must do their business fast. No time to smell pretty; just bloom and get it over with. At Logan Pass, walk toward Hidden Lake Overlook or out along the Garden Wall toward Granite Park Chalet to see colors a Monet would envy.

While winter retreats, yellow glacier lilies and white spring beauties force their blooms up, even through inches of snow. They are the harbingers of summer. Later, the lily bulbs

become prized food for grizzly bears, which rototill large swaths like good gardeners.

Flower shows fluctuate; some years three-foot-tall beargrass grows so thick that slopes appear to be snow-covered. Nodding onion, wild chives, saxifrage, shooting stars, arnica, deep blue gentians, and monkey flowers line trails. For one of the best midsummer flower displays, hike three miles from Siyeh Bend to Preston Park. Seemingly endless fields of fuchsia paintbrush, lavender fleabane, and yellow St. John's wort make you wonder what artist walked here.

ALPINE

Alpine wildflowers struggle. High winds with no protection from small trees, drying altitude, and rocky soils lacking organic matter ravage these diminutive wildflowers during their short few-week season. They survive by hugging the ground. No roads access the alpine zone in Glacier; to see these beauties requires hiking, usually uphill.

In **Two Medicine,** hike a short but steep three miles to Scenic Point, where you'll see mats of pink moss campion – some several hundred years old – spread on crumbled rock. Small bluebells crumple over to protect themselves, and the red tops of king's crown cower between slabs. To see blue Jones columbine and creamy mountain avens cling to the talus for dear life, hike to Siyeh Pass, a 10.5-mile trail grunting up to an 8,000-foot saddle through flower shows in Preston Park.

TOP 10 DAY HIKES

Glacier is a hiker's park. With over 700 miles of trails, it's a place to explore on foot. Ten days in Glacier-Waterton during July, August, or September will allow you to sample the top 10 trails. Hiking these can easily be combined with camping or staying in the historic lodges—one trail even connects to a backcountry chalet. Shuttles running from July through Labor Day help accommodate point-to-point hiking, especially over Going-to-the-Sun Road.

MCDONALD VALLEY

Two distinctly different hikes stand out as icons here. Located at Lake McDonald's foot, **Apgar Lookout** requires a less than three-mile climb to attain a panoramic view of Glacier's peaks, the North Fork Valley, and Lake McDonald. Trains rumble like tiny inchworms along tracks far below. Since the 2003 Robert Fire, the views – once occluded by trees – are much improved.

Although you won't feel like you're getting away from it all, a two-mile trail leaves the McDonald Creek Valley, heading up a red rock side canyon to **Avalanche Lake.** It's the most easily accessed subalpine lake – hence the crowds. Fed by Sperry Glacier above, waterfalls spew thousands of feet down the cliffs at the head of the lake below the Little Matterhorn.

GOING-TO-THE-SUN ROAD

Beginning at Logan Pass, the stunning, nearly 12-mile point-to-point **Highline Trail** tiptoes through high wildflower meadows along the jagged Garden Wall arête to historic Granite Park Chalet before dropping through the 2003 Trapper Fire to The Loop. You'll feel like you're walking in the realm of mountain goats as the trail clings to the Continental Divide.

Acrophobes may clench their stomachs, but others will feel like soaring.

Just east of Logan Pass, Siyeh Bend marks the trailhead for one of the best point-to-point hikes. Over a high elevation saddle with glaciers and alpine tundra flowers, **Siyeh Pass** loops 10.5 miles from Siyeh Bend on Going-to-the-Sun Road to Baring Creek. The trail wanders through Preston Park, with one of the most colorful collections of wildflowers, as it circumnavigates Going-to-the-Sun Mountain. Piegan and Old Sun Glaciers gleam in the sun, and bighorn sheep often browse in the upper slopes.

TWO MEDICINE

High above Two Medicine Lake, **Scenic Point** lets you look for miles across the plains and then turn around to stare at rugged peaks. A half-day bop up 3 miles puts you atop a promontory of the Lewis Overthrust Fault, where tiny alpine bluebells and pink moss campion struggle to grow in the incessant wind.

In a long loop plus a boat ride across Two Medicine Lake, the 16-mile **Dawson-Pitamakin Loop** actually crosses three passes: Dawson, Cutbank, and Pitamakin. You'll feel like you're walking on top of the world as the narrow path hangs dizzyingly thousands of feet above the valley floor. It traverses an arête between Flinsch and Morgan peaks, and bighorn sheep vie for space on the trail.

MANY GLACIER

For the rarity of seeing icebergs in August, a 4.5-mile gentle ascent in Many Glacier leads to **Iceberg Lake**, a glacial remnant set below the mountain-goat-dotted cliffs of the Continental Divide. Tradition dictates a quick dive in, but be ready to experience chill like you've never felt before. Not only the view, but the frigid water will take your breath away.

In Many Glacier, the **Grinnell Glacier** trail provides the quickest trail to reach a glacier in the park. In its scenic climb, its 5.5-mile path delights en route with wildflowers, bighorn sheep, and often grizzly bears. You'll stare down at turquoise Grinnell Lake, and above, you'll see the smaller Gem and Salamander Glaciers.

WATERTON

Beginning at Cameron Lake in Waterton, the nearly 12-mile **Carthew-Alderson** trail climbs high into alpine tundra with panoramic views before dropping past sparkling tarns to Waterton Townsite. While the hike begins and ends in thick forests, the midsection sees only stunted subalpine firs struggling to grow in the sheltered lee of windblown ridges.

Requiring boat access, **Crypt Lake** throws a ladder, tunnel, and cliff walk in its five miles. The lake itself is in a hanging valley, but be prepared for hiking with hordes — everyone begins the hike together from the boat dock and races at the end of the day to catch the return boat.

WILDLIFE-WATCHING

With 57 animals and over 210 varieties of birds to spot, wildlife watchers shouldn't be bored. Bring your binoculars and scopes, for your own safety as well as the animal's well being. Several locations offer good chances of spying on animal activities. With a week in the park, you should be able to see a wide diversity of wildlife and birds. Die-hard birders will want to hit June and July because migrations prompt some birds to head south as early as August. Animal watchers will find suitable subjects for their binoculars throughout July and August.

Both Glacier and Waterton Parks have wildlife and bird checklists. Ask for them at visitors centers or check on park websites.

NORTH FORK VALLEY

For birders, the North Fork Valley is prime. Over 196 species of **birds** have been recorded here, 57 percent of which are nesters. Listen carefully for woodpeckers drumming. Fens bustle with red-winged blackbirds, snipes, and soras, while killdeer, sandpipers, American dippers, and great blue herons hound waterways. Songbirds chatter everywhere: sparrows, thrushes, nuthatches, and warblers. Keep your eyes open for the flash of the western tanager's striking yellow and red.

From Canada, **gray wolves** migrated into Glacier's North Fork Valley in the 1980s. While their numbers have grown and packs spread to other northwest Montana locales, the North Fork is still a good wolf spot. Two packs inhabit the area. For your best chances, drive Inside Road, watching carefully around Sullivan meadows. **Moose** and **elk** also inhabit the North Fork Valley: Keep your binoculars handy while driving Camas Road, North Fork Road, or Inside Road. Look for moose in willow bogs and elk in open grasslands.

GOING-TO-THE-SUN ROAD

Birds of prey inhabit Glacier's woodlands, waterways, and cliffs. To spot bald eagles, watch Lake McDonald's north end. At Logan Pass, birds abound. Grosbeaks, rosy finches, and mountain chickadees flit between subalpine firs while blue grouse and ptarmigan strut in open meadows. When dropping down Going-to-the-Sun Road's east side, hike to St. Mary and Virginia Falls to see American dippers. Then stop at Two Dog Flats to watch woodpeckers, flickers, sapsuckers, flycatchers, wrens, mountain bluebirds, and several species of owls in the aspen trees. Listen for the ruffed grouse's drumming.

Mammals also make frequent appearances on Going-to-the-Sun Road. In early July, survey avalanche slopes during mornings and evenings on Going-to-the-Sun Road's west side, where **bears** paw through debris for animal carcasses or after snowmelt dig up glacier lily bulbs. Around Logan Pass, white descendants of old-world antelopes roam: **Mountain goat** nannies and newborn kids often cluster around Oberlin Bend Overlook and Hidden Lake Overlook trail. Look hard for small herds of **bighorn sheep** that may blend in with the rocks above the road just east of Logan Pass.

MANY GLACIER

Abutting aspen groves and grasslands, the high subalpine-lake-strewn valleys of Many Glacier make for rich **bird** habitat for white-crowned sparrows, loons, ptarmigans, gray-crowned rosy finches, Townsend's solitaires, hummingbirds, Steller's jays, and kinglets. Zoom in on Clark's nutcrackers, usually found gathering seeds from white bark pines. With binoculars, scan high cliffs

for golden eagles soaring where winds are good along the Continental Divide.

Sniffing out food sources, **grizzly and black bears** congregate in Many Glacier on the slopes of Mount Altyn and Mount Henkel as they forage for berries, ground squirrels, and bulbs. With a good pair of binoculars, you can watch them from the deck of Many Glacier Hotel. For a chance to spot **moose,** hike to Red Rocks and Bullhead Lakes. Look on cliffs for **mountain goats,** but on slightly lower scree fields for **bighorn sheep.** Often the park service sets up a spotting scope in the Swiftcurrent parking lot for public wildlife viewing.

WATERTON

For birders, the wetlands around Maskinonge and Linnet Lakes abound with **waterfowl.**

Osprey, ducks, teals, mergansers, swans, and kingfishers haunt the waterways, as does a plethora of hawks and songbirds. Over 250 avian species pass through here on two major migratory flyways because of the rich wetlands and varied habitats.

Sometimes, **bighorn sheep** hang out in Waterton Townsite. Often huddling in small groups, sheep cluster in bachelor herds and nanny colonies in summer, although their numbers may be declining due to isolated habitats and disease. While **bison** once roamed these areas in great numbers, none remain wild in Glacier. In Waterton, stop at the bison paddock to see the small bison herd maintained there. Take the boat down Waterton Lake and hike to Kootenai Lakes to spot **moose,** which frequently inhabit the mosquito-ridden wetlands.

WEST GLACIER AND APGAR

Two miles apart, West Glacier and Apgar span Glacier Park's southern boundary—the Middle Fork of the Flathead River. While West Glacier sprouted up outside the park along Great Northern Railway's line, Apgar's early trapper and logger homesteads dug in the southwestern foothold on Lake McDonald—the port to the park's wild interior before Going-to-the-Sun Road was built. Connected by the "new bridge," the park entrance road, and a two-mile paved bicycling and walking pathway, the pair are doorways for exploring Glacier's western wilderness. As such, they throng with cars and visitors in summer. The pair also launch sightseers in two disparate directions: to the untrammeled North Fork Valley and to Glacier's crowning highway, Going-to-the-Sun Road.

Today, many concessionaires headquarter themselves in West Glacier, just outside national park boundaries, because 60 percent of park visitors access via the west entrance. The tiny town evolved into the seasonal mecca for rafting, guided hiking and backpacking, guided fishing trips, trail rides, and helicopter tours. Along with the train station, campgrounds, restaurants, motels, shops, and even an espresso stand, West Glacier is a place to gas up the car one last time before seeking Glacier's interior. On Lake McDonald's shores and inside the park, Apgar resounds with calm in comparison. Although its restaurant, lodging, camping, shopping, boat ramp, and petite west-side visitor center swarm in high season, miles of lake sprawl with blue space to unwind and lakeshore enough to find a niche off by itself.

© BECKY LOMAX

HIGHLIGHTS

☾ Belton Chalet: As old as the park, the chalet stands as a tribute to a bygone era of tourism. On chillier days, enjoy the ambience by its stone fireplace; on warmer days, lounge at sunset on its deck with a local brew (page 36).

☾ Robert Fire: Evidence of the 2003 fire fills much of West Glacier and Apgar. From Rubideau Basin to Apgar Mountain and Howe Ridge, the fire forced the evacuation of both West Glacier and Apgar, as well as the McDonald Valley (page 38).

☾ Lake McDonald: Apgar's boat ramp provides the only public ramp access to Lake McDonald, the largest lake in the park. Lake McDonald is great for boating, kayaking, fishing, swimming, or just plain skipping rocks (page 38).

☾ Apgar Lookout: A half-day hike puts you where you can survey all Lake McDonald, West Glacier, and the North Fork, backdropped with a huge panorama of Glacier's skyline of peaks (page 39).

☾ Huckleberry Lookout: Climb to a top-of-the-world ridge walk where views stretch from Flathead Lake to Canada on this 12-mile round-trip hike (page 40).

☾ Middle Fork of the Flathead: Whitewater rafting puts a little spice in your westside stay. The Wild and Scenic River drops through rapids such as Screaming Right Hand Turn, Bonecrusher, Jaws, and Could Be Trouble (page 43).

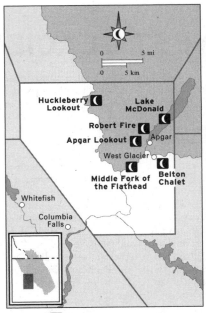

LOOK FOR ☾ TO FIND RECOMMENDED SIGHTS, ACTIVITIES, DINING, AND LODGING.

HISTORY
Native Americans

For the Ksanka or Standing Arrow people (known today as the Salish and Kootenai, whose tribal lands are at Flathead Lake's south end), Glacier's Lake McDonald area held special significance. Ten thousand generations ago, as legend says, the Ksanka were first given a ceremonial dance by the spirits at their winter camp near Apgar. Originally called the Blacktail Deer Dance, the ceremony became an annual event for the tribe, and the area became known as "the place where people dance." Today, the annual dance—now called the Jump Dance—takes place on the Flathead Reservation, but rapids on McDonald Creek still hold the original name, Sacred Dancing Cascade.

Early Tourism

When the Great Northern Railroad completed

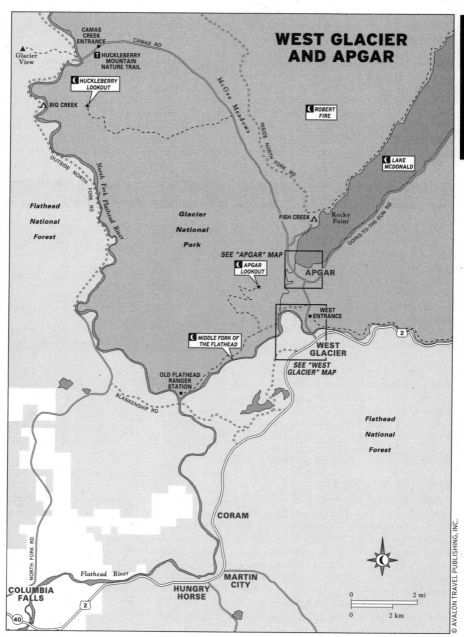

WEST GLACIER AND APGAR

CAMAS CREEK ENTRANCE

Glacier View

HUCKLEBERRY MOUNTAIN NATURE TRAIL

CAMAS RD

HUCKLEBERRY LOOKOUT

BIG CREEK

McGee Meadows

ROBERT FIRE

OUTSIDE NORTH FORK RD

North Fork Flathead River

INSIDE NORTH FORK RD

LAKE McDONALD

Flathead National Forest

Glacier National Park

FISH CREEK

Rocky Point

GOING-TO-THE-SUN RD

SEE "APGAR" MAP

APGAR LOOKOUT

APGAR

WEST ENTRANCE

2

MIDDLE FORK OF THE FLATHEAD

WEST GLACIER

SEE "WEST GLACIER" MAP

OLD FLATHEAD RANGER STATION

BLANKENSHIP RD

Flathead National Forest

CORAM

NORTH FORK RD

Flathead River

COLUMBIA FALLS

2

40

HUNGRY HORSE

MARTIN CITY

0   2 mi

0   2 km

its westbound track in 1891, early tourists jumped off the train in Belton (West Glacier) to launch their Glacier foray. With no bridge across the Middle Fork of the Flathead, visitors rowed across the river and then saddled up for a horseback ride to Apgar. Finally, in 1895 a rough dirt road eased the two-mile journey, followed two years later by a bridge across the river.

As the railroad dumped visitors in Belton, Lake McDonald homesteaders leaped into the tourism business, offering cabins, meals, pack trips, boat rides, and guided tours. After Glacier became a national park in 1910, local landowners along the lake retained their property as inholdings. While private summer homes still exist here within the park boundaries (to the envy of everyone), when sellers are ready, the National Park Service purchases these properties at fair market value.

To coincide with Glacier's first summer as a national park, the railway company opened Belton Chalet in 1910 across from the depot.

Exploring West Glacier and Apgar

ENTRANCE STATION

Crossing the Middle Fork of the Flathead River on the West Glacier Bridge officially enters you into Glacier National Park. There's even a pullout before the park entrance sign for those who photo-document their travels by park signage. The park entrance is usually staffed during daylight hours all summer long and off-season on weekends. But don't sweat it if you miss someone in the station: you can use the self-pay cash-only kiosk on the right just beyond the booth. At the entrance station, pick up a map and a copy of the *Waterton-Glacier Guide,* the park's newspaper, which is updated twice annually.

You can also enter Apgar via the Camas Entrance from the rough dirt North Fork Road. On its north end, an entrance station sits unstaffed along with a self-pay cash-only kiosk.

VISITORS CENTERS
Apgar Visitor Center

The tiny Apgar Visitor Center (on Apgar Rd. 0.2 mile from Camas Rd. or 0.9 mile from Going-to-the-Sun Rd., 406/888-7800, 9 A.M.–5 P.M. daily May–late June and after Labor Day–Sept., 8 A.M.–7 P.M. daily late June–Labor Day, 9 A.M.–4:30 P.M. winter weekends) is crowded with 15 people, but it sees 190,000 visitors annually. Thank goodness future plans include replacing it with the West Side Discovery Center and Museum, to

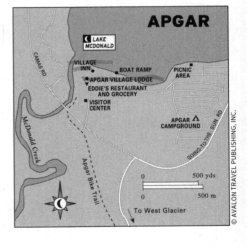

be located at the Apgar T junction on Going-to-the-Sun Road. In the small shell of what was once a two-room house, the visitor center building houses a few displays, an information desk, and a small Glacier Natural History Association bookstore. The backcountry permit office (May–Nov. 406/888-7859, winter 406/888-7800) is now a few doors west opposite the old red schoolhouse. In spite of the visitor center's diminutive size, park personnel are big on information. Pick up maps, naturalist activity guides, and Junior Ranger Program newspapers, and get the latest up-

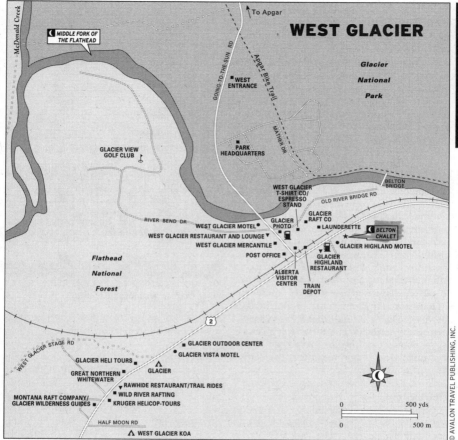

To Apgar

WEST GLACIER

MIDDLE FORK OF
THE FLATHEAD

McDonald Creek

Glacier

National

Park

WEST
ENTRANCE

Apgar Bike Trail

GOING-TO-THE-SUN RD

MATHER DR

GLACIER VIEW
GOLF CLUB

PARK
HEADQUARTERS

BELTON
BRIDGE

WEST GLACIER
T-SHIRT CO/
ESPRESSO
STAND

OLD RIVER BRIDGE RD

RIVER BEND DR

GLACIER
RAFT CO

GLACIER
PHOTO

WEST GLACIER MOTEL

LAUNDERETTE

BELTON
CHALET

WEST GLACIER RESTAURANT AND LOUNGE

WEST GLACIER MERCANTILE

GLACIER HIGHLAND MOTEL

POST OFFICE

Flathead

National

Forest

ALBERTA
VISITOR
CENTER

GLACIER
HIGHLAND
RESTAURANT

TRAIN
DEPOT

(2)

WEST GLACIER STAGE RD

GLACIER OUTDOOR CENTER

GLACIER VISTA MOTEL

GLACIER HELI TOURS

GLACIER

GREAT NORTHERN
WHITEWATER

RAWHIDE RESTAURANT/TRAIL RIDES

MONTANA RAFT COMPANY/
GLACIER WILDERNESS GUIDES

WILD RIVER RAFTING

KRUGER HELICOP-TOURS

HALF MOON RD

WEST GLACIER KOA

0   500 yds

0   500 m

© AVALON TRAVEL PUBLISHING, INC.

dates on trail, road, campground, fishing, and boating information. Restrooms are around the side of the building.

For some free, fun, hands-on activities especially for children, stop by the **Discovery Cabin** in the woods across the street from the Apgar Visitor Center. With the help of interpretive rangers, learning stations teach about wildlife, geology, and natural history. Hours are limited and varied; consult the visitor center for the current schedule and walking directions to the cabin.

Alberta Visitor Center

Located in West Glacier, the Alberta Visitor Information Center (125 Going-to-the-Sun Rd., 800/252-3782, www.travelalberta.com, 8 A.M.–7 P.M. daily late May–early Sept., expect closures around 5 P.M. during late Sept.) is a building-size advertisement for Canada, complete with dinosaur bones. For those heading over the border to Waterton, the center is worth a stop to help with travel planning. Staff have plenty of brochures and maps to give away, and there are big, clean public restrooms here!

TOURS AND SHUTTLES

Red Bus Tours

Glacier Park's fleet of **Red Buses** (406/892-2525, www.glacierparkinc.com) are the best way to tour in historic style, with roll-back tops allowing for the most scenic ride. For those with oversized vehicles not permitted on Going-to-the-Sun Road, these tours are the easiest way to see Logan Pass. Reservations are strongly recommended, especially in high season, but sometimes visitors can hop on the same day. Half- and full-day tours are based out of Lake McDonald Lodge but have pickups scheduled 20–30 minutes in advance of Lake McDonald departure times at West Glacier KOA, Glacier Campground, and Belton Chalet in West Glacier and the Village Inn in Apgar.

With a pickup at the Alberta Visitor Center or your campground, **Sun Tours** (406/226-9220 or 800/786-9220, www.glaciersuntours.com, July–Aug., adults $35, kids ages 12 and under $15, kids under 5 free, park entrance fees not included) departs at 9 A.M. daily from West Glacier for four-hour tours to Logan Pass and back. The air-conditioned 25-passenger coaches are extremely comfortable, with extra-big windows assisting the views, and Blackfeet guides give insight into the park's Native American heritage.

Helicopter

Two helicopter tour companies—both within one mile of the train depot—fly half-hour and one-hour tours over Glacier Park. Per person rates vary $95–660, based on the number of passengers and flight duration. Even though tours are weather dependent, make reservations from home, especially if you want to be able to keep the cost down by sharing the ride with other passengers. You may have to adjust your schedule when you're here, but you'll still have your reservations. **Glacier Heli Tours** (11950 Hwy. 2 E., 406/387-4141 or 800/879-9310, www.glacierhelitours.com, 8 A.M.–8 P.M. daily May–Oct.) flies two helicopters, seating 4–6 guests. **Kruger Helicop-Tours** (11892 Hwy. 2 E., 406/387-4565 or 800/220-6565, www.krugerhelicopters.com, daily mid-May–

The Alberta Visitor Information Center in West Glacier promotes Canada.

Sept., office hours vary with weather) loads up to four passengers in its helicopter.

Shuttles

July–Labor Day, **Glacier Park, Inc.** (406/892-2525, www.glacierparkinc.com, $8–40 per person, kids half price) operates a daily shuttle service between West Glacier and St. Mary, departing 7:30 A.M.–4:15 P.M. From St. Mary, you can connect with the east-side shuttle linking with East Glacier, Two Medicine, Many Glacier, and Waterton. For hikers, shuttles are the best way to get to trailheads—especially in high season when popular parking lots burst at the seams with too many vehicles. No reservations are taken for this service, and you must pay in cash when you board. In West Glacier, catch the shuttle at the Alberta Visitor Information Center; in Apgar, the stop is the Village Inn. Shuttle schedules are available online and on the signs at pickup locations.

Running late May through late September, Glacier Park, Inc. also shuttles train arrivees for $5 per person from the Belton Depot to lodging

in West Glacier, Apgar, and Lake McDonald Lodge. Contrary to the hiker shuttle policy, reservations are mandatory for this service.

West Side Transit Center

To accommodate increased traffic and construction over Going-to-the-Sun Road, Glacier Park will begin building a West Side Transit Center in 2006 at the Apgar T junction on Going-to-the-Sun Road. The center, in conjunction with the new West Side Discovery Center and Museum, will have parking and a shuttle stop for those traveling over Going-to-the-Sun Road. Call park headquarters for updates (406/888-7800).

SERVICES

Gas services are *not* available inside the park, on Going-to-the-Sun Road, up the North Fork Valley, or on Highway 2 until East Glacier. The last chance for gasoline is West Glacier: **Glacier Highland** (gas available year-round with a credit card) across from the train depot or **West Glacier MRC Gasoline** (mid-May–Sept.) across from the Mercantile.

The **West Glacier Laundromat** (8 A.M.– 10 P.M. daily mid-May–mid-Sept.) is behind the Alberta Visitor Center. If the West Glacier launderette is packed, there's one in Coram, 5.5 miles west, but sometimes it hasn't been exceptionally clean. Hungry Horse 9 miles west on Highway 2 also has one next to the grocery store.

You can get a hot shower ($3–5) at most of the commercial campgrounds between West Glacier and Hungry Horse, with West Glacier Campground and West Glacier KOA being the closest options.

The post office is across the street from the Alberta Visitor Center in West Glacier. Adjacent to the post office, **Going-to-the-Sun Gift Shop** (8 A.M.–7 P.M. daily May–Sept.) has a wireless Internet hotspot. ATM machines are located in Apgar at Eddie's and in West Glacier between the MRC gas station and the film store.

Glacier Heli Tours (11950 Hwy. 2 E., 406/387-4141 or 800/879-9310) rents cars.

Shopping

West Glacier and Apgar provide a wee bit of shopping. Of the four gift shops in Apgar, **Montana House of Gifts** (406/888-5393, on Apgar Rd. next to the visitor center, 9 A.M.– 8:30 P.M. daily in summer, until 5 P.M. in winter) is worth a stop for its locally made pottery, weaving, jewelry, crafts, and arts, some by Native Americans. West Glacier also has several gift, souvenir, and T-shirt shops, along with a film store. Limited outdoor supplies for hiking, rafting, and fishing are also sold at West Glacier's rafting companies.

Located in the historic Belton Railway Station in West Glacier, the **Glacier Natural History Association** (GNHA, 406/888-5756, www.glacierassociation.com) headquarters sells books, posters, and maps of Glacier. This is the place to go for all park-reference, natural-history, guide, and picture books. GNHA also runs a small bookstore in the Apgar Visitor Center and six other park locations. Products may be ordered from the GNHA website.

Newspapers and Magazines

In northwestern Montana, look for three daily newspapers: Kalispell's *Daily Interlake, The Missoulian* from Missoula, and the *Great Falls Tribune* from the east side of the Continental Divide. But for the scoop on park news and adjacent west-side communities, the *Hungry Horse News*—a weekly—will give you better insight about life here. *Flathead Living,* a local free magazine, also features cultural and lifestyle tidbits.

Emergencies

For emergencies within park boundaries, contact a ranger or call 406/888-7800. Outside park boundaries, call 911. The nearest hospitals are in the Flathead Valley: Kalispell Regional Hospital (406/752-5111) and North Valley Hospital in Whitefish (406/863-2501).

The nearest ranger station inside the park is **Glacier National Park Headquarters** (406/888-7800), on Going-to-the-Sun Road just west of the park entrance station. The side road is well-signed; turn onto it and take the first right into the parking lot for the adjacent headquarters building. The nearest U.S. Forest Service ranger station for Flathead National

Forest (406/387-3800) is in Hungry Horse on Highway 2 at milepost 143.1.

DRIVING TOUR
Camas Road

Outside Apgar, the 11.3-mile Camas Road heads north across Lower McDonald Creek toward the North Fork of the Flathead River on one of the best paved roads in Glacier, open only in summer. The havoc of weather, time, geology, and massive traffic has not taken its toll on the Camas Road as on other park roads. Climbing along the base of the Apgar Range, the road traverses through the areas of the **2003 Robert Fire** and the **2001 Moose Fire,** which offer a contrast in forest succession. Several pullouts en route are worth a stop: If you can stand the mosquitoes, grab binoculars to peruse **McGee Meadows** (at 5.5 miles) for moose, deer, and bear. Just west of the Camas entrance station at 11.1 miles, a turnoff leads to **Huckleberry Mountain Nature Trail,** a 0.9-mile self-guided loop. The parking lot itself stares at the remote Livingston Range. After crossing the park boundary, the North Fork River, the Camas Road terminates at North Fork Road. If bears frequent the Camas Road, you may see bear management rangers hazing them away from the roadway in attempts to condition the bears to steer clear of trafficked areas for their own safety.

SIGHTS

While most visitors head straight to Lake McDonald, the biggest attraction in the area, there's plenty more to see in West Glacier and Apgar.

West Glacier

The town of West Glacier (originally known as Belton) centered historically around the Belton Train Depot and Belton Chalet. Today, Highway 2 divides the pair, and West Glacier centers now around recreational concessions such as rafting, backpacking, hiking, helitours, and fishing. To leave the highway bustle, drive through the railroad tunnel and enter a historic world preserved by the Lundgren family, operators for over 50 years of the West Glacier Mercantile Company. The 1938 brown national park buildings house a bar, restaurant,

gift shops, grocery, and motel. Fall finds lazy birch leaves covering the ground as shops board their windows, leaving the town's 224 year-round residents to themselves.

Belton Chalet

In 1910, Glacier became a park, and the Belton Chalet opened its doors to guests arriving via Great Northern Railway. The first in a series of chalets built by the railroad company, the hotel increased train ridership and eased access to Lake McDonald Valley. Following a Swiss chalet theme, milkmaid-attired hostesses and flowered walkways greeted guests. Over the years, the chalet changed hands, serving as everything from housing for Civilian Conservation Corps crews building Going-to-the-Sun Road to a pizza parlor and bakery. After heavy snows destroyed roofs and floors in the late 1990s, owners Andy Baxter and Cas Still restored the lodge and cabins to the tune of $1 million. In 2000, Belton Chalet was recognized on the National Register of Historic Places.

Historic Belton Bridge

In 1920, the historic Belton Bridge opened, offering park visitors a way to cross the river without rowing. Ironically, this wood and cement bridge remained standing during the 1964 flood while torrents of water destroyed the new bridge downstream. For a time, this bridge became the west entrance again as the new bridge was repaired. The park service recently rehabilitated the historic bridge, open now for foot traffic only. The "old bridge," as locals call it, accesses Boundary Trail, fishing spots along the Middle Fork, and calm but deep chilly pools for swimming. To find it, turn right in West Glacier on Old Bridge Road and drive to the end.

Middle Fork of the Flathead

The Middle Fork of the Flathead collects its waters from deep within the Bob Marshall Wilderness Complex and Glacier National Park, with the national park boundary on the north shore high-water mark. Designated a Wild and Scenic River, the Middle Fork—the shortened moniker most people use for the

WILDFIRES

In an average summer, 13 wildfires burn in Glacier, altering the forest landscape on 5,000 acres. Most are lightning-caused, with over 80 percent of strikes touching down in the park's heavily timbered west side. Some are unseen while others send huge smoke plumes thousands of feet in the air, but all fires create biodiversity in Glacier's ecosystem.

Two large fire seasons ripped through Glacier in recent summers. In 2001, the **Moose Fire** burned almost 30,000 acres in the North Fork Valley and Apgar Mountain Range. In 2003, 135,000 acres burned inside Glacier Park from an onslaught of lightning strikes and illegal campfires – one of the largest fire seasons in the park's history; 39,000 of those acres belonged to the **Robert Fire,** only one of many burning around the park, but one of the largest that summer. (You can see the evidence from Going-to-the-Sun Road across Lake McDonald and at The Loop.) But even in these recent fire zones, plants and forests already regenerate.

As flames eat up wood, ash falls to the ground, releasing nutrients. Similar to putting a good fertilizer on a garden, the ash fosters energetic plant growth, especially with the open tree canopy. As a natural succession of greenery takes over, wildlife dependent on plant foraging finds improved habitat. In short, fires help maintain a natural balance. They also remove deadfall and infested insects, reduce the power of future fires, and create forests more resistant to drought and nonnative plant invasions.

Some species even rely on fires for reproduction: The lodgepole's serotinous cones require high heat to release its fast-growing seeds from the sticky resin. Ceanothus, hollyhock, and morel mushrooms flourish after fires. Others, like the larch or ponderosa, will survive a fire through thick resin-less bark and minimal low branches.

In Glacier, each fire is managed on an individual basis. From 1916 to 1968, federal policy suppressed all fires – resulting in excessive fuel build up, bug infestations, and elimination of some floral species. Today, this policy has changed. If fires threaten human life or structures, they will be suppressed along with most human-caused fires, but lightning fires ranging in the wilds will often be monitored, allowing the ecosystem's natural cycle to take place. Sometimes, park crews set intentional fires to reduce fuel buildup or protect a resource, such as a prairie, from invasion by other species.

In Glacier, wildfires used to be monitored from 17 different lookouts. Today, satellite and airplane surveys have reduced the need for staffed lookouts to four: Huckleberry, Scalplock, Numa, and Swiftcurrent.

Fire isn't the end of a forest, but part of an ongoing process of succession in an ever-changing landscape.

---

river—vacillates between raging rapids and mesmerizing meanders. Anglers and swimmers gravitate to its blue-green pools. Rafters and kayakers splash through rapids known as Bonecrusher and Jaws. Hikers tootle along the Boundary Trail. To enter the park, the West Glacier Bridge crosses the Middle Fork as does the historic Belton Bridge upriver.

Apgar

Two miles from West Glacier, Apgar sits on the shore of the park's largest body of water—Lake McDonald. With Apgar Campground within walking distance and Fish Creek Campground a couple of miles away, Apgar is crowded in high season but still quiet compared to the West Glacier highway hubbub. It's the quintessential national park community. The tiny west-side visitor center, a restaurant, a camp store, two inns, Lake McDonald's only boat ramp, swimming beaches, and picnic areas all cluster here at Lake McDonald's foot. One local gift shop is in Apgar's historic schoolhouse. Like West Glacier, most of Apgar shuts down by October and opens again in May.

(Robert Fire

Summer 2003 unleashed some of the biggest flames in Glacier Park's history. Starting possibly from an illegal campfire, the Robert Fire leaped across the North Fork of the Flathead into Glacier National Park, aided by high winds that sped the fire 1.5 miles in less than two hours. It forced local evacuations of campers, motel guests, and park headquarters personnel from West Glacier and Apgar while helicopters and CanadaAir "Duck" planes scooped water out of Lake McDonald to douse the fire. High winds battered the fire as it moved over Apgar Mountain and ran up Howe Ridge, burning 7,000 acres in four hours. While more than 135,000 acres burned within Glacier's boundaries during summer 2003, the Robert Fire's 39,000 acres comprised 29 percent of the park's aflame forests. More than seven weeks after the fire started, rain and snow finally suppressed its growth.

To see the fire's aftermath and speedy forest regeneration, a short drive up Camas Road tours you through the burn. For a closer look, walk Lake McDonald Trail starting at Fish Creek Campground. For a spectacular overview of the entire Robert Fire, hike to Apgar Lookout. While many visitors lament the charred timbers—a visible memory of the fire—fast-growing new vegetation isn't singing a funeral dirge. From the fire's ash, soils with increased nutrients prompt prolific flower blooms, like pink fireweed. Three-toed woodpeckers have a heyday digging bugs out of the dead timber, and some species of trees that require fire to germinate sprout again. It is by no means a dead zone to lament.

(Lake McDonald

Catching waters from Glacier's longest river, Lake McDonald is 10 miles long by 1.5 miles

© BECKY LOMAX

multicolored rocks from different sedimentary layers in Lake McDonald

wide—the largest lake in Glacier National Park. Squeezed between Mount Brown and Stanton Peak at its head, the lake plummets to depths of 472 feet—the deepest waters in the park. Resting in an ice age–scoured trough, the 6,823-acre lake is buffered on both sides by larch forests that turn gold in fall. Here, visitors fish, boat, and swim in its quiet no-jet-skis-allowed waters. While waterskiing attracts a few wetsuited diehards, the lake's cold temperatures and hefty breezes deter many. Access the lake's shores via Fish Creek or Apgar Picnic Area, the Apgar boat ramp, or the many pullouts along Going-to-the-Sun Road.

Recreation

If Glacier has a recreation center, it's West Glacier and Apgar. For between them you can hike, bike, riverraft, ride horses, kayak, boat, fish, swim, and golf. It's the unofficial park headquarters for riverrafting; two Wild and Scenic Rivers are a short step from the back door.

HIKING

Hiking in Apgar improved substantially with the 2003 Robert Fire. Views opened up amid the once-thick forest, and the nutrient-enriched soil from the fire sprouted lush growth. Wildflowers now run amok on slopes that once had meager color. This also is the only park area where a trail permits dogs: The two-mile paved Apgar Bike Trail connecting West Glacier and Apgar is open to walkers, leashed dogs, and bicyclists.

Apgar Lookout is the climax of one of the park's most scenic hikes.

Rocky Point

- Distance: 2 miles round-trip

- Duration: 1 hour

- Elevation gain: none

- Effort: easy

- Trailhead: Fish Creek Campground by Apgar

Rocky Point is a short romp along Lake McDonald Trail through a larch forest to a promontory on Lake McDonald's north shore. The walk meanders through remnants from the 2003 Robert Fire. You'll notice places of heavy burn with slow regrowth and lighter burn packed now with lush greenery. Don't forget your camera: The view from Rocky Point looks up lake toward the Continental Divide and grabs grand shots of Mounts Jackson and Edwards to the south. If the lake is calm, you'll nab some stunning reflection photos.

(Apgar Lookout

- Distance: 5.6 miles round-trip

- Duration: 3.5 hours

- Elevation gain: 1,835 feet

- Effort: moderate

- Trailhead: end of Glacier Institute Road 1.9 miles from Going-to-the-Sun Road

- Directions: Take the first left after the West Entrance Station at the Glacier Institute sign. At the first fork, follow the sign to the horse barn; at the second, go left, crossing over Quarter Circle Bridge. Drive approximately one mile up the hill to a small clearing at the trailhead.

Beginning with a gentle walk along an old dirt road, Apgar Lookout Trail soon climbs steeply uphill toward one of three long switchbacks. As the trail ascends, large burned sentinels stand as relics from the

HIKING ESSENTIALS

When hiking in Glacier National Park, go prepared. Unpredictable, fast-changing weather can mutate a warm summer day into wintry conditions in a matter of hours. Different elevations see temperatures, winds, and visibility vary. Sun on the shore of Two Medicine Lake may hide knock-over winds barreling over Dawson Pass six miles away. Hot valley temperatures may give way to chilly breezes at Grinnell Lake as winds blow down from the Continental - Divide and across the ice. To be prepared in Glacier's backcountry, take the following:

- **Extra clothing:** Rain pants and jackets can double as wind protection, while gloves and a lightweight warm hat will save fingers and ears. Carry at least one extra water-wicking layer for warmth. Avoid cotton fabrics that stay soggy and fail to retain body heat.

- **Extra food and water:** Depending on the hike's length, take a lunch and snacks, like compact high-energy food bars. Low-odor foods will not attract animals.

Always carry extra water as heat, wind, and elevation can lead quickly to dehydration. Do not plan to drink directly from streams or lakes. Because giardia and other bacterial organisms may be present, always filter (with at least a one-micron filter) or treat water sources before drinking.

- **Map and compass or GPS device:** Although Glacier's trails are extremely well-signed, a map can be handy for ascertaining distance traveled and location. A compass or GPS device will also help, but only if you know how to use it.

- **Flashlight:** Carry a small flashlight or headlamp. In an emergency when you're out after dark, the light becomes invaluable. Take extra batteries, too.

- **First-aid kit:** Two bandaids may not be enough! Carry a fully equipped standard first-aid kit with blister remedies. Many outdoor stores sell suitably prepared kits for hiking. Don't forget to add personal

2003 Robert Fire. Because of the fire, hikers during the climb now have views of the Middle Fork drainage, Rubideau Basin, the railway line, and West Glacier. Following the third switchback, the trail traverses across the ridge to the recently rebuilt lookout. The North Fork Valley sprawls its forested expanse. A panoramic view unfolds from Canada to the park's southern sector: You can pick out all six park peaks over 10,000 feet.

From this 5,236-foot aerie, the path of the Robert Fire is evident, where it raced over Apgar and out Howe Ridge, burning 7,000 acres in four hours. The fire left a mosaic of burn and forest, sure to provide habitat for a variety of species during regrowth. Prior to the fire, heavy timber and brush occluded views, but Apgar Lookout now ranks as one of the park's most scenic hikes. While fire improved the views, increased installation of park communication radio antennas has not, but at least

they are clustered in one location instead of spread throughout the park.

◖ Huckleberry Lookout

- Distance: 12 miles round-trip

- Duration: 5–6 hours

- Elevation gain: 3,403 feet

- Effort: strenuous

- Trailhead: six miles up Camas Road from Apgar just past McGee Meadows

Huckleberry Lookout trail is aptly named, for huckleberries do abound in this area. During certain times of the season, usually late summer to early fall, the trail may be closed due to bear activity. The heavy concentration of huckleberries attracts a significant bruin population looking to bulk up for the winter. Check with visitors centers or ranger stations

items like bee-sting kits and allergy medications.

- **Sun protection:** Altitude, snow, ice, and lakes all increase ultraviolet radiation. Protect yourself with 30 SPF sunscreen, sunglasses, and a sunhat or baseball cap.

- **Emergency bathroom supplies:** Not every hike conveniently places a pit toilet at its destination. To accommodate an alfresco bathroom, move at least 200 feet away from water sources. For urinating, aim for a durable surface, such as rocks, logs, gravel, or snow. "Watering" fragile plants, campsites, or trail sides attracts mineral-starved animals that dig up the area. Bury feces 6–8 inches deep in soil. Carry a small trowel, plastic baggies, and toilet paper for bathroom activities. Do not bury toilet paper; use a baggie to pack it out.

- **Feminine hygiene:** Carry heavy-duty Ziploc baggies and pack tampons, pads, and everything out. Do not dispose of any feminine hygiene products in backcountry pit toilets.

- **Insect repellent:** Summer can be abuzz at any elevation with mosquitoes and blackflies. Insect repellents containing 50 percent DEET tend to work best. Purchase applications that rub or spray in a close range rather than aerosols that become airborne onto other people, plants, and animals.

- **Pepper spray:** If you want to carry pepper spray, purchase an eight-ounce can as nothing smaller will be effective, but do not bother unless you know how to use it and what influences its effectiveness. It is not to be used like bug repellent.

- **Miscellaneous:** A knife may come in handy, as can a few feet of nylon cord and a bit of duct tape (wrap a few feet around something small like a flashlight handle or film canister). Many hikers have repaired boots and packs with duct tape and a little ingenuity.

for current status. When the trail is closed, the trailhead will have obvious closure signage.

The trail begins with a gentle walk through a lodgepole forest. Shortly, the path climbs, steadily gaining elevation among larch until it emerges in high meadows and reaches the ridge at 4.5 miles. In a short reprieve from the climb, the trail traverses a wide bowl until it crests the Apgar Range for the final ascent to the lookout at 6,593 feet. A spectacular view of the North Fork Valley and the park's Livingston Range unfolds. During fire season, the lookout is staffed. Evidence of the 2001 Moose Fire clings to Huckleberry Mountain as well as Demers Ridge below and the North Fork Valley.

Lake McDonald Trail

- Distance: 6.6 miles one-way

- Duration: 3 hours

- Elevation gain: none

- Effort: easy

- Trailhead: Fish Creek Campground or North McDonald Road

This trail follows the north shore of Lake McDonald, sometimes back in the trees, sometimes close to shoreline. While its views of Lake McDonald flanked by peaks are dramatic, more remarkable is the study of fire behavior and forest succession along the trail. Burned by the 2003 Robert Fire, the trail passes through all phases of a fire: cool burns, areas where fire swept just along the forest floor, treetop blazes, and hot burns. Regrowth is fast and lush as the ash returns nitrogen to the soil. With a car shuttle, hikers can walk this point-to-point, but most opt to saunter out for a few miles from either direction, perhaps drop a fishing line into the lake, and turn around again.

South Boundary Trail

- Distance: 10.6 miles round-trip to Lincoln Creek
- Duration: 5 hours
- Elevation gain: minimal
- Effort: easy
- Trailhead: behind park headquarters on Mather Drive's south end or the old bridge in West Glacier

After parking at headquarters, walk through the headquarters housing area to the trailhead. Follow the old Glacier Park Entrance Road to the historic Belton Bridge, where a trail continues upstream. You can also access this trail via the Belton Bridge, but the trailhead here does not have as much parking. With gentle ascents and descents, the trail hugs the north-shore hillside above the Wild and Scenic Middle Fork of the Flathead River.

This trail won't feel like wilderness: Noise from the railroad and highway competes with the river's roaring white water. But it's a good place to watch rafters shoot rapids, swim in deep pools, or fish. The trail descends to a fine rocky beach at Lincoln Creek, a stopping point for rafters before they hit the white water. From here, backpackers can opt to continue another 15 miles upriver to Coal Creek or turn 9.4 miles up Lincoln Creek to Lincoln Lake.

Guided Hikes

National Park Service **naturalist rangers** guide hikes and walks around Apgar from mid-June through mid-September. Days and times vary, but they lead easy strolls to more difficult hikes. Some winters, they offer guided snowshoe trips to look for animal tracks. Grab a copy of *The Glacier Explorer* at visitors centers to check for the current schedule. And they're the best price of all: free!

Glacier Guides (11970 Hwy. 2 E., 406/387-5555 or 800/321-7238, www.glacierguides.com, $65 person, $400 flat fee per day) leads day hikes for groups of five or more and custom hikes by reservation only. Sometimes solo travelers or couples can hook up with other interested parties through their office. Rates include guide service, deli lunch, transportation to the trailhead, and park entrance fees. The guide service also leads backpacking trips, with three-, four-, and six-day trips departing weekly; however, most of the overnight backcountry trips explore other park areas rather than West Glacier and Apgar.

Rentals

Three West Glacier companies rent gear for day hiking and backpacking: **Glacier Outdoor Center** (11957 Hwy. 2 E., 406/888-5454 or 800/235-6781, www.glacierraftco.com), **Glacier Guides** (11970 Hwy. 2 E., 406/387-5555 or 800/321-7238, www.glacierguides.com), and **Great Northern Whitewater** (12127 Hwy. 2 E., 406/387-5340 or 800/735-7897, www.gnwhitewater.com). Expect to pay $10–20 per day for a pack.

BIKING

Bicycling Glacier National Park is not for everyone. Roads are narrow, shoulderless, and packed with curves, and bikes are prohibited on trails. However, West Glacier–Apgar is one area in the park that does provide two off-road biking options.

Bike Trails

A level, newly repaved bicycle trail connects West Glacier with Apgar. Approximately 2.6 miles long, the **Apgar Bike Trail** begins on the north side of the West Glacier bridge. After dropping through the woods, it crosses through the park service employee housing area before entering the forest again, where it continues on to Apgar, connecting finally with the campground. Be cautious at two road crossings en route. This is one park trail where dogs are permitted on a leash, and it's good flat riding for kids.

A fun 10-mile round-trip ride on a combination dirt road and trail that was once a road, mountain biking to the **Old Flathead**

Ranger Station provides little-seen views of the confluence of Flathead River's North and Middle Forks. Access the route from midway between West Glacier and Apgar on the Apgar Bike Trail, turning west on the unnamed, dirt Glacier Institute road. At the first junction, follow the sign to the horse barn; at the second, hang a left toward Quarter Circle Bridge. About 0.5 mile past the bridge, the Old Flathead Ranger Station Trail begins. Turn left here, biking 3.7 miles to the Old Flathead Ranger Station site and the confluence. Although the trail continues north, bikes are not permitted beyond here.

Bicycle Road Tours

Many bicyclists enjoy short road rides from Apgar up Camas Road, the dirt Inside Road (see *North Fork* chapter for details), or just to Fish Creek Picnic Area.

For a longer mountain-bike tour (approximately 37 miles, four hours) on a mix of dirt and paved roads, the **Apgar Mountain Loop** takes off from West Glacier heading west over Belton Stage and Blankenship Roads to connect with North Fork Road. From here, ride north, parallel with the North Fork River to the Camas Road entrance and back into the park. Follow rolling Camas Road back to the Apgar Bike Trail. The scenic loop is well worth a ride, especially in late spring before Going-to-the-Sun Road is open, but be prepared to suck serious dust on the dirt sections during dry spells and to encounter bears and mosquitoes along Camas Road.

West Glacier is also the launch point for those bicycling Going-to-the-Sun Road. For details, see the *Going-to-the-Sun Road* chapter.

Rentals

No bicycle rentals are available inside the park. Outside the park in West Glacier, **Glacier Outdoor Center** (11957 Hwy. 2 E., 406/888-5454 or 800/235-6781, www.glacierraftco.com) rents mountain bikes for adults and children ($15–30 per day) as well as bike racks for cars ($4–10 per day). The center also has maps of local bicycle tours.

TRAIL RIDING

For riding in the park, you'll have to drive to Lake McDonald Lodge for the horse concession. However, just outside the park in West Glacier, **Rawhide Trail Rides** (12000 Hwy. 2 E., 406/387-5999 or 800/388-5727, www.rawhidetradingpost.com, mid-May–mid-Oct.) leads horseback tours through the lodgepole foothills of Flathead National Forest. Rides begin daily at 8 A.M. with one-, two-, or three-hour rides ($23–50 per person, no children's rates); the last ride leaves at 4 P.M. Rawhide also guides half-day ($58) rides. You can just show up for these, but if you want to guarantee a time, make reservations. By reservation only for a minimum of four people, you can also do a full-day ride ($100 per person, including lunch). For riding, be sure to wear long pants and sturdy shoes rather than sandals; you'll be a lot less sore afterward. Rawhide can accommodate kids 4–7 years old, whereas the park concessionaire will only take kids over 7.

RAFTING
◖ Middle Fork of the Flathead

Bordering Glacier's southern boundary, the Middle Fork of the Flathead interrupts scenic float sections with raging white water. Designated a Wild and Scenic River, the Middle Fork draws its headwaters from deep within the Bob Marshall Wilderness Complex and drains Glacier's immense southern valleys. Together with the North Fork of the Flathead, the rivers provide 219 miles of wildness, scenery, and recreation; the rafting season runs May–September, with high water peaking usually in June.

If there's one thing you should do while you're in the area, it should be a raft trip on Middle Fork. While the white water cannot compete with the Grand Canyon, the Middle Fork is a fun, splashy place to raft. It's lightweight enough for kids and good introductory fun for a first-time river trip.

Managed by the Forest Service, the Middle Fork River offers several put-ins and take-outs easily accessed along U.S. Highway 2. Different sections are appropriate for overnights, day trips, fishing, and short floats. While a

© BECKY LOMAX

Tunnel Rapid, on the Middle Fork of the Flathead River outside West Glacier

few rapids at certain water levels are rated Class IV, the river along Glacier's boundary is primarily Class II and III. No permits are required; however, all camping must be done on the south shore; no camping is permitted on Glacier's shoreline. Since private property abuts some of the south shore, you'll need to be knowledgeable about where and where not to camp. Consult the Flathead National Forest Ranger Station (milepost 143.1 on Hwy. 2, 406/387-5243) in Hungry Horse, nine miles west of West Glacier, for assistance in planning a self-guided overnight trip.

North Fork of the Flathead

From Canada, the North Fork of the Flathead flows through the remote North Fork Valley. As the river enters the United States, it forms the western boundary of Glacier. Accessed via the bumpy, dirt Outside North Fork Road, the Class II river is great for multiday float trips, day rafting, and fishing. Put-ins and take-outs range up and down North Fork Road. No permits are required, but campsites must all be set up on the western shore; no camping is permitted on Glacier's bank. Just past its confluence with the Middle Fork, the take-out at Blankenship is 10 minutes from West Glacier.

Guides

All four West Glacier rafting companies lead half-day, full-day, and scenic float trips on the Middle Fork River. All four also guide overnight and multiday trips as well as dinner, barbecue, or evening floats. Expect to pay in the $40 per person range for an adult half-day raft trip or in the high $70s for full day; kids run about $10 cheaper. For more fun rafting, tackle the white water in an inflatable kayak, otherwise known as a rubber ducky! Guides instruct inflatable kayakers on routes as they tag along with their raft trips; rates for rubber duckies run about $10–13 more per person than rafting rates. A 7 percent service fee is added on to all river trips. Paddles and lifejackets are included in all rates, but some companies charge additional fees for wetsuits and/or

booties. Clarify fees when you make your reservation.

The commercial rafting season runs May–September with high water peaking usually in June. Overnight rafting trips range 2–4 days; longer ones are usually paired up with hiking, horseback riding, or backpacking. Expect to pay around $130–150 per person per day (not night) for an overnight rafting trip and $30–40 less per day for children. When making reservations, clarify what you'll need to bring for your overnight. The companies usually can provide tents, sleeping bags, pads, and dry bags for your gear.

Glacier Raft Company (6 Going-to-the-Sun Rd., 406/888-5454 or 800/235-6781, www.glacierraftco.com) departs six times daily with half-day rafting trips. Guides also lead excursions on the Class III–IV Upper Middle Fork of the Flathead River. These white-water trips require flight access or a six-mile hike to a remote put-in inside the Great Bear Wilderness, south of Glacier Park. A 2.5-day horseback trip can also be combined with an Upper Middle Fork rafting trip. Per person rates for overnight trips range $265–1,500.

Great Northern Whitewater (12127 Hwy. 2 E., 406/387-5340 or 800/735-7897, www.gnwhitewater.com) departs five times daily with half-day trips. Overnights on the Middle Fork River range $150–365 per person, depending on duration.

Montana Raft Company (11970 Hwy. 2 E., 406/387-5555, 800/521-RAFT or 800/521-7238, www.glacierguides.com) departs five times daily with half-day trips. It also offers overnight rafting on the North Fork of the Flathead River, along with cabin stays and hike-raft or backpack-raft combinations—full day trips to week-long adventures. Overnights range $275–1,035 per person, depending on length of trip.

Wild River Adventures (11900 Hwy. 2 E., 406/387-9453 or 800/700-7056, www.river wild.com) departs four times daily for half-day rafting trips. Three-day overnight trips on the North Fork River run $375 per person.

Rentals

Rent a raft or inflatable kayak from **Glacier Outdoor Center** (11957 Hwy. 2 E., 406/888-5454 or 800/235-6781, www.glacierraftco.com) in West Glacier and guide yourself. Rates range $45–175 and include paddles, helmets, life-jackets, pump, and repair kit. Get your vehicle shuttled from put-in to take-out for $20 and up, depending on distance.

BOATING

With its vast acreage of water, Lake McDonald attracts boaters, but it's never crowded—usually just a few quiet anglers in the early morning and a couple die-hard water-skiers, sightseers, and kayakers touring the shoreline. Because the frigid waters inhibit tons of water-skiers and jet skis are not permitted, the lake never has a frenzied hubbub of noise. In fact, national park regulations enforce a maximum noise level of 82 decibels. As at many of the park's lakes, you'll rarely see a sailboat or windsurfer: unpredictable, swirly winds on Lake McDonald make other lakes outside the park more appealing. Located adjacent to Village Inn, Apgar's boat ramp provides the lake's only public ramp access.

Rentals

For boating and fishing on Lake McDonald, **Glacier Park Boat Company** (406/257-2426, www.glacierparkboats.com) rents rowboats and eight-horsepower motorboats for $10–20 per hour from the Apgar boat dock next to Village Inn. Paddles, lifejackets, and fishing regulations are included in the rates. Come prepared with cash, for the company does not take credit cards out of its tiny boat dock office.

Regulations

Two shoreline closures affect boaters: from the Apgar boat ramp north to the lake's outlet, and between the Apgar Amphitheater and Going-to-the-Sun Road. To protect swimmers here, boaters must stay 300 feet off the shoreline and are not permitted to beach. Watch also for additional temporary wildlife closures marked with

FISHING IN GLACIER

With 27,023 acres of lakes, 563 streams, and 22 species of fish, in Glacier no angler should sit with a slack line. Although only a scant 10 percent of park visitors fish, those that do typically enjoy calm vistas and a few native fish. While all kinds of variables from weather to skill can influence success, a few tips for Glacier's waters can help.

FISHING TIPS

- Avoid making a long hike to a remote lake to fish, unless you want to go there for the sake of the journey. While many anglers find more success fishing waters away from roads, just because a lake is remote doesn't make it good fishing. Waterfalls may prevent fish from reaching a stream or lake.

- Arrival at a high mountain lake will most likely be at midday when fishing is not the best. Hence, if you can stay overnight in the backcountry at a lodge nearby you can fish in the morning or evening for best results; that's when fish feed. Low light on overcast days can also make for good fishing.

- Early in the season, during runoff when river waters cloud with sediments, fish hang on the bottom to feed. Try lures that mimic insect larvae. Or fish lakes instead.

- Later in the season when streams run clear, fly-fishing is the most productive. Try to match a prominent hatch, but traditional high-floating attractor patterns will also move fish.

- At lakes, look for inlets and outlets to fish, but be considerate of heavily trafficked areas.

- Trolling from a motorboat (where allowed) or canoe is the most effective way to fish for lake trout.

FISHING AND BEARS

- Fishing in bear country poses special considerations. Since smells attract bears and bears travel along waterways, minimize your chances of a bear encounter by keeping fishy smells away from your clothing. In general, catch-and-release fishing minimizes the chances of attracting a bear.

- For cleaning fish in the front country, dispose of fish entrails in bear-resistant

buoys, especially at the lake's east end, where bald eagles nest.

While any craft over 12 feet must be registered in Montana, temporary use of out-of-state boats is permitted without registration. On Glacier's waters, federal boating regulations and water travel etiquette apply. For a complete list of boating regulations, check with visitors centers or Glacier's website: www.nps.gov/glac.

KAYAKING AND CANOEING

The West Glacier–Apgar area offers two types of kayaking: river and lake. The **Middle Fork of the Flathead** churns up Class III white-water rapids for kayakers with skills or calm Class II riffles for beginners. You'll find kayakers playing in the rapids between Moccasin Creek put-in and the West Gla-

cier take-out, surfing the waves on Tunnel Rapid. The scenic section of the Middle Fork is flat enough for canoeing from West Glacier downriver to Blankenship. One very scenic canoe route starts at Lake McDonald's west end and follows Lower McDonald Creek past Quarter Circle Bridge, where it intersects with the Middle Fork; you can then take out at Blankenship.

With its monstrous shoreline, **Lake McDonald** is a treat for both canoeing and sea kayaking, but watch for winds whipping up large whitecaps. When glassy calm waters prevail, you'd be hard-pressed to beat canoeing or kayaking Lake McDonald at sunrise or sunset. Touring the shoreline, you may encounter wildlife closures, especially for nesting bald eagles at the lake's head.

garbage cans. In the backcountry, do not bury or burn the innards as that may attract bears. Instead, be at least 200 feet away from a campsite or trail, puncture the air bladder, and throw the entrails into deep water. If you plan to eat your fish, keep only what you can eat, and eat as soon as you can.

NATIVE SPECIES

Glacier Park's fishing regulations enforce protection of native species through selected area closures and limits on the taking of native species. The park service no longer stocks fish, as many of the introduced species took a toll on native fish through competition for food and predation. Until 1972, an estimated 45-55 million fish and eggs were planted in Glacier's waters, introducing **arctic grayling, rainbow trout, kokanee salmon, brook trout,** and **Yellowstone cutthroat trout. Lake trout** and **lake whitefish** also invaded the park's west side water systems through stocking in Flathead Lake, although lake trout are native to park waters east of the Continental Divide and **mountain whitefish** are native throughout the park.

Of Glacier's 10 sport and 12 non-sport fish, the **bull trout** is the one listed as a threatened species under the Endangered Species Act. In Montana, this predatory fish, which can grow to two feet long, now inhabits less than half of its original streams, due to a number of factors, including habitat degradation. No fishing for bull trout is allowed; any incidentally caught must be immediately released.

Glacier is also a one of the few remaining strongholds for **westslope cutthroat trout,** which now inhabit only 2.5 percent of their original range. Mostly threatened by genetic contamination or interbreeding with rainbow trout, genetically pure populations of cutthroat remain in 15-19 park lakes.

While bull trout are protected by law, other native fish need conscientious anglers to help preserve the native fishery. Learn to identify native and nonnative species and follow park guidelines for which fish to harvest and which native fish to release. But in general, release native fish; keep only your limit of nonnative species.

For the best fishing recommendations, grab a copy of Russ Schneider's *Fishing Glacier National Park.*

Rentals and Lessons

At the Apgar boat dock next to Village Inn, **Glacier Park Boat Company** (406/257-2426, www.glacierparkboats.com) rents canoes and kayaks (rowboats, too) for $10 per hour. Boats come with paddles and lifejackets. Bring cash; the company does not take credit cards.

In West Glacier, **Glacier Outdoor Center** (11957 Hwy. 2 E., 406/888-5454 or 800/235-6781, www.glacierraftco.com) rents one- and two-person inflatable kayaks for $45–75, including paddles, helmets, lifejackets, pump, and repair kit. The center will also shuttle your vehicle from put-in to take-out starting at $20; shuttle rates depend on distance.

Great Northern Whitewater (12127 Hwy. 2 E., 406/387-5340 or 800/735-7897, www.gn

whitewater.com) rents canoes for $35 per day. For white-water kayakers and kayaker-wannabes, guides lead both half- and full-day kayak trips and teach a **kayak school** on the Middle Fork. Instructors, who are all Whitewater Certified by the American Canoe Association, walk beginners through the basics or teach playboating skills to intermediate and advanced kayakers. Day trips start at $105 per person with all equipment included.

FISHING

While Lake McDonald may be the biggest body of water in Glacier, expert anglers head to other lakes. Those who want to troll for lake trout here should use a boat. For catch-and-release fly-fishing, Lower McDonald Creek from the lake to Quarter Circle Bridge

works, but it's also heavily fished because of its easy access. For several miles in both directions from West Glacier, the Middle Fork of the Flathead presents good fishing, but be ready to contend with rafters and fishing outfitters. Because of the concentration of visitors in the West Glacier–Apgar area during high season, you may not feel like you're off in the wilderness when you toss a line in here.

Guides

Four angling companies guide half-, full-, and multiday fly-fishing trips on Glacier's boundary waters in the Middle Fork or North Fork of the Flathead River. For beginners, all four offer fly-fishing schools to teach the basics of casting, mending, and catch-and-release. Reservations and fishing licenses are mandatory. Although no companies guide fishing adventures on Glacier's front country lakes, Glacier Guides is the only outfitter permitted to guide trips into Glacier's backcountry.

For a half-day guided fishing trip for one or two people, expect to pay $260–280 and add on about $100 more for full days. It's pricey, but the instruction is often well worth the cost. Rates include all equipment, such as lifejackets, rods, and flies. As with rafting trips, a 7 percent service fee is added to all fishing trips.

Glacier Anglers (Glacier Outdoor Center, 11957 Hwy. 2 E., 406/888-5454 or 800/235-6781, www.glacierraftco.com) leads fishing trips and a fishing school on the Middle Fork and North Fork of the Flathead April 15–October 15. There's also a fly shop on-site.

Glacier Guides (11970 Hwy. 2 E., 406/387-5555 or 800/521-7238, www.glacierguides.com) has fly-fishing trips and a fly-fishing school on the North Fork and Middle Fork of the Flathead River July–September. For those looking for a guided fishing trip into Glacier's backcountry, Glacier Guides operates the only backpacking concession in the park with three-, four-, and six-day trips going out weekly all summer long. Per person rates for backpacking trips begin at $115 per day. For those with specific fishing agendas, custom backpacking trips are a bet-

ter idea; rates begin at $140 per person per day with a four-person minimum.

Montana Fly-fishing Guides (Great Northern Whitewater, 12127 Hwy. 2 E., 406/387-5340 or 800/735-7897, www.gnwhitewater.com) leads trips on the Middle Fork River and offers fly-fishing instruction April–October.

Wild River Adventures (11900 Hwy. 2 E., 406/387-9453 or 800/700-7056, www.riverwild.com, July–early Sept.) provides anglers with day trips and a fly-fishing school on the Middle Fork of the Flathead and overnight trips on the North Fork.

Rentals

Glacier Outdoor Center (11957 Hwy. 2 E., 406/888-5454 or 800/235-6781, www.glacierraftco.com) rents fishing gear ($5–50)—from rods to waders and float tubes. Along with rowboats and motorboats, **Glacier Park Boat Company** (406/257-2426, www.glacierparkboats.com) at the Apgar boat dock rents some fishing gear, but remember to bring cash, for they don't take credit cards.

Licenses and Regulations

Fishing inside Glacier Park does not require a license, but fishing outside on Flathead River drainages does.

Lake McDonald has no limit on lake trout or whitefish. Lower McDonald Creek from the lake outlet to Quarter Circle Bridge is catch-and-release only. Despite its name, Fish Creek is closed to fishing.

GOLF

Glacier View Golf Club (640 River Bend Dr., 406/888-5471 or 800/843-5777) may tax your concentration as you tee off. Moose, elk, bears, and deer wander across the fairways, and the park view is hard to ignore. The 18-hole course has a pro shop, restaurant, practice green, lessons, and cart rentals ($24). Open daily to the public April–October (snow permitting), the course charges only $24–29 for 18 holes. To locate the golf course in West Glacier, turn west onto River Bend Drive and follow signs to the clubhouse.

skiing to Fish Creek on Lake McDonald's northwest corner

CROSS-COUNTRY SKIING AND SNOWSHOEING

Winter converts the roads and trails around Apgar into easy cross-country skiing and snowshoeing paths usually between late November and April. Quiet and scenic, road skiing makes for easy route finding with little avalanche danger in lower elevations. For access during winter, roads are plowed into Apgar and up Lake McDonald's south shore. Popular ski tours follow roads and trails to Fish Creek Campground, Rocky Point, McGee Meadows, and the Old Flathead Ranger Station near the Middle Fork and North Fork confluence. Those with gumption and stamina climb to Apgar Lookout. For route descriptions, pick up *Skiing and Snowshoeing* in visitors centers or online: www.nps.gov/glac. Skiers and snowshoers should be well-equipped and versed in winter travel safety before venturing out even on snow-covered roads.

Glacier Outdoor Center (11957 Hwy. 2 E., 406/888-5454 or 800/235-6781, www.glacier raftco.com) rents cross-country ski gear and snowshoes for $10–15 daily; weekly rates run $60 for snowshoes and $90 for cross-country ski gear.

Guides

November–April as snows permit, **Glacier Park Ski Tours** (406/862-2790, www.glacier parkskitours.com, $165–275 for 1–4 people per day, $35 for each additional person) guides full-day ski tours for a variety of skill levels into Glacier—road schussing to backcountry telemark. If you're a solo traveler, it's the best way to get accompanied into the backcountry. Tours usually meet at the West Glacier post office. Lunch and snacks are included. For something different, ski in to an igloo to spend the night (add $35 per person per day to above rates). On full-moon nights, you can also take a ski tour, skiing by ethereal moonglow ($30 per person).

ENTERTAINMENT

If you're looking for nightlife, don't expect much. You can hang at the West Glacier bar to shoot pool with the river-rafters or head into

the Flathead Valley. Instead of nightlife, most park visitors take advantage of the long daylight hours (dark doesn't descend until almost 11 P.M. in June) to explore everything they can.

Park Naturalist Evening Programs

Fish Creek Campground Amphitheater and Apgar Campground Amphitheater host park naturalists with evening programs on wildlife, fires, and natural phenomena. Check a current copy of *The Glacier Explorer* for subjects, times, and dates for these programs, which usually run mid-June through mid-September; the 45-minute talk topics are usually posted in campgrounds, hotels, and visitors centers, too. Best of all, park naturalist programs are free!

Accommodations

With the ambience of Lake McDonald, the limited lodging inside the park at Apgar is extremely popular, so West Glacier options often serve as backup. But given that the communities are only two miles apart and connected by a bike path, they are equally convenient to each other and their unique activities. Keep in mind that Montana tacks on a 7 percent bed tax to each lodging night, so your bill will be a higher than your quoted room rate.

APGAR

Adjacent to each other, two lodges sit in Apgar at the foot of Lake McDonald, with Eddie's Restaurant and Grocery, the visitor center, Lake McDonald boat dock, and several gift shops all within the same block. The Apgar Bike Trail begins here, and there's access to McDonald Creek for fishing or canoeing. The Apgar Campground Amphitheater for naturalist talks is a seven-minute walk away. Reservations are a must. Although the area is a busy hive during the day, at night it's very quiet.

Near Lake McDonald's shores are set back in huge old-growth cedars, **(Apgar Village Lodge** (on Apgar Rd. 0.3 mile from Camas Rd. or 0.8 mile from Going-to-the-Sun Rd., 406/888-5484 or 888/838-2363, www.westglacier.com, early May–early Oct., $116–213 per night) clusters 20 motel rooms and 28 rustic cabins—most with kitchens—within a two-minute walk to the lake. The cabins along McDonald Creek are particularly quiet and serene—mixed with a wonderful ambience of wildlife and the sound of the stream. Although older, the nonsmoking cabins have all been upgraded since the mid-1990s with new linoleum, bathrooms, and appliances. All rooms have televisions, but no phones. (Pay phones are outside the lobby.)

On Lake McDonald's shore, every one of the 36 nonsmoking rooms in the **(Village Inn** (on Apgar Rd. 0.3 mile from Camas Rd. or 0.8 mile from Going-to-the-Sun Rd., 406/892-2525, www.glacierparkinc.com, late May–early Oct., $108–170 per night) wakes up to a striking view uplake toward the Continental Divide. Some rooms include kitchenettes, but to preserve the get-away-from-it-all ambience, none of the rooms have phones (a pay phone is outside the lobby) or televisions, nor is there an elevator to the second floor. Although it's been redecorated, not much else has changed since the inn was built with its 1956 architecture. Even though the rooms are rather nondescript, the stunning view makes the stay worthwhile.

WEST GLACIER

Lodging in West Glacier is convenient for hopping the train, going river-rafting or fishing, and heading off on guided backpacking trips. It's also such a quick jaunt to Lake McDonald that if park lodging is full, West Glacier options work as an easy backup. Be prepared, however, for nightly noise—not from people (they're crashed from packing in so much activity during the long days), but from almost 30 trains that ride the Burlington Northern Santa Fe rail daily. Bring earplugs if you're a

light sleeper. During high season, most West Glacier lodging options fill nightly with bookings, so reservations are a good idea.

Lodges and Cabins

Located across from Belton Train Depot, the National Historic Landmark **◖ Belton Chalet** (12575 Hwy. 2 E., 406/888-5000 or 888/235-8665, www.beltonchalet.com, late May–mid-Oct. plus two cottages year-round) improved its main summer-only lodge rooms ($130–155) and private year-round cottages ($285 summer, $95 winter) with a $1 million restoration. The chalet's restaurant serves outstanding dinners; other restaurants serving breakfast and lunch are within a five-minute walk, as are gift shops, rafting, the Middle Fork of the Flathead, and the West Glacier Mercantile. Remedies Day Spa offers its refreshing services on-site. It's one of the best places to stay in West Glacier, but bring the earplugs to sleep through the highway and railroad noise.

Sitting on a hill above the highway, the **◖ Glacier Outdoor Center** (11957 Hwy. 2 E., 406/888-5454 or 800/235-6781, www.glacierraftco.com, open year-round, $210–310, off-season discounts available) has three non-smoking one- and two-bedroom log cabins that sleep 6–14 people. Set way back from the road amid birch trees around a trout pond with views of Glacier, the cabins come with fully equipped kitchens, televisions, log furniture, decks, grills, and gas fireplaces, and the deluxe cabin has a washer and dryer. Horseshoe pits, an outdoor pavilion, and a volleyball court sit adjacent, and amenities include rentals for hiking, biking, skiing, snowshoeing, and fishing. Multinight stays chop off $5–15 per night depending on the duration.

Part of the Great Northern Whitewater complex with the rafting, fishing, and kayaking company located on-site, **Great Northern Chalets** (12127 Hwy. 2 E., 406/387-5340 or 800/735-7897, www.gnwhitewater.com, open year-round, $225–295, discounts available off-season) rents two small (six-person) and two large (eight-person) nonsmoking log chalets with fully equipped kitchens. Set around

historic Belton Chalet in West Glacier, across from the train depot

© BECKY LOMAX

a landscaped garden pond, the cozy chalets are decorated in Glacier outdoor themes, and several have views of the park. A three-night minimum stay is required during high season. West Glacier's restaurants and shops are one mile away: You can walk down the highway, but it's not the most pleasant walk with big trucks zipping by.

Motels

For basic rooms and nothing fancy, motels in West Glacier work for a good place to flop after hiking. Located in West Glacier's shopping, rafting, and restaurant hub, **West Glacier Motel** (200 Going-to-the-Sun Rd., 406/888-5484 or 888/838-2363, www.westglacier.com, open mid-May–late Sept.) has nonsmoking motel units ($75–100) and three cabins ($125–156)—all with televisions but no phones (pay phones are outside the lobby), and the motel does have a wireless Internet hotspot. Sitting directly across Highway 2 from the Belton Train Depot, the **Glacier Highland** (12555 Hwy. 2 E., 406/888-5427 or 800/766-0811,

open mid-Apr.–Oct., $80–95, off-season discounts available) has 33 nonsmoking modern rooms that include satellite television and access to a hot tub, adjacent to the Glacier Highland Restaurant.

Perched on a hill above the highway a half mile west of the Belton Train Depot, the family-run, older, nonsmoking **Glacier Vista Motel** (milepost 152.5 on Hwy. 2 E., 406/888-5311, www.glaciervistamotel.com, open mid-May–mid-Sept., $67–125) is the only motel with an outdoor heated swimming pool, and rooms facing the highway have an amazing view into Glacier.

OUTSIDE WEST GLACIER

Typically, lodging facilities in West Glacier and Apgar both book up for high season, well before summer's onset. However, plenty of motels and cabins line the nine miles of Highway 2 from West Glacier to Hungry Horse—good alternatives, with just a short drive down the highway to reach the West Glacier park entrance.

Cabins

A new cabin complex built in 2003, **Glaciers Mountain Resort** (1385 Old Hwy. 2 E., 406/387-5712 or 877/213-8001, www.glaciers mountainresort.com, open year-round, $160 per night, off-season rates drop 20–30 percent) has five one-bedroom knotty pine cabins—with fully equipped kitchens with dishwashers, satellite television, VCRs, log furniture, private bathrooms, and barbecue grills—lined up on landscaped property. There's a two-night minimum stay mid-June–mid-September.

Touted for its "designer chalets," ◖ **Silverwolf Log Chalet Resort** (Gladys Glenn Rd. and Hwy. 2 E., 406/387-4448, www.silverwolf chalets.com, open mid-May–mid-Oct., $158, off-season discounts available) rents 10 modern, two-person log chalets decorated with log furniture and set in a landscaped lawn under lodgepoles. Separated from the road by a privacy fence, the resort is a neat, well-maintained, sharp-looking adults-only place, with

kids, smoking, and pets not allowed. Multi-night stays reduce rates by $10–13 per night. Built in 1907, the **Tamarack Lodge** (9549 Hwy. 2 E., 406/387-4420 or 877/387-4420, www.historictamaracklodge.com, year-round $99–119) renovated its six main log-beam lodge rooms in 1994—running them now as a bed-and-breakfast, with a full breakfast served in the morning. The lodge also has eight motel units ($79–94) and three private chalets ($130–290) with fully equipped kitchenettes.

Bed-and-Breakfasts

For those who want the intimacy of a B&B setting, two operate near West Glacier, both serving full, hearty breakfasts. Within sight of but off the highway on seven partially landscaped acres, **A Wild Rose Bed and Breakfast** (10280 Hwy. 2 E., 406/387-4900, www.awildrose.com, year-round, $120–150 per night) has four nonsmoking luxury Victorian rooms with all-natural linens and cushy robes. Amenities include an outdoor hot tub and breakfast served in the dining room, which is furnished with 1920s antiques. In 2005 the venue was listed for sale, so call ahead to confirm availability and rates.

Sitting below the highway, overlooking the Flathead River, the **Glacier Park Inn** (9128 Hwy. 2 E., 406/387-5099, www.glacierpark inn.com, open year-round, $80–140) tucks five rooms in its remodeled, octagonal, nonsmoking home with a giant wraparound deck—the perfect place to unwind with a view of the Apgar Mountains.

CAMPING
Apgar

In Apgar, two campgrounds sit amid thick forests with easy access to Lake McDonald. Rustic—with no hookups—both Fish Creek and Apgar Campgrounds have flush toilets, disposal stations, hiker-biker sites, amphitheaters for evening naturalist talks, and sites that accommodate large RVs. Because of their location inside the park, they are popular campgrounds away from highway and railroad noise.

Fish Creek (end of Fish Creek Rd., 406/888-7800, June–early Sept., $17 per night), one of two campgrounds in the park that can be reserved through the National Park Reservation System (800/365-CAMP, http://reservations.nps.gov), is one of the largest campgrounds in the park, with 180 sites tucked among cedars, lodgepoles, and larch and accessing Lake McDonald through the picnic area. Eighteen campsites accommodate RVs up to 35 feet long; 62 sites fit RVs up to 27 feet. To find Fish Creek, which is a six-minute drive from Apgar, drive 1.25 miles north on Camas Road and turn right, dropping one mile down to the campground. Lake McDonald Trail departs from the campground.

Apgar Campground (on Apgar Rd. 0.4 mile from Going-to-the-Sun Rd., 406/888-7800, May–early Sept., $15 per night) is within short walking distance to Apgar Village and Lake McDonald. The 192-site campground is the park's largest. Large group campsites are available, and 25 sites accommodate RVs up to 40 feet. Primitive camping ($6) is available before and after dates listed, but the water is turned off and only pit toilets are available. The Apgar Bike Trail begins nearby, and a restaurant, gift shops, visitor center, and boat dock are in adjacent Apgar Village.

Free winter camping is permitted at the Apgar Picnic Area. However, no services are available: no water, no toilets, just a plowed lot. Check the winter camping instructions on the bulletin board here for details.

West Glacier

Commercial campgrounds in the West Glacier vicinity are convenient for rafting, fishing, biking, and trail rides, but are located outside the park. If you require hookups, this is where you'll need to be. Standard amenities in these campgrounds include flush toilets and hot showers. Also, these campgrounds can handle the big RV rigs, whereas the park campgrounds have limited sites. If you're a light sleeper, bring your earplugs, for many of the campgrounds hear the rumble and screech from nearly 30 trains per day.

Although most commercial campgrounds lean toward servicing RVers and car campers, bikers and hikers should ask about special rates in shared area sites, for they can often pay much less, around $6 per person. Many of the campgrounds also offer rustic camping cabins or yurts, which have no kitchens or bathrooms, and you'll need to bring sleeping bags or pay extra for clean linens, blankets, and towels (around $9–15 per person). Commercial campgrounds tack on a 7 percent Montana bed tax to their rates. When you make your reservations, check for deals; many give 10 percent discounts over the Internet or to Good Sam, AAA, or Woodall's members. Reservations are highly recommended for July and August, especially for big rigs requiring sites with a certain amount of room.

On 40 timbered acres only a half mile from West Glacier, **Glacier Campground** (12070 Hwy. 2 E., 406/387-5689 or 888/387-5689, www.glaciercampground.com, May–Sept., $19–26) is one mile west of the park entrance. Sites are very private, separated by birch and fir trees as well as lush undergrowth, so you don't feel you are camping in a parking lot. Amenities include laundry, camp store, propane, picnic tables, fire pits, and a dump station. A playground, cabins ($35–45), and **Cajun Mary's Café** are here. Leashed pets are totally welcome. With the campground set back from the road, trees reduce highway and railroad sounds to quiet. For evening entertainment, the campground sponsors Forest Service presentations.

Set back in the woods one mile off Highway 2 and 2.5 miles west of the park entrance, the **West Glacier KOA** (355 Half Moon Flats Rd., 406/387-5341 or 800/562-3313, www.westglacierkoa.com, May–Sept., $22–50) is the only campground with a heated swimming pool (June–mid-Sept.) and a couple of hot tubs. It also has evening programs, cabins ($45–70), a playground, modem dataports, flush toilets, hot showers, picnic tables, fire pits, a laundry, camp store, horseshoes, and a pancake breakfast and evening barbecue. Due to its location away from the highway and

railroad, this is one of the quietest campgrounds around.

Outside West Glacier

If you can't find a campsite at the campgrounds listed above, there are plenty more sprawled in the nine miles between West Glacier and Hungry Horse. At 2.5 miles from the park entrance, **San-Suz-Ed RV Park** (11505 Hwy. 2 E., 406/387-5280 or 800/305-4616, www.sansuzedrvpark.com, May–Oct., $20–27) centers its campground around a nightly community campfire pit: BYOM (bring your own marshmallows) or BYOHD (bring your own hot dogs) to roast. For those needing open space for clear satellite reception, the **North American RV Park and Campground** (10784 Hwy. 2 E., 406/387-5800 or 800/704-4266, May–Sept., 18–31) sits in a big grassy parking lot-type setting where the windows of one RV look into the next. One of the quietest campgrounds, **Mountain Meadows RV Park** (9125 Hwy. 2 E., 406/387-9125, www.mmrvpark.com, May–Sept., $20–30) sites span 77 acres of forested hillside with sites separated for privacy and a stocked catch-and-release rainbow trout pond.

Food

A few seasonal restaurants cater to summer visitors, but don't expect much open between October and May. Glacier is a place for good down-home cooking where tasty, freshly baked fruit pie is still the rage, rather than upscale or ethnic delicacies.

RESTAURANTS

Apgar

Eddie's Restaurant (on Apgar Rd. 0.3 mile from Camas Rd. or 0.8 mile from Going-to-the-Sun Rd., 406/888-5361, open early June–mid-Sept., 7 A.M.–9:30 P.M. daily in high season, 8 A.M.–8 P.M. daily in shoulder seasons) is the only game in town, but it has decent family-friendly meals. Open for breakfast ($6–8), lunch ($7–9), and dinner ($7–19), the restaurant is often very crowded with long waiting lines in high season. Takeout can be more convenient, especially when eaten a few steps away on Lake McDonald's shore. For dinner, you can order sandwiches ($8), fiesta chicken salad ($11), or a 14-ounce Montana rib-eye ($19). Leave room for the Bear Paw pie ($5); it takes the cake. Hiker lunches are available for $8.

West Glacier

Open daily for breakfast, lunch, and dinner, the **❰ West Glacier Restaurant and Lounge** (200 Going-to-the-Sun Rd., 406/888-5403, 7 A.M.–10 P.M. mid-May–mid-Sept.) serves good tasting cafe fare. Located in West Glacier between the park entrance bridge and the railroad tunnel, the restaurant can pack out with a line in high season. You can wait for a table in the fully licensed bar next door (or eat off the restaurant's menu in there), or with kids plan to go early. Breakfasts, which specialize in blueberry pancakes, and lunches run $6–9; full dinners ($9–17) feature fish, pasta, and steaks. You can also order sandwiches or salads for dinner, if you're looking for something lighter. Ironically, you'll find the best thing to sate a hungry hiker stomach—the Glacier Monster Cheeseburger—listed under "Lighter Appetites," but it's no such thing with bacon and cheese atop a half-pound hamburger, with fries.

Located conveniently across Highway 2 from the Belton Train Depot, the **Glacier Highland** (12555 Hwy. 2 E., 406/888-5427, 7 A.M.–10 P.M. mid-Apr.–Oct.) bakes great huckleberry muffins and cinnamon rolls to start the day. It's open daily for breakfast, lunch, and dinner. The basic cafe menu can please four different family eaters. Dinners can be sandwiches and burgers ($5–7) or steaks (up to $18). Beer and wine are served, too. The restaurant closes at 8 or 9 P.M. in shoulder seasons.

Whether you're eating on the deck watching

trains stop at the Belton Train Depot, in the dining room, or by the fireplace in the taproom, the historic 🄲 **Belton Chalet** (12575 Hwy. 2 E., 406/888-5000 or 888/235-8665, www.beltonchalet.com, taproom 3 P.M.– midnight daily, dining room 5–10 P.M. daily June–early Oct.) is a treat—not just for its ambience, restored to its 1910 grandeur, but for its fine-dining flavors with a local flair ($16– 27). Try the yummy Montana meatloaf ($16), a buffalo meatloaf wrapped in apple-smoked bacon with chipotle gravy. The well-stocked taproom is loaded with a full wine cellar and Montana microbrews. Lighter taproom meals ($7–9) feature goodies such as goat cheese tamales. In winter, the taproom opens on Saturday and Sunday 2–8 P.M., serving everything from buffalo beer chili to steak ($7–21) for hungry skiers.

Located in Glacier Campground, one mile west of Belton Train Depot, **Cajun Mary's Café** (12070 Hwy. 2 E., 406/387-5689, 5– 9 P.M. daily June–early Sept.) serves only dinners in an open-air pavilion. Specials ranging $6–20 vary nightly except for weekends, which always feature barbecues. Try the huckleberry barbecue sauce on your grilled goodies!

For the trail ride crowd, the **Rawhide Trading Post Restaurant and Steakhouse** (12000 Hwy. 2 E., 406/387-5999 or 800/388-5727, 8 A.M.–9 P.M. daily mid-May–mid-Oct.) serves a reasonably good burger and fries ($6), or you can pig down on the house specialty of mesquite grilled steak—a 10-ounce cowgirl ($18) or 14-ounce cowboy ($20)—which comes with homemade mini-loaves, veggies, and potatoes. Don't forget the huckleberry pie ($5). Open for breakfast, lunch, and dinner (except until mid-June and after Labor Day when it is only open 4–8 P.M.), the restaurant also does take-out meals for an easy dinner around the campfire. The restaurant is one mile west of the Belton Train Depot.

Outside West Glacier

Don't be fooled by its gas station exterior or the fact that it's down the road in Coram, 5.5 miles west of West Glacier. Open daily year-round for breakfast ($5–7), lunch, and dinner, the 🄲 **Spruce Park Café** (10045 Hwy. 2 E., 406/387-5614, 6:30 A.M.–10 P.M. Mon.–Fri. and 7 A.M.–10 P.M. Sat.–Sun. in summer, 7 A.M.– 8 P.M. daily in winter) bakes the best homemade fruit pie ($3–5) on the west side; you can even buy whole pies ($18–24) to go. Lunch and dinner feature burgers and sandwiches ($7), such as the homemade corn beef Rueben and the Rafter's Wrap of chicken, tomatoes, red onion, and Caesar dressing. Or try the Mexican entrees ($8–9), such as the Mountain Burrito in veggie, chili, or spicy beef Grande.

Located in Coram, **Canyon Deli and Pizza** (10026 Hwy. 2 E., 406/387-4223, 11 A.M.– 11 P.M. daily) serves cafe fare ($5–10) year-round, but the main reason to go here is the pizza ($11–16). The loaded all-meat pizza is packed wall-to-wall with sausage, Canadian bacon, and pepperoni; the Mediterranean special with feta cheese is baked with a delightful twist on spices.

CAFFEINE

The **Glacier Espresso** stand (8 A.M.–3 P.M.-ish daily June–mid-Sept.) is near the Alberta Visitor Center in West Glacier. A few baked goodies— cookies and muffins—are also sold. If temps climb, you can get an Italian soda or granita instead. In high season, it stays open sometimes as late as 7:30 P.M.

GROCERIES

Groceries (food, beer, wine) and camping items (ice, firewood, stove gas) may be purchased in both West Glacier and Apgar. **Eddie's Campstore** (on Apgar Rd. 0.8 mile from Going-to-the-Sun Rd. or 0.3 mile from Camas Rd., 8 A.M.–10 P.M. daily in high season, closes at 6 P.M. in shoulder seasons, open June–mid-Sept.) in Apgar also has a little outdoor seating for dining. In the West Glacier shopping area, the **West Glacier Mercantile** (0.1 mile west of Hwy. 2 junction on Going-to-the-Sun Rd., 8 A.M.–10 P.M. daily in high season, early and late season closure at 5 P.M., open May–Sept.) has the bigger selection of meats, fresh veggies,

and fruits. Convenience store items are also available at **Glacier Highland** (across from the Belton Train Depot on Hwy. 2, 7 A.M.–9 P.M. daily mid-Apr.–Oct., may close earlier in shoulder seasons); you'll find the cheaper beer and wine prices here.

The nearest year-round grocery store is in Hungry Horse, on Highway 2 nine miles west of the park entrance. Its sign calls it a supermarket, but it's not really that big. You'll have to drive 30 minutes into Flathead Valley to hit the megastores that carry huge brand selections.

PICNIC AREAS

Two picnic areas, both with beach access, rim Lake McDonald's western shores. **Apgar Picnic Area** is just off Going-to-the-Sun Road on the lake's southwest corner, with a beautiful uplake view to the Continental Divide. **Fish Creek Picnic Area** sits next to Fish Creek Campground, where a one-mile hike leads out to Rocky Point for more views. Both have picnic tables, flush toilets, and fire grates, but firewood is not provided and gathering is prohibited, so plan to purchase firewood in Apgar or West Glacier before heading here for your picnic.

NORTH FORK

It's remote. It's wild. And it's definitely not for everyone. The North Fork Valley defines rustic. Not rustic as in cute, comfortable rustic, but real rustic as in you nearly have to fend for yourself. No gas stations, no electricity, and pit toilets are de rigueur. But for those who want to get away from the mayhem, it's the place to go, if for no other reason than to slow the pace of life and experience the ambience of the Polebridge Mercantile and Northern Lights Saloon.

The North Fork Valley spans diverse habitats from grassland prairies to alpine glaciers, home for an immense range of wildlife—from grizzly bears to pygmy shrews. Spruce trees 300 years old root the valley in deep history. A visit to the North Fork transports you back in time. For the average traveler, the dirt roads alone deter interest. Potholes and washboards go on forever. But trails from the North Fork have only a few people, even in high season. Surrounded by thick subalpine fir forests, Bowman and Kintla Lakes have miles of empty shoreline dotted with only a boat of anglers or a few kayaks. For those who have patience and time to see, wildlife-watching and birding are the best. Nothing chills the soul quite like the wild call of wolves in the dead of night.

HISTORY

In the late 1800s, handfuls of homesteaders, loggers, hunters, and trappers eked out a living in the North Fork Valley, connected only by a network of trails. In 1900, a Butte business, on a quest for oil at Kintla Lake, built the Inside North Fork Road—a 65-mile wagon track

© BECKY LOMAX

HIGHLIGHTS

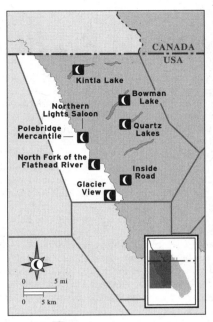

◖ Inside Road: Not to be missed in the annals of rough roads, this byway presents a real challenge for both vehicles and mountain bikes. Drive or ride its 28 miles for a closer encounter with its wildlife and rugged ups and downs (page 63).

◖ Polebridge Mercantile: With its freshly baked cookies and breads, this is clearly the historic hub of the North Fork Valley. It harkens back to another era with no electricity, where an old-fashioned cash register clangs up your groceries (page 64).

◖ Northern Lights Saloon: In spite of its remote location, the saloon serves incomparable food in its tiny log cabin. Order a microbrew and sit outside to enjoy the view or just soak up the chatter from locals (page 65).

◖ North Fork of the Flathead River: Floating the river is akin to throwing your watch away, for River Time takes over. Forming the western boundary of Glacier National Park, the river courses through prairielands and forests where grizzly bears and wolves hunt prey (page 65).

◖ Bowman Lake: Look down the lake and you're looking straight into wild country. Rainbow Peak juts straight up 4,500 feet from the lakeshore, while Thunderbird Mountain scrapes the sky behind nesting bald eagles (page 65).

◖ Kintla Lake: Although it may have been the site for oil drilling a century ago, today it's about as far away from civilization as you can get. It's a mean 42 miles from pavement and launches into some of the park's most remote backpacking terrain (page 65).

◖ Quartz Lakes: Lined up like pearls on a

LOOK FOR ◖ TO FIND RECOMMENDED SIGHTS, ACTIVITIES, DINING, AND LODGING.

necklace, the three Quartz Lakes lure anglers for their native westslope cutthroat trout—but pack the bug spray, for they're mosquito havens as well (page 66).

◖ Glacier View: A short grunt with scenery galore, the climb up may tax your lungs, but your nose will love the smell of wild roses and your eyes will relish Glacier's panorama at the top (page 68).

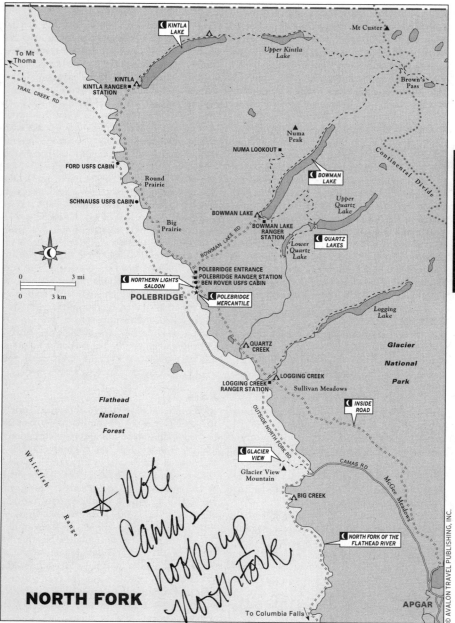

NORTH FORK

NORTH FORK

APGAR

© AVALON TRAVEL PUBLISHING, INC.

riddled with ruts, bogs, and stumps. It was sufficient, however, for hauling drilling equipment from Belton (West Glacier) to Kintla Lake, where sleds skidded supplies across the frozen lake to drill Montana's first oil well in 1901. The road attracted more homesteaders, but talk of Glacier becoming a national park was already afoot, a change the homesteaders disliked because it meant an end to their livelihoods.

When Glacier achieved national park status in 1910, construction of the rough Outside North Fork Road two years later prompted many of the 35 homesteading families within the park boundaries to move across the North Fork of the Flathead River, outside the park boundary. One resident, Bill Adair, built a new mercantile in 1914 near Hay Creek—a two-story plank building. The "Merc," as locals call it, is now listed on the National Register of Historic Places. The area today is known as Polebridge—named for the funky bridge over the North Fork River, a one-lane lodgepole affair burnt in the 1988 Red Bench Fire.

Culture

The North Fork is unique. It's a small intimate community that prides itself on its rustic nature—not L.L.Bean squeaky-clean look-alike rustic, but real bucolic earthiness with no electricity and few phone lines. The population of the four-mile-wide floodplain comprises year-round residents living off-the-grid and summer cabins. Most residents could care less if visitors complain about dust and potholes on the roads, and talk of paving the North Fork Road raises the hackles of many. The hub of valley life, the Merc and Northern Lights Saloon are where residents catch up on news, sometimes not much differentiated from gossip.

In Polebridge, you'll meet several of the town's dogs, who run amok freely and lounge on the Merc's front porch. However, as a visitor, you have a different responsibility with your dog in town. Visitors' dogs must be leashed. Hand-painted signs will tell you so: "Local dogs at large—please leash pets." One of the warning signs on the Northern Lights Saloon says, "Unleashed dogs will be eaten."

Ecological Significance

The North Fork area contains all five of Glacier's ecosystems: grassland prairies, aspen parklands, montane forests, subalpine, and alpine tundra. Rich floodplains teem with wildflowers, berries, shrubs, and trees. Fens abound with plantlife—orchids, bladderworts, sundews, mosses, sedges, ferns, and bulrushes. McGee Meadows, which is actually a fen, houses at least 50 species of flora. The valley is rife with grizzly and black bears, moose, coyotes, mountain lions, elk—all manner of wildlife down to its tiniest occupant, the pygmy shrew, which preys on 25 species of bugs, insects, and snails. Birders have documented woodpeckers, owls, raptors, waterfowl, and songbirds—196 species in the valley, over half of which nest here.

Since the natural migrations of wolves from Canada in the 1980s, Glacier saw its first wolf pack in 50 years with its first litter of pups in 1986. Numbers have since expanded to several wolf packs across northwestern Montana. However, don't expect to see a wolf; their numbers vary year to year, they range far (up to 300 square miles), and they are elusive. But you may hear them—especially at night. High deer and elk concentrations make the North Fork Valley prime habitat; to maintain its health, every day a wolf must eat 10 percent of its body weight in meat.

Fires

Rich timberlands of the North Fork are prime fire lands. Years of fire suppression policies led to thick lodgepole stands and bug infestations. The 38,000-acre Red Bench Fire in 1988 saw a change in policy, for the fire ran its natural course, nearly wiping Polebridge off the map. Silver sentinels stand as a reminder near town. In 2001, the Moose Fire shot over Demers Ridge, burning 71,000 acres, over one-third inside Glacier. In 2003, the Wedge Canyon Fire burned 53,315 acres, jumping the North Fork River into the park and traveling up the side of Parke Peak, while the Robert Fire burned the valley's south end. Evidence of each of these fires is obvious, but swift new growth is building a new forest with rampant blooms of fireweed, arrowleaf balsamroot, and pussytoes.

NORTH FORK WONDERS

TINY FAUNA

The North Fork Valley is home to the rare **northern bog lemming,** a small, brown-backed, gray-underbellied rodent that seeks mats of thick, wet sphagnum moss for habitat. Weighing only one ounce – the same as one heaping tablespoon of sugar – but growing up to six inches long, the tiny lemming is a relic of the Pleistocene Ice Age, which began two million years ago. It's also cousin to the arctic lemming. Although it's rarely seen, look for small, neat piles of clipped grass along the mossy thoroughfares en route to nests tunneled six inches underground. One study found that bog lemmings make up 2 percent of the pine marten's diet.

Glacier's smallest predator, the **pygmy shrew,** inhabits floodplains in the North Fork Valley. This tiny carnivore is one of North America's rarest mammals. Less than 2.5 inches in size and weighing less than a quarter ounce, this shrew's voracious appetite for insects, slugs, snails, and carrion can put larger shrews to shame. One study watched a female eat three times her own body weight daily for 10 days. Their high metabolism echoes their respiration rate – 25 times more than humans – and their hearts beat up to 1,320 times per minute when excited. To feed their high metabolic rates, pygmy shrews eat every couple of hours both night and day year-round.

PLANTS

Carnivorous plants inhabit North Fork fens. The **sundew** attracts insects to its sparkling droplets like morning dew on leaves. Sitting atop hairs lining its leaves, the sticky droplets entrap unsuspecting visitors like cement. Slowly, the leaves curl around their victim as digestive juices work their magic. Like the sundew, the **bladderwort** refined trapping. Bouyant bladders trap anything that swims by – mosquito larvae to fish fry. When the prey passes, it brushes hairs, opening a trap door that sucks water in along with the naive prey. Digestive enzymes make short work of the meal, and the trap is reset in 15 minutes to two hours.

BIRDS

Birders find a feast for their eyes and ears in the North Fork. With 196 species of birds documented here – at least 112 nesters – the valley teems with avian activity. Migratory birds stop on their flight highways to wintering ranges or summer nesting.

Raptors: Birds of prey find abundant food in the North Fork Valley. Numerous rodents, ground squirrels, songbirds, and carrion feed their appetites here. The valley's forests attract sharp-shinned and Cooper's hawks. Bald eagles nest on Kintla and Bowman Lakes. Northern harriers, red-tailed hawks, goshawks, and American kestrels all prowl above the prairies. At night, the hoots of large great-horned and pygmy owls haunt the air.

Waterfowl: Between the North Fork of the Flathead River, the many large lakes lining Glacier's western valleys, and swamps and wetlands, waterfowl have no shortage of suitable habitat. Herons, ducks, grebes, geese, loons, and swans migrate through or nest in the plentiful waters here.

Songbirds: The North Fork could be considered downright noisy at times – not from traffic, but from the scads of songbirds flitting among its trees and cattails. American redstarts, warbling vireos, kinglets, nuthatches, crossbills, sparrows, and warblers are just a few of the neotropical songbirds that migrate annually into the valley. In winter, you'll spot tree sparrows and redpolls.

Woodpeckers: After the recent Moose (2001) and Wedge Canyon Fires (2003), dead standing timber attracted the three-toed woodpecker, picking away for bugs. Watch also for the large, red-headed pileated woodpecker looking for a favorite food – carpenter ants. To help with identification of Glacier's birds, pick up a bird list from visitors centers or on the park's website.

NORTH FORK

Exploring North Fork

ENTRANCE STATION

The North Fork River is the boundary between national forest and national park lands here. From the North Fork Valley, two roads enter the park, both with entrance stations. Paved **Camas Road** enters from the dirt North Fork Road, with an unstaffed entrance station and a self-pay cash-only kiosk. A mile northeast of Polebridge, the **Polebridge entrance station** is staffed during summer only, but a self-pay cash-only kiosk is available, too.

TOURS AND SHUTTLES

The closest thing to guided tours in the North Fork is guided outdoor recreation: river-rafting the North Fork of the Flathead River, backpacking the Quartz Lakes Loop, or Goat Haunt via Kintla or Bowman Lake. However, the companies that guide these trips are based in West Glacier (see the *West Glacier and Apgar* chapter for contact info and pricing). You can also hook up with a **Glacier Institute** course that might be wildlife-watching in the area (covered in the *Background* chapter).

The North Fork does not see any daily or even weekly shuttle service; however, **Flathead-Glacier Transportation** (FGT, 406/892-3390 or 800/829-7039, www.fgtrans. com) provides a taxi service to Polebridge ($70 from the airport). Because of Glacier's concessionaire contracts, visitors can get shuttled to Bowman or Kintla Lake only by renting a vehicle from FGT to drive themselves to the lake; then FGT picks up the vehicle the following day ($200).

SERVICES

You won't find strip malls nor much in the way of services up the North Fork. The nearest gas stations are in Columbia Falls and West Glacier. Forget the ATMs, newspapers (unless they are a couple days old), a post office, satellite television, visitors centers, and shopping. But the Polebridge Mercantile does have a pay phone on its front deck.

With the re-opening of the **Home Ranch Store,** you can now get hot showers ($7) and do laundry ($3.50 wash, $3.50 dry), which is somewhat pricey due to the power source—a generator. A phone is available for calling-card calls and Internet with a dial-up modem (20 minutes for $5). Consider using the woods or a pit toilet elsewhere, as using the restroom here costs $2 because of the power consumption involved in flushing the toilet.

Emergencies

For emergencies within park boundaries, contact a ranger or call 406/888-7800. Outside park boundaries, call 911. The nearest hospitals are in the Flathead Valley: Kalispell Regional Medical Center (310 Sunny View Ln., 406/752-5111) and North Valley Hospital in Whitefish (6575 Hwy. 93, 406/863-2501).

The **Polebridge Ranger Station** (staffed year-round, 406/888-7800) sits one mile from Polebridge across the North Fork River next to the park entrance; backcountry camping permits are available here when someone is available to write one. During summers only, Logging Creek Ranger Station on the Inside North Fork Road is staffed, as are stations at Bowman and Kintla Lakes; however, these seasonal rangers may be out on backcountry duties.

DRIVING TOURS
Outside North Fork Road

Open year-round, the Outside North Fork Road is the easier drive of the two dirt and gravel access roads. Although it's wide enough for two cars to pass, be prepared for washboards, potholes, ruts, dust in summer, slush in fall or spring, and ice in winter. Locals refer to the road as simply the North Fork, dropping the "Outside," for it is the main gateway to the valley. From time to time, clamor arises about paving the North Fork, but many locals are opposed to that because pavement would promptly change the valley's nature. North Fork Road is plowed in winter to the Canadian border, but do

TIPS FOR WILDLIFE-WATCHING

- Safety is important when watching wildlife: safety for you and safety for the wildlife. The easiest tool for watching wildlife is a pair of binoculars. Invest in a pair for seeing up close.

- Do not approach wildlife. Although our inclinations tell us to scoot in for a closer look, crowding wildlife puts yourself at risk and endangers the animal, often scaring it off in fright. Sometimes simply the presence of people can habituate an animal to hanging around people; with bears, this can lead to more aggressive behavior.

- Let the animal's or bird's behavior guide your behavior. If the animal appears twitchy, nervous, or points eyes and ears directly at you, back off: You're too close. The goal is to watch wildlife go about their normal business, rather than seeing how they react to disruption. If you behave like a predator stalking an animal, the creature will assume you are one. Use binoculars and telephoto lenses for moving in close rather than approaching an animal.

- Most animals tend to be more active in morning and evening. These are also optimum times for photographing animals in better lighting.

- Blend in with your surroundings. Rather than wearing loud colors, wear muted clothing that matches the environment.

- Relax. Animals sense excitement. Move slowly around them because abrupt, jerky movements can startle them. Look down, rather than staring animals directly in the eye.

- Don't get carried away watching big, showy megafauna like bears and moose only to miss a small carnivore like a short-tailed weasel.

- Use field guides to help with identification and understanding the animal's behavior.

- If you see wildlife along a road, use pullouts or broad shoulders to pull completely off the road. Do not stop in the middle of the road. Use the car as a blind to watch wildlife, but keep pets inside. If you see a bear, you're better off just driving by slowly. Bear jams tend to condition the bruin to become accustomed to stopped vehicles, one step toward getting into more trouble.

not attempt it without good snow tires. Carry chains and emergency supplies in the car.

Running from Columbia Falls to Canada, the road leaves pavement just past Blankenship Road, where it follows the North Fork River for 13 miles. After a junction with the paved Camas Road (another access you can use from Apgar), the road travels past a few small bucolic ranches whose pastures provide browse for cows as well as elk herds. You'll hit six miles of rough pavement again at Home Ranch, where cattle may be on the road, so drive with caution, especially when coming around corners. At 32 miles and a little over one hour's drive, the road meets Polebridge Loop—the main road for the town and the cutoff to Inside North Fork Road and **Bowman and Kintla Lakes.** You'll see hand-painted signs when you enter town: "Slow Down, People Breathing"

and "10 mph: Bear, dog, kid, wolf, rabbit, squirrel crossing." Respect residents here; speed kicks up a tremendous amount of dust in summer!

From the Polebridge junction, the road continues north 22 more miles toward Canada—another hour's drive—and accesses the upper Whitefish Range, the North Fork River, and Forest Service cabins. Although drivers used to be able to cross into Canada, the port of entry (Trail Creek) is no longer open, since the road washed out on the Canadian side.

◖ Inside Road

Not for everyone, the summer-only (usually May–Oct.), gravel Inside North Fork Road throws precipitous drops, curves, and climbs at drivers. Huge potholes and washboards are commonplace; spaces wide enough for two

© BECKY LOMAX

North Fork of the Flathead River, Glacier's western boundary, in Flathead National Forest

vehicles to pass are rare. You're definitely off the beaten path on this bumpy trek where speeds top out at 20 mph. Marked as Glacier Route Seven on some maps and known as simply the Inside Road to locals, the Inside North Fork Road is the rougher of the two North Fork Valley choices and requires high-clearance vehicles. Big RV rigs will definitely have trouble, and it's a rough ride for a trailer. Although it's only 29 miles to Polebridge, it will take two hours to drive. For a 53-mile loop drive, many link it up with Outside North Fork and Camas Roads.

From the south, the Inside Road begins at Fish Creek Campground and climbs past peek-a-boo views of **McGee Meadows,** good wildlife-watching spots if you can squeeze your vehicle off the road and tolerate swarms of mosquitoes. Soon, it passes through remnants of the 2001 Moose Fire, madly popping with fireweed. After dropping down steep Anaconda Hill (12.5 miles from Fish Creek) and crossing the creek, the road bisects Sullivan Meadows, famous for Glacier's wolves, and passes two small campgrounds—Logging Creek (17.5

miles) and Quartz Creek (20 miles). At 28 miles, the road intersects with the Polebridge park entrance. From here, cross the North Fork River, drive one mile to **Polebridge,** and connect with Outside North Fork Road.

If continuing farther up the Inside Road, you'll reach **Bowman** and **Kintla Lakes.** A few minutes north of the Polebridge Ranger Station, the curvy Bowman Lake road turns off, a 6-mile (25-minute) snake-like drive eastward up the valley. Farther north, the Inside Road crosses **Big Prairie,** the largest of the North Fork's unique grasslands. Round Prairie follows at one-third the size. The road re-enters the forest and passes through the 2003 Wedge Canyon Fire site before dead-ending at Kintla Lake, 14 miles north of the North Fork entrance station.

SIGHTS
◖ Polebridge Mercantile
Located 25 miles north of Apgar, the hub of the North Fork community is the red-planked Polebridge Mercantile—known as the Merc—

built in 1914 and listed on the National Register of Historic Places. It is more than a place to buy that forgotten can of pork and beans for camping. It sells everything from local handmade jewelry to not-to-be-missed bakery goods fresh from the oven. While the smell of cookies and pastries fills the small room, an old-fashioned cash register clangs up sales.

Northern Lights Saloon

Next door to the Merc, the tiny Northern Lights Saloon looks like a ramshackle log cabin but packs out with diners, extras spilling outside onto picnic tables. Open nightly in summer and weekends in winter for dinner, it may be the only restaurant in the North Fork, but the food clearly beats many eateries elsewhere. After hiking, order whatever Montana microbrew is currently on tap and lounge outside while staring at Rainbow Peak.

North Fork of the Flathead River

Forming the western boundary of Glacier National Park, the North Fork of the Flathead River draws its headwaters from Canada and ends near West Glacier at its confluence with the Middle Fork. Fifty-nine miles of waters flow through private, state, and federal lands while descending the North Fork Valley's diverse habitats. Designated as a Wild and Scenic River in 1976, the Class II–III river with six accesses is great for multiday float trips, day rafting, fishing, and scenic floating.

McGee Meadows

Actually a fen, McGee Meadows is a wildlife-watching spot. Too wet to walk due to its soggy nature, it is also a haven for mosquitoes. As a fen, its waters retain low oxygen levels and build up dead plant matter, but nutrients feed it from precipitation and ground water, making it fertile ground for a great diversity of plants. The meadow is home to rare plants and over 50 species of flora—bulrushes, bladderworts, sphagnum moss, sundews, and orchids. It is also a place to see bears, moose, deer, and a host of birds. Access McGee Meadows from the Camas Road (six miles from Apgar) or from the Inside Road (four miles from Fish Creek), but bring bug spray if you plan on wildlife-watching.

Bowman Lake

The easier of Glacier's northwestern lakes to reach, but still not a cakewalk with its jarring dirt road, Bowman Lake sits in a narrow trough seven miles northeast of Polebridge. Its six-mile span sprawls uplake toward nesting bald eagles and Thunderbird Peak; its half-mile width squeezes in between the hulks of Numa Peak and Rainbow Peak, which rises 4,500 feet straight up from the south lakeshore. In summer, lake waters offer solitude: Drop in a canoe to tour its shoreline. In winter, the lake's icy expanse and snow-laden crags call to cross-country skiers, who ski in on a road pockmarked with wildlife tracks.

Big Prairie

Located 30 miles up the Inside North Fork Road, just two miles past the Bowman Lake turnoff and three miles from Polebridge, Big Prairie is the largest of four Palouse prairies in the North Fork. At one mile wide and four miles long, the prairie is a grassland community with wheatgrass, fescues, oatgrass, and sagebrush. Because the Whitefish Range causes a rain shadow effect, the North Fork receives only 20 inches of precipitation per year, which fosters this drier flora.

Kintla Lake

Kintla Lake is a place to go only on purpose. Fifteen miles north of Polebridge, it is a chore to get here over the washboard, rutted road. But its tiny, remote campground tucked deep in the trees offers quiet, a place to decompress. Cowering between Starvation and Parke Ridges, the half-mile-wide lake curves a little over five miles upvalley, a prelude to Upper Kintla Lake. Only one trail takes off along the north shore toward the isolated Kintla-Kinnerly peak complex. Haul a canoe or kayak to Kintla Lake, for the secluded paddling or fishing can't be beat.

Recreation

HIKING

Hiking in the North Fork can lead to stunning vistas, but be prepared for tromping through long, heavily forested valleys to earn your views. While day hikes trek to lakes and lookouts, backpacking trips gain altitude into stunning glaciated alpine bowls above tree line. In this undeveloped area, you're on your own to get to trailheads; no shuttle service runs up the North Fork. On opposite sides of the valley, hikes depart in Glacier and in the Whitefish Range (Flathead National Forest). For those looking for hikes for the pooch, Flathead National Forest is the answer.

While trails in Glacier Park are well-signed, Flathead National Forest trails are less so. Trail signs may consist of just a number with no distances, destinations, or directions. For that reason alone, always hike with a topographical map in Flathead National Forest, and know how to read it. Trails also in the national forest are maintained less frequently: Expect to encounter deadfall and downed trees as well as brushy routes. For hiking maps of Flathead National Forest, contact the Glacier View Ranger District in Hungry Horse (406/387-3800). Topographical quads of the Whitefish Range can be purchased at outdoor sporting-goods stores in Flathead Valley. For hiking Glacier's trails, take along a topographical map, available through Glacier Natural History Association (406/888-5756, www.glacierassociation.org).

◖ Quartz Lakes

- Distance: 12.4-mile loop
- Duration: 6 hours
- Elevation gain: 1,470 feet to Upper Quartz, 1,000 feet on return over ridge
- Effort: moderate
- Trailhead: backcountry parking area at Bowman Lake Campground

In June, early parts of the trail burst with calypso orchids while the part crossing Cerulean Ridge is still buried under snow. In less than a half mile, the trail splits—the junction you will loop back to at the end. Take the left fork, heading to Quartz Lake. The trail climbs through thick spruce and fir forests with peek-a-boo views of Numa Peak until it crests Cerulean ridge. As the trail drops 1,000 feet to Quartz Lake, it enters the 1988 Red Bench burn, where open meadows afford views of Vulture Peak's steep north face.

At Quartz Lake, the trail cuts through the backcountry campsite and rounds the lake through boardwalk bogs, passing Middle Quartz Lake. Even as the trail moves away from water, mosquitoes will pester. The trail drops to a backcountry campsite at Lower Quartz Lake's outlet. From here, the trail climbs 1.5 miles with good views to the top of Cerulean Ridge before dropping back to the junction. For families with kids, an out-and-back excursion just to Lower Quartz Lake may be easier at 7 miles round-trip.

Numa Lookout

- Distance: 11.2 miles round-trip
- Duration: 5.5 hours
- Elevation gain: 2,930 feet
- Effort: moderately strenuous
- Trailhead: from Bowman Lake Campground near lakeshore

Although the bulk of the trail crawls through thick forests, the view from Numa Lookout is well worth the climb. Following the northwest shore of Bowman Lake, the trail winds 0.7 mile through deep, damp forest to a junction. Take the left fork. The trail climbs steadily uphill to a saddle with a small boggy pond. During mosquito season, hike fast to get by the swarms.

After the trail switchbacks up the final climb, finally within eyesight of the lookout, the treed

slope breaks into dry open meadows. At 6,960 feet high, the lookout, which is staffed during fire season, stares across Bowman Lake at the massif of Square, Rainbow, and Carter Peaks.

Bowman Lake

- Distance: 14.2 miles round-trip to head of lake
- Duration: 6 hours
- Elevation gain: none
- Effort: easy, but lengthy
- Trailhead: from Bowman Lake Campground near lakeshore

This easy walking trail wanders the forested northeast shoreline of Bowman Lake. For a stroll, walk it as far as you want and then turn around. In a few places, the trail nears the shore, close enough for beach access, although June water levels sometimes flood beaches. Intermittent views of the Square, Rainbow, and Carter massif poke out from the trees.

At the head of the lake, a backcountry campground with a marvelous pebble beach is a great place to lunch, but do so by the community cooking site rather than in or near backcountry sleeping sites. Bring binoculars, because bald eagles nest at the lake's head. For backpackers, the trail continues on, climbing to Brown's Pass atop the Continental Divide, where it splits, either heading east to Goat Haunt on Waterton Lake (23 miles total) or climbing over Boulder Pass to Kintla Lake (37 miles total).

Kintla Lake

- Distance: 12.4 miles round-trip
- Duration: 6 hours
- Elevation gain: none
- Effort: easy, but lengthy
- Trailhead: from Kintla Lake Campground near lakeshore

The gentle trail follows Kintla Lake's north shore. Much of the trail is deep in the trees

with few views, but it does offer a collection of woodland flowers: trilliums, twisted stalk, queen's cup, fairybells, bunchberry, and bog orchids. The trail also passes through the 2003 Wedge Fire, which opened up some views.

At 6.3 miles, the trail reaches the Kintla Lake backcountry campground. Pull out the binoculars, for you might see moose, bear, or bald eagles from its shoreline. When eating lunch, do so by the community cooking site rather than in or near backcountry sleeping sites. For backpackers, the trail continues on to Upper Kintla Lake before beginning a substantial climb to Boulder Pass. From there it drops to Brown's Pass on the Continental Divide, where it splits, either heading east to Goat Haunt on Waterton Lake (32 miles total) or dropping down to Bowman Lake (37 miles total).

Logging Lake

- Distance: 8.8 miles round-trip
- Duration: 4 hours
- Elevation gain: 477 feet
- Effort: easy
- Trailhead: Logging Creek Campground on the Inside North Fork Road

With no peak views until the lake, the trail attracts mostly anglers fishing for cutthroat, some with gumption enough to haul in float tubes to get away from the brushy shoreline. Above Logging Creek, the trail climbs quickly at the start but then levels out across a timbered ridgeline that offers a glimpse or two of the creek canyon. At the lake, far beyond its opposite shoreline 8 miles away, you can spot Mount Geduhn and Anaconda Mountain.

Mount Thoma

- Distance: 10 miles round-trip
- Duration: 5 hours
- Elevation gain: 2,917 feet
- Effort: strenuous

NORTH FORK

- Trailhead: on north side 3 miles up Trail Creek Road

- Directions: Drive north of Polebridge on the Outside North Fork Road approximately 13 miles to Trail Creek, 6 miles from the Canadian border. Turn left and drive 3 miles to the trailhead.

This trail in the Flathead National Forest is a great place to garner solitude and some incredible views. The heavily forested trail starts off with a gentle pitch that soon rocks into a definite uphill grunt. Brushy and rarely maintained, the trail frequently has downed trees barring the path, requiring climbing and worming through branches. But soon it breaks out into a high ridgeline meadow with bluebells. At the end of the ridge, it climbs a series of switchbacks to the summit.

The summit is well worth the hike, for the views are extensive. The peaks of Glacier sprawl southeasterly. The border swath between Canada and the United States cuts an unnaturally straight line across the North Fork Valley. In Canada, a mosaic of clearcuts leads up to the mountains bordering Waterton National Park. To the south, the Whitefish Range layers off peak after peak as far as the eye can see.

❰ Glacier View

- Distance: 4.5 miles round-trip

- Duration: 4 hours

- Elevation gain: 2,687 feet

- Effort: strenuous

- Trailhead: at the junction of Camas and North Fork Roads

A steep climb up the side of Demers Ridge in Flathead National Forest leads to Glacier View. Its name says it all: views from the top span the length of the park's peaks. You'll even see Flathead Lake in the distance. The trail passes right through the 2001 Moose Fire area with charred stumps and silver toothpick trees. In the valley below, you can see the fire's mosaic as

Glacier View hike in Flathead National Forest

© BECKY LOMAX

it burned with different intensities and leaped to stands of trees. In June, you'll hike with the scent of wild roses amid a botanical dream of wildflower species.

Right from the start, the trail makes no bones about going uphill. No flats to catch your breath, no lingering for views. But with a decent pair of lungs, it's not bad. Just adopt a slow, steady plod, and you'll reach the top where meadows afford a scenic top-of-the-world place to lunch with your view. The fire removed shading timber from the slopes, so the trail is a baker in hot August heat. In winter, snowshoers make the trek up.

Guides

Glacier Guides (406/387-5555 or 800/521-7238, www.glacierguides.com), in West Glacier, has the sole guiding concession for Glacier Park. Some day-hiking trips tackle hikes in the North Fork area, but mostly the multiday backpacking trips begin or finish at Bowman and Kintla trailheads. See the *West Glacier and Apgar* chapter for details. No companies have guiding services for hiking in the Whitefish Range of Flathead National Forest.

BIKING

With the North Fork's rough gravel roads, mountain biking is the only way to go; road bikes won't cut it here. Bike rentals are not available in the North Fork—only in West Glacier and Flathead Valley.

While mountain bikers can easily access Bowman and Kintla Lakes, many choose to make a 54-mile loop from Apgar up the Inside North Fork Road, overnighting in Polebridge, and down the Outside North Fork and Camas Roads. Because the Inside Road packs in serious elevation gain as it climbs and drops through five creek drainages, the loop is a good two-day ride, but it requires carrying only minimal supplies. (Some do the trip in one long day, but then you don't have much time for exploring.) By staying at the North Fork Hostel and renting linens, you can leave the tent and sleeping bag home. Plan dinner at the Northern Lights Saloon

and breakfast on baked goodies at the Merc. All you need to carry is your lunch, the day's water, emergency supplies, and, of course, bug juice. In June, while moisture still clings in the gravel, the ride is less dusty, but you'll eat your share of mosquitoes on the Inside Road. By late July, you might need a dust mask to survive the ride back south on the Outside North Fork Road.

RAFTING

Floating on the Wild and Scenic **North Fork of the Flathead** decompresses you to river pace on its Class II waters. Six river put-ins range up and down the river's length from the Canadian border to its confluence with the Middle Fork: the border, Ford, Polebridge, Big Creek, Glacier Rim, and Blankenship. High water hits in June, with the lowest water in August. In July, the average float time from the border to Blankenship is 16 hours. Most rafters tend to break that into three days. The nearest rentals for rafting and camping gear are in West Glacier and Flathead Valley. If you need your vehicles shuttled from the put-in to your take-out, contact **Glacier Outdoor Center** (406/888-5454 or 800/235-6781) in West Glacier.

Overnight Permits

No permits are required for overnights, but all camps must be set up on the western shore rather than Glacier's eastern shoreline. Camps in Flathead National Forest and on state lands are first-come, first-serve. Round Prairie is the one exception on Glacier's bank, and it requires a permit ($4 per person per night). Permits are available by advance reservation ($20 per trip) and must use the official Backcountry Camping application: download it at www.nps.gov/glac. Or you can stop in a permit office the day before your departure and hope it is available. Located near the Polebridge entrance station, Polebridge Ranger Station is the closest, but call ahead to be sure someone is available to write the permit (406/888-7742). Apgar Backcountry Permit Center (406/888-7859) in Apgar may be

more convenient as you launch your trip up the North Fork. Hours are generally 8 A.M.–4:30 P.M. for both permit centers.

Respect the rights of private property owners along the river. Signage at river accesses identifies land ownership en route. For questions regarding rafting on the North Fork, call Glacier View Ranger District (406/387-3800).

Guides

Several raft-guiding companies lead overnight trips down the North Fork; however, none base their operations in the North Fork Valley. All commercial outfitters begin their trips in West Glacier. Due to the Class II nature of the river, most trips are camping and float trips, appropriate for families and kids. In June and early July, **Glacier Guides** (406/387-5555 or 800/521-7238, www.glacierguides.com) runs a unique three-day North Fork float trip that combines rafting with overnight cabin stays rather than camping ($532 adults, $424 kids).

BOATING

All types of rowed boats and sail craft are allowed on both Bowman and Kintla Lakes; however, swirly winds from their narrow canyons make sailing and sailboarding almost impossible. While Kintla does not permit any motorboats or jet skis, Bowman allows motors of 10 horsepower or less. Bowman Lake, however, is closed to jet skis and waterskiing. No boat rentals are available in the North Fork Valley; the closest rentals are in Flathead Valley.

Be aware of wildlife closures on the lakes. Both lakes harbor nesting bald eagles at their heads; seasonal closures marked with orange buoys protect the nests.

KAYAKING AND CANOEING

River kayakers and canoers who can handle Class II ripples head to rapids on the Wild and Scenic **North Fork of the Flathead.** For access, six river put-ins range up and down the length of the North Fork from the Canadian border to its confluence with the Mid-

dle Fork. Sea kayakers and most canoers aim for the larger waters of **Bowman and Kintla Lakes.** While the lakes on calm days make for stellar paddling, both waters can kick up with lusty winds in a matter of minutes. Be aware, too, of wildlife closures marked with orange buoys at the heads of both Bowman and Kintla Lakes, where bald eagles nest. The nearest rental shops for kayaks, canoes, and camping gear are in West Glacier and Flathead Valley.

No permits are required for those overnighting along the North Fork River, but all camping must be done on the western shore rather than Glacier's eastern shoreline. Round Prarie, however, does require a permit. See Rafting permit information for details.

FISHING

Anglers are attracted to the North Fork for its indigenous fish: westslope cutthroat and bull trout. However, you should be able to identify bull trout; they are a protected species and must be returned to the wild immediately.

Kintla and **Bowman Lakes** are the main lakes accessible by car for fishing. Bowman allows motorized boats, but not Kintla. For those willing to hike to a worthy fishing lake, the three **Quartz Lakes** hop with native trout and whitefish. Along the Inside North Fork Road, most of the western creek drainages provide some fishing, with various degrees of accessibility. Fishing closures in the area include Upper Kintla Lake and Kintla Creek between the two Kintla Lakes, Bowman Creek above the lake, and Logging Creek between Logging and Grace Lakes.

The most popular North Fork Valley fishing is on the **North Fork River** itself, where six river accesses (Canadian border, Ford, Polebridge, Big Creek, Glacier Rim, and Blankenship) allow for raft or boat launching and fishing. The Camas Bridge also provides fishing access.

Several commercial outfitters guide overnight fishing trips on the North Fork River;

however, all fishing outfitters base their operations out of West Glacier.

Licenses and Regulations

The North Fork River's high water line on the eastern shore provides Glacier's western boundary. Inside the park, fishing licenses or permits are not required, but outside the park, anglers must possess a Montana State Fishing License. This includes anglers on the North Fork River. Purchase one before you come up the North Fork, for there are none sold in Polebridge. Check details on licenses in the *Background* chapter.

CROSS-COUNTRY SKIING

Roads in the North Fork convert to cross-country ski and snowshoe trails in winter. But don't expect pristine smooth snows: The North Fork thrives as a winter habitat for moose, wolves, deer, elk, snowshoe hares, coyotes, and bobcats, which pockmark their tracks across roads. If the roads make easy skiing, they also make for easy animal travel. Grab a track identification book to help in deciphering the footprints splattered across your trail. If you need rental gear, pick it up in West Glacier or the Flathead Valley before coming up the North Fork; no rentals are available in Polebridge.

Bowman Lake makes a perfect day ski; park at the Polebridge entrance station and ski less than a half mile north on the Inside Road before climbing six miles up to Bowman Lake's frozen shores. Be cautious about continuing out onto the ice. You're better off sticking close to shore if you want to ski the lake. Big Prairie, the Inside Road, and Hidden Meadows all provide other routes starting from the same point. Pick up a copy of *Skiing and Snowshoeing* from visitors centers and ranger stations for route descriptions.

For an overnight, skiers traverse 12 miles up Whale Creek Road to stay in one of the Forest Service cabins—Ninko—on the flanks of Thompson-Seton Mountain. For information on this trip, call Glacier View Ranger Station (406/387-3800).

SNOWMOBILING

While snowmobiles are not permitted in Glacier, they are allowed in Flathead National Forest in the Whitefish Range, where snowfall piles up 6–12 feet. December–April, unplowed roads heading west off the North Fork Road are used by snowmobilers, and a few are groomed by Flathead Snowmobile Association. Contact Montana Snowmobile Association (406/788-2399, www.snowtana. com) for current information on the local association and maps. Glacier View Ranger Station (406/387-3800) regulates the snowmobile use, season, and closures; check for current conditions and restrictions. The nearest rentals are in Flathead Valley.

ENTERTAINMENT

Instead of the usual red, white, and blue marching bands and floats, witness cross-dressers, beer-can draggers, bicycles, the 1956 Polebridge fire truck, and rafts in Polebridge's **Fourth of July Parade**—the more slightly off-kilter, the better. Hundreds of people line the one dirt main street for the noon parade-that's-really-not-a-parade. (Warning: Parking is an absolute nightmare!) It's a two-for-one show as the parade goes up the street and then back down the same street. Enter for free, watch for free. Who's in charge? No one knows.

The second weekend in August, the Northern Lights Saloon (406/888-5669) and Polebridge Mercantile (406/888-5105) sponsor **Aurorafest,** a one-day outdoor music festival featuring bands from North America with international flavors—marimba, Celtic, Middle Eastern, Jamaican, African. It's a bring-your-own-chair affair, with drumming, jamming, dancing, and camping going on deep into the night. Tickets ($22.50 advance, $25 at the door, kids 12 and under free) are usually limited to 500 to protect the Polebridge ecosystem and often sell out. A shuttle bus runs from West Glacier to alleviate parking. Call for current information.

NORTH FORK

Accommodations and Food

North Fork lodging is seriously off-the-grid. With no electricity, power comes from generators, lights are most often propane, and woodstoves provide heat. Telephone lines reach only as far north as Polebridge. However, despite conditions in this outpost, the state of Montana still charges its 7 percent bed tax.

IN POLEBRIDGE

Located a quarter mile south of the Mercantile, the **(North Fork Hostel** (80 Beaver Dr., 406/888-5241, www.nfhostel.com, May–Oct., $15 per person) may be off the electric grid, but you'd never know it. A huge storage battery powers phone, fax, and computer with Internet access. You can even recharge your digital camera batteries from it. Propane powers lights, a cooking stove, and a refrigerator, with a few kerosene lights added in. Amenities include a shared living room, fully equipped kitchen, outhouses, washrooms with hot showers, rooms

for couples, cabins, bunks for six women and seven men, and a wood-fired hot tub. Bring linens (or rent them for $5) or sleeping bags and food. In addition, the hostel rents tipis ($10), tent camping spaces ($10), and cabins ($30 per night, $150 per week). The Northern Lights Saloon is an eight-minute walk away.

Nearby at **Square Peg Ranch,** the hostel also rents two log homes (sleeping 6 each)— one a 1918 homestead—with daily ($65 per night) or weekly rates ($325). Propane lights, refrigerator, and cooking ranges stock the equipped kitchens, and wood heats the buildings. Cold running water, solar showers, and outhouses complete the rustic stay. Bring sleeping bags, food, and water containers for hauling potable water from the hostel.

A two-story guesthouse in Polebridge, **(Sweet Loretta's** (215 Skyline Dr., 406/539-8785, www.sweetlorettas.com, mid-May–mid-June and mid-Sept.–mid-Nov. $154 per

USFS Schnauss Cabin looks across Glacier's western Livingston Range.

night, mid-June–mid-Sept. $220 per night, contact for winter rates) is a fully furnished, three-bedroom house complete with generator, propane-powered appliances, phone, flush toilets, cedar sauna, campfire pit, and tent space. The guesthouse sleeps 7 people; additional people up to 10 total may be included at $25 per person per night beyond the original 7. Rates go down $7–30 per night for multiple-night stays. Birders will love staying here, as the many bird feeders outside attract summer songbirds.

Cabins

Open year-round, the units at **Polebridge Cabins** (265 Polebridge Loop, 406/888-5105, $35–45 per night double occupancy, $5 additional adult, kids under 16 free, dogs $5) are stark. Some visitors complain of smoky woodstoves and lack of amenities, but then the accommodations don't cost much either. Adjacent to the Mercantile and Northern Lights Saloon, the cabins come equipped with beds, tables, chairs, and propane refrigerators. Bring your sleeping bag, pillow, cooking utensils, a water jug, and a flashlight for middle-of-the-night trips to the outhouse. Call ahead to see if you need to bring firewood.

OUTSIDE POLEBRIDGE

For those looking to get away from it all, ◖ **The Way Less Traveled Bed and Breakfast** (16485 North Fork Rd., 406/261-5880, www.thewaylesstraveled.com, open year-round) is about as far away as you can get and still have the comforts of civilization. Here, proprietors Paul and Nancy Winkler encourage guests to forget about the outside world. Located 17 miles north of Polebridge near the Canadian border, the smoke-free, alcohol-free B&B has three themed rooms. Two of the rooms ($75) share a bathroom, but the Lewis and Clark room ($95) has a private bath and deck. The dining room, where the full breakfast features goodies like cinnamon-raisin-vanilla French toast, is surrounded by wildlife-watching windows; in summer, breakfast on the deck is accompanied by loons singing on a nearby lake. A generator provides power for lights, hot water,

a satellite television for those who just cannot live without noise, and wireless Internet. While phone lines don't reach this far, you can make calls through net2phone.

Cabins

The Flathead National Forest (Glacier View Ranger District in Hungry Horse, 406/387-3809, www.fs.fed.us/r1/flathead) maintains five cabins for rent scattered throughout the North Fork. All with a three-night maximum stay, the cabins ($20–50 per night) come with beds, vault toilets outside, equipped kitchens, and outdoor fire pits. Water is carried from streams or pumped, and firewood is supplied. Bring your own bedding and food. They are all nonsmoking and do not permit pets, tents, or RVs. Reservations are mandatory for all the cabins; you can make them for the following year beginning the first Monday in November. After you pay for and sign the permit, the Forest Service issues directions and the cabin combination. You must clean up at the end of your stay and pack any garbage out with you.

In a rather drafty building, **Hornet Lookout** (open year-round, sleeps 2) has a 1-mile hike in summer or 11-mile ski or snowmobile trek in winter. The deck at **Schnauss** (open year-round, sleeps 12) yields sweeping views of the Livingston Range, making it a local favorite for its sunrises and sunset alpenglow over Glacier. It has vehicle access right up to the front door and a less than one mile walk to the North Fork River. Located right on the North Fork River, **Ben Rover** (open year-round, sleeps 8) is convenient for skiing to Bowman in winter, walking to Polebridge in summer, and fishing right out the front door. In a remote forested setting, **Ninko** (Dec.–Mar., sleeps 7) is reached via a 12-mile ski or snowmobile trek. Adjacent to the North Fork Road, **Ford** (May 20–Mar. 10, sleeps 8) has drive-up access but little else to commend it.

CAMPING

No commercial campgrounds are up the North Fork Valley, only the more rustic national park or national forest campgrounds. If you require hookups, your nearest options are West Glacier

and Columbia Falls. While the campgrounds—all first-come, first-serve—have fire pits, picnic tables, and drinking water, you'll need to bring your own firewood. In Glacier, firewood gathering is prohibited, except along the Inside North Fork Road; here you can stop to collect downed twigs, sticks, and limbs. However, cutting live timber is not permitted. After the season, you can camp primitively ($6) with pit toilets and no drinking water at Bowman and Kintla after mid-September and Quartz and Logging after Labor Day until winter closures. You can haul water from lakes and streams, but you'll need to boil or purify it.

Glacier National Park Campgrounds

At the foot of Kintla Lake, **⟨ Kintla Lake Campground** (406/888-7800, May–mid-Sept., $12 per night) is accessible only by 42 miles of dirt road (15 miles north of Polebridge) not appropriate for large RVs and huge trailers. Even by park standards, the small 13-site campground set in deep forest is rough, with pit toilets, hand-pumped water, and smaller sites that do not accommodate larger RVs. It is, however, very attractive for its quiet. A trail leads up Kintla Lake to a backcountry campsite and on to Upper Kintla Lake before continuing on over Boulder Pass. With no reservations, you should plan on arriving early enough that if all campsites are full, you can still drive back toward Bowman Lake.

At the foot of Bowman Lake, **⟨ Bowman Lake Campground** (406/888-7800, mid-May–mid-Sept., $12 per night) is accessible only by 34 miles of dirt road (7 miles from Polebridge). Rough roads and smaller sites do not accommodate larger RVs. With 48 sites sprinkled throughout a mixed conifer forest, the campground is larger than Kintla's but still does fill up sometimes in high season. It has running water and pit toilets. The boat ramp is adjacent to the campground, and trails lead to Quartz Lakes, Numa Lookout, Akokala Lake, and up Bowman Lake to Brown's Pass.

On Inside North Fork Road, **Quartz Creek Campground** (406/888-7800, July–Labor Day, $12 per night) is accessible only by dirt road from Polebridge or Apgar. Rough roads and smaller sites do not accommodate larger RVs. Set in the woods along Quartz Creek, the tiny 7-site campground has only pit toilets and hand-pumped water. Since reservations cannot be made, plan on arriving by midafternoon, which should allow plenty of time to go elsewhere if the campground is full. From the campground, a 6.8-mile rough trail with infrequent maintenance follows Quartz Creek up to Lower Quartz Lake.

Also on Inside North Fork Road, **Logging Creek Campground** (406/888-7800, July–Labor Day, $12 per night) is accessible only by dirt road. Between the rugged access road and smaller sites, larger RVs will have trouble. Only 8 sites, pit toilets, and pump water make up this somewhat buggy forested campground adjacent to Logging Creek Ranger Station. With no reservations available, you should plan on arriving by midafternoon. This is a popular site for anglers heading to Logging Lake.

National Forest Campgrounds

Located 20 miles north of Columbia Falls and 13 miles from Apgar on North Fork Road, **Big Creek Campground** (Glacier View Ranger District, 406/387-3800, mid-May–mid-Oct., $10 per night) sits in Flathead National Forest rather than Glacier Park. It can be accessed via a five-minute gravel road drive from the Camas Road park entrance. The campground can accommodate 40-foot RVs and trailers among its large cottonwoods. Drinking water is available, along with vault toilets. Since the campground sits between the North Fork Road and the North Fork of the Flathead River, fishing access is easy. While you can technically collect firewood here, the surrounding woods have been pretty well scoured. Plan on bringing your own.

FOOD

A chalkboard proudly proclaims the ever-changing menu in the **⟨ Northern Lights Saloon** (255 Polebridge Loop, 406/888-5669, nightly at 5 P.M. and Sunday 8:30 A.M.–3 P.M.)

© BECKY LOMAX

sign outside Northern Lights Saloon in Polebridge, center of the North Fork Valley

Memorial Day–Oct., only Friday and Saturday nights in winter, entrees $9–16), with seasonal specialties ranging from stuffed morel mushrooms to buffalo, fish, and elk entrees sided with colorful fruit chutneys. Served in bottles or fishbowls, Montana beers or your favorite cocktails accompany healthy portions of food. Friday nights pack the dinky log building with pizza night, and breakfast and lunch are served on Sunday. It may be the only game in town, but it can outclass any restaurant with ambience and flavors, as its waiting lines will attest.

Open year-round, the **Polebridge Mercantile** (265 Polebridge Loop, 406/888-5105, 8 A.M.–6 P.M. daily, until 9 P.M. in summer), or The Merc, as it is called, stocks limited groceries, white gas, propane, film, fishing tackle, and beer. You can pick up forgotten camping items, but don't expect a broad selection of choices, and there might just be some road dust on the canned foods. However,

it's the place to go for yummy baked goodies yanked fresh from the oven—pastries, lunch breads, and snacks. For being out in the boonies, the prices beat out airport prices any day: three cookies for $1, a brownie for $1.25. The Merc also sells sandwiches to go.

Closed for several years after a grizzly ripped apart the building, **Home Ranch Store** (8855 North Fork Rd., 406/888-5572, www.home ranchstore.com, 7:30 A.M.–7 P.M. late May–Oct.) opened again in 2005 after new owners rebuilt the cabin. A few miles south of Polebridge and well-signed with hand-painted advertising, the small store sells convenience-type groceries, beer, coffee, pop, T-shirts, firewood, ice, and frozen foods such as ice cream, pizza, and hamburgers. (You can microwave the pizza and hamburgers here). It's worth a stop just to see the preserved grizzly-clawed section of floor and photos of the damage displayed on the wall.

GOING-TO-THE-SUN ROAD

Historic Going-to-the-Sun Road is a testament to human ingenuity and nature's wonders. Tunnels, switchbacks, arches, and a narrow two-lane highway cutting across precipitous slopes nod to engineering feats—marvels in themselves. Yet in the road's 52 miles, an incomparable diversity unfolds with surprises around each corner: cedar rainforests give way to aspen groves, broad lake valleys lead into glacial corridors, thousand-foot cliff walls abut wildflower gardens, and waterfalls spew from every pore. Above all, ragged peaks rake the sky defying conventions of gravity.

This National Historic Landmark is a highway to taste and savor every nook and cranny. With myriad pullouts, many sightseers run through an entire roll of film only halfway up the alpine section. To stretch your legs, well-signed short paths guide hikers through a dripping rainforest, along a glacial moraine, amid mountain goat nannies and kids, and beside a roaring waterfall. Those ready to put miles on their boots should tackle at least one of the longer high alpine trails. The Sun Road, as locals call it, leaves a lasting impression. Its spectral color and the sheer immensity of its glacier-chewed landscape send the human spirit soaring and leave visitors bemoaning, "I can't fit it all in my camera!"

HISTORY
Early Development
By 1895, Lake McDonald boomed with tourism brought on by the railroad's arrival in West Glacier. To shuttle guests from Apgar to his 12-room hotel where Lake McDonald Lodge

HIGHLIGHTS

◖ Red Bus Tour: Ride over Logan Pass in historic style. The 1937 vintage touring sedans, designed especially for national parks, roll their canvas tops back for superb views and maybe a bit of dousing from the Weeping Wall (page 80).

◖ Boat Tours: This is the best way to see St. Mary, the second-largest lake in the park. The lake spans an array of color and features one of the oldest geological formations on the park's east side (page 81).

◖ Lake McDonald: Glacier's largest lake fills a monstorous valley gorged out by an ancient ice age glacier. Rent a boat from Lake McDonald Lodge to fish its depths or explore by kayak from any of the pullouts on Going-to-the-Sun Road (page 86).

◖ Lake McDonald Lodge: A historic final outpost heading up Going-to-the-Sun Road's west side graces the shore of Lake McDonald. Its rustic hunting lodge appearance harkens back to a pre-national park era when the area served as a hunting preserve (page 86).

◖ Logan Pass: The apex of Going-to-the-Sun Road crests the Continental Divide, where waters stream toward the Pacific and the Atlantic. Broad alpine meadows teem with wildflowers, where mountain goats cluster (page 89).

◖ Wild Goose Island Overlook: Hands down the most photographed spot in the park, Wild Goose Island stares up St. Mary Lake to Glacier's rugged interior. Fusillade Mountain dominates the view along the Continental Divide (page 91).

◖ Trail of the Cedars: Through the easternmost rainforest in the U.S., the trail follows a boardwalk and paved pathway under a tree canopy that keeps temperatures cool even in midsummer (page 94).

◖ Highline Trail and Granite Park Chalet: Only the spectacular Highline Trail reaches Granite Park Chalet, one of the most dramatic settings for a backcountry chalet. Its rustic appeal transports you back in time, where bear-watching is a worthy pastime (page 95).

◖ Siyeh Pass: One of the most dramatic and diverse trails in Glacier climbs among wildflower parks and descends through amazing colorful sedimentary strata—perhaps touching every color in the spectrum (page 96).

◖ Mule Shoe Outfitters: For the best trail ride in the park, join Mule Shoe Outfitters for a ride to Sperry Chalet, where you can lunch in the historic dining room and smack your lips on freshly baked pie (page 99).

GOING-TO-THE-SUN ROAD

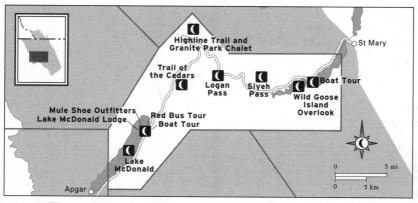

LOOK FOR ◖ TO FIND RECOMMENDED SIGHTS, ACTIVITIES, DINING, AND LODGING.

GOING-TO-THE-SUN ROAD

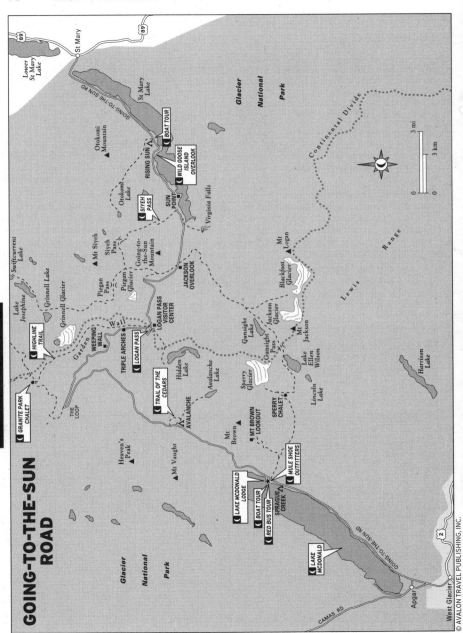

Glacier National Park

West Glacier

Apgar

CAMAS RD.

GOING-TO-THE-SUN RD

LAKE McDONALD

RED BUS TOUR

BOAT TOUR

LAKE McDONALD LODGE

SPRAGUE CREEK

MULE SHOE OUTFITTERS

MT BROWN LOOKOUT

Mt Brown

SPERRY CHALET

AVALANCHE

TRAIL OF THE CEDARS

THE LOOP

Mt Vaught

Heaven's Peak

GRANITE PARK CHALET

HIGHLINE TRAIL

Garden Wall

WEEPING WALL

TRIPLE ARCHES

LOGAN PASS

Hidden Lake

Avalanche Lake

Sperry Glacier

Lincoln Lake

Lake Ellen Wilson

Gunsight Pass

Mt Jackson

Gunsight Lake

LOGAN PASS VISITOR CENTER

Jackson Glacier

JACKSON OVERLOOK

Blackfoot Glacier

Mt Logan

Lewis Range

Continental Divide

Harrison Lake

Lake Josephine

Grinnell Glacier

Grinnell Lake

Lake Swiftcurrent

Swiftcurrent Lake

Mt Siyeh

Siyeh Pass

Piegan Pass

Piegan Glacier

Going-to-the-Sun Mountain

SIYEH PASS

SUN POINT

Otokomi Lake

Virginia Falls

RISING SUN

WILD GOOSE ISLAND OVERLOOK

BOAT TOUR

Otokomi Mountain

St Mary Lake

GOING-TO-THE-SUN RD

Glacier National Park

Lower St Mary Lake

St Mary Lake

St Mary

89

89

Glacier National Park

3 mi

3 km

0

0

© AVALON TRAVEL PUBLISHING, INC.

2

currently sits, George Snyder hauled a 40-foot steamboat up from Flathead Lake. With the discovery of Sperry Glacier in 1896 by Dr. Lyman Sperry, Snyder's guests had a popular destination above his lodge, enhanced by the Gunsight Pass and Sperry spur trail funded by Great Northern Railway and built by Sperry and 15 of his students. While the west side surged with turn-of-the-century tourism, on the Continental Divide's east side, Roes Creek (Rose Creek at Rising Sun) boomed as a short-lived mining town—vacated with the Alaska gold rush.

Lodges and Chalets

Under dubious circumstances—perhaps a poker game—ownership of Snyder's hotel went to John and Olive Lewis in 1906, who moved the old hotel and built a cedar and stone lodge facing Lake McDonald. Opening in 1914, Lewis's Glacier Hotel imitated the Swiss theme of Great Northern Railway's hotels and chalets springing up parkwide. Lewis promoted Going-to-the-Sun Road, spending his own money to cut part of the route along the lake, grade the road, and build bridges. From West Glacier, the road reached his hotel in 1922, increasing the hotel's visitorship with increased automobile popularity.

Because of Lewis's foothold in McDonald Valley, Great Northern Railway ignored the area around the park's largest lake, instead frenetically erecting its chalets at Sun Point, Gunsight Lake, and Sperry between 1912 and 1914 and using Sperry's trail over Gunsight Pass to link the three. A year later and quite behind schedule, Granite Park Chalet was finally completed—a destination from Many Glacier Hotel and Sun Point. With bunk-bed dorms packed to the gills and additional canvas tents, Granite and Sperry could house 144 and 152 guests, nearly four times the number each sleep today. Their popularity increased in the 1920s as wealthy easterners spent an average of 21 days in the park, much of it touring on horseback with Park Saddle Company. However, Gunsight Chalet lasted only five years, wiped out by an avalanche.

In 1930, Great Northern Railway purchased Lewis's hotel, adding it to its lodging arsenal. When ownership changed, so did the name—to Lake McDonald Lodge. Two years later, the lodge was sold to the National Park Service.

Ironically, Going-to-the-Sun Road itself hastened the demise of the chalets, along with the Depression and increased auto travel. Horse-trip visitation dropped from 26 to 3 percent, and the chalets suffered. Natty automobile drivers sought more affordable places to stay. In 1940, the railroad company built East Glacier Auto Cabins (now Rising Sun Motor Inn), where two people could rent a cabin without a shower for $1.75. Finally, World War II park closures, deteriorating buildings, and increased costs of supplying the chalets taxed the railway company to the point where it razed Going-to-the-Sun Chalets and sold Sperry and Granite Park to the National Park Service for $1.

Building the Road

Nearly 20 years of planning and construction went into building Going-to-the-Sun Road, fueled by burgeoning excitement over the automobile. While proponents proposed various passes for the "Transmountain Highway," its original name, in 1918 Logan Pass won the park service selection. However, the plan called for 15 switchbacks up the west side, replaced later with one long switchback. Over several years, Congress appropriated $2 million for its construction.

Surveying the route required tenacity to hang by ropes over cliffs and tiptoe along skinny ledges—perhaps causing the 300 percent crew turnover in three months. Over six seasons, three companies excavated rock using only small blast explosives and minimal power tools to create tunnels, bridges, Triple Arches, and guard walls. With power equipment unable to reach the East Side Tunnel, crews cleared its 405-foot length by hand-boring 5.33 inches per day.

In 1932, during late fall, the first automobile chugged over Logan Pass. The following July, over 4,000 people attended dedication ceremonies at the pass, celebrating the road's completion

and ending with a peace ceremony for the Black-feet, Kootenai, and Flathead tribes.

Although guardrails, surfacing, and grading were not completed until 1935, nearly 40,000 visitors in its first year flocked to the road de-spite its rough tread and the Depression. Until the late 1930s, crushed rock covered its surface. Finally, in 1938, the park service embarked on a 14-year project to pave the scenic highway—at last completed in 1952.

Exploring Going-to-the-Sun Road

Going-to-the-Sun Road connects West Glacier and St. Mary by 52 miles of one of the most scenic highways in America. The road joins two immense glacier-carved valleys—McDonald and St. Mary—via Logan Pass atop on the Con-tinental Divide at 6,646 feet. From Lake Mc-Donald, the road ascends well over 3,400 feet to the pass; from St. Mary, it rises about 2,200 feet. Given the road's extremes in elevation, it takes rash punishment from brutal weather.

ENTRANCE STATIONS

Both ends of Going-to-the-Sun Road have en-trance stations: one at West Glacier, the other at St. Mary. Staffed during daylight hours all summer long and off-season on weekends, the stations have national park maps and the *Waterton-Glacier Guide,* the park's newspaper updated twice annually. If you miss working hours, you can use the self-pay cash-only ki-osks on the right just beyond the booths.

VISITOR CENTER

It's crazy: The one place everyone wants to go is Logan Pass, but its visitor center is small and the parking lot cramped on sunny days. But we all put up with the hassle, for no one wants more pavement and a larger building impinging the meadows. Unprepared visitors arrive expect-ing a resort atmosphere at **Logan Pass Visitor Center** (406/888-7800, 9:30 A.M.–4:30 P.M. daily early June and Labor Day–Sept., 9 A.M.–7 P.M. late June–Labor Day), but it's a seasonal outpost with a tiny Glacier Natural History Bookstore (406/888-5756, www.glacierasso-ciation.org), an information desk, and a few displays. Set your hand in the grizzly paw cast to marvel at the size difference!

While a fireplace crackles upstairs on cold days, one bench allows only a few to snuggle up to its heat. Restrooms downstairs have the coldest running water you'll ever stick your fingers in. During October, portable toi-lets in the parking lot replace the flush toi-lets here. No food or beverages are sold here, not even coffee and candy bars, so bring your own goodies. Due to the elevation, expect harsher weather—wind, rain, and snow even in August. Don't be surprised if you left the lowlands in sunny summer only to arrive at Logan Pass in winter.

TOURS AND SHUTTLES
(Red Bus Tour

In historic style, red jammer buses tour visi-tors over Going-to-the-Sun Road in vintage 1930s White Motor Company sedans oper-ated by **Glacier Park, Inc.** (406/892-2525, www.glacierparkinc.com, late May–Sept., $25–45; kids 11 and under half price, meals and park entrance fees not included). On good weather days, the jammers (tour bus drivers known for their storytelling) roll the canvas tops back for spectacular views of the Continental Divide. Without a roof, it's one of the most scenic ways to feel the expanse of the glacier-carved terrain. From Lake McDonald Lodge, two tours depart daily to explore Going-to-the-Sun Road: the 6.5-hour Crown of the Continent tour departing at 9 A.M. and 2:30 P.M. for Logan Pass and Rising Sun and a 3-hour Logan Pass tour departing at 9 A.M., 1 P.M., and 4:30 P.M. You can make reservations by phone or at the hotel activity desk. Early-season tours may not be able to cross Logan Pass due to

© BECKY LOMAX

historic red jammer buses

snows, but a ride in the historic buses is still a treat.

For those staying at Rising Sun Motor Inn, daily tours originating at Many Glacier Hotel or Glacier Park Lodge will stop to pick up riders. Inquire at the motel's front desk.

Sun Tours

A Blackfeet-led tour provides a different perspective with emphasis on Native American cultural history as well as the park's natural history. Sun Tours (406/226-9220 or 800/786-9220, www.glaciersuntours.com, mid-May–mid-Oct., adults $35–55, kids ages 12 and under $15, kids under 5 free, park entrance fees not included) trips depart daily from East Glacier, St. Mary, and Rising Sun for 4- to 8-hour tours over Going-to-the-Sun Road. In July and August, they also depart at 9 A.M. from West Glacier in a 4-hour tour to Logan Pass and back. The air-conditioned 25-passenger coaches are extremely comfortable, with extra-big windows for views. Make reservations at least one day in advance—especially in high season.

Boat Tours

Lake McDonald and St. Mary, the park's largest lakes, dominate the lowlands here, and **Glacier Park Boat Company** (406/732-4430 summers only, or 406/257-2426, www.glacier-parkboats.com) runs boat tours on both. You buy tickets (cash only) at the boat docks. In high season, purchase your spot a few hours in advance; midday, cocktail, and sunset cruises fill up. Some launches have ranger naturalists aboard (check *The Glacier Explorer* for scheduled times).

At the boat dock behind Lake McDonald Lodge, hop on the historic *DeSmet* (late May–late Sept., adults $10.50; kids half price) for a one-hour tour down the lake at 10 A.M. (through early Sept. only) and 1:30, 3:30, 5:30 (July–late Aug. only), and 7 P.M. With a 90-passenger capacity, the 1930 vintage 57-foot wooden boat tours to the lake's middle, where surrounding snow-clad peaks pop into sight. Go for a prime seat on the top deck, even in marginal weather—just bring along a jacket.

At the Rising Sun boat dock on St. Mary

RED BUSES AND RED BIKES

In the 1930s, red buses led sightseeing tours in Glacier. Built by Ohio's White Motor Company specifically for national park touring, the red buses became a symbol of the country's western parks. Yosemite, Yellowstone, Zion, Mount Rainier, Grand Canyon, and Bryce all had their own fleets, and so did Glacier. Nearly 500 red buses toured visitors in Glacier, Yosemite, and Yellowstone alone.

Although red bus fleets disappeared from the other parks in the 1950s, Glacier steadfastly held on to its 33 scarlet prizes, upgrading parts as necessary. The canvas tops rolled back to create an open-air touring car, so guests rode in historic style over Going-to-the-Sun Road, covering up with blankets if temperatures chilled down. Nicknamed "jammers" or "gear jammers" for the tremendous noise their gears made while shifting, the vintage 25-foot-long 17-passenger vehicles first drove Glacier's curvy roads in 1937 as the park's second generation of touring sedans. Sixty years later, as automatic transmissions replaced the manual transmissions and power steering eased driving Going-to-the-Sun Road's curves, jammers continued to tour folks through Glacier until 1999, when safety concerns sidelined the red rigs.

Glacier Park, Inc., operator of the historic park lodges, owned the jammers, but after the fleet was donated to the National Park Foundation, Ford Motor Company jumped aboard to rehabilitate the vehicles in keeping with their historic appearance. In the process, Ford also converted them to bi-fuel, able to run on gasoline or propane. New wiring, interiors, and paint jobs completed the project. (Check a jammer up close: You'll see both White and Ford logos.) Thirty-two of the red buses are back in service; one was kept intact for historical value.

Red seems to be the color, for at least 20 red bikes pedal Glacier's back roads. These retro-wonders are part of a National Park Service program to employ alternative transportation in the park. The bikes, retro in style and red to match the historic red buses, are used by park service employees to travel short distances, saving fuel costs and helping to reduce emissions.

You may see park service employees in uniform riding the bikes to check on campgrounds or traveling to do their jobs. The bikes were purchased with help from The Glacier Fund, a nonprofit organization.

Lake, catch a ride on *Little Chief* (mid-June–early Sept., adults $12–15; kids half price) as it braves the lake's choppy waters. Views of Sexton Glacier and Wild Goose Island can't be beat, but be ready for some healthy wind. Five daily departures offer different options for the 90-minute cruise: at 9 and 11 A.M. and 2, 4, and 6:30 P.M. Two continue on optional guided two-hour hikes to St. Mary Falls (check with the boat company for which ones), and the sunset cruise includes a 15-minute guided walk to Baring Falls.

Shuttles

To avoid Logan Pass parking lot hassles, shuttles are the way to go. Better yet, they enable point-to-point hiking on some of Glacier's most spectacular trails. **Glacier Park, Inc.** (406/892-2525, www.glacierparkinc.com, July–Labor Day, $8–40 one-way, kids half price, cash only) operates a daily shuttle service linking West Glacier, Logan Pass, St. Mary, and Many Glacier. No reservations are taken for this service, and you pay when you board. Shuttle schedules are available online, at visitors centers and lodges, and on the signs at pickup locations. Major stops en route on Going-to-the-Sun Road include Apgar, Lake McDonald Lodge, Avalanche Campground, The Loop, Logan Pass, Rising Sun, and St. Mary. The shuttle also stops at popular trailheads for Granite Park Chalet, Highline Trail, Piegan and Siyeh Passes, and Sun Point for Baring, St. Mary, and Virginia

Falls. At St. Mary, the shuttle links in with the east-side route running between East Glacier and Waterton.

SERVICES

Prepare for driving Going-to-the-Sun Road because no services exist on Logan Pass. The closest gas stations are outside the park at St. Mary and West Glacier. With no food services available at the pass, you'll enjoy your time better in less of a rush if you pack a lunch.

Restrooms are few and far between on this historic highway. Flush toilets and (at least cold) running water are available at Lake McDonald Lodge, Logan Pass Visitor Center, and Rising Sun. Older, somewhat smelly pit toilets are available at Logan Creek and Sun Point. New vault toilets are available at Avalanche Picnic Area, The Loop, and Jackson Glacier Overlook; they even have sanitizing hand cleaner since there's no running water.

Hot showers (one token $1.25 for eight minutes) are available at Rising Sun. For laundries, you'll have to hit West Glacier or St. Mary.

While some cell phones pick up service at Logan Pass, most do not work throughout the road's length due to the high surrounding peaks and narrow valleys. No Internet service is available at the lodges or chalets; if you have a laptop, you can plug in at Lake McDonald Lodge to dial up your own service long distance. Public pay phones are at Lake McDonald Lodge and Rising Sun as well as Avalanche Campground.

Shopping

The gift shops in Lake McDonald Lodge and Two Medicine Grill at Rising Sun and both camp stores carry a good selection of guidebooks, coffee-table photo books, maps, and natural-history books along with gifts, T-shirts, postcards, and jewelry. And if you need cash, you'll find ATM machines at Lake McDonald Lodge and Rising Sun Motor Inn. Lake McDonald Lodge area has a small seasonal post office across from the camp store; hours vary throughout the season with current hours posted on the door.

Newspapers

In gift shops and camp stores at Lake McDonald Lodge and Rising Sun, you'll be able to find local newspapers like the *Great Falls Tribune* or Flathead Valley's *Daily Interlake*.

Emergencies

If you have an emergency on Going-to-the-Sun Road, contact the park service (406/888-7800). If you cannot leave the scene to make a phone call, flag down a vehicle heading up or down the pass to notify the nearest ranger (usually at Logan Pass, St. Mary Visitor Center, or by phone from Lake McDonald Lodge). The nearest hospitals are North Valley Hospital (6575 Hwy. 93 S., Whitefish, 406/863-2501), Kalispell Regional Medical Center (310 Sunny View Ln., Kalispell, 406/752-5111), or Northern Rockies Medical Center (802 2nd St. E., Cut Bank, 406/873-2251).

DRIVING TOUR

Of all the driving tours in Glacier National Park, **Going-to-the-Sun Road,** the 52-mile historic transmountain highway bisecting Glacier's heart, stands in a class by itself. Its beauty, diversity, color, flora, fauna, and raw wildness will leave an impression like no other. For that reason, many park visitors drive it more than once in their stay.

In July and August, expect crowds, especially in the alpine section around Logan Pass. To avoid the hordes, drive in early morning or early evening, when lighting is often better for photography and wildlife is more active. In high season, Logan Pass parking lot crams full by 11 A.M. Signs at the entrance will indicate so and include an estimated wait of 30–60 minutes for a parking space. If the parking lot is full, there are very few alternatives. While there are pullouts a half-mile east and west of the pass, the shoulderless road does not afford safe walking to the pass, and tromping across the fragile alpine Oberlin meadows is taboo. You're better off forgoing Logan Pass for the time being and returning later in the day.

The road is definitely not average highway driving. Although it's possible to drive the

GOING-TO-THE-SUN ROAD

Logan Pass Visitor Center and Clements Peak in late spring

the-Sun Road is closed to vehicles from Avalanche to Rising Sun, snow-free sections are open for bikers and hikers—a treat without cars. During winter, the road is closed from St. Mary to Lake McDonald Lodge, but cross-country skiers and snowshoers trek its corridors.

Road Restrictions for Vehicles

Large vehicles are restricted on Going-to-the-Sun Road between Avalanche Campground and Sun Point. Because the road is narrow and overhung, vehicles must be under 21 feet in length, 10 feet high, and 8 feet wide. These dimensions include side mirrors, bumpers, towed units, and bike racks. Every summer, you can see a side extension mirror or two reflecting from the road—the vehicle's driver having forgotten to pull the mirrors in. Even though a camper unit may be smaller than the restrictions, camper drivers will still feel pinched between the guardrail and wall while squeezing in the skeletal lane left in construction areas.

Road Maintenance

Maintenance work seems interminable on Going-to-the-Sun Road. Avalanches, torrential downpours, and snows all wreak havoc. Summer snowstorms and heavy rains cause washouts, and annual repair reduces two lanes to one. Here, road construction is a fact of life, but it's also a unique chance to watch how workers cling to the side of thousand-foot cliffs.

The alpine section of Going-to-the-Sun Road is in critical status—from drainage damage to wear-and-tear from the 475,000 vehicles that travel the road annually. Because heavy snows constrict road work to 4–6 months, construction must happen during summer. The park plans to embark in 2007 on a major long-term $140–170 million rehabilitation project to improve road safety, parking, guardwalls, drainage, cracks, and deteriorating road beds—all while maintaining the historic character, fabric, and width of the road and done without closing the road during the peak visitor season. New facilities are also planned:

historic road in less than two hours with no stops, most visitors take all day. Summer construction, sightseeing, and traffic slow travel. Don't be anxious with it; just sit back and enjoy the view. Pack a lunch to avoid frustration over lack of food services; the road passes through a wonderland whose development has been kept in check, and no one wants to see that changed simply to accommodate hunger.

Season

Going-to-the-Sun Road is usually open June to October. Memorial weekend sees the most common opening, but it has opened as early as May 16 and as late as June 28. Closure is set for the third Monday in October, unless unseasonably dry weather permits an extension or snows force an earlier closure. During the season, snowstorms, washouts, and accidents may cause temporary closures. The park updates road status reports regularly: 406/888-7800 or www.nps.gov/glac.

During spring and fall, when Going-to-

DRIVING TIPS: GOING-TO-THE-SUN ROAD

Follow posted speed limits and turn on your headlights.

Rather than gawking from the vehicle, use the many pullouts to park, get out, and photograph.

Use second gear for descents for slowing speeds rather than riding the brakes all the way down the mountain. Don't be a vehicle that smells of burning brakes by the valley bottom.

If you use extension mirrors to see around a fifth wheel or trailer, remove the extensions or push them in before driving the narrow upper sections of the road.

During high season (mid-July–mid-Aug.), Logan Pass parking lot fills up by late morning with long waits for parking spaces. Consider getting an early start for touring Going-to-the-Sun Road. Alternative parking is available at Oberlin Bend and just east of Logan Pass; however, walking on the road is dangerous – it's narrow with no shoulders.

Take lunch, snacks, and drinks. Between Lake McDonald Lodge and Rising Sun, no food or drinks are sold.

Watch for bicyclists. Although bicycle restrictions are in effect during July and August on Going-to-the-Sun Road's west side, the narrow roadway, lack of shoulder, and curves squeeze cyclists. Show them courtesy by slowing down and easing around them.

Expect construction delays. Repair work usually reduces traffic to a single lane controlled by construction personnel. When workers are not present, timed traffic lights control flow. Obey both, for the single lanes allow for no pullover room for passing.

Although the road is narrow along cliff sections, do not hug the center line. Remember, traffic goes both ways. Use your own lane.

Check for summer closures. Heavy rains, summer snowstorms, fires, and accidents may close portions of the road. Entrance and ranger stations as well as lodges have current updates of the road status available.

Pull over when you have more than five cars behind you. Look for the nearest pullout and let them pass. Locals especially become irked at excessively slow drivers gawking while driving rather than stopping.

Be prepared for all types of weather. Sunny skies may prevail in the valleys while visitors at Logan Pass cower in frigid high winds or creep along slowly in a dense fog.

Passengers with a fear of heights should sit on the driver's side of the car for ascending the west side and descending the east. This will put you farthest away from the cliff edges.

While a hand-held video camera hanging out a vehicle window on Going-to-the-Sun Road seems like a good idea, the road is bumpy. Videos don't come out clear (and locals make fun of folks who do it).

For updates on Going-to-the-Sun Road status, call 406/888-7800 or check www.nps.gov/glac.

GOING-TO-THE-SUN ROAD

more toilets, interpretive areas, and the West Side Transit Center.

Prior to mid-June and after mid-September, some road portions may be closed to speed up construction. But during high season and peak hours, drivers should see a maximum traffic delay of 30 minutes. Usually this is true. Longer delays are scheduled for early mornings and evenings. By 2007, a beefed-up shuttle system should reduce vehicle congestion, too.

While road construction elicits complaints and moans, repairing this road is not like repaving a local highway! You can watch state-of-the-art road technology at work in a cliffy environment: Cranes and bobcats jockey for position along one narrow lane, somewhat akin to working on a tightrope. Anyone with a mild engineering interest will be blown away, and you get a feel for the immensity of the original road building.

Plowing Going-to-the-Sun Road

Every April, snowplows take to Going-to-the-Sun Road to heave over 100,000 cubic yards of snow off the pavement. It's a big deal here. Drifts range 30–50 feet thick from The Loop to the pass. Just east of Logan Pass, a 50- to 80-foot snowdrift, the Big Drift, clings to a 35- to 40-degree slope. No wonder the job takes several months—into Memorial Day weekend or later! For the duration, 25–30 equipment operators, mechanics, and snow specialists dig in with over 20 different machines—excavators, bulldozers, sweepers, loaders, and rotary blowers.

With over 60 avalanche swaths between The Loop and Siyeh Bend, slides smash into the road, forcing crews to replow the same pavement over and over or plow themselves out at night. Compounding the snow removal difficulties, heavy rains, fog, and whiteouts hamper progress.

When spring snows prohibit the road opening until late June, everyone gets nervous: local businesses to the governor of Montana. The opening of the road is inextricably bound to the local economy's well-being. Glacier Park's website tracks plow progress with daily reports (www.nps.gov/glac), and the park's communications center phones (406/888-7800) post updates. Annually, the National Park Service leads a "Show Me Day" to show visitors the plowing operations in the road's upper reaches. Call the park for details. If avalanches threaten, the event will be canceled in favor of safety.

SIGHTS

Going-to-the-Sun Road is a favorite. The following sights are listed as visitors will see them from Lake McDonald to St. Mary. For those traveling from east to west, the sights will be reversed. Approximate mileposts are listed parenthetically with eastbound first, beginning at the road's junction with Highway 2, followed by westbound mileposts beginning with the junction with Highway 89. The total mileage is actually 50.8 miles, yet the road's signs claim 52 miles. Where the missing 1.2 miles has gone, no one knows, nor is anyone too concerned about the mathematical error.

◖ Lake McDonald

The largest lake in the park, Lake McDonald (2.8–11, 39.9–47.9) hogs a valley hollowed out by a monstrous glacier some several thousand feet high. Lining both sides, Howe and Snyder Ridges are lateral moraines left from that Pleistocene ice age bulldozer. At 10 miles long and 1.5 miles wide, the lake is big enough to plummet to a chilly depth of 472 feet. Its deep waters collect from melting glaciers and snowfields high atop the Continental Divide. Kayakers and boaters tour the shoreline, anglers pull trout from its depths, and a few water-skiers brave the cold. The road hugs its southeastern shore with frequent pullouts for access. If calm waters reflect Stanton Peak, shoot off some film, for glassy waters here are uncommon.

◖ Lake McDonald Lodge

At Lake McDonald's east end, the historic Lake McDonald Lodge (11.2, 39.2) was designed to resemble a hunting lodge. A taxidermist's delight or an animal-rights activist's nightmare, the tall, stately cedar-log lobby is cluttered with stuffed goats and mounted heads of bighorn sheep, deer, elk, and moose. Look for the woodland caribou—still represented among the furry creatures here, even though it no longer exists in the park. Because the lodge was built prior to the road, the front door actually opens on the lake side, facing the original boat approach. In 1976, the lodge was listed on the National Register of Historic Places. Even if you're not staying here, explore the lobby, take a boat tour, or sit a spell in a log rocker on the back porch.

McDonald Creek

Originating near the Continental Divide, McDonald Creek (12.8–22, 29.6–38) is the longest river in the park at 25.8 miles and definitely more than a creek, but we won't quibble about nomenclature here. The road follows the river path until it begins its ascent to Logan Pass. In the seven miles where the road borders the river, several tumbling rapids and waterfalls with pullouts are worth a stop.

© BECKY LOMAX

Upper McDonald Creek Falls Overlook, along the west side of Going-to-the-Sun Road

But be extremely cautious of hazardous slippery rocks. Unseen algae, mosses, and swift cold waters have been lethal for the unwary. At **Upper McDonald Creek Falls** (14.7, 36.2), waters roil through scoured rock and wooden stairs drop you onto a convenient observation platform right over the falls.

Trail of the Cedars

Trail of the Cedars (16.6, 34.1) walks through a rainforest, the easternmost in the country. On a 0.7-mile wheelchair-accessible boardwalk and pavement, the shaded trail passes water-carved Avalanche Gorge. Several-hundred-year-old western red cedars, hemlocks, and towering black cottonwoods form a dense canopy that cools the forest floor where mosses, lichens, Pacific yew, and devils club grow in the rich duff. Fire has bypassed this small ecosystem, leaving monstrous old grandfather trees—some toppling from heavy rains, snows, and winds. One giant cedar requires many arms to encircle its trunk; it might be the best chance you'll have to hug a tree.

Avalanche Paths

As the road sneaks through a slim corridor between the Glacier Wall—an arm of Heavens Peak—and Mount Cannon (19.5, 31.3), look for avalanche paths. Snow, set in motion sometimes thousands of feet above, roars down gullies uprooting trees and snapping them like toothpicks. In early summer, scour the slope for remnants of avalanches—ice, snow, and rock rubble piled up. Grizzly and black bears forage for carcasses along these avalanche paths in hopes of stumbling across some unfortunate mountain goat. Bring binoculars or spotting scopes to aid in bear-watching from a safe distance.

West Side Tunnel

An engineering marvel, the West Side Tunnel (24, 26.8) is 192 feet long with two stunning alcoves framing Heavens Peak. In early season, the alcoves drip in a thin-sheeted waterfall, but you can easily pop through the spray to reach the dry rock-hewn guardwalls. Photographers, especially, will enjoy working the alcoves into framing their pictures of Heavens Peak. To

walk into the tunnel, park below, where large pullouts are on both sides. Above the tunnel, the road narrows, making walking hazardous. In early season, a waterfall on the tunnel's uphill side will splatter your car's windshield. If you're driving a convertible, too bad.

The Loop

Going-to-the-Sun Road has one gigantic hairpin turn known as The Loop (24.7, 26.1). With parking lots both below and above the switchback, it's a popular stop for views and a trailhead to Granite Park Chalet. Across the valley, the 8,987-foot **Heavens Peak** makes a stunning backdrop for a family photo. In early season, it will be snow covered; by late August, only a few icefields remain. In 2003, the **Trapper Fire** blew through The Loop; evidence of the burn lingers here in the acres of charred trees.

Bird Woman and Haystack Falls

About two miles past The Loop, look for the sign marking Bird Woman Falls (mile 27, 24.7). However, the sign doesn't name the cascade crossing under the road, which is **Haystack Creek,** whose steps were created from eroding layers of Belt Sea sedimentary rock created 8 million to 1.6 billion years ago. To see Bird Woman Falls, look across the valley for waters tumbling nearly 500 feet from a hanging valley, carved by a glacier in the last 6,000 years and lounging like a hammock in between Mount Oberlin, Mount Cannon, and Clements Peak. Early summer runoff pumps these falls full of water that dwindles to trickles by late August.

Glaciation Exhibit

Look for a signed interpretive pullout (28.3, 22.5) with terrific views of McDonald Valley's glaciated expanse. Once filled with several-thousand-foot thick ice, the valley's U shape shows the gouging, scouring, and carving of the monstrous glacier as it moved around the Glacier Wall approximately two million years ago. Through the glaciated trough, McDonald Creek courses 26 miles and ends at Lake McDonald. If you can handle the vertigo of gazing

2,500 feet below, you'll see Going-to-the-Sun Road with cars looking tiny like ants as they drive the narrow corridor between the Glacier Wall and Mount Cannon.

Weeping Wall and Big Bend

As its name implies, the Weeping Wall (29.5, 21.3) does weep, but it's a moody thing. In early summer, the wall wails profusely, enough to douse cars driving the inside lane. Roll up your windows unless you want a shower! In August, drips slow as the wall merely simpers. At the Weeping Wall, the road affords no room to pull over; drive instead to the aptly named Big Bend (29.7, 21) just in front of you to find ample parking on both sides of the road. Here, where avalanches careen from the flanks high on Bishop's Cap into the bowl, snow often remains until mid-July.

Triple Arches

One of the most striking engineering marvels on Going-to-the-Sun Road, Triple Arches

Weeping Wall, on Going-to-the-Sun Road, below Haystack Butte

© BECKY LOMAX

(30.4, 20.2) requires a slow drive to see, for no pullouts offer a good view. You can see this feature only driving uphill, for it is at the back of downhill traffic. Approximately 1.5 miles past Big Bend, you'll come upon the arches abruptly. Start watching for them as you enter a very narrow, curvy part of the road. At several sharp S turns, you'll see them. As you drive over the arches, don't think about the repairs that shore up the stonework hanging over hundreds of feet of air!

Garden Wall

From Big Bend to Logan Pass (29.7–32, 18.8–21), the peaks above the road actually form an arête, a wall carved by glaciers on two sides. Below its top cliffs, wildflower meadows bloom with every color of the rainbow: white cow parsnip to pink spirea, yellow columbine, purple nodding onion, and blue gentian. In a short half mile, you may pass over 30 varieties of plants. For this reason, this wild botanical wonderland has been dubbed the Garden Wall. For the best look at the Garden Wall, hike the Highline Trail, which departs from Logan Pass.

Oberlin Bend Overlook

As Going-to-the-Sun climbs its final mile to Logan Pass, it sweeps around a large turn below Mount Oberlin. Park on the uphill lane side for the wheelchair-accessible walk to Oberlin Bend Overlook (31.4, 18.4), the best spot for photographing the road's west-side climb, as well as viewing the Continental Divide and peaks marching northward toward Canada. Far to the north, you can see Mount Cleveland, the park's highest peak. Mountain goats wander in the subalpine fir thickets here; look for newborns with only nubbins for horns.

◖ Logan Pass

Logan Pass (32.6, 18.2) sits atop the Continental Divide at 6,646 feet. With its altitude and location between mountainous hulks, weather can be chilly here even in midsummer. For evidence, look at the trees, gnarled, growing low in krummholz or thick mats for protection against

THE CONTINENTAL DIVIDE

At Logan Pass, you can take your photo next to a sign that says you're atop the Continental Divide. But what is it?

The Continental Divide runs the length of North America from Alaska and the Yukon to Mexico. Along the Rocky Mountains, it is the highest point in the land dividing snowmelt and stream runoff in two directions: the Pacific and the Atlantic. In Glacier Park, the Continental Divide runs along the tops of the Livingston Range from Canada south to Trapper Ridge and West Flattop, where it leaps to Mount Kipp on the Lewis Range.

To cross the Continental Divide, drive over Logan or Marias Pass. To hike across the divide, Brown's Pass is the only trail that crosses the Livingston Range. In the Lewis Range, several trails cross the Continental Divide on passes: Swiftcurrent, Hidden Lake, Gunsight, Cut Bank, Dawson, Two Medicine, and Firebrand. Beginning in New Mexico, the 3,100-mile Continental Divide Trail finishes its length with its last 110 miles in Glacier National Park.

Glacier's Continental Divide also stands in a class by itself, for it houses a tri-oceanic divide – the only one in the United States. (Canada's Mount Columbia is the continent's other significant three-way oceanic divide.) Not particularly high by Glacier Park standards, Triple Divide Peak stands at only 7,397 feet above sea level, while many of the park's peaks climb above 9,000-10,000 feet. But its placement on the Continental Divide with connecting spurs of mountains and ridges splits waters in three streams: Hudson Bay Creek, Atlantic Creek, and Pacific Creek. Their names cite their eventual destinations in the continent's major watersheds of the Saskatchewan, Missouri, and Columbia.

On the southeast corner of St. Mary Lake, Divide Mountain with St. Mary Ridge forms the division between waters flowing to Hudson Bay and the Gulf of Mexico. To drive over this unmarked divide, head from St. Mary south on Highway 89.

GOING-TO-THE-SUN ROAD

the elements. Explore the visitor center and scan surrounding slopes for goats, bighorn sheep, and bears. In late July, the wildflowers usually are at their prime—pink alpine laurel, paintbrush, and monkeyflower. Two hikes depart from Logan Pass: Hidden Lake and the Highline Trail to Granite Park Chalet. Try to fit one or both of these unsurpassed trails into your agenda. Meadows at this elevation are fragile with short-lived flora, so stick to the paths.

Big Drift

Those driving over Logan Pass when it first opens get a treat: Big Drift (32.8, 18.1) towers on both sides of the road, making a thin corridor bounded by immense snow towers. Because of the Continental Divide, winds deposit heavy snows in this zone below Logan Pass on the east side. Often 80 feet thick, Big Drift remains the last obstacle for road clearing in the spring. By August, snow piles melt to small patches and disappear. In the next few miles, the guardwall is sporadic—just for some added thrill.

Lunch Creek

Spilling from a cirque between Piegan and Pollock peaks, Lunch Creek (33.4, 17.4) makes for a scenic stop at the first bend east of Logan Pass. Although no picnic tables line the road, the pullout's rock guardwall serves as a good impromptu lunch counter. Drag out your binoculars; often bighorn sheep cruise the slopes here, but they're hard to see with their tans camouflaged with the rocks. Waterfalls spew from the side of Piegan Mountain, fed by the glacier on the mountain's opposite side.

East Side Tunnel

The largest tunnel, the East Side Tunnel (33.8, 17), was excavated entirely by hand—all 408 feet. For safety, flip your headlights on as you drive through this tunnel. To stop for photos, drive through to its downhill side to find pullouts, also good stops for spotting bighorn sheep and photographing the large peak looming ahead—**Going-to-the-Sun Mountain,** from which the road acquired its name.

Siyeh Bend

Three miles below Logan Pass, the road swoops through Siyeh Bend (35.5, 15.5), with ample parking above and below the turn. The trailhead leads to Piegan and Siyeh Passes via Preston Park, a meadowland of fuchsia paintbrush and purple fleabane. For a short stroll, walk up the creek crossing under the road to the junction of two creeks. The city-block-long walk passes gorgeous wildflower blooms in late July. From Siyeh Bend ("Siyeh" means "Mad Wolf"), named for the 10,014-foot barren peak towering above, you can see Blackfoot Glacier toward the south.

Jackson Glacier Overlook

This is the best view of a glacier on Going-to-the-Sun Road, but due to its distance, binoculars and scopes are handy to aid vision. Although trees are beginning to occlude the view from Jackson Glacier Overlook (mile 37.3, 13.4), you can still spot Jackson Glacier six miles away. One of the six highest peaks in the park, Jackson Peak, rises to its west. Jackson Glacier joined its neighboring Blackfoot Glacier in the early 1900s, but the two glaciers melted into separate icefields by 1939. A trail departs here for Gunsight Lake and Pass.

Sunrift Gorge

A narrow canyon, Sunrift Gorge (40, 10.5) requires a short 75-foot uphill walk to see it. Baring Creek cascades through the dark gorge like a knife slicing cake. The dank rock walls create a perfect grotto for ferns and mosses. Parking on both sides of the road is somewhat crowded here, and it is a trailhead for Siyeh Pass, although most hikers opt to start at Siyeh Bend and finish here. You may find hitchhikers thumbing for a ride back to their cars two miles up the road.

Sun Point

The often windy Sun Point (40.6, 10) at St. Mary Lake marks the site of the park's most popular early chalet colony: Going-to-the-Sun Chalets. Accessed via boat from St. Mary, the chalet launched visitors into Glacier's interior.

For the best views, walk five minutes on the nature trail from the parking lot to the top of the red-rock promontory, where you'll have great views of Going-to-the-Sun Peak, Fusillade, and the Continental Divide. The trail leads 0.6 mile to Baring Falls and on another mile to connect with the St. Mary Falls Trail.

St. Mary Lake

The second-largest lake in the park, St. Mary Lake (42.2–49.8, 1–8.6) fills a much narrower valley than its larger counterpart—Lake McDonald. At nine miles long and 292 feet deep, it forms a blue platform out of which several stunning red argillite peaks rise. Its width shrinks in The Narrows (44.1, 6.6) to less than half a mile, where buff-colored Altyn Limestone resisted erosion—the most ancient exposed rock sediments on the park's east side. While its waters attract boaters, anglers, water-skiers, and windsurfers launching from Rising Sun, frequent high winds whip up wicked whitecaps in minutes.

◖ Wild Goose Island Overlook

One of the most photographed spots in Glacier Park, Wild Goose Island (43.8, 7) is dwarfed in St. Mary Lake's blue waters. Locate parking on both sides of the road from the signed viewpoint and walk the few steps to the overlook. The Continental Divide serves as the backdrop for the tiny island, with Fusillade Mountain as the prominent central pyramid. For the best

lighting, visit this spot in early morning or at sunset. Shoot a photo, then check the nearest gift shop for the same photo—you'll find it on postcards, on calendars, and in photo books.

Rising Sun

Rising Sun (44.5, 6.3) on St. Mary Lake is not really a scenic stop so much as one for necessity and services. A picnic area, campground, boat dock and ramp, camp store, restaurant, and cabins make up the area's amenities. It's also a jumping-off spot for hiking to Otokomi Lake and touring St. Mary Lake on the *Little Chief.* To access a beach, head to the picnic area (44.7, 6), but hold on to your hats, for winds often send large whitecaps down the lake.

Two Dog Flats

A series of grassland meadows interspersed by aspen groves lines the road from Rising Sun to St. Mary. Known as Two Dog Flats (46.5–49, 1.8–4.3), the meadows can be good elk-, coyote-, bear-, and bird-watching areas in early morning or late evening. From here, you can see two hydrological wonders to the south—Triple Divide Peak and Divide Mountain. Triple Divide Peak sits atop the Continental Divide, where its waters head to three seas—the Pacific Ocean, Hudson Bay, and the Caribbean. Divide Peak, along with the sweeping moraine heading east, marks the division between the huge Saskatchewan and Missouri watersheds.

Recreation

HIKING

Hikes off Going-to-the-Sun Road are top-notch, no matter what time of the summer. On the west side around Lake McDonald, trails all begin in the forest, but several climb to undaunted heights—Sperry Chalet, Sperry Glacier, and Mount Brown Lookout. At Logan Pass and eastward, most trails access high alpine meadows and spectacular glacially carved scenery fairly quickly.

Due to their ease, shorter hikes are often crowded in midsummer: you may feel like you're walking in a long parade to St. Mary Falls or Hidden Lake Overlook. If you want to get away from the masses, head for longer hikes that will take you farther in the backcountry: Granite Park Chalet, Siyeh Pass, Piegan Pass, or Gunsight Lake. The hikes described here are in order of their trailheads from west to east.

TWO CHALETS: GETTING AWAY FROM IT ALL

To sample a few of Glacier Park's top trails and historic charm, head to the backcountry chalets. Here, you get away from the hubbub of modern life – no phones, no televisions, no electricity, no hot running water, and no flush toilets. Load up day packs with a few extras like toothbrushes, and you can relish backpacker advantages without lugging huge heavy packs. Backcountry solitude, sunrises, and sunsets are prime amenities at the two rustic historic chalets, reached only by trail. Plan a five-night lodging itinerary that includes two nights each at Granite Park and Sperry Chalets. In between the two chalet stays, treat yourself to a night at Lake McDonald Lodge for a shower.

Make chalet reservations early, for high season often books up by March. Trails to the chalets usually open in early July, although heavy snow years see delayed access via high passes until mid-July. Access trails bloom with wildflower shows during the end of July and early August. Open until mid-September, the chalets often have rooms available at the last minute midweek in early fall. For point-to-point hiking, hop on hiker shuttles.

The two historic chalets still stand as enclaves of comfort in the backcountry and as tributes to a bygone era of horse tours. Their stone and log edifices are set in spectacular surroundings, and each offers different amenities. Don't forget earplugs, for noise from heavy snorers travels between rooms.

SPERRY CHALET

Leave your vehicle at Lake McDonald Lodge and catch the earliest hiker shuttle over Logan Pass to Jackson Glacier Overlook. Hike the long 14-mile route over **Gunsight Pass.** As it traverses the Continental Divide, it climbs roughly 3,500 feet and crosses two passes, so you need a very early start and plenty of stamina. (For a shorter access, hike up the 6.5-mile route from Lake McDonald Lodge.)

Set in a cirque, the full-service Sperry Chalet provides everything, including mountain goats clomping on walkways. With the package including meals – dinner, breakfast, and sack hiker or dining room lunches – and rooms complete with

fresh linens and bedding, you need to carry only your water, clothes, and a few snacks. If you can handle the weight in your pack; throw in a bottle of your favorite beverage for evening sipping.

On your second day at Sperry, pack up your lunch and head for **Sperry Glacier.** The 8-mile round-trip trail climbs past bedrock tarns before it squeezes up a narrow stairway through a cliff into the ice-scoured basin housing the glacier, moraines, and crevasses. To exit Sperry on your final day, prep your toes, knees, and nose for a 3,500-foot descent down the 6.5-mile horse-manure-laden trail to **Lake McDonald Lodge,** where a hot shower awaits.

GRANITE PARK CHALET

Get an early start and drive to Logan Pass (or hop the hiker shuttle). Walking with the goats, hike the **Highline Trail** heading north along the Garden Wall. With only an 800-foot climb, the 7.6-mile trail heads out to a knoll with a 360-degree view of the Livingston Range, Logan Pass, and the Continental Divide.

Granite Park Chalet functions as a hiker hostel: You bring and cook your own food in a fully equipped kitchen or purchase package meals on-site to cook yourself. Either tote your sleeping bag or order linen service. In the evening, bring your binoculars outside to watch bears foraging in the valley below; at sunset, walk to the chalet's northwestern side as orange and pink hues spread across the sky.

On your second day at Granite, pack in two half-day hikes: one to **Swiftcurrent Lookout** for views of the park from end to end, and the other to **Grinnell Glacier Overlook** to see the melting glacier from the crest of the Continental Divide. Together, the hikes total 8 miles.

To depart on your last day at Granite, either drop 4 miles downhill through the 2003 Trapper Fire burn to The Loop and catch the shuttle back to Logan Pass, or cross over Swiftcurrent Pass. The 7.6-mile Swiftcurrent Trail descends through a spectacular cliff wall dripping with waterfalls before leveling out for an easy walk past moose browsing in lakes along the valley floor. From Swiftcurrent, grab the shuttle back over Logan Pass to your vehicle.

Mount Brown Lookout

- Distance: 10.8 miles round-trip
- Duration: 6 hours
- Elevation gain: 4,325 feet
- Effort: strenuous
- Trailhead: Sperry Trailhead across from Lake McDonald Lodge parking lot

Only one word describes this hike: steep. While the trail starts out climbing through moderate switchbacks, once you turn off the Sperry trail at 1.8 miles, the next 5 switchbacks are lung-busters. After these, the remaining 20-some switchbacks level out into a more reasonable ascent.

While trees preclude views on most of this trail, snippets of Mount Edwards poke through from time to time. Toward the top, alpine meadows open with beargrass and huckleberry patches as the trail works its way along the ridge to the recently renovated lookout. From this false summit (Mount Brown is higher to the east), a dizzying look down to Lake McDonald and the lodge can't be beat. While you pick out Granite Park Chalet and Swiftcurrent Lookout on the Continental Divide with binoculars, keep your lunch from the overly curious mountain goats.

Sperry Chalet

- Distance: 12.8 miles round-trip
- Duration: 6.5 hours
- Elevation gain: 3,432 feet
- Effort: strenuous
- Trailhead: Sperry Trailhead across from Lake McDonald Lodge parking lot

The historic chalet is an attraction in itself, serving lunch and homemade desserts to hikers, but many overnight at the chalet to access Sperry Glacier. The climb begins with moderate switchbacks through a hemlock forest. After crossing Snyder Creek at two miles, the trail takes a long traverse around Mount

Edwards, slowly easing up in elevation before switchbacking again up alder-strewn avalanche slopes. Because of the mules and horse-packing trips using this same trail, the route sometimes can be miserable, as you dodge horse droppings buzzing with black flies and smelling like a barnyard.

With more than a mile still to go, you will catch sight of the chalet clinging to a clifftop high above. The trail crosses Sperry Creek before climbing its final switchbacks, passing the turnoff to Sperry Glacier en route. If mountain goats don't stand in your way, you'll arrive at the dining hall's door, ready for lunch goodies inside, served 11:30 A.M.–5 P.M. For those spending the night, reservations are required.

Sperry Glacier

- Distance: 8 miles round-trip
- Duration: 4 hours
- Elevation gain: 1,600 feet
- Effort: strenuous
- Trailhead: Sperry Chalet

From the chalet, drop down several switchbacks to the Sperry Glacier trail sign. From here, the trail climbs gently as it wraps completely around a glacial cirque below waterfalls and immense cliffs. The trail switchbacks up past alpine tarns, flower gardens, snowfields lingering in to August, and glacially carved rock ledges before it seemingly disappears into a cliff. But, voilà: A steep stairway leads through the cliff into the basin above.

In the Sperry Glacier basin, a different world awaits. Snowfields, moraines, and ice mark this environment, with trees and flowers very sparse. From here, follow vertical markers across the snow-covered trail to the glacier overlook. Glaciers have hidden crevasses and waterways: Do not attempt to walk out on the glacier. Seasoned hikers pull a 21-mile round-trip Sperry Glacier hike off in one day from Lake McDonald Lodge: It's a 10-hour-plus day

with a 5,000-foot climb followed by a knee-pounding descent.

◀ Trail of the Cedars

- Distance: 0.7-mile loop
- Duration: 30 minutes
- Elevation gain: none
- Effort: easy
- Trailhead: adjacent to Avalanche Campground and Picnic Area

A boardwalk guides hikers through the lush rainforest with interpretive signs. Here, fallen cedars become nurse logs, fertile habitat for hemlocks and tiny foamflowers. Immense black cottonwoods are furrowed with deep bark Ansel Adams could have photographed. A huge cedar requires more than three people to reach around its girth. At the boardwalk's end, the trail crosses Avalanche Creek, spewing and spitting from its narrow gorge. To make a loop, continue on the paved walkway past large burled cedars to return to the trailhead.

Avalanche Lake

- Distance: 4 miles round-trip
- Duration: 2–3 hours
- Elevation gain: 500 feet
- Effort: moderately easy
- Trailhead: use Trail of the Cedars adjacent to Avalanche Campground

One of the most popular hikes, Avalanche Lake is the easiest-to-reach subalpine lake on the west side. Sitting in a steep-cliffed cirque tumbling with waterfalls, the lake attracts anglers and hikers alike. High season sees an endless stream of hikers, some incredibly ill-prepared with no drinking water and inappropriate footwear like flip-flops or heels. Avoid midday crowds by hiking this trail earlier or later in the day, but not at dawn or dusk.

When Trail of the Cedars crosses Avalanche Creek, turn uphill onto the lake's trail. A short

grunt leads up to the dramatically carved gorge's top. Be extremely careful: Far too many people have had fatal accidents here. From the gorge, the trail climbs steadily through woods littered with glacial erratics—large boulders strewn when the ice receded. Some still retain scratch marks left from the ice abrading the surface. At the lakeshore, enjoy watching waterfalls, mountain goats, and bears.

The Loop Trail to Granite Park Chalet

- Distance: 8 miles round-trip
- Duration: 4 hours
- Elevation gain: 2,400 feet
- Effort: moderately strenuous
- Trailhead: The Loop

The Loop trail is mostly used for hikers exiting the Highline Trail; however, in early season when you can drive only to The Loop, this trail makes a worthy hike with Granite Park Chalet as a scenic destination. Due to the 2003 Trapper Fire, the trail is much more open than it used to be—improving views, but on hot days offering little relief from the sun's blazing heat.

At its beginning, the trail crosses a tumbling creek before joining up with the Packer's Roost trail at 0.6 mile. Note this junction: You do not want to miss it hiking back down. From here, the trail climbs two long switchbacks before it crests into the upper basin to the chalet. In June, you'll have snow in the last mile. Open July–mid-September, the chalet has no running water but does sell candy bars. Bring cash to purchase bottled water, carry your own, or filter water from the campground stream just below the chalet.

Hidden Lake Overlook

- Distance: 6 miles round-trip
- Duration: 2 hours
- Elevation gain: 550 feet

- Effort: moderate
- Trailhead: behind Logan Pass Visitor Center

Regardless of crowds, Hidden Lake Overlook is a spectacular hike. The trail is often buried under feet of snow until mid-July or later, but tall lodgepoles mark the route. Once the trail melts out, a boardwalk climbs the first half through alpine meadows where fragile shooting stars and alpine laurel dot the landscape with pink. The trail ascends through argillite layers: Look for evidence of mud-cracks and ripple marks from the ancient Belt Sea.

The upper trail climbs past moraines and waterfalls, where mountain goats and bighorn sheep browse on tiny alpine plants. At Hidden Pass, the trail reaches the overlook with views down to Hidden Lake's blue waters. For ambitious hikers or anglers, the trail continues down to the lake. Just remember: What goes down 675 feet, must come up!

Highline Trail and Granite Park Chalet

- Distance: 7.6 miles to Granite Park Chalet, 11.6 miles to The Loop
- Duration: 5–6 hours
- Elevation gain: 830 feet
- Effort: moderate
- Trailhead: across Going-to-the-Sun Road from Logan Pass parking lot

Many first-time hikers fail to pack enough film and shoot most of it within the first three miles. Also, severe acrophobes need to be aware of several exposed thousand-foot drop-offs. The trail drops from Logan Pass through a cliff walk above the highway before crossing a flowerland that gave the Garden Wall arête its name. At three miles, it packs all of its elevation gain into one climb: Haystack Saddle appears to be the top, but it is only halfway. After the high point, the trail drops and rounds through several large bowls before passing Bear Val-

ley to reach Granite Park Chalet atop a knoll at 6,680 feet.

En route, side trails lead to Grinnell Glacier Overlook (1.6 steep miles round-trip) and Swiftcurrent Lookout (4.6 miles round-trip). To exit the area, some hikers opt to hike out over Swiftcurrent Pass to Many Glacier (7.6 miles); backpackers continue on to Fifty Mountain (11.9 miles farther) and Goat Haunt (22.5 miles farther). Most day hikers head down The Loop trail (4 miles) to catch the hiker shuttle to Logan Pass.

The chalet (open July–mid-Sept.) does not have running water. Plan on purchasing bottled water here, carrying your own, or filtering water from the campground stream below the chalet. Day hikers may also use the outdoor picnic tables or chalet dining room but do not have access to the kitchen. On a rainy day, a warm fire offers respite from the bluster and a chance to dry out. Pop and candy bars are sold, too.

Piegan Pass

- Distance: 9 miles round-trip, 12.8 to Many Glacier
- Duration: 4–5 hours
- Elevation gain: 1,670 feet
- Effort: moderate
- Trailhead: Siyeh Bend on Going-to-the-Sun Road

Piegan Pass, named for the Pikuni or Piegan tribe of Blackfeet, is a reasonably unpopulated trail. After climbing two miles through subalpine forest and turning north at the first trail junction, the trail breaks out into Preston Park, bursting with purple fleabane, blue gentians, white valerian, and fuchsia paintbrush. As the trail gains altitude, Piegan Glacier is visible above. A signed trail junction splits the Piegan Pass trail from the Siyeh Pass trail.

Shortly after the junction, the Piegan Pass trail heads into the seemingly barren alpine zone as it crosses the base of Siyeh Peak. But

look carefully, for all kinds of miniature flowers bloom here. In a long traverse, the trail sweeps around a large bowl to Piegan Pass, tucked under the Continental Divide. Rather than returning to Siyeh Bend, some hikers opt for continuing another 8.3 miles to Many Glacier Hotel.

◖ Siyeh Pass

- Distance: 10.3 miles

- Duration: 5 hours

- Elevation gain: 2,240 feet

- Effort: strenuous

- Trailhead: Siyeh Bend on Going-to-the-Sun Road

Siyeh Pass trail crosses through such different ecosystems that the entire trail nearly captures the park's diversity in one 10-mile segment. The trail begins with a 2-mile climb through subalpine forest broken by meadows, where it passes two well-signed junctions.

Siyeh Pass trail

© BECKY LOMAX

(Go left at the first, right at the second.) The trail waltzes through Preston Park, one of the best flower meadows around, with purple fleabane and fuchsia paintbrush, before switchbacking up above tree line.

The switchbacks appear to lead to a saddle, which is a false summit. Eight more turns continue above the saddle before swinging through a cliff to the pass. Be wary of your lunch here as the golden-mantled ground squirrels can be quite aggressive. Due to the elevation, snow can pack the switchbacks down until mid-July and sometimes later. The trail descends past goats, bighorn sheep, and a multicolored cliff band before traversing the flanks of Goat Mountain and dropping to Going-to-the-Sun Road. The shuttle does not have a stop here, but a short hitchhike will put you back at Siyeh Bend.

Gunsight Lake

- Distance: 12.4 miles round-trip

- Duration: 6 hours

- Elevation gain: 550 feet

- Effort: moderate

- Trailhead: Jackson Glacier Overlook on Going-to-the-Sun Road

Gunsight Lake is a tantalizer. For those who hike in for the day, more high country lures beyond. The trail begins with a one-mile drop down to Reynolds Creek before gently climbing through a forest of boggy moose ponds that kick up a horde of mosquitoes. After passing a spur trail leading to Florence Falls, the trail breaks out into flower meadows, climbing along the flanks of Fusillade Mountain. Incomparable views of the wild Blackfoot and Jackson Glaciers sprawl through the scoured basin.

Surrounded by avalanche corridors, the lake sits at the base of Jackson Peak (10,064 feet), one of the six highest peaks in the park. From here, a two-mile spur trail wanders back into Jackson Glacier basin before disappearing in meadow seeps. Another trail climbs

to Gunsight Pass (3 miles farther) and on to Sperry Chalet (7.8 miles farther) before descending to Lake McDonald Lodge (20 miles total). Well-seasoned hikers do the entire trail over Gunsight Pass to Lake McDonald Lodge in one day.

St. Mary and Virginia Falls

- Distance: 3.6 miles round-trip
- Duration: 2 hours
- Elevation gain: 280 feet
- Effort: easy
- Trailhead: on Going-to-the-Sun Road between Jackson Glacier Overlook and Sunrift Gorge (mile 39.3, 11.3)

In midsummer, the trail will see a constant stream of people, but the two falls are still worth a look. The trail drops through two well-signed junctions en route to St. Mary Falls, where a wooden bridge crosses blue-green pools. From here, the trail switchbacks up to Virginia Falls, a broad falls whose waters spew mist. At both falls, look for water ouzels, or American dippers. The dark gray birds nest near streams and waterfalls and are easily recognized by their dipping action, doing up to 40 bends per minute. Be wary of slippery rocks on the sides and strong, cold currents.

Baring Falls

- Distance: 1.2 miles round-trip
- Duration: 1 hour
- Elevation gain: 50 feet on return
- Effort: easy
- Trailhead: southeast corner of Sun Point parking lot

As soon as you start hiking the trail, you'll need to pop up to Sun Point, a large promontory in St. Mary Lake, the site of the original Sun Point Chalets. From here, a sign identifies peak names circling the upper lake. Be prepared for winds, as St. Mary frequently brews up whitecaps. After you return to the trail, follow it around the knoll as it gradually descends to lake level through intermittent forests and dry grassy meadows of yellow arrowleaf balsamroot and stonecrop. The trail crosses the creek below Baring Falls, originally named "Weasel Eyes" in Blackfeet, meaning "huckleberries." For a longer hike, you can connect to St. Mary and Virginia Falls via the trail that continues up the lake (7.2 miles round-trip).

Otokomi Lake

- Distance: 10 miles round-trip
- Duration: 5 hours
- Elevation gain: 1,882 feet
- Effort: moderate
- Trailhead: behind Rising Sun Motor Inn

While Otokomi Lake can be a good early-season hike, its sights pale in comparison to higher trails. Climbing immediately uphill, the trail soon levels out into a gentle timbered traverse above Rose Creek. Pause for breaks at the two scenic creek sections where fragile shooting stars grow next to rock slabs sliced by the creek. As the trail continues uphill, it has very few views until the last mile, where it crosses open beargrass meadows and red argillite talus slopes. At the lake, you may have to rummage through scrubby subalpine firs for places to sit as no great beaches flank the shore. But, do scan the cliffs above, which usually cluster with mountain goats.

Guides

Mid-June through mid-September, park naturalists (406/888-7800, www.nps.gov/glac) guide free hikes, particularly at Avalanche, Sun Point, and Logan Pass. Both the Avalanche Lake and Hidden Lake Overlook hikes are extremely popular, so expect to walk in a rather long line. They also guide longer hikes, like Siyeh Pass, and hikes with boat tours on St. Mary Lake. Pick up a copy of *The Glacier*

GOING-TO-THE-SUN ROAD

Explorer from visitors centers for current destinations and schedules, also online. You can also check at Lake McDonald Lodge activity desk and the front desk at Rising Sun.

The folks at **Glacier Guides** (406/387-5555 or 800/521-7238, www.glacierguides.com), in West Glacier, lead day-hiking trips ($65 per person with 5 people minimum—$400 for custom) off Going-to-the-Sun Road. Solo travelers can sometimes hook up with their day hikes. Call for availability. They also guide three-day chalet trips ($750 per person, all meals, transportation from West Glacier to trailhead, guide services, park entrance, linens, and lodging included) to Granite Park Chalet or Sperry Chalet. Travelers are guided, cooked for, and catered to—a cushy way to enjoy the backcountry. For those looking to hit both backcountry chalets, the six-day Chalet Tour spends two nights at Granite Park Chalet, a night at Belton Chalet for a shower, and two nights at Sperry ($1,397 per person, all meals except one dinner, transportation, park entrance, and lodging included). These trips fill up early, so make your reservations by March.

BIKING

Bicycles are restricted on Going-to-the-Sun Road during summer due to high traffic during midday. From June 15 to Labor Day, bicycles are not permitted between the Apgar Road junction and Sprague Creek or climbing uphill between Avalanche Campground and Logan Pass 11 A.M.–4 P.M. If starting from the west side, head out from Lake McDonald by 6:30 A.M. at the latest to give yourself adequate time to reach Logan Pass. In late June and early July, long daylight hours allow for riding after 4 P.M. West Glacier has the closest bike-rental location.

While helmets are not mandatory by law, it would be stupid not to wear one—especially considering most drivers are gaping at the views rather than paying attention to the road. Wear bright colors for visibility and consider tacking a flag on the bike. At dusk or night, tail reflectors and a front light are required. Be sure to

bicycling Going-to-the-Sun Road's west side in spring

© BECKY LOMAX

carry plenty of water: exertion, wind, and altitude can lead to a fast case of dehydration.

Going-to-the-Sun Road

Bicycling here is only for the very stout of heart. Because Going-to-the-Sun Road is narrow with no shoulders, it is not the place to take the family riding, except in early spring or late fall when the road is gated at Avalanche but permits bikes on the road beyond. In spring, without cars, even tricycles and training wheels will be on the road!

Going-to-the-Sun Road is a bicycle trip you won't forget. While the 3,500-foot climb in elevation seems intimidating, it really is not steep. During construction, the road grade was limited to 6 percent because in the 1920s cars shifted at a 7 percent grade. But, the ascent is downright relentless. Before heading out, be sure to check bikes for safety, especially the brake pads, for the screaming downhill off the Continental Divide can wear them down to nubbins. Both mountain bikes and road bikes are appropriate, but with skinny

tires, be wary of obstacles: debris, grates, rockfall, and ice.

Biking Going-to-the-Sun Road begins as soon as snowplows free up pavement in May on both sides of the Continental Divide. Riders climb up as far as plowing operations permit. As soon as Logan Pass opens, bicyclists head for the top, some returning the way they came, others continuing on to the other side. Local racers make a 142-mile one-day loop (Going-to-the-Sun Road, Hwy. 89, Hwy. 49, and Hwy. 2); tourers ride the loop in two days. Locals also celebrate the full moon by riding the road at night. A dangerous undertaking (injuries and at least one fatality have occurred) and most times bone-chilling cold, the full-moon ride is nevertheless an other-worldly experience.

TRAIL RIDING
Mule Shoe Outfitters

Only one trail-riding concession operates along Going-to-the-Sun Road, and that's in McDonald Valley. Rides here offer a scenic way to see McDonald Valley highlights and the creek. Mule Shoe Outfitters (mile 11.2 or 39.2, 406/888-5121 summers, 928/684-2328 winters, http://mule-shoe.com, late May –early Oct., $47–68) trips depart from the horse barn across from McDonald Lodge parking lot several times daily with two- and three-hour rides. These rides tour on trails through heavy cedar and fir dripping with lichen. You'll get peek-a-boo views of peaks, but mostly a good close look at McDonald Creek. Wear long pants and hiking boots or tennis shoes. For trail rides, kids need to be at least seven years old, and they cost the same as adults, so rates for families add up fast. For all rides, registration at least a day ahead is recommended; pay in cash, for Mule Shoe does not take credit cards.

July–mid-September, the specialty all-day ride (six hours, $120)—the best trail ride in the park—departs at 9 A.M. and climbs to Sperry Chalet, where you can lunch in the historic dining hall. In the last two miles of the ride, you break out of thick trees into avalanche chutes, where you'll have better views of the steep-walled valley as it ascends. Lunch is not included in the rate, so be sure to bring cash to eat at Sperry Chalet, and plan on ordering fresh homemade pie for dessert!

BOATING

Lake McDonald and St. Mary permit motorized boats, kayaks, sailboards, and canoes on both lakes, but Lake McDonald imposes a 10-horsepower limit on motorboats. As with all lakes in the park, jet skis are banned. Due to vehicle length restrictions (21 feet), towed boats may not cross Going-to-the-Sun Road between Avalanche and Sun Point.

Lake McDonald

Because Lake McDonald has only one boat ramp, you must drive to Apgar to launch anything larger than what you can carry. For hand-carried crafts, you can launch from Sprague Creek Picnic Area or several pullouts along the lake. For boating and fishing on Lake McDonald, **Glacier Park Boat Company** (406/888-5727 summers only, 406/257-2426, www.glacierparkboats.com) rents rowboats for $10 per hour and eight-horsepower motorboats for $20 per hour. Paddles, lifejackets, and fishing regulations are included. Find the rentals at the boat dock behind Lake McDonald Lodge. Bring cash, though, because no credit cards are accepted.

St. Mary

St. Mary Lake permits motorboats with unlimited horsepower. Its boat ramp is at Rising Sun. Hand-carried crafts can also launch easily from Rising Sun Picnic Area. Be aware, though, that wild winds whip up quickly here on the Continental Divide's east side, so keep your eye on conditions. No boats are available to rent on St. Mary Lake.

McDonald Creek

In spite of its attractive rapids for rafting and kayaking, McDonald Creek is closed to all forms of boating between Mineral Creek and Lake McDonald's head in order to protect nesting

GOING-TO-THE-SUN ROAD

harlequin ducks. These colorful ducks fly from the Pacific coast to Glacier for its swift, cold streams and then return to the coast with their young.

KAYAKING AND CANOEING

Both sea kayaking and canoeing are popular on Lake McDonald and St. Mary Lake. On calm days, shoreline tours are exceptionally scenic, and evening paddles are relaxing. On Lake McDonald, the north shore offers up-close views of the 2003 Robert Fire. You can launch from Apgar boat ramp or any of the pullouts on Going-to-the-Sun Road. On St. Mary Lake, Silver Dollar Beach below Red Eagle Mountain is a popular destination; however, keep one eye on the weather as high winds churn up monstrous waves quickly in the narrow valley. Launch boats from Rising Sun at the boat dock or the picnic area. Although river kayakers drool at the rapids on McDonald Creek, the creek is closed to all boating due to nesting harlequin ducks.

Glacier Park Boat Company (406/888-5727 summers only, 406/257-2426, www.glacier-parkboats.com) rents canoes and kayaks ($10 per hour, cash only) on Lake McDonald at two locations: Apgar and Lake McDonald Lodge. They do not rent boats on St. Mary Lake.

FISHING
McDonald Valley

Heavily fished, Lake McDonald is a haven for kokanee, lake trout, whitefish, and cutthroat. Lake McDonald has no limit on lake trout or lake whitefish. Since boat fishing tends to produce better results than shore fishing here, you'll have more luck if you rent a boat at the Lake McDonald Lodge dock. If you have your own boat to launch (heavier than what you can carry), you'll have to go to Apgar for the lake's only public ramp.

Other than Lake McDonald, fishing in Mc-Donald Valley is sporadic at best. Although scads of anglers rim McDonald Creek, the river actually has a reputation for leaving hooks bare. As for Fish Lake, a steep three-mile hike from Lake McDonald Lodge ac-cesses the tiny lily-padded shallow lake; a few westslope cutthroats reside here. Snyder Lake, a 4.4-mile climb from Lake McDonald Lodge, also has small cutthroat and is a little more open than Fish Lake's brushy shore. Ignore Avalanche Creek and head instead for the lake, where indigenous westslope cutthroat have been kept genetically pure by the gorge's falls. This lake is fished extensively, so drop your line far away from the trampled outlet or wade to one of the inlet streams to fish its chilly south end.

Logan Pass

With a quick three-mile access from Logan Pass, Hidden Lake holds good-sized westslope cutthroat trout in spite of its elevation and its reputation as the highest lake in the park with fish. However, the lake is catch-and-release only, and during spawning both the lake and the outlet are closed.

St. Mary Valley

St. Mary Lake's reputation is similar to Lake McDonald's: beautiful scenery, but not spec-tacular fishing. The larger lakes are best fished from boats rather than the shoreline. Upper St. Mary River doesn't fare much better: You often see anglers up and down its reaches especially around St. Mary Falls, but with few catching fish. Gunsight Lake, the best fishing lake, rests 6.2 miles from Jackson Glacier Overlook, but be prepared for wind and late snowpack along the shoreline.

Rentals and Guides

For those in need of fishing gear, the camp stores at Lake McDonald Lodge and Rising Sun sell a few items like line and flies. The nearest rental-gear location is **Glacier Outdoor Center** (11957 Hwy. 2 E., 406/888-5454 or 800/235-6781, www.glacierraftco.com) in West Glacier. The park has no fishing guides for its road-accessible lakes and streams, but **Glacier Guides** (11970 Hwy. 2 E., 406/387-5555 or 800/521-7238, www.glacierguides.com), based out of West Glacier, is licensed for all backcountry trips. For the best bet for fishing backcoun-

try lakes, hire one of the guides for a custom overnight backcountry trip ($560 per day), and they'll get your permit, transport you to the trailhead, bring all the food, and do all the cooking.

Glacier requires no fishing license, but be aware of regulations (as detailed in the *Background* chapter).

WATERSKIING

While both Lake McDonald and St. Mary permit waterskiing (although Lake McDonald has a 10-horsepower limit), you won't find the lakes packed shore to shore with skiers, and that's frankly because the lakes are frigid. Those who do water-ski the glacier-fed waters wear wetsuits. Because precocious winds whisk up sizable whitecaps—especially on St. Mary Lake—serious water-skiers head to Flathead Valley for its warmer, less whimsical lakes. Flathead Valley has the nearest ski boat and water-ski rentals.

WINDSURFING

Of all the park's lakes, St. Mary Lake is the one windsurfers occasionally use. Lake McDonald attracts a few, but its winds are too inconsistent to appeal to avid windsurfers. On St. Mary Lake, winds can rage down the valley; however, its winds are also swirly due to the high mountains and erratic confluence of valleys. For that reason, the lake is really not a beginner windsurfing area; experience is helpful, and know how to self-rescue. Those who do want to try its frigid waters usually launch from Rising Sun Picnic Area and wear a wetsuit. No windsurfing equipment is available for rent in the vicinity.

CROSS-COUNTRY SKIING AND SNOWSHOEING

Since plowing in winter ends at Lake McDonald Lodge, most skiers simply continue up the gated road on their skis through a relatively avalanche-free zone. The gentle grade makes for good gliding suitable for beginners as the road leads past McDonald Creek and Upper McDonald Creek Falls to Avalanche Camp-ground (at six miles). Some skiers cross the bridge at Sacred Dancing Cascade to loop back on the river's north side, but snow coverage is more variable and sometimes low in the trees. For snowshoers on Going-to-the-Sun Road, etiquette requires blazing a separate snowshoe trail rather than squishing the parallel ski tracks flat.

In McDonald Valley, John's Lake can provide a ski through the trees, but for a destination, it's not much more than a pond. Some skiers head up to Snyder Lakes, but the narrow trail descending through tight trees on the way back down makes for a hair-raising adventure; most winter tourers prefer to tackle that trail on snowshoes instead.

On the east side, Going-to-the-Sun Road is closed in winter at St. Mary. It can be a good, relatively avalanche-free six-mile ski up to Rising Sun along Two Dog Flats; however, high winds frequently blow the snow to the plains of eastern Montana, leaving bare sections on the road. For skiers, this means repeatedly taking the skis off to walk on bare road between the snowy sections.

Between Rising Sun and Avalanche Creek, Going-to-the-Sun Road sees significant avalanche activity. Do not attempt to ski any of this section without experience and know-how. Avalanche transceivers, shovels, and probes must be carried. Check current conditions at www.glacieravalanche.org.

Rentals and Guides

For guided winter ski or snowshoe excursions, call **Glacier Park Ski Tours** (406/862-2790, www.glacierparkskitours.com, $165–275 for 1–4 people per day, $35 per person for each additional). They usually meet at the West Glacier post office and then tour up the road or on side trails as conditions permit. You'll need to bring along a pack, water, extra clothes, and a lunch, and you must have your own equipment. The nearest ski and snowshoe rental location is **Glacier Outdoor Center** (11957 Hwy. 2 E., 406/888-5454 or 800/235-6781, www.glacierraftco.com, $10–15 per day) in West Glacier.

GOING-TO-THE-SUN ROAD

ENTERTAINMENT
Park Naturalists

Lake McDonald Lodge, Avalanche Campground Amphitheater, and Rising Sun Amphitheater offer 45-minute evening park naturalist programs usually starting around 8 P.M. Check for schedules at campground information boards and hotel activity desks or pick up a copy of *The Glacier Explorer* at visitors centers. Topics range from fires to birds. If you can catch a presentation by Professor Avian Guano or Critterman (a.k.a. Denny Olson), you'll laugh your socks off. Best of all, they're free. Once a week at Rising Sun, the program features a Native American speaker, a great way to gain an understanding of the park's rich Native American culture and history.

Jack Gladstone

Grammy-nominated Jack Gladstone, a Blackfeet, presents his multimedia **Legends of Glacier** (adults $5, kids 12 and under $2) usually once a week at the Lake McDonald Lodge auditorium. The show blends slides, storytelling, and original music. His highly entertaining show provides insight into Blackfeet history, culture, and legends that have sprung from parklands. For showtimes and days, pick up the current newspaper copy of *The Glacier Explorer* at visitors centers or check online: www.nps/gov/glac.

Accommodations

Accommodations on Going-to-the-Sun Road are scarce. The west side has Lake McDonald Lodge, 16 miles west of Logan Pass. Twelve miles east of the pass, Rising Sun offers plain cottages and motel units. For those with the feet to carry them, there are two more outstanding options—Granite Park and Sperry Chalets—but both require hiking and, for Granite Park, the ability to carry your own food. All chalets and inns charge a 7 percent state bed tax.

LAKE MCDONALD

Historic ◖ **Lake McDonald Lodge** (milepost 11.2 or 39.2 on Going-to-the-Sun Road, 406/892-2525, www.glacierparkinc.com, late May–early Oct., $96–147 double, $10 for each additional adult) sits on the lakeshore with access to activities from boating and trail riding to red bus and boat tours. Located on Lake McDonald's east end and centering around its hunting lodge–themed lobby full of trophy specimens hung by John Lewis, the complex offers three types of accommodations: rooms in the main hotel, rooms in adjacent cottages, and motel rooms a five-minute walk away. The lodge and cottage exteriors have a quaint cabin look with lakeside rooms having views, but the motel is 1950s in architecture and set in deep trees with no views. While all the rooms are small with their age clearly showing, cottage rooms tend to be the tiniest, many with space for only two twin beds; main lodge rooms tend to be the largest. Be prepared for all three room types to have petite bathrooms—dinky sinks and skinny elbow-knocking shower stalls—in many cases closets converted into bathrooms. Rooms have phones but no televisions, air-conditioning, or elevator access, and the entire facility is nonsmoking. While the rooms are not what you'd call modern, this is a place to get out and explore—not sit in a room. Dial back your expectations to the 1940s or 1950s, and you'll be delighted with its location and historic ambience. Restaurants, a lounge, gift shop, and camp store are in the lodge or within a five-minute walk. Best of all, trails to Mount Brown Lookout, Snyder Lake, Sperry Chalet, and Sperry Glacier depart right across the street. Reservations are highly recommended in June and September and an absolute must in July and August.

RISING SUN

Rising Sun Motor Inn (milepost 44.7 or 6 on Going-to-the-Sun Road, 406/892-2525, www.glacierparkinc.com, open mid-June–mid-Sept., $94–110 for two people, $10 each additional) became the answer for motorists traveling to Glacier during World War II as it was the only facility that stayed open. Built in 1940, the inn still retains its old-time feel with no television, air-conditioning, in-room phones, or elevators. (A pay phone is in front of the camp store.) The compound comprises nonsmoking cottages and motel units, all with very diminutive private bathrooms; expect to bump your elbows in the shower stalls. The motel also has a restaurant, camp store, and hiker shuttle stop. The trail to Otokomi Lake begins right behind the motor inn, and access to St. Mary Lake is right across the street, along with the boat tour dock.

While not much has changed at this funky old-time motor inn with its board-and-batten construction, it's hard to beat its location 12 miles from Logan Pass—the nearest lodging to the pass. Although the rooms don't have much in the way of amenities, you won't want to spend your time there anyway with so much outside to explore right at your fingertips. In the evening, go on a gorgeous sunset cruise on St. Mary Lake or drive to look for wildlife on Two Dog Flats between Rising Sun and St. Mary.

BACKCOUNTRY CHALETS

One of two historic chalets remaining in Glacier's backcountry, **Sperry Chalet** (406/387-5654 or 888/345-2649, www.sperry chalet.com, $155 for first person per night, $100 for each additional person per night in same room) offers hikers and horseback riders full service. Three meals and a warm bed means hauling only a day pack with some extra clothing for that 6.5-mile hike up from Lake McDonald or 14-mile hike over two passes from Jackson Glacier Overlook. To ease the point-to-point hike, hiker shuttles stop at both trailheads. Set in a timbered cirque, the chalet has rock and log buildings—a dining hall, a

© BECKY LOMAX

historic Sperry Chalet, below Mt. Edwards

GOING-TO-THE-SUN ROAD

dorm, and several park service buildings. Seventeen dorm rooms sleep 2–6 people each in bunks or beds, but pack along earplugs because snores resound through the historically thin walls. With no electricity, no phones, and no televisions, evening entertainment entails watching goats and sunsets and, in the dead of night, grabbing a flashlight to find the composting toilet (with cold running water).

While Sperry's buildings are owned by the park service, the concession has been operated by the same family since 1954, when Great Northern sold its interest. Country meals with roasted turkey sate ravenous hiker appetites, but the menu has maintained culinary sensibilities from the late 1950s with canned fruits and vegetables. Trail lunches packed for you are plain, with a meat and cheese sandwich (no lettuce nor tomato), candy bars, and raisins. However, bakery goods—yummy cookies, freshly baked breads, and pies—are outstanding, using traditional recipes passed down from decades ago. No alcohol is sold on the premises or allowed in the dining hall; you can pack along your favorite beverage for elsewhere, though, and you will need to pack the containers out with you. Reservations are required and often fill up by spring.

Set at the same elevation as Logan Pass, **(Granite Park Chalet** (888/345-2649, www.graniteparkchalet.com, July–early Sept., $66 per person per night) is a historic backcountry chalet accessed only by trail from Logan Pass (7.6 miles), The Loop (4 miles), or Swiftcurrent (7.6 miles). Hiker shuttles stop at all three trailheads, making point-to-point hiking from the chalet simple. Sitting atop a knoll, where a 360-degree view alone makes the stay worth it, the chalet has three stone and log buildings—the main chalet (kitchen, dining room, and guest rooms), a dorm, a park service building, and the composting outhouse. Twelve private guest rooms sleep 2–6 people each. Bring earplugs, for you will hear everything your neighbors say plus someone snoring next door. This chalet functions somewhat like a hostel. You must bring your own sleeping bag, or if you don't want to carry one, you can purchase linen service ($10). Meals are not supplied, so hikers must haul their own food to cook in the kitchen, whatever you can carry—from lasagna to stir fry. If you don't want to carry food, you can purchase freeze-dried meals on-site, along with candy bars, juices, pop, and bottled water. A new concessionaire (same operators as Sperry Chalet) took over in 2005 with some planned changes in past practices, such as expectations for carrying out garbage, hauling water, and use of pots, pans, plates, cups, and silverware. Clarify these details when you make your reservation.

The chalet building, owned by the park service, has no running water or electricity, but propane runs the stoves. Water filters will be available, but guests may have to haul water from a quarter mile away. No alcoholic beverages are allowed in the dining room, but they are permitted in private rooms. Good weather evenings begin with binoculars focused on bears and finish with sunsets over the Livingston Range. Reservations are mandatory, with high season often filling up by early spring.

CAMPING

In the 52 miles of Going-to-the-Sun Road, five campgrounds stretch along the corridor, but none sit in the 28-mile central Logan Pass section. On the west side, Apgar, Sprague Creek, and Avalanche offer more sites than Rising Sun and St. Mary on the east side. (Details on Apgar and St. Mary are listed in their respective chapters.) Given their coveted location, in high season Avalanche, Sprague Creek, and Rising Sun fill up usually by noon with all sites first-come, first-serve. For all campgrounds on Going-to-the-Sun Road, the only amenities are flush toilets, running water, picnic tables, and fire grates; bring your own firewood, as collecting is not permitted. For hookups, hit commercial campgrounds in St. Mary or West Glacier. For bicyclists, hikers, and motorcyclists along Going-to-the-Sun Road, shared hiker-biker sites with bear-resistant food storage and held until 9 P.M. are available at all five campgrounds for $5 per person.

Because vehicles over 21 feet cannot travel

between Avalanche Campground and Sun Point, if campgrounds are full, oversized RVs on the west side must backtrack to Fish Creek at Apgar and commercial campgrounds in West Glacier. If Rising Sun is full on the east side, large RVs have to head to the park service or commercial campgrounds in St. Mary.

Lake McDonald

Sprague Creek Campground (milepost 10.2 or 40.5 on Going-to-the-Sun Road, 406/888-7800, mid-May–mid-Sept., $15 per site) sits right on Lake McDonald's shore one mile west of the lodge in a timbered setting with shaded sites. Unfortunately, several sites also abut Going-to-the-Sun Road, with a nice view of cars driving by. After dark, thank goodness, the road noise calms down substantially, so it's not like tenting next to a major highway. As the smallest campground—only 25 sites accessed via a paved road, Sprague Creek does not allow towed units; however, a few sites can accommodate small RVs up to 21 feet. No trailheads depart from here, but sunset from the beach can be spectacular, and for kayakers and canoers, you can't beat the lakefront access. At 23 miles from Logan Pass, it still has quick access to the high country.

Set in a cedar-hemlock rainforest, **(Avalanche Campground** (milepost 16.6 or 34.1 on Going-to-the-Sun Road, 406/888-7800, mid-June–early Sept., $15 per site) opens for a shorter season than Sprague Creek. Six miles

east of Lake McDonald Lodge, Avalanche makes the closest west-side base for exploring Logan Pass 16 miles away and is convenient for hiking to Avalanche Lake, since the trailhead departs from the back of the campground. You'll know you're in a rainforest with its dark overgrown forest canopy allowing little sunlight to enter the campground. The moist area sprouts thick patches of thimbleberries and sometimes a good collection of mosquitoes. Although the campground can fit RVs up to 26 feet in over half of its sites, no disposal station is available.

Rising Sun

Located 12 miles east of Logan Pass and six miles west of St. Mary, **(Rising Sun Campground** (milepost 44.5 or 6.3 on Going-to-the-Sun Road, 406/888-7800, late May–mid-Sept., no reservations, $15 per site) tucks at the base of Otokomi Mountain by St. Mary Lake. Adjacent to Rising Sun Motor Inn, the campground is a few-minutes' walk to a restaurant, camp store, hot showers, and a hiker shuttle stop. Beach access is across Going-to-the-Sun Road at the boat ramp or picnic area, and boat tours also depart from here. Otokomi Lake trailhead is behind the inn. The campground has 83 sites and a dump station, but only 10 sites that can accommodate small RVs up to 25 feet. This is a favorite for its ease of access to Logan Pass, but the sun drops down early behind Goat Mountain, so expect a rather long twilight.

GOING-TO-THE-SUN ROAD

Food

No food services are available at Logan Pass. The nearest restaurants on the west side are at Lake McDonald Lodge, 21 miles from the pass. On the east side, Rising Sun has the only restaurant, 12 miles from Logan Pass and 6 miles from St. Mary.

RESTAURANTS
Lake McDonald

Located in Lake McDonald Lodge,

(Russell's Fireside Dining Room (milepost 11.2 or 39.2 on Going-to-the-Sun Road, 406/892-2525, daily late May–early Oct.) is worth a meal, just for its ambience with woven seats and painted Native American chandeliers. The north windows have a peek-a-boo lake view, but during dinner the blinds usually need to be pulled down as the sun blazes in fairly hot. The food is decent, but don't expect to find anything really inventive on the

menu. Breakfasts (6:30–9:30 A.M., $5–9) are the same in all the lodges run by Glacier Park, Inc.—a massive buffet spread with fruit, pastries, waffles, eggs, pancakes, French toast, sausage, and bacon. It offers a huge selection and enough to fill big eaters, but entrees will not be steaming hot off the grill. Those looking for something smaller can order à la carte. The nonsmoking dining hall is also open for lunch (11:30 A.M.–2 P.M., $6–9) and dinner (5–9:30 P.M., $15–24). While wild game, pasta, and fish take on a decidedly Montana taste at the lodge, your waitstaff is from around the globe. When you dine here, don't pass up a northern Rocky Mountain dessert—huckleberry ice cream. Because reservations are taken only for groups larger than 12, you'll often have to wait in a line for a table at dinner. The restaurant also makes hiker lunches to go ($7–10); order these one day in advance for pickup in the morning.

If you want a lighter dinner than is offered in the lodge dining hall but don't want to leave the lakeside or Lake McDonald Lodge, check out the cozy **Stockade Lounge** (406/892-2525, 11:30 A.M.–midnight daily late May–early Oct.). It serves a respectable $6–9 appetizer and sandwich menu 2–10 P.M., which includes the requisite burger and fries. The nonsmoking bar also stocks plenty of local microbrews along with wine and cocktails.

Across the parking lot from Lake McDonald Lodge and operated by the same concession that runs the lodge dining room and Stockade Lounge, **Jammer Joe's Grill and Pizzeria** (406/892-2525, 11:30 A.M.–9:30 P.M. daily late May–Sept., $6–9) serves lunch and dinner in a nonsmoking, cafeteria-type atmosphere. Pizzas, pasta, and sandwiches, including buffalo burgers, dominate the menu, making it the best place to take the kids. It also recently added an Italian buffet, which includes a large salad bar and desserts.

Rising Sun

Located at Rising Sun Motor Inn, **Two Dog Flats Grill** (milepost 44.7 or 6 on Going-to-the-Sun Road, 406/892-2525, 6:30–10:30 A.M.

and 11 A.M.–9:30 P.M. daily mid-June–mid-Sept.) serves breakfast ($4–7), lunch ($6–9), and dinner ($8–15). Fare is standard American: soups, salads, sandwiches, steaks, and fish. Montana microbrews and wine, too. Ask for a south window table to view Red Eagle Peak. Because the nonsmoking restaurant—a slightly upgraded old coffee shop—sometimes crowds with bus tours, and no reservations are taken for groups smaller than 12 people, you may have to wait for a table in high season. If the line is really long, you can bop six miles down the road to St. Mary. The restaurant also makes hiker lunches to go ($7–10); order these one day in advance for pickup the following morning.

GROCERIES

Camp stores are located at Lake McDonald Lodge 21 miles west of Logan Pass (a five-minute walk from Lake McDonald Lodge) and Rising Sun 12 miles east of the pass. Open 7 A.M.–9 P.M. daily mid-June–mid-September, both camp stores carry limited brand selections, but you can pick up ice, firewood, stove gas, and other camping supplies as well as convenience store groceries, beer, wine, gifts, and newspapers. For hikers, both stores are a suitable place to buy trail lunch supplies—crackers, cheese, chips, fruit, and cookies.

PICNIC AREAS

Only four areas accommodate the picnic basket on Going-to-the-Sun Road: Sprague Creek, Avalanche Creek, Sun Point, and Rising Sun. For those that allow fires, you'll need to bring your own firewood, as gathering is prohibited. To the right as you drive in the campground, **Sprague Creek Picnic Area** (milepost 10.2 or 40.5) is tucked tightly between Going-to-the-Sun Road and Lake McDonald in the trees, with more road view than scenery; however, short paths access the shoreline. It has access to flush toilets, picnic tables, and fire pits. ◖ **Avalanche Creek Picnic Area** (milepost 16.6 or 34.1) sits across the street from the campground and has newly rebuilt larger vault toilet restrooms. Picnic sites with tables

and fire pits under cedar shade access McDonald Creek and are adjacent to Trail of the Cedars and the Avalanche Lake trail. **Sun Point Picnic Area** (milepost 40.6 or 10) is more or less a parking lot with tables (no fire pits) scattered around its perimeter; however, it has great views up St. Mary Valley to the Continental Divide, and its trails access spectacular Sun Point and Baring Falls. Be prepared for wind here. An old, yucky wooden outhouse services the area. **(Rising Sun Picnic Area** (milepost 44.7 or 6) sits adjacent to St. Mary Lake, but its open sites are somewhat buffered from wind by aspen trees. Short paths through the trees access the shoreline. It has flush toilets, picnic tables, and fire pits.

Logan Pass has no picnic area, and the park service does not allow coolers outside of vehicles (although you can pack a sack lunch and eat it anywhere). If you want to "picnic" up with the views, the best method is to pack a sack lunch to eat on a trail or at one of the many pullouts along the road. Especially scenic and aptly named, Lunch Creek pullout (milepost 33.4 or 17.4) just east of Logan Pass has a good historic rock wall that makes a great place to sit for lunch, but keep the cooler inside the car.

ST. MARY AND MANY GLACIER

Mountains don't pinch the scenery here, but instead drop abruptly to wide open grasslands—eastern Montana's prairieland. Wildflowers grow rampant. Elk browse. Aspen leaves chatter quietly in the slightest breeze below sheer cliffs. A wild panorama of Glacier's peaks draws across the western skyline, dominated by burgundy sediments and milky-blue sapphire lakes. Here on the Continental Divide's east side, wind is a constant companion, shaping trees and whipping up whitecaps, but every minute yields another view to burn up film. No wonder the Blackfeet called Glacier the "Backbone of the World."

While St. Mary is the eastern portal to Glacier's famed Going-to-the-Sun Road, Many Glacier is a setting of dreams: rugged, idyllic, pastoral. On the east side, morning sunrise gleams gold across a rampart of peaks speckled with glaciers clinging for dear life to cliffy north faces. Loons call across glassy lakes. Grizzly bears forage on hillsides, clawing at the ground for glacier lily bulbs. By evening, when trails vacate, the sunset paints royal hues above the Continental Divide. Dark descends, with a multitude of stars. And if you're lucky, the northern lights dance across the sky.

HISTORY
Parkhood
George Bird Grinnell first set eyes on his namesake glacier in 1887. The editor of *Forest and Stream,* the precursor to *Field and Stream,* speckled over two decades with several excursions to Glacier, during which he lobbied Congress for support for the area's preservation.

© BECKY LOMAX

HIGHLIGHTS

◖ Boat Tours: The Many Glacier boat tour offers travelers two boats and a short stroll. Begin the excursion on Swiftcurrent Lake and walk to Lake Josephine for the second boat. Both have unbeatable views (page 114)!

◖ Many Glacier Road: Enjoy a scenic evening drive into Many Glacier. Sunsets turn the peaks rosy with alpenglow, and wildlife is frequently afoot (page 116).

◖ Divide Mountain: Commanding the southern point above St. Mary before its ridge drops low across the plains, this aptly named wonder demarcates the continental division between waters flowing north to the Saskatchewan drainage and those heading south in the Missouri (page 118).

◖ Many Glacier Hotel: Built to be the grandest of the park's lodges, this historic hotel lives up to its reputation for beauty. Its enormous four-story log lobby and two-story floor-to-ceiling dining room windows make it nothing less than grand (page 119).

◖ Grinnell Glacier: Ice calves off in huge chunks, floating the milky blue waters of Upper Grinnell Lake, while waterfalls tumble from Salamander Glacier above. See it up close by hiking. (page 123).

◖ Swiftcurrent Valley and Lookout: It takes gumption to accomplish this hike and stand atop the Continental Divide to survey glaciers and peaks for as far as the eye can see (page 123).

◖ Iceberg Lake: Tucked below goat-studded cliffs, the lake gleams with icebergs floating its waters even in late August. You might just have to go swimming here, just to say you did (page 123)!

◖ Ptarmigan Tunnel: Built in the 1930s, this is a hiker's treat. A walk through its dark corridor spits you out with a burst of color: Red argillite smears across hillsides with Elizabeth Lake's blue waters below (page 124).

◖ Duck Lake: For anglers, the world-famous lake is known for its large rainbow trout. The views aren't bad either with Chief Mountain looming above the lake (page 130).

◖ Native America Speaks: Gain an understanding of Blackfeet culture and heritage by catching one of these programs, which feature storytellers, singers, and dancers. Some popular shows have standing room only (page 130).

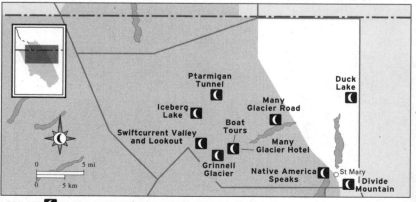

LOOK FOR ◖ TO FIND RECOMMENDED SIGHTS, ACTIVITIES, DINING, AND LODGING.

ST. MARY AND MANY GLACIER

ST MARY AND MANY GLACIER

To Browning

To Browning
and East Glacier

DUCK LAKE

Goose Lake

Lake

CHEWING
BLACKBONES

SEE "ST MARY" MAP

St Mary

DIVIDE
MOUNTAIN

USA

CUSTOMS

CHIEF MOUNTAIN INTERNATIONAL HWY

BLACKFEET

INDIAN

RESERVATION

Babb

MANY GLACIER ROAD

Lower
St Mary
Lake

GOING-TO-THE-SUN RD

Red Eagle
Lake

St Mary
Lake

Red Eagle
Mountain

CUSTOMS

Chief
Mountain

BELLY RIVER
RANGER
STATION

SEE "MANY GLACIER" MAP

Poia
Lake

Apikuni
Mountain

Lake
Sherburne

MANY GLACIER
HOTEL

Cracker Lake

Mt Siyeh

Otokomi
Mountain

Goat Haunt
Mountain

GOAT HAUNT

Cosley
Lake

Glenns
Lake

Elizabeth
Lake

Helen
Lake

Iceberg
Lake

Upper
Waterton
Lake

Mt
Cleveland

Stoney
Indian
Lake

GOING-TO-THE-SUN RD

Kootenai
Lakes

Kootenai
Peak

Glacier

National

Park

Continental Divide

Logging
Lake

Congress agreed to purchase lands from the Blackfeet to open to the public, and Grinnell helped negotiate the sale.

After the federal government purchased the land from the Blackfeet, Glacier became a forest reserve thrown open to prospecting and hunting. The Many Glacier Valley attracted hordes of would-be miners, digging for copper, silver, and gold. In 1898, the mining boom gave rise to Altyn, a townsite located where Sherburne Reservoir is today. At its peak, the burg housed 800 residents, but by December of 1902 it was a ghost town, its yields meager and its inhabitants lured north into Klondike's gold rush.

Grinnell pressed on in his efforts to preserve Glacier. Finally, in 1910, President Taft signed the act creating Glacier National Park, America's 12th national park. In recognition of Grinnell's efforts, a glacier, a peak, a point, and two lakes have been named after him, all in Many Glacier Valley.

Lodges and Chalets

From wagon roads, the Great Northern Railway built a dirt road 1911–1912 from Midvale (East Glacier) to St. Mary and Swiftcurrent Valley—soon home to the "Showplace of the Rockies," Many Glacier Hotel. When dry, the road was drivable; when rains fell, it mutated into treacherous muck. In the hustle to create guest lodging for train riders, the train company threw up Many Glacier and St. Mary Chalets in 1912–1913. Guests rode the 36 miles from Midvale to St. Mary by car in 2.5 hours or stagecoach in four hours. Others arrived via the Inside Trail on an overnight saddle horse trip, stopping at Cut Bank Chalets. After avalanches demolished two of the Many

Glacier chalets and the dining hall, poor site selection prompted choosing another location for the grand Many Glacier Hotel. Finally, the luxury hotel on Swiftcurrent Lake opened its doors in 1915 with running water—both hot and cold—steam heat, telephones, and electric lights in every room.

Blackfeet Highway

In the late 1920s, the State of Montana rerouted and paved the road connecting Midvale and St. Mary—the Blackfeet Highway, found on most maps today as Highways 49 and 89. The new route bypassed St. Mary Chalets, which fell into disuse as growing automobile traffic diverted toward Going-to-the-Sun Road and sprouted the town of St. Mary. Saddled with the Depression and fewer people who could afford pricey hotels, the park service pressured the railroad company into building Swiftcurrent Cabins in 1933—immediately a popular place to stay at $2.25.

1936 Fire

When high winds forced the 1936 Heavens Peak fire over the Continental Divide, it beelined down Swiftcurrent Valley, eating up 33 of the auto cabins en route to Many Glacier Hotel. Employees doused the hotel roof with water to protect their lodge. After the fire spared the hotel, employees telegrammed the railway vice president, apprising him of the success. His reply: "Why?" The hotels and chalets had become a financial noose around the railway's neck. The St. Mary chalets were torn down in 1948; Many Glacier chalets succumbed to fire and avalanches. Only the historic showplace Many Glacier Hotel remains.

Exploring St. Mary and Many Glacier

Glacier's eastern ecosystem sprawls across national park lands and the Blackfeet Reservation—divided by an artificially straight border. Bears and elk know no boundaries, and sometimes neither do cattle, ranging astray inside Glacier.

Blackfeet Reservation

Bordering the park's eastern boundary are 1.5 million acres of Blackfeet tribal lands. The boundary slices across the summits of Chief Mountain, Napi Point, and Divide Peak, crossing the lower end of Sherburne Reservoir and sliding between the two St. Mary Lakes. Tribal permits are required for recreating on the reservation: camping, fishing, hiking, and boating.

St. Mary

St. Mary is the eastern portal to Going-to-the-Sun Road. Sitting at the junction of the historic road and the Blackfeet Highway (Hwy. 89,) the town sprawls across the park boundary. Only the visitor center and St. Mary Campground are within the park; the town, restaurants, grocery stores, lodging, and commercial campgrounds are all on the Blackfeet Reservation. A park-staffed park entrance station and cash-only self-pay kiosk lead up Going-to-the-Sun Road.

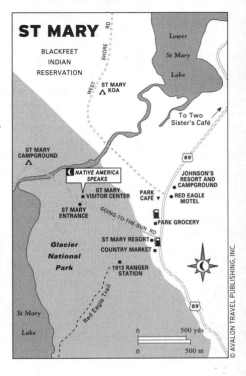

Many Glacier

You'll have to become used to the lingo here: Although the popular Many Glacier Hotel sits in the Swiftcurrent Valley, locals refer to the whole valley area simply as Many Glacier, even though that technically is not its name. (Only two features actually use that name—the hotel and the campground.) Many Glacier derived its name from the string of small glaciers that populated its peaks: Grinnell, Salamander, Gem, North Swiftcurrent, and South Swiftcurrent. Many Glacier Road has a staffed park entrance station and a self-pay cash-only kiosk.

Babb

Between St. Mary and Many Glacier sits Babb, a blink-and-you'll-miss-it village about one block long. A few houses cluster behind a petite year-round grocery store, along with two bars, two restaurants, and a tiny motel. It seemingly has no purpose in the middle of nowhere, but its year-round post office and elementary school service families ranching between St. Mary and the Canadian border.

Belly River

A confluence of two valleys lined with good fishing lakes, the Belly River is home to tales of one of the park's most notorious rangers—Joe Cosley. Guides and rangers tell stories of his exploits—from poaching to womanizing. The Belly, as locals call it, is undeveloped backcountry; there are no hotels and restaurants.

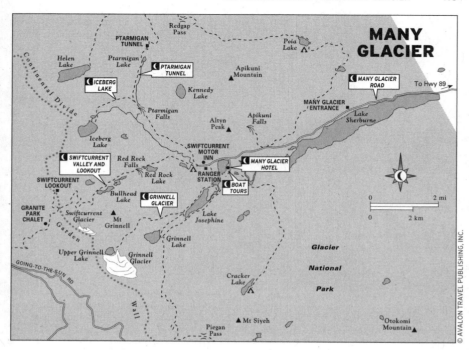

While hikers can reach a couple of the Belly River's lakes in one long day, most of the valley's lakes require backpacking.

VISITOR CENTER

In St. Mary, **St. Mary Visitor Center** (0.4 mile west on Going-to-the-Sun Rd., 406/732-7751, 8 A.M.–8 P.M. mid-May–late June and Labor Day–Sept., open until 9 P.M. late June–Labor Day) is the largest visitor center in the park. Its two parking lots are set on both sides of the building. Indoor facilities comprise displays, a small Glacier Natural History Association bookstore, and a theater. In 2005, the center added a tipi, the first step in developing a tipi encampment with outdoor dancing and a performance stage for the popular Native America Speaks program. Plans also include renovation of the center's indoor exhibits to emphasize more Native American cultural park history.

Inside the center, you'll find backcountry permits, fishing regulations, Going-to-the-Sun Road updates, Junior Ranger newspapers, and information on free guided park naturalist hikes and presentations in *The Glacier Explorer.* The small indoor theater also shows slide presentations and schedules evening naturalist programs. The visitor center is a shuttle stop for hikers: To avoid parking hassles at Logan Pass, you can park your car here all day for free and catch the shuttle up Going-to-the-Sun Road.

TOURS AND SHUTTLES
Red Bus

Glacier Park, Inc. (406/892-2525, www.glacierparkinc.com, mid-June–mid-Sept., adults $36–50, kids 11 and under half price, prices do not include meals or park entrance fees) runs three daily tours leaving Many Glacier Hotel on the historic red buses. These scenic buses

A Blackfeet tipi sits outside the St. Mary Visitor Center.

are charmers; on good weather days, the jammers (tour bus drivers) roll the canvas tops back for unlimited skyward views—no air-conditioning needed then! The 7.5-hour Crown of the Continent tour departs at 9 A.M. for Lake McDonald Lodge, hitting almost every scenic stop on Going-to-the-Sun Road. The 4.5-hour Logan Pass tour departs at 1 P.M., goes to the pass, sees the Garden Wall, and then returns. Both of these tours stop in St. Mary to pick up riders at St. Mary KOA, Johnson's of St. Mary, and St. Mary Lodge.

The 5-hour International Peace Park Tour departs daily at 11:30 A.M. for an excursion to Waterton and arrives at Prince of Wales Hotel in time for afternoon tea. This tour, which originates in East Glacier, also picks up riders in St. Mary. Reservations can be made by phone or at Many Glacier Hotel's activity desk.

Sun Tours

Departing St. Mary daily at 9 A.M., **Sun Tours** (406/226-9220 or 800/786-9220, www.glaciersuntours.com, mid-May–mid-Oct., adults

$35–55, kids ages 12 and under $15, kids under 5 free, meals and park entrance fees not included) drives 25-passenger air-conditioned buses over historic Going-to-the-Sun Road to Lake McDonald and back. Extra-large windows make for big views, an asset on the scenic highway. Led by local guides who live on the reservation, the tours highlight Glacier's rich historical and present-day connection with the Blackfeet. Call for reservations at least 24 hours in advance.

Boat Tours

In Many Glacier, jump on a pair of historic wooden boats for a tour of two lakes with **Glacier Park Boat Company** (406/732-4480 summers only, 406/257-2426, www.glacierparkboats.com, mid-June–mid-Sept., adult round-trip $13.50; kids half price.). Catch the 1961-vintage *Chief Two Guns* on Swiftcurrent Lake's boat dock behind Many Glacier Hotel. In 1.25 hours, you'll cruise across the lake, hike 0.2 mile over a hill, hop aboard the 1945 *Morning Eagle,* and return. On this tour, you're right in the thick of moose, bear, and deer country. Tours depart six times daily: 9 and 11 A.M., 1 (July–Aug. only), 2, 3 (July–Aug. only), and 4 P.M. Two of the daily launches (9 A.M. and 2 P.M.) offer a guided walk farther up the valley to Grinnell Lake. Don't forget your camera, but you may have difficulty cramming the view into the lens. In high season, the guided hike tours fill up fast, so buy your tickets (cash only) at the dock a few hours early. Once the Grinnell Glacier trail melts out, the boat company adds an 8:30 A.M. launch to the schedule, allowing hikers quicker access across the valley. Hikers may also catch a return boat at the upper Lake Josephine dock (pay as you board); you may have to wait for a few launches to get on, but the captain runs the boat until all hikers are shuttled.

On St. Mary Lake, boat tours on the *Little Chief* depart from Rising Sun. Check the *Going-to-the-Sun Road* chapter for details.

Shuttles

Glacier Park, Inc. (406/892-2525, www.glacierparkinc.com, $8–40 depending on destination,

kids under 11 half price) operates the hiker shuttle departing from Swiftcurrent Motor Inn, Many Glacier Hotel, and St. Mary Visitor Center. Between late May and late September, the east-side shuttle runs north–south along the Blackfeet Highway, connecting Waterton, Many Glacier, St. Mary, Two Medicine, and East Glacier. A second shuttle runs between July and Labor Day from Many Glacier to West Glacier along Going-to-the-Sun Road, with a stop at St. Mary Visitor Center. Schedules are available on shuttle stop signs, online, at hotel activity desks, visitors centers, and ranger stations. No reservations are accepted; pay cash when you board.

Shuttles make point-to-point hikes a pleasure—no time-consuming setup of your own shuttle or hitchhiking back to retrieve a car! For details of point-to-point hikes ending in Many Glacier, like Piegan Pass or the Highline Trail over to Swiftcurrent Pass, see *Going-to-the-Sun Road* chapter.

SERVICES

Two gas stations are in St. Mary on Highway 89, one on either side of the Going-to-the-Sun Road junction. One more gas station is in Babb across from Thronson's General Store. Many Glacier has no gas services.

In Many Glacier, public showers ($1.25 for eight minutes)—which are often cold-to-lukewarm—and laundry facilities are available behind Swiftcurrent Campstore; purchase tokens for both in the store. In St. Mary, you'll find $5 showers and a coin-op laundry at St. Mary KOA, and $3 showers and coin-op laundry at Johnson's Campground. In Many Glacier, public pay phones are located at the Many Glacier Hotel and adjacent to Swiftcurrent Campstore. ATMs are found at Many Glacier Hotel, Swiftcurrent Motor Inn, Country Market, and The Resort at Glacier: St. Mary Lodge. At the junction of Many Glacier Road and Highway 89, Babb has the nearest post office to Many Glacier; St. Mary has a seasonal post office in the Country Market. The local newspaper is the *Great Falls Tribune*. In St. Mary, you can find public restrooms at the visitor center and behind Curly Bear Café.

Planning to use your cell phone? Keep dreaming. There's no coverage in Many Glacier; however, some cell phones may work in St. Mary and Babb.

Shopping

Several gift shops in St. Mary offer a break from the same selections found in all the park hotel gift shops, but expect to see merchandise heavily branded with popular moose and bear themes. The only place on the east side of the park to pick up hiking gear, **Trail Creek Outfitters** (junction of Hwy. 89 and Going-to-the-Sun Rd., 406/732-4431, late May–early Oct.), carries good lines of hiking, backpacking, and camping gear at specialty store prices.

Emergencies

If you are inside the park, contact a ranger or call 406/888-7800 for emergencies. The nearest hospital is in Cut Bank—the Northern Rockies Medical Center (802 2nd St. E., 406/873-2251).

The **Many Glacier Ranger Station** (milepost 12.4 on Many Glacier Rd., 406/732-7740, 8 A.M.–5 P.M. daily late May–mid-Sept.), between the picnic area and Swiftcurrent parking lot on Many Glacier Road, is a good place to pick up maps, backcountry camping permits, trail closure information, and advice for hikes. Rangers like to keep apprised of all bear sightings—especially bears close to the trail—so report your sightings here.

DRIVING TOURS

St. Mary is the eastern portal for Going-to-the-Sun Road. Winding along St. Mary Lake and Two Dog Flats, the road reaches Logan Pass in 18 miles before dropping 32 miles to West Glacier. The seasonally open Chief Mountain Highway connects the St. Mary Valley with Waterton and crosses the Canadian-U.S. border.

Blackfeet Highway

The Blackfeet Highway, otherwise known as Highway 89, runs entirely on the Blackfeet Reservation along the east side of Glacier Park from

the Canadian border at Piegan-Carway to East Glacier—the last portion on Highway 49. Its only gas services are at Babb, St. Mary, and East Glacier. From the town of St. Mary, the highway rolls northward undulating on a fairly wide road past **Lower St. Mary Lake,** where you'll see Thunderbird Island. This section of the highway is one of the few roads around with shoulders, making the driving significantly easier. As you round the lake's outlet, watch for waterfowl and spectacular views to the north of Chief Mountain and Old Sun Glacier on Mount Merritt. En route north from St. Mary, the road travels through ranchland, passing Duck Lake Road (7.3 miles), Many Glacier Road and Babb (9 miles), and Chief Mountain Highway (14 miles) before reaching the Canadian border (24 miles). At the boundary, the highway turns into Alberta Highway 2 as it continues north in Canada.

On the Blackfeet Highway, be prepared for impediments! Much of the road crosses open range where you may encounter cattle on the road. Drive slowly if you run into a small herd. Ole Bessy may just stand there staring at you and refuse to budge. If so, a toot on the horn can sometimes help, but avoid being obnoxious about it. If necessary, carefully pass in the other lane. In the seven miles north of St. Mary, horses frequently run alongside or across the road. Slow down and give them room. Because of livestock, slow down your driving at night, even though the speed limit sign says 70 mph. You'll frequently hear the screech of brakes as drivers come too quickly upon a cow in the middle of the road.

From St. Mary, the Blackfeet Highway heads south toward **Two Medicine, Browning,** and **East Glacier.** Even if you have only a couple of minutes, bop southward two miles up the hill from town to grab a panoramic view of the St. Mary Valley. Several unmarked wide pullouts afford good places to stop for a photo, and it's a sight worth blowing off a bit of film. As the road climbs St. Mary Ridge at 6,015 feet, it crosses the Hudson Bay Divide—sending waters to the Missouri or Saskatchewan. Several lanes allow for passing, but within a few miles the road shrinks to a curvy, rolling, narrow

shoulderless trek through willow bogs and beaver ponds divided by aspen groves. Turns are blind; take them slowly in case bicyclists or cows are on the road. (Remember: It's open range here.) At 20 miles, you can turn off onto Highway 49—a road with more curves than a snake and part of the original Blackfeet Highway—toward Two Medicine (38 miles) or East Glacier (33 miles). If you continue on Highway 89, you'll reach Browning (32 miles).

◖ Many Glacier Road

The 12-mile-long Many Glacier Road—also called Glacier Route Three on some maps—provides a scenic entrance to the **Swiftcurrent Valley.** On this road, there are two reasons to drive slowly and take your time: Motorists here have a good chance of spotting wildlife, and the road is chockfull of potholes and torn up pavement. From Babb, the road follows Swiftcurrent Creek upstream across Blackfeet tribal lands, where open range may put you nose-to-nose with cows on the road. Give them room, and drive at a snail's pace around them. Watch for bears, particularly around dusk. If you spot a bear, drive by slowly to watch rather than stopping and creating a bear jam, which conditions bears to be around vehicles. Above all, stay in the car for safety.

After the road rises to reach Sherburne Dam (mile 4.8), it follows the reservoir's north shore, crossing into the park over the cattle grate, but you won't reach the park entrance station for another three miles. Check the shoreline for deer, bears, and sometimes a wolf or two. Errant cows straying into the park sometimes graze on the reservoir's shores. Aspen groves and wildflower meadows with July's pink sticky geraniums line the road. Scenic stops lend views of Sherburne Reservoir and up the valley to **Grinnell, Salamander,** and **Gem Glaciers.**

At **Many Glacier Hotel** (turn south at 11.6 miles), stop to tour the historic building if you are not staying here. After the hotel turnoff, the road passes Swiftcurrent Lake with the picnic area (mile 12.2), followed by the ranger station, campground, and Swiftcurrent Motor Inn, where the road terminates in Swiftcurrent parking lot.

historic Lubec Ranger Station Barn, adjacent to the 1913 Ranger Station

© BECKY LOMAX

Duck Lake Road

Montana Highway 464, known as the Duck Lake Road, leaves the Blackfeet Highway at the east end of Lower St. Mary Lake (7.3 miles north of St. Mary, 1.7 miles south of Babb). Locals tend to use this road via Browning for a faster access between the park's northeast sections and East Glacier. Although the mileage is longer (53 miles from St. Mary to East Glacier rather than 33 miles via Hwy. 89), the straighter road offers easier driving. It's also faster driving as speed limits reach 70 mph on stretches, and fences keep cattle off the road. Large RV drivers and those pulling trailers in particular find it easier to handle than the curvy Blackfeet Highway from St. Mary to East Glacier. It climbs over St. Mary Ridge, passing Duck Lake at 3 miles. From the top of the ridge above Duck Lake—the divide between the Missouri and Saskatchewan river drainages—the highway heads southward across the Blackfeet Reservation through bison and cattle ranchland with Glacier's peaks dominating the western skyline across the prairie to Browning (34 miles from Highway 89).

SIGHTS

St. Mary River

Between St. Mary Visitor Center and St. Mary Campground, Going-to-the-Sun Road crosses St. Mary River, a waterway connecting the two St. Mary Lakes. You can park near the bridge to take a look, but a better option is to park at the visitor center and walk a third of a mile through prairie smoke flowers to a scenic wooden bridge—the same one Forrest Gump jogged across in his run across America. Watch for killdeer among other birds. For anglers, this river offers some of the best opportunities around for fishing. You can drop a line in from the wooden bridge, but not the Going-to-the-Sun Road bridge.

St. Mary Lakes

In pockets left from 1,200-foot-deep Pleistocene ice age glaciers that gouged out St. Mary Valley, **St. Mary Lake** and **Lower St. Mary Lake** fill most of the valley floor. The lakes collect water from snowmelt and some of the largest glaciers left in the park—Blackfoot and Jackson Glaciers. Their waters then meander

ST. MARY AND MANY GLACIER

toward the Canadian border and into the Saskatchewan River to Hudson Bay. With the valley sucking air down from the Continental Divide, frequent winds swirl up large whitecap waves. Both lakes can be easily seen from roads: Going-to-the-Sun Road and Highway 89.

(Divide Mountain

Divide Mountain rises 8,665 feet in elevation, the last in a string of peaks lining St. Mary Valley's south. From its summit, it drops to tree-covered St. Mary Ridge, which runs for miles out onto the prairie. The ridge actually is a lateral moraine, deposited by the Pleistocene glacier that formed the valley. This ridge, along with Divide Mountain, separates the waters flowing into the Saskatchewan drainage and those heading toward the Missouri.

1913 Ranger Station

Follow the signs on a five-minute drive off Going-to-the-Sun Road (0.2 mile from the Hwy. 89 junction) just south of St. Mary Visitor Center to the historic 1913 Ranger Station. A small parking area leads uphill on a three-minute walk to the historic building. Adjacent to it stands the Lubec Ranger Station Barn, which was moved here in 1977 for its preservation. However, with its restored weather-split logs and chinking, the barn is more photo-worthy than the original ranger station.

Grinnell Glacier

Like all glaciers in northwest Montana, Grinnell Glacier is sadly melting. Located in Many Glacier, the icefield reached its peak size around 1850, when it filled the entire upper lake pocket

THE EXTINCTION OF GLACIERS

"Where's the best place to go to watch the glaciers go by?" Every so often, a tourist asks this crazy question. But in reality, the question carries certain poignancy. For Glacier National Park's icefields are moving rapidly. Melting, that is.

Climatologists from the United States Geological Survey (USGS) estimate northwestern Montana will be devoid of glaciers in 25 years. Relics from a mini ice age that peaked around 1850, these once glamorous diamonds strung along the Continental Divide now look barely different from snowfields hanging late into August. But 37 of them do remain, tiny in comparison to Alaska's rivers of ice.

When Glacier National Park was formed in 1910, more than 150 glaciers were documented within its borders. Today, only 25 percent of those remain. And not for long.

A glacier's upper end is called the accumulation zone, for that is where snows pile up, adding to the ice's mass. Downslope, summer's heat brings on melt. When more ice turns to water at the bottom end than is created at the upper end, a glacier shrinks.

While tree-ring studies show that a warming trend began about 1850 causing glaciers to

retreat, melting rates tended to be relatively slow. But in the latter 1920s, warmer summers and less snow triggered rapid melting, splitting some larger glaciers in two, like Grinnell and Salamander Glaciers. In 1850, Sperry Glacier stretched across 960 acres, but today it covers less than one-fourth that area. Likewise, 27 glaciers clustered over 5,300 acres in the Mount Jackson area; now 15 of those glaciers have disappeared and those remaining split into several pieces.

As glaciers retreat, they break into patches. Some form lakes at their snouts. Since 1927, Grinnell Glacier's recession has formed a lake, which grows in size as the glacier recedes. Within 20 years, the lake had grown to 20 acres and was named Upper Grinnell Lake.

Today, no glaciers remain in Waterton or in Two Medicine Valley. Climatologists estimate that current rates of recession will lead to the extinction of all glaciers within Glacier National Park by 2030.

Because small glaciers are susceptible to worldwide climate change, the USGS monitors the park's glaciers as climate barometers. For information on melting glaciers, see www.nrmsc.usgs.gov.

© BECKY LOMAX

Ptarmigan Tunnel cuts through an arête in the Ptarmigan Wall.

under Mount Gould and connected with Salamander Glacier. You can see lateral moraines marking its original size. By 1930, the glacier receded to the point where a lake formed at its snout, and it separated from Salamander above. Today, the ice has shrunk to less than one-third its 1850 size. By 2030, the glacier's moving ice is expected to be completely gone. Then it will appear more like Iceberg Lake. In the meantime, you can see the glacier with binoculars from the Many Glacier Road. For a closer inspection, hike to the glacier while you can; it's the most easily accessed glacier in the park.

Swiftcurrent Lake

Originally called McDermott Lake, Swiftcurrent Lake took its name from the Blackfeet term for swift-flowing water—a name that George Bird Grinnell promoted for the area and also used on a peak, glaciers, creek, falls, and ridge. The lake, however, does not have fast-flowing waters. Located in Many Glacier, its bays attract waterfowl like loons and mergansers. Moose browse in the willows along the shoreline. A beaver lodge sits at the inlet of

Swiftcurrent Creek. Enjoy the lake from Many Glacier Hotel's deck, launch a canoe from its boat ramp, ride across it on the tour boat, or walk an easy two miles around it.

(Many Glacier Hotel

Built in 1915 and placed on the National Register of Historic Landmarks in 1987, the five-story 211-room Many Glacier Hotel sits on Swiftcurrent Lake's shores in Many Glacier. Listed as one of the 11 most endangered places in the country, the hotel, owned by the National Park Service and operated by Glacier Park, Inc., began a $30 million restoration in 2001. Beginning with structural damage, the rehabilitation has repaired exterior walls, windows, doors, decks, the roof, and siding. Further interior improvements are planned to continue as Congress appropriates more money for its preservation. The hotel's massive lobby with its huge fireplace is a great place to warm up on a cold day, and the large deck is perfect for lounging with dramatic views of the Continental Divide. Join park naturalists for a one-hour tour of the historic hotel: Check *The Glacier Explorer* for the current schedule.

ST. MARY AND MANY GLACIER

Iceberg Lake

Tucked in a cirque below Mount Wilbur and Iceberg Peak in Many Glacier, Iceberg Lake is a treat for the eyes. The lake itself sits in a glacial pocket, once carved by the moving ice that left a small moraine along the beach. With winter snows depositing heavy loads in the bowl protected by Wilbur's shadow, summer icebergs float in the lake—even on the hottest of August days. It's worth a quick dive in, just to say you swam with the icebergs. But be ready for icy waters that suck the air out of your lungs!

Ptarmigan Tunnel

Built in 1931 to access the Belly River Valley from Many Glacier, Ptarmigan Tunnel is a phenomenon found on few trails. Large steel doors prevent winter snows from piling up inside; good thing, too, as those snows would never melt out. The doors open usually in July and close in early October. The 183-foot-long tunnel is high enough to permit riders on horseback without bonking heads. A walk through its dark corridor doesn't require a flashlight, but more than one hiker has encountered a bear racing through its bowels.

Recreation

HIKING

Hiking in the St. Mary vicinity doesn't offer the wealth of options that Many Glacier does. Easy trails access mosquito-ridden beaver ponds, while rough trails or scrambles lead to high peaks and bluffs. For this reason, most visitors at St. Mary choose to travel back up Going-to-the-Sun Road to trailheads, where well-marked paths access high alpine meadows and passes, or bop 21 miles to Many Glacier's trailheads. St. Mary Visitor Center has a free non-topographical map of hiking trails in St. Mary Valley, and it's also online (www.nps.gov/glac). For hiking outside the park on Blackfeet tribal lands, pick up a $10 annual Tribal conservation permit at the St. Mary Visitor Center.

Using the hiker shuttle, visitors staying in St. Mary can easily avail themselves of point-to-point hikes. Logan Pass to Swiftcurrent (15.2 miles) and Piegan Pass to Many Glacier Hotel are the most popular. (For both of these options, see the *Going-to-the-Sun Road* chapter for details). Hikers can catch shuttles from Many Glacier, too, for both of these trails.

Hiking Many Glacier is a treat. Trails trot up fast into the high country, and there's not much old-growth forest to obliterate views. Most trailheads are accessed from Many Glacier Hotel, Swiftcurrent parking lot, or the picnic area. Although trail junctions are extremely well signed, you'll find a map helpful to navigate the maze of trails—especially those crisscrossing the Grinnell Valley. Free area non-topographical hiker maps are available at St. Mary Visitor Center, Many Glacier Ranger Station, in park lodge front desks, and online (www.nps.gov/glac). In Many Glacier, seasonal footbridges are usually installed in late May and removed in October. Check with the ranger station or on the trail status report online for installation or removal dates.

Because of dense bear populations and high hiker traffic in Many Glacier, trails see closures from time to time to let an aggressive bear cool off. Check for current trail status with the ranger station or Many Glacier Hotel's activity desk, or online.

Backcountry camping permits are available at St. Mary Visitor Center or Many Glacier Ranger Station for Red Eagle, Otokomi, Gunsight, Cracker and Poia Lakes and the Belly River drainage. No backcountry camping is permitted at Iceberg, Ptarmigan, Red Rocks, Bullhead, and Grinnell Lakes, or at Grinnell Glacier and Piegan Pass.

Hikes listed below begin in the south at St. Mary and head north to the Canadian border.

Divide Peak and Fire Lookout

- Distance: 5 miles round-trip
- Duration: 3.5 hours
- Elevation gain: 1,800 feet
- Effort: strenuous
- Trailhead: unmarked end of dirt road
- Directions: Depart off Highway 89 south of St. Mary at the dirt road at milepost 25.5 on top of St. Mary Ridge south of town.

On Blackfeet land, this hike requires a Tribal recreation label ($10) available at St. Mary Ranger Station. You'll have to poke around a bit to find the trail (of which there are several). Not only is the trail unmarked, but it's very steep—only those confident in their backcountry skills should attempt this. Several trails lead up steeply to an old hexagonal fire lookout on Divide's northeast ridge. Pick one, scouting constantly ahead for where it goes. If you don't like the steepness of what's ahead, back down and try another trail.

At the lookout, incredible views span the St. Mary Valley up to the Continental Divide and sprawl eastward across the plains. From the lookout, a 45-minute scramble leads to the top of the peak, where you can stand atop staring down both the Saskatchewan and Missouri drainages.

Red Eagle Lake

- Distance: 15 miles round-trip
- Duration: 7.5 hours
- Elevation gain: 300 feet
- Effort: easy, but long
- Trailhead: at 1913 Ranger Station parking lot at St. Mary

After following an old road for one mile, the trail climbs gently through wildflower meadows raging with shooting star or blue camas amid aspen groves to a rolling plateau. Watch for bear diggings here—places where grizzlies rototill for glacier lily bulbs or chase after ground squirrels. Red Eagle Mountain looms ahead, and grand views upvalley to Going-to-the-Sun Mountain unfold. About halfway, the trail crosses Red Eagle Creek twice on swinging bridges. In between the two bridges, the St. Mary Lake trail splits off.

At the lake, surrounded by heavy timber, it's hard to get a great view. For the best views upvalley, wander to the small bluff at the lake's end or wade out in the lake. In the 1920s, Red Eagle Lake held a large tent camp, famous for its fishing. Today, die-hard anglers hike in with float tubes hitched to their packs.

Apikuni Falls

- Distance: 2 miles round-trip
- Duration: 1 hour
- Elevation gain: 550 feet
- Effort: moderate
- Trailhead: Grinnell Glacier Interpretive site 10.4 miles on Many Glacier Road

Named for the green unoxidized argillites that layer between reds, Apikuni Falls is nice, but not anything stunning. The short walk starts out across a flat meadow but soon climbs uphill. In July, wildflowers bloom thickly here: geraniums, arrowleaf balsamroot, paintbrush, lupine, and stonecrop. The trail climbs to the cliffs between Altyn Peak and Apikuni Mountain where the falls drops out of the basin above.

Cracker Lake

- Distance: 12.2 miles round-trip
- Duration: 6 hours
- Elevation gain: 1,400 feet
- Effort: moderate
- Trailhead: south end of Many Glacier Hotel parking lot

If you can stand the muddy, horse-rutted, manure-filled first 1.3 miles where trail rides travel four times a day, the rest of the hike is extremely scenic and not nearly as crowded as other Many Glacier hikes. If you meet horses, step below, not above the trail to let them pass. At the Cracker Flats junction, leave the messy trail behind and stomp the mud and manure from your boots. Climb up switchbacks into the Cracker Valley, where the forested trail breaks out into bluebell and lupine meadows about halfway up.

Once you reach Cracker Lake, bypass the backcountry campground and drop to the inlet for the best lunch spot along the shore. Glacial flour clouds the lake water, turning it a rich milky turquoise. Some historic mining debris still litters the cirque above the lake; it's protected by law, so leave items where you see them. Siyeh Peak at 10,014 feet rises abruptly up a gigantic cliff face, a skyscraping 4,000 feet above the lake shore.

Josephine and Grinnell Lakes

- Distance: 1.8–7.8 miles round-trip
- Duration: 1–4 hours
- Elevation gain: minimal
- Effort: easy
- Trailheads: on the south side of Many Glacier Hotel, at the picnic area, or via the tour boat

With the maze of trails through the Grinnell Valley, a map is helpful to navigate even though trails are well signed. Pick up a free non-topographical map from the hotel desk or the ranger station. For a short walk, catch the tour boat to the head of Josephine Lake to begin hiking to Grinnell Lake. For a longer hike, begin from Many Glacier Hotel, following the trail winding around Swiftcurrent Lake to the boat dock opposite the hotel. A third starting point begins at the picnic area, where it follows Swiftcurrent Lake to that same boat dock.

Grinnell Lake and the Angel Wing in Many Glacier

© BECKY LOMAX

From here, bop over the hill to Josephine Lake, where the trail hugs the north shore until it splits off to Grinnell Glacier. Stay on the lower trail to wrap around Josephine's west end until you reach the Grinnell Lake junction. Turn toward the lake and follow the trail over a swinging bridge. At the lakeshore, enjoy Grinnell's milky turquoise waters and the falls tumbling into the lake from the glacier basin above. Although you can return to the trailheads via the south lakeshore trail, it is not as scenic, sticking mostly in deep forest. You can also shorten the hike by catching the tour boat back.

Grinnell Glacier

- Distance: 11 miles round-trip
- Duration: 6 hours
- Elevation gain: 1,600 feet
- Effort: moderately strenuous
- Trailheads: on the south side of Many Glacier Hotel, at the picnic area, or via the tour boat

In early summer, a large steep snowdrift frequently bars the path into the upper basin; check with the ranger station for status before hiking. The most accessible glacier in the park, Grinnell Glacier still requires a bit of stamina to access, for most of its elevation gain packs within two miles. For that reason, many hikers take the hiker boat shuttle, cutting the length to 7.8 miles round-trip or just trimming 2.5 miles off the return. From the picnic area, follow Swiftcurrent Lake's west shore to the boat dock. From Many Glacier Hotel, round the southern shore to meet up with the same dock. Bop over the short hill and traverse around Lake Josephine's north shore.

Toward Josephine's west end, the Grinnell Glacier trail diverts heading uphill. As the trail climbs up through multicolored rock strata, Grinnell Lake's milky turquoise waters come into view below. Ascending through a cliff where a waterfall douses hik-

ers climbing a stairway, the trail passes a rest stop with outhouses before climbing steeply up the moraine to the glacier pocket where a maze of trails crosses the bedrock to Upper Grinnell Lake's shore. Do not walk out on the glacier's ice where hidden crevasses can turn the hike deadly.

Swiftcurrent Valley and Lookout

- Distance: 3.6–16 miles round-trip
- Duration: 2–8 hours
- Elevation gain: 100–3,500 feet
- Effort: easy to strenuous
- Trailhead: Swiftcurrent parking lot in Many Glacier

This popular trail provides various destinations along a scenic trail dotted with lakes, waterfalls, moose, glaciers, and wildflowers. The trail winds through pine trees and aspen groves as it climbs up gently to Red Rocks Lake and Falls at 1.8 miles. At the top of the falls, a knoll provides a viewpoint to scan hillsides with binoculars for bears. The trail continues level through meadows rampant with sitka valerian in July to Bullhead Lake at 3.9 miles, a good destination with bighorn sheep wandering above on talus slopes.

From the lake, the trail knows nothing but uphill switchbacks. It cuts through a cliff face before reaching the pass at 6.6 miles. From here, Granite Park Chalet is a 0.9 mile downhill. To reach the lookout, take the spur trail up 1.4 miles of more switchbacks—you'll lose count of them. From the lookout, the view surveys almost the entire park: glaciers, peaks, wild panoramas, and the plains. Many Glacier Hotel looks minuscule. For a different descent, drop to The Loop, but you'll need to be there by 5:25 P.M. to catch the last shuttle.

Iceberg Lake

- Distance: 9.4 miles round-trip
- Duration: 4.5 hours

Icebergs float all summer in Iceberg Lake at Many Glacier.

- Elevation gain: 1,200 feet
- Effort: moderate
- Trailhead: behind Swiftcurrent Motor Inn cabins in Many Glacier

One of the top hikes in Glacier, the trail to Iceberg Lake begins with a short-lived steep jaunt straight uphill with no time to gradually warm up the muscles. However, within a half mile, you reach a junction. Take note of the sign here and watch for it when you come down. Some hikers in zombie-walk mode blaze right on past it on the return. From here, the trail maintains an easy railroad grade to the lake. Make noise on this trail known for frequent bear sightings.

Wildflowers line the trail in July: beargrass, bog orchids, penstemon, and thimbleberry. A mile past the junction, the trail rounds a red argillite outcropping with views of the valley. As the trail heads north, it enters a pine and fir forest and crosses Ptarmigan Falls, a good break spot where aggressive ground squirrels will steal your snack. Do not feed them; feed-ing only trains them to be more forceful. The trail traverses avalanche paths until it climbs the final bluff, where a view of icebergs stark against blue waters unfolds.

◖ Ptarmigan Tunnel

- Distance: 10.4 miles round-trip
- Duration: 5 hours
- Elevation gain: 2,300 feet
- Effort: moderately strenuous
- Trailhead: behind Swiftcurrent Motor Inn cabins in Many Glacier

Depending on snowpack, the tunnel doors usually open in July and close in early October; check with the ranger station to confirm status. Traversing the same trail as Iceberg Lake, the route begins with a steep uphill climb be-fore leveling out into a gentle ascent around Mount Henkel. Just past Ptarmigan Falls at 2.5 miles, the Ptarmigan Tunnel route leaves

© BECKY LOMAX

the Iceberg Trail. From here, it climbs aggressively uphill for nearly a mile before assuming an easier uphill grade through meadows to Ptarmigan Lake.

From the lake, the route to the tunnel switchbacks another 800 feet up a talus slope. Tiny fragile alpine plants struggle to survive on this barren slope: Protect their existence by staying on the trail rather than cutting switchbacks. The 183-foot tunnel cuts through Ptarmigan Wall and is six feet wide by nine feet tall. When you walk through, a burst of red will greet you on the other side. Admire the trail engineering along the north side's cliff wall and drop down 0.25 mile to see Old Sun Glacier on Mount Merritt.

Belly River Ranger Station

• Distance: 12.6 miles round-trip

• Duration: 6 hours

• Elevation gain: 750 feet on return

• Effort: moderate

• Trailhead: Chief Mountain Customs parking lot on Chief Mountain Highway

A trail used by backpackers to access Elizabeth, Helen, Cosley, Glenns, and Mokowanis Lakes and Stoney Indian Pass, the Belly River Trail attracts day hikers more for the views along the way of Chief Mountain and Pyramid Peak in the distance. Anglers also drop lines into the Belly River. The trail begins with a descent down to the valley floor. Look en route for scratches in the aspen bark where elk have rubbed to remove the velvet from their antlers.

As the trail undulates gently across the valley floor, it traverses aspen groves and open meadows blooming with lupine and paintbrush. At the pastoral Belly River Ranger Station, listed in 1986 on the National Register of Historic Places, you can envy the backcountry rangers who spend their summers staring at Gable Mountain's colorful strata, the spires of the Stoney Indian Peaks, and Mount Cleveland, the highest peak in the park.

Guides

In Many Glacier and St. Mary, options abound for guided hikes. The National Park Service leads hikes to various scenic destinations mid-June through mid-September, including full-day hikes to Grinnell Glacier and Iceberg Lake in Many Glacier and the short stroll around the beaver ponds in St. Mary, where you can see moose if you can stand the mosquitoes. Some trips combine with boat tours to cross Swiftcurrent and Josephine Lakes. Although park naturalist hikes are free, you'll need to pay for the boat. The park's guided hikes are great for solo hikers to be in the company of others in bear country and to glean tidbits of natural history, but be prepared for hiking in very large groups—some upwards of 30 people in high season. For schedules, pick up a copy of *The Glacier Explorer* from the visitors centers, online (www.nps.gov/glac), at ranger stations, or hotel activity desks. For full-day hikes, pack along water, snacks, lunch, and extra clothes.

Glacier Guides (406/387-5555 or 800/321-7238, www.glacierguides.com, $65 per person with a minimum of five people; $400 flat rate per day for custom groups) operates the sole hiking concession in the park. Expert guides can meet you in St. Mary or Many Glacier for a hike here, or pick you up to hit another trailhead elsewhere. Deli lunch, snacks, and transportation to the trailhead are provided; you just need to bring a day pack with extra clothes, water bottle, bug spray, and sunscreen. Sometimes solo travelers can link up with other groups of day hikers; call to see what's on the schedule. Reservations are required.

BIKING

Bicycling the east side of Glacier Park is pretty much relegated to road biking as trails do not permit mountain bikes. No bike rentals are available in Many Glacier, so bring your own. But in St. Mary, you can rent a bike ($10–20) at St. Mary KOA.

St. Mary and Many Glacier campgrounds provide shared biker-hiker campsites on a first-come, first-serve basis for $5 per person. The sites have bear-resistant food storage containers and are held daily until 9 P.M. for cyclists.

BELLY RIVER COUNTRY

North of Many Glacier, the Belly River is wild backcountry. It isn't easy to get there! No roads access the valley, making the entrance via foot or horseback. From Many Glacier, two routes cross into the Belly – Ptarmigan Tunnel and Red Gap Pass via Poia Lake. Three other trails reach the Belly via other routes: the shortest from Chief Mountain Customs, one from Goat Haunt over Stoney Indian Pass, and one from Lee Ridge.

Possibly named for the Gros Ventre (French for "Big Belly") tribe, the Belly River is a tributary of the Saskatchewan River, which heads to Hudson Bay. Thirty-three backcountry campsites string up and down two valleys – the Belly River and Mokowanis (a Blackfeet term that refers to a buffalo's stomach) Valleys. The Belly River drainage cradles Elizabeth and Helen Lakes, while the Mokowanis houses Cosley, Glenns, Mokowanis, Atsina, Sue, Margaret, and Ipasha Lakes, not all reachable by trail. At the confluence of the two valleys, the historic Belly River Ranger Station, which is staffed in summer, sits amid aspen groves and fields of wild sticky geraniums staring up at the three fingers of the Stoney Indian Peaks and Mount Cleveland, the highest peak in the park.

THE LEGEND OF JOE COSLEY

Belly River Country is rife with legend. For here, one of the park's favorite renegade rangers, Joe Cosley, literally made his mark carving his name into trees. A fur trapper since 1890, long before Glacier became a national park, Joe Cosley scoured the Belly River for hides. He wandered both Glacier and Waterton gouging his name on thousands of trees.

When Glacier achieved parkhood in 1910, superintendent William Logan hired Cosley as the Belly's first ranger. What man knew Glacier's remote northeastern corner better than one who wandered its mountains for 20 years hunting and trapping? For Cosley, ranger duties became a vehicle to continue poaching.

A year later, near West Glacier under the superintendent's nose, Joe was caught poaching and fired. His firing failed. Perhaps communication of new hunting prohibitions posed confusion; perhaps officials needed Cosley's mountain skills. Regardless, he wore the Belly's ranger badge for two more years.

Sprouting from truth and fiction, Cosley's mountain man reputation grew, his self-generated legend watered with changeable facts. He told more than one woman he named Elizabeth Lake for her, said he buried a diamond ring in a Belly River poplar, and claimed to have hiked between Polebridge and Waterton in 3.5 hours for a dance, returning be-

Going-to-the-Sun Road

Bicyclists riding on Going-to-the-Sun Road have no restrictions heading westbound until reaching Sprague Creek Campground on the west side. Due to heavy traffic during July and August, riding earlier or later in the day is easier on the narrow, shoulderless road. See the *Going-to-the-Sun Road* chapter for details.

Blackfeet Highway

Cycling the Blackfeet Highway (Hwy. 89) from the Canadian border to St. Mary is easier than pedaling other roads in the area. The undulating road is wider, straighter, and has at least a bit of a shoulder. However, the wide open space

on the Continental Divide's east side means only one thing—high winds. Expect strong headwinds blowing mostly eastward. If you're heading the right direction, it will be a nice tailwind. Otherwise, you'll be cursing under your breath as you push against its bluster.

Riding south from St. Mary to East Glacier on Highway 89, however, is a different story. A wide thoroughfare with big shoulders climbs atop St. Mary Ridge, luring you into breathing comfortably with the width in spite of the huffing climb. But atop the ridge, the spacious road suddenly squeezes into a narrow, curvy ribbon with blind corners and little place to go when large vehicles hog the road. From a cycling per-

fore breakfast the next morning – 70 miles round-trip.

During his years as a park ranger, Cosley supplied big game to paying customers and sold hides in Canada. Eventually, heeding local gossip, park officials dispatched rangers to snag him poaching. Joe evaded them, and despite lack of evidence, in 1914 the superintendent ousted Joe from the payroll.

Cosley vanished northward, joining up with Canadian forces heading to Europe's escalating war. In 1919, Joe snuck back into the Belly to trap and hunt, selling hides across the border in Canada. Meanwhile, young Joe Heimes inherited the Belly's ranger badge. In his fifth season, he stumbled over a footprint leading to one of Cosley's caches. When Cosley sauntered into camp, 24-year-old Heimes leaped from hiding to arrest the legend twice his age. Cosley bolted three times and was tackled repeatedly by the shorter Heimes. Afraid of chasing Cosley all night, the young ranger sat on him and tied his feet.

The only route to jail demanded a snow slog over 7,200-foot Gable Pass to Slide Lake, a car to East Glacier, and a train to Belton. Heimes loaded Joe's own pack with traps and beaver pieces, evidence against him, and marched him toward West Glacier.

In 1929, Glacier Park witnessed its most in-famous trial. Accused of poaching and possession of seven traps, three muskrat hides, and one beaver carcass, Cosley stood before the park commissioner. Heimes testified. Cosley pled guilty. But he claimed the evidence was not his. The commissioner fined Cosley $125 and sentenced him to 90 days in jail.

In an Oscar performance, Cosley professed a fatal disease, begging for clemency. Fearful of a death in his jail, the commissioner reduced the sentence to 30 days and then suspended it due to Joe's fast-failing health. After longtime local friends paid his fine, Cosley strolled free.

Two hours post-sentencing, gifted with snowshoes and trail grub – and cured – Cosley hiked 30 miles over the Continental Divide. Though years earlier Ahern Pass's crags had killed his horse and mule, Cosley snowshoed over and beelined for his cache in the Belly.

When Heimes reached the camp, one log pole marked Cosley's presence like a lonely bone left after a wolf kill. Canada had swallowed Cosley and his pelts whole. Two days after his trial, Cosley visited a Lethbridge fur buyer. He sold 55 beaver, 21 marten, and 22 mink hides for $4,129.

For more details of Joe Cosley's adventures, read *Belly River's Famous Joe Cosley,* by Brian McClung.

---

spective, it's a fun ride with the rolling terrain, but you'll find yourself nearly steering off the road while watching for vehicles coming up behind you. Blind corners have a tendency to make riders brake for safety and then curse the loss of momentum. To avoid the heavier traffic in high season, ride early or late in the day. Since the highway is open range, be prepared to brake; you may round a corner into cattle and may need to dodge a few cow pies.

Many Glacier Road

Bicycling Many Glacier Road is extremely picturesque. However, keep at least one eye on the road for potholes, cattle grates, and a few short gravel sections pockmarking the road. Also, be prepared for possible bear encounters, especially early or late in the day. While riding this road, some cyclists even whoop or holler to make noise to alert bears to their presence. With bears capable of running up to 40 mph, you won't be able to outbike a bear, so muster up all your bear country savvy when riding here.

TRAIL RIDING
Mule Shoe Outfitters

Adjacent to the Many Glacier Hotel parking lot, Mule Shoe Outfitters (406/732-4203, www.mule-shoe.com, mid-June–mid-Sept., $47–120, depending on length of ride, cash only)

ST. MARY AND MANY GLACIER

guides two-hour rides departing several times daily for Josephine Lake and Cracker Flats. Half-day rides leave twice daily for Grinnell Lake's milky blue waters. Departing at 9 A.M., all day rides (lunch not included) head through aspen parklands and wildflower meadows toward Poia Lake or to Cracker Lake, which hovers at the base of Siyeh Peak's several-thousand-foot north face. Be aware that this is trail riding; the nose of one horse will be in the tail of another—sometimes in a long string of 15 horses. This is not the horse riding of the movies where you're galloping across Montana's prairies. However, the scenery is well worth a ride. Wear long pants and hiking boots or tennis shoes for these rides. Unfortunately, kids under seven are not allowed, and kids over seven pay the same rate as adults. Reservations are highly recommended.

BOATING

Power boating is restricted on Glacier's east side. Many Glacier's public boat dock on **Swiftcurrent Lake** sits adjacent to the picnic area, but no motorized boats are allowed on the lake. Sans motors, only sailboats, kayaks, rowboats, and canoes ply the waters quietly. On **Lake Sherburne** in Many Glacier, motorized craft are permitted (except jet skis), but the big dilemma is the lack of a boat ramp! Only crafts small enough to be carried are used here. **St. Mary Lake** does allow motorized craft with no horsepower limit as well as nonmotorized boats such as canoes, kayaks, rowboats, and rafts.

On the Blackfeet Reservation, you can launch onto **Lower St. Mary Lake** via the public boat ramp at Chewing Blackbones Campground (milepost 37.3 on Hwy. 89), which is no longer an operational campground, but you can still access the boat ramp. Boating is also allowed on the reservation at **Duck Lake,** at milepost 29 on Duck Lake Road (Hwy. 464). Both lakes require a $20 Blackfeet recreation label, which you can purchase at St. Mary KOA (103 West Shore, 406/732-4122) or Montana's Duck Lake Lodge (milepost 32 on Duck Lake Rd., 406/338-5770) to affix to your boat. If you plan on fishing, your boat label is included in your Tribal fishing permit.

No motorized boat rentals are available in St. Mary, Rising Sun, or Many Glacier. On Swiftcurrent Lake in Many Glacier, however, **Glacier Park Boat Company** (406/732-4480 summers only, 406/257-2426, www.glacierparkboats.com, mid-June–mid-Sept., $10 per hour) rents rowboats, canoes, and kayaks with oars and lifejackets at the boat dock behind Many Glacier Hotel. Bring cash; no credit cards are accepted. On Lower St. Mary Lake, **St. Mary KOA** (106 West Shore, 406/732-4122 or 800/562-1504, www.goglacier.com; mid-May–early Oct.) rents rowboats and canoes ($10 per hour); you can launch right from the dock at the shallow inlet of St. Mary River.

KAYAKING AND CANOEING

High east side winds deter many kayakers and canoers from the larger lakes. Instead, most paddlers head to more protected waters. Because Many Glacier's lakes are smaller with less chance to kick up big whitecaps, most paddlers head there rather than St. Mary Lakes. A popular kayak trip crosses **Swiftcurrent Lake** and paddles the connecting slow-moving Cataract Creek upstream to Lake Josephine, where a shoreline loop makes a wonderfully scenic tour. Launch this tour from the public boat dock adjacent to Many Glacier Picnic Area. In spite of the potential for gusty wind, some kayakers tour **St. Mary Lake.** A Tribal recreation label ($10 per year), available at St. Mary KOA or Duck Lake Lodge, is required for kayaking or canoeing on Lower St. Mary Lake or Duck Lake.

Rentals

In Many Glacier, **Glacier Park Boat Company** (406/732-4480 summers only, 406/257-2426, www.glacierparkboats.com, mid-June–mid-Sept., $10 per hour) rents both kayaks and canoes on Swiftcurrent Lake from the boat dock behind Many Glacier Hotel. Paddles and lifejackets are included in the rates. Bring cash to rent a boat, as no credit cards are accepted. On Lower St. Mary Lake, **St. Mary KOA** (106 West Shore, 406/732-4122 or 800/562-1504, www.goglacier.com; mid-May–early Oct.) rents canoes with paddles and lifejackets ($10 per hour, $50 per day).

FISHING

Glacier's east side is more noted for lake fishing than having luck in streams or rivers. Glacier's Red Eagle Lake has yielded state record trout, and Duck Lake on the Blackfeet Reservation claims a reputation for world-class fishing.

Inside Glacier, no license is required for fishing, although you must be aware of fishing regulations (for details, see the *Background* chapter). Outside park boundaries, visitors are on the Blackfeet Reservation and need a Tribal fishing permit. Tribal fishing permits may be purchased at St. Mary KOA (103 West Shore, 406/732-4122) and at Duck Lake Lodge (milepost 32 on Hwy. 464, 406/338-5770, www.ducklakelodge.com).

St. Mary

St. Mary Lake doesn't support much in the way of good fishing, especially with its raging winds. But it does have lake whitefish, brook trout, and rainbows. For better fishing, head instead to St. Mary River's deep channels below the lake for rainbow trout. The best fishing in the area requires a 7.5-mile hike to **Red Eagle Lake;** here a 16-pound state record westslope cutthroat was caught. Those with a serious commitment, and an incredible amount of willpower, hike in float tubes.

Many Glacier

With its number of lakes, the Many Glacier Valley offers lots of fishing holes. Grinnell, Josephine, Swiftcurrent, Red Rocks, Bullhead, Windmaker, and Ptarmigan Lakes all support varying trout populations, but don't be deceived into carrying your rod to Iceberg, Upper Grinnell, or Poia Lakes, which have no fish. Cracker Lake is closed to fishing. A dam-controlled reservoir partly on tribal lands and partly in the park, Sherburne Lake supports northern pike. Cataract Creek between Josephine and Swiftcurrent Lakes contains brookies, but other creeks in the area don't offer much.

Those willing to heft a backpack should hike through Ptarmigan Tunnel into the **Belly River** drainage (or hike from Chief Mountain Highway). Here, pools and riffles in the Belly

World-famous angling can be found in Duck Lake below Chief Mountain.

© BECKY LOMAX

ST. MARY AND MANY GLACIER

and Mokowanis Rivers along with Elizabeth, Cosley, Glenns, and Mokowanis Lakes provide endless angling for arctic grayling and trout.

Duck Lake

Outside the park on Blackfeet tribal lands at 5,015 feet in elevation, Duck Lake (milepost 29 on Hwy. 464) attracts serious lake anglers year-round. One can easily spend a day of catch-and-release, pulling 8-pound rainbow trout from its waters. Some anglers commonly catch 10–12 pounders, and a rainbow or brown trout may reach 15 pounds! Although you can keep the fish from this tribally stocked and managed fishery, you may find your fishing over within an hour or so if you don't throw some back. The fishing is better from a boat or a float tube: Motorized boats are allowed with a 10 mph speed limit, and lots of float tubers launch from shore. In winter, the lake permits ice fishing. The lake is surrounded by tribal and private land, so be respectful of private property.

WATERSKIING

Waterskiing is not a big sport on Glacier's east side. But for diehards, waterskiing is permitted on both upper and lower St. Mary Lake; however, brisk winds and cold waters inhibit the activity for most. All folks choosing to waterski here wear wetsuits or dry suits, as the water is extremely cold. On **Lower St. Mary Lake**, the public boat launch is at Chewing Blackbones Campground (milepost 37.3 on Hwy. 89). For Lower St. Mary, a Tribal recreation label ($10 per year per person) and boat permit ($20 per year) are required for waterskiing. Purchase the permits at St. Mary KOA (103 West Shore, 406/732-4122). Duck Lake does not permit waterskiing.

WINDSURFING

Because St. Mary Lake kicks up good winds, it attracts windsurfers from time to time, launching from various locations along Going-to-the-Sun Road from Rising Sun Picnic Area and east. (See the *Going-to-the-Sun Road* chapter for details.) Although sailboards are permit-

ted on Swiftcurrent Lake and Sherburne Reservoir in Many Glacier, the winds there are swirly. Most serious windsurfers head instead for **Duck Lake** (seven miles north of St. Mary and three miles up Duck Lake Rd. #464), where winds blow more consistently—usually in the afternoon—and waters are warmer. Private land surrounds much the shoreline; be considerate of property here. Tribal recreation labels ($10 per person per year and $20 per sailboard per year) are required for windsurfing; purchase them at Duck Lake Lodge (milepost 32 on Hwy. 464, 406/338-5770, www.ducklakelodge.com).

ENTERTAINMENT
Park Naturalist Programs

Evening programs about natural history and wildlife are presented by park naturalists in Many Glacier Hotel, Many Glacier Campground Amphitheater, and St. Mary Visitor Center during summers. The free 45-minute programs run nightly at 8 P.M. in Many Glacier and at 7:30 P.M. at St. Mary Visitor Center. Indoor programs include slide shows; outdoor programs feature park naturalists.

Native America Speaks

For more than 20 years, Glacier's naturalist programs have included the extremely well-liked Native America Speaks program. Free campground evening amphitheater schedules usually feature once a week the 45-minute program with members of the Blackfeet, Salish, and Kootenai tribes. Speakers use storytelling, humor, and music to share their culture and heritage. You'll walk away with a new appreciation of Glacier's Native American history.

Two acclaimed Native American programs with standing-room-only performances visit St. Mary Visitor Center's auditorium. Tickets for both shows are available at the visitor center desk. The **Two Medicine Lake Dancers and Singers** show demonstrates Blackfeet dances in full traditional regalia usually once a week during the summer. Tickets (adults $6, kids 12 and under $2) go fast for this popular show. Jack

ON STAGE WITH NATIVE AMERICANS

During summer months, a variety of Native American performance artists feature their talents around Glacier Park. Look for shows in park lodges, at campground amphitheaters, and in various Flathead Valley venues.

During summers in Glacier, Blackfeet, Salish, and Kootenai tribal members share stories and legends from their history in the **Native America Speaks** program, free 45-minute presentations. Speakers include several renowned storytellers and performance artists. Noted for his humorous storytelling, Curly Bear Wagner shares his expertise on Blackfeet culture, tradition, and heritage. Darrell Norman, a Blackfeet artist, narrates Blackfeet history. Blackfeet musicians, such as Jack Gladstone and Ernie Heavy Runner, convey legends and the Blackfeet heritage through original songs. You can catch the Native America Speaks series usually at the Apgar, Many Glacier, Rising Sun, and Two Medicine campground amphitheaters and Lake McDonald Lodge. Check *The Glacier Explorer* for the current times and days.

An award-winning and Grammy-nominated singer, songwriter, and storyteller, **Jack Gladstone** combines music and slides to create a narrative weaving Native American tradition with current cultural history. Gladstone packages a unique vision that gives insight into Blackfeet roots and Glacier's roots as sacred tribal land. Look for his **Legends of Glacier** (adults $5, kids 12 and under $2) performances at St. Mary Visitor Center and Lake McDonald Lodge; check *The Glacier Explorer* for showtimes and dates.

At St. Mary Visitor Center, the **Two Medicine Lake Dancers and Singers** (adults $6, kids 12 and under $2) with Ray Croff, a Blackfeet school teacher, stage traditional Blackfeet dances in full regalia with narration by Joe McKay. The performances include traditional dances as well as jingle, fancy, and grass dances – each with different footwork, body movement, and costumes. For the finale, visitors can join in their Round Dance. This show packs out, so buy your tickets early. Check *The Glacier Explorer* for current showtimes and dates.

Gladstone, a Blackfeet, presents his multimedia **Legends of Glacier** (adults $5, kids 12 and under $2) show, blending slides, storytelling, and music into a walk through Glacier's history from the Blackfeet perspective. For showtimes and days, pick up the current newspaper copy of *The Glacier Explorer* at visitors centers or check online: www.nps/gov/glac. Ticket sales for both shows help support the Native America Speaks program and the development of the St. Mary Visitor Center tipi encampment.

David Walburn Programs

Montana singer-songwriter-guitarist David Walburn (adults $7, kids 11 and under free) performs multimedia shows nightly in Many Glacier Hotel at 9 P.M. He entertains with live folk music, scenic photography, and stories in a series of rotating 90-minute shows. Celebrate the 200th anniversary of the west's most famous explorers and their epic trip with Walburn's outstanding narrative **Lewis and Clark: West for America,** or catch his re-creation of homesteading in Alaska in **Cabin Song,** or the colorful regional history with **Montana: Life Under the Big Sky.** Check the sign in the hotel lobby for a current schedule.

Accommodations

St. Mary has access to Going-to-the-Sun Road; Many Glacier has location. While St. Mary is convenient for exploring Logan Pass and taking day trips to Many Glacier, Waterton, and Two Medicine, Many Glacier is the best place to be right in the heart of hiking country. Here, you can park the car for a few days without getting back in it. In St. Mary and Many Glacier, that 7 percent Montana bed tax will still find its way to your bill.

ST. MARY

◖ **The Resort at Glacier: St. Mary Lodge** (junction of Hwy. 89 and Going-to-the-Sun Rd., 406/732-4431 or 800/368-3689, www.glcpark.com, late May–early Oct.) offers several options for accommodations. In 2001, the resort added the 48-room **Great Bear Lodge** ($189–249), aimed at luxury and draped with flower baskets in high summer. For those looking for the comforts of a modern hotel, it's high end with satellite televisions, air-conditioning, wet bars, and private decks that have views of the Continental Divide—especially those on the top floor. The resort also added six two-bedroom **Pinnacle Cottages** ($349) with fully equipped kitchens, satellite television, river-rock fireplaces, and large decks looking across St. Mary Valley with a Glacier peak skyline.

Less pricey, the resort still has its older hotel rooms in the main lodge and renovated rooms in the West Lodge ($139–159), which now include satellite television and air-conditioning. For those wanting to cook their own meals, the small, cozy Glacier Cabins ($169) and three larger cabins ($219–249) each have kitchenettes. For deals, check the resort's website for packages, some that add golf, boat tours, fishing, and horseback riding. Although the resort surrounds itself with parking lots rather than natural grounds, it provides convenience with shopping, restaurants, cafes, and a bar as part of the complex.

In 2005 the venue was listed for sale, so call ahead to confirm availability and rates.

Located 2.5 miles north of St. Mary, the units at **Glacier Trailhead Cabins** (milepost 34.4 on Hwy. 89, 406/732-4143 or 800/311-1041, www.glaciertrailheadcabins.com, mid-May–Oct. $105–120) are quiet, removed from the bustle of town, and set back from the highway in aspens. The 12 simply furnished smoke-free knotty pine log cabins built in 1999 maintain a silence without televisions and phones (a guest phone is available in the office). Each cabin has one or two queen beds with a private bathroom, electric heat, and a secluded porch with a mountain view; one cabin is wheelchair accessible. Cook your own dinner at the community outdoor grill, where a covered kitchen area has sinks, a stove, picnic tables, and running water. St. Mary restaurants are five minutes away by car.

A rather plain, older motel in St. Mary, the **Red Eagle Motel** (above Hwy. 89 just 0.5 mile north of Going-to-the-Sun Rd. and Hwy. 89 junction, 406/732-4453, www.redeaglemotel.com, May–Oct., $65–84) is good if you're just looking for an inexpensive place to crash. On a bluff above town between Johnson's Campground and Johnson's Café, its 23 rooms look out toward Napi Point. A five-minute walk connects with shops and restaurants.

On a bluff above St. Mary with an incomparable view into the park, the third generation family-owned **Johnson's of St. Mary** (0.5 mile north of Going-to-the-Sun Rd. and Hwy. 89 junction, 406/732-5565, www.johnsonsofstmary.com, late May–late Sept.) added a new homey bed-and-breakfast ($125) and three cabins ($105 for two people) to its resort. Log beds with handmade quilts decorate both, and the cabins (sleeping 2–5) come with fully equipped kitchens, private decks, and air-conditioning. Johnson's Café is right next door; shopping and other restaurants are a five-minute walk away.

Eight miles northeast of St. Mary, **Montana's Duck Lake Lodge** (milepost 32 on Hwy. 464, 406/338-5770, www.ducklake-

lodge.com, open year-round, $59–130) is a friendly family-owned lodge mostly attracting anglers, hunters, and snowmobilers with Duck Lake one mile away and access to local Native American hunting and fishing guides. The quiet lodge is surrounded by ponds, aspen parklands, and views of Glacier—especially from west-facing rooms. Clean but spartan rooms decorated in outdoor themes range from two twin beds with a shared bathroom and shower down the hall to a queen bed with in-room bathroom. A great room has a guest phone, satellite television, fireplace, restaurant, and bar.

MANY GLACIER

Historic **(** Many Glacier Hotel (milepost 11.5 on Many Glacier Rd., 406/892-2525, www.glacierparkinc.com, mid-June–mid-Sept., $114–225 double, $10 for each additional person) sits centrally in the Swiftcurrent Valley right on Swiftcurrent Lake with access to activities from boating and trail riding to red bus and boat tours. Centering around its massive four-storied lobby with a large fireplace, the nonsmoking hotel rooms and suites face lakeside staring at the Continental Divide's ragged peaks or toward the sunrise with a unique morning wake-up as the pack horses jangle to the corral.

For being the "Showplace of the Rockies," the hotel sadly slipped into disrepair, prompting Congress to fork over funds to renovate the National Landmark. An extensive five-year rehabilitation straightened the structure, repaired decks, and replaced windows. The bathrooms are small—many created from the original closets—with tiny sinks and skinny shower stalls. Some rooms have old-fashioned clawfoot tubs. The rooms have phones but no television, air-conditioning, or elevator access for its four stories. A restaurant, lounge, convenience store, and gift shop are on-site. When the hotel opened in 1915, it was considered the epitome of luxury; today, that is hardly the case, but what the hotel lacks in amenities it makes up for in historical ambience, unbelievable scenery, and convenience to trailheads.

© BECKY LOMAX

ST. MARY AND MANY GLACIER

Historic Many Glacier Hotel sits below Mt. Wilbur in Swiftcurrent Valley.

Trails to Cracker Lake, Grinnell Lake, Piegan Pass, and Grinnell Glacier depart from the hotel. Other trails depart from Swiftcurrent one mile away. Because of the renovation, this hotel has received lots of press, making reservations an absolute must.

At Many Glacier Road's terminus, **Swiftcurrent Motor Inn** (end of Many Glacier Rd., 406/892-2525, www.glacierparkinc.com, mid-June–mid-Sept., $73–110 double with private bath, $43–53 without bath, additional guests $10 each) has older cottages and a single-story motel. Units come with or without baths. For those without, a central comfort station and shower house awaits. It's similar to camping, especially with a the lukewarm-to-cold shower, but with a bed, heat, walls, and a roof for inclement weather. The nonsmoking rooms have no televisions, air-conditioning, or in-room phones. Pay phones are outside the camp store; the complex also has a laundry and restaurant. Historic charm isn't the lure, but rather its price and utter convenience. A stone's throw away are trailheads for Red Rocks and Bullhead Lakes, Granite Park Chalet, Swiftcurrent Pass and Lookout, Iceberg Lake, and Ptarmigan Tunnel.

CAMPING

While Many Glacier has only one park service campground with no hookups, St. Mary has both commercial campgrounds and a park service campground. The commercial campgrounds have flush toilets, hot showers, picnic tables, and hookups for electric, water, and sewer (and will add a 7 percent state tax to your bill) while the park service campgrounds are limited to flush toilets, dump stations, picnic tables, fire grates, and running water. Bring your own firewood for the park service campgrounds; collecting it is illegal within the park. In September after the campground water is turned off, you can camp primitively ($6, pit toilets only). If the park service campgrounds fill up, head to a commercial one in St. Mary, rather than up Going-to-the-Sun Road to Rising Sun, which usually fills up first.

St. Mary is convenient for exploring Going-to-the-Sun Road, and it works as a home base for day trips to Waterton, Many Glacier, and Two Medicine. However, if you envision parking the car and setting up a tent for a couple days to hike straight from the campground, then Many Glacier is where you need to be, instead.

St. Mary

At St. Mary Lake's east end, but with no lake access, **◖ St. Mary Campground** (milepost 0.9 on Going-to-the-Sun Rd., 406/888-7800, late May–late Sept., $17) has 183 sites right inside the park boundary, some in open meadows, others tucked between aspens. For the best views, the C loop sites stare at Divide and Red Eagle mountains, but in August heat, they can be hot. The campground can fit RVs up to 35 feet in 25 sites. Reservations here are highly recommended through the National Park Service Reservation System (800/365-2267, http://reservations.nps.gov). A trail crosses St. Mary River on a wooden bridge to connect with the visitor center, St. Mary's restaurants, and shops (0.6 mile).

Away from the hubbub of St. Mary and one mile down a paved road, **St. Mary KOA** (106 West Shore, 406/732-4122 or 800/562-1504, www.goglacier.com; mid-May–early Oct., tents $23, RV hookups $24–34, Kamping Kabins and Kottages $52–150) sits on the St. Mary River and Lower St. Mary Lake in a huge meadow where elk often browse. Open, with views of surrounding peaks, the campground has little shade and can be quite windy. It rents canoes and paddleboats ($10 per hour), mountain bikes ($10–20 per day), and cars for driving Going-to-the-Sun Road—a great option for RVers whose rigs are too big. In addition to the usual commercial campground amenities, it has a grocery store, espresso, outdoor hot tubs, laundry, gift shop, playground, and the A-OK Grille (June–Aug.), which serves $3–6 sourdough pancake breakfasts and highly acclaimed ribs at an evening barbecue.

Sitting atop a bluff with premium RV sites

having a gorgeous view of Glacier, the older **Johnson's Campground** (0.5 mile north of Going-to-the-Sun Rd. and Hwy. 89 junction, 406/732-4207, www.johnsonsofstmary.com, late Apr.–late Sept.) sprawls in a grassy setting broken up by chattering aspens just above St. Mary. With 75 tent sites ($16) plus 82 RV sites with hookups ($20–30)—some with fire pits—the campground can usually accommodate latecomers when park service campgrounds are full. The bathrooms are by no means modern, but amenities include a camp store, laundry, dump station, and 18-hole mini-golf. Both Sun Tours and the red buses stop at the campground, an easy solution to see Going-to-the-Sun Road for those with rigs too big. Restaurants and shops in St. Mary are a five-minute walk away.

Many Glacier

At the end of Many Glacier Road, **(Many Glacier Campground** (406/888-7800, late May–late Sept., $15 per site) packs 110 shaded sites into a treed setting at the base of Grinnell Point. Because of the popularity of its location, it fills up early in high season. Plan to arrive by 11 A.M. to claim a site as they are all first-

(handwritten: But 12 miles)

come, first-serve. Thirteen sites can accommodate RVs up to 35 feet. Here, trails depart for Red Rocks, Bullhead, and Iceberg Lakes as well as Ptarmigan Tunnel and Swiftcurrent Pass. From the picnic area, a five-minute walk down the road, trails depart to Josephine and Grinnell Lakes or farther to Grinnell Glacier or Piegan Pass. Across the parking lot at Swiftcurrent Motor Inn, you have access to a restaurant, laundry, hot showers, and a camp store. If bears frequent the campground, tent camping may be restricted, with only hard-sided vehicles allowed. Check www.nps.gov/glac or 406/888-7800 for status.

Duck Lake

Open year-round, but snow-covered in winter (Nov.–Apr.), **Montana's Duck Lake Lodge** (milepost 32 on Hwy. 464, 406/338-5770, $59–130) has 10 RV full-hookup sites ($25) and tent sites ($15) with propane available at every site. Amid aspen trees and ponds, the quiet campground centers around the family-owned lodge with a restaurant and bar and a communal bonfire pit. For anglers looking to fish Duck Lake one mile away, this is the most convenient campground.

Food

Because Many Glacier has only two restaurants, locals staying here for several days will drive to Babb (12 miles away) or St. Mary (21 miles away) to hit their favorite eateries. Nothing beats driving back in to Many Glacier at sunset with ample opportunities for wildlife-watching! Be aware that restaurants and grocery stores in Babb and St. Mary do not serve alcohol during Indian Days, a reservation-wide four-day celebration beginning the second Thursday in July. Other select days also prohibit alcohol sales, such as graduation in June. Because of location in the park rather than on the reservation, the restaurants in Many Glacier can still serve beer, wine, and cocktails on those days.

RESTAURANTS
St. Mary

Located in The Resort at Glacier: St. Mary Lodge, **(Snowgoose Grille** (junction of Going-to-the-Sun Rd. and Hwy. 89, 406/732-4431 or 800/368-3689, www.glcpark.com, late May–early Oct.) is the resort's headliner restaurant. Overlooking Divide Creek, the dining room serves breakfast (7–11 A.M., à la carte $6–8, buffet $10), lunch (11:30 A.M.– 4 P.M., $7–11), and dinners (5:30–10 P.M., $14–26). During early and late seasons, the restaurant sometimes shortens its hours; call to confirm times in the shoulder season, and you'll definitely need to make reservations for dinner in high season. Dinner specialties range

from prime rib to wild game. Fork-tender elk and buffalo tenderloins are favorites, and the requisite huckleberries are baked into various tempting pastries to finish off your meal. To accompany dinner, try the resort's own private label California wine. After dinner, cuddle up on country log furniture in front of the river-rock fireplace in the **Mountain Lounge** next door or on warm days sit on the deck overlooking Divide Creek to watch the sunset. Try, if you dare, one of the martini concoctions ($7–8)—the Montini with chocolate or the Huckletini with huckleberry-infused vodka.

Also in the resort, **Curly Bear Café and Rainbow Pizza Company** (junction of Going-to-the-Sun Rd. and Hwy. 89, 406/732-4431, late May–early Oct., 11 A.M.–7 P.M.) is the best place to take the kids as it has the closest thing to a fast food menu: buffalo burgers ($6.25), pizza ($3.50 for a slice and soda), ice-cream cones, and espresso. During high season, hours for the pizza shop extend to 10 P.M., or you can order pizza to go ($10–18). Try the gourmet house specialties—buffalo chicken or puttanesca pizza.

The **(Park Café** (0.2 mile north of Hwy. 89 and Going-to-the-Sun Rd. junction, 406/732-4482, late May–Sept., 7 A.M.–10 P.M.) cranks out daily the best homemade fruit pies. Try the triple berry or peach ($3.50). If your heart is set on a particular pie, order it when you order dinner, in case they run out by the time you get around to dessert. The restaurant serves breakfast, lunch, and dinner with an eclectic menu all of its own: creative veggie meals, burgers, and southwest style. Most items range $6–12. Be ready for long waiting lines in high season, for they don't take reservations, and it's a favorite haunt of locals. (But grab a beer at the store next door while you wait, as no alcohol is served in the restaurant.) In early June and after Labor Day, it opens at 7:30 A.M. and closes at 9 P.M.

Four miles north of St. Mary in a multicolored building with a wall inside covered with license plates and bumper stickers, **(Two Sisters Café** (milepost 36 on Hwy. 89, 406/732-5535, late May–mid-Sept., 8 A.M.–

10 P.M.) serves up great eclectic homemade fare for breakfast, lunch, and dinner. Most menu items range $6–14, with its St. Mary whitefish and Cajun grilled chicken dinners (often accompanied by corn on the cob and freshly baked bread) topping out at $16–20. The Red burger and chili cheeseburger ($9) fly off the grill all day. Best of all, be sure to order a plate of the sweet potato fries ($5). Montana microbrews and margaritas are available, too. For dessert, try the ice cream sandwich ($6) but share the monstrous thing with a friend. It's a popular place with waiting lines sometimes in high season.

For a different experience, **Johnson's World Famous Historic Restaurant** (0.5 mile north of Hwy. 89 and Going-to-the-Sun Rd. junction, 406/732-5565, www.johnsonsofstmary.com, late May–late Sept., 7 A.M.–9 P.M.) serves up its daily specials family-style along with creative pricing for kids—they charge by age. Located at Johnson's Resort of St. Mary, the small old-fashioned restaurant with red-checked tablecloths serves its eggs, bacon, and hash browns all on one big platter for the entire table ($5–7 per person). Lunch soup shows up in a large tureen; you ladle it yourself. Dinner features country foods with fried chicken on Sunday (adults $7–10, kids $0.50–0.75 per year to age 12). On Sunday, lunch is replaced by the dinner menu starting at 11:30 A.M. No alcohol is served, and contrary to other Montana unlicensed restaurants that permit beer and wine to be brought in, Johnson's does not.

At the north end of St. Mary just on the edge of town, the **BNC Taco Shack** (milepost 32 on Hwy. 89, 406/732-9202, www.bnctacoshack.com, Apr.–Oct., 11 A.M.–10 P.M., closes earlier in spring and fall) is much more than a shack. With its full Mexican menu ($5–10), specially ordered green chiles from New Mexico, and 55 kinds of burritos, it's a crowd pleaser. Even vegans and vegetarians will find lots of appealing options. Of course, the local favorite is the bean, rice, and corn Logan Pass burrito. But you can also try great named burritos like the Cow Grazer or The Heater, which is stuffed with 12-hour slow-cooked pork. It's

not really a dine-in restaurant; only a couple of tables fill the room and the outdoor deck. But if you want to dine, you can bring in your own wine or beer. You order at the counter, and you can get anything to go.

Babb

Clearly, the **(Cattle Baron Supper Club** (junction of Hwy. 89 and Many Glacier Rd., 406/732-4033, or before 3 P.M. 406/732-4532, weekends only mid-May–mid-June, daily mid-June–Sept., 5–10 P.M.) ranks as the best place around to get a melt-in-your-mouth steak. Up the log spiral staircase in the Babb Bar, once known as the roughest bar in Montana, the restaurant serves dinners ($14–29) where the baked potato isn't the biggest thing on the plate. You'd better be ready to gorge, for steak cuts are humongous—16–20 ounces. Salads with homemade dressings, grilled veggies, baked bread yanked fresh from the oven, and potato accompany most meals. The log lodge gives tribute to Blackfeet history with painted wall stories, a sculpture of a buffalo jump, and table placemats that narrate the family history of the Blackfeet owners. In high season, you'll be glad you made reservations.

Many Glacier

The **(Ptarmigan Dining Room** (milepost 11.6 on Many Glacier Rd. in Many Glacier Hotel, 406/892-2525, daily mid-June–mid-Sept.) doesn't have a bad seat in it. Known more for its views than its cuisine, the restaurant's massive two-story floor-to-ceiling windows look out on Swiftcurrent Lake, Grinnell Point, and Mount Wilbur. For the best views to watch bears while you eat, ask to sit near the north windows facing Altyn Mountain. Like all the park's historic hotels, breakfast (6:30–9:30 A.M., $5–9) is a multi-table spread of fruits, pastries, eggs, French toast, bacon, sausage, biscuits and gravy, pancakes, waffles, or à la carte. While the buffet has a breadth of selection and enough to feed hikers ready for a long day, lukewarm entrees lose their appeal; sometimes you're better off sticking to fruit and oatmeal. The nonsmoking dining

hall is also open for lunch (11:30 A.M.–2 P.M., $6–9) and dinner (5–9:30 P.M., $15–24), which theme around Swiss and Continental styles. No reservations are accepted for groups less than 12 people, so you may have to wait in high season for a table. The restaurant also makes hiker lunches ($7–10); order these one day in advance.

For a lighter meal, grab a sandwich at the nonsmoking **Swiss Room and Interlaken Lounge** (2–10 P.M. daily mid-June–mid-Sept., $6–9). Instead of sitting in the dark Swiss cut-out motif lounge, you can order drinks and eat in the lobby just outside the bar with views of the sunset over the Continental Divide. The bar serves Montana microbrews along with wine and cocktails 11:30 A.M.–midnight.

At the Many Glacier Road terminus at Swiftcurrent Motor Inn, **Italian Garden Ristorante** (milepost 12.5 on Many Glacier Rd., daily mid-June–mid-Sept.) is open for breakfast (6:30–10:30 A.M., $4–7), lunch (11 A.M.–3 P.M., $6–9), and dinner (5–9:30 P.M., $8–15). Breakfast and lunch menus are standard café fare in the nonsmoking restaurant; dinner menu is pasta and pizza. Montana microbrews and wines are available, but no cocktails. Since reservations are not taken for groups smaller than 12 people, you may have to wait for a table in high season, for it's popular because of its convenient location. The restaurant also makes hiker lunches ($7–10); order these one day in advance.

CAFFEINE

Located in The Resort at Glacier: St. Mary Lodge, the **Glacier Perk** (junction of Going-to-the-Sun Rd. and Hwy. 89, late May–early Oct., 406/732-4431, 8 A.M.–8 P.M.) is the place to grab an espresso before driving over Going-to-the-Sun Road. If temperatures outside are too hot, order it iced. Although it's incredibly sweet, many folks enjoy the huckleberry fudge, too.

GROCERIES

In Many Glacier, you'll find only two options for groceries—both convenience-type

stores. In the basement of Many Glacier Hotel, **Heidi's Store** (406/892-2525, mid-June–mid-Sept., 8 A.M.–9 P.M.) sells hot dogs, coffee, pop, snacks, newspapers, beer, wine, and other convenience store items. Located at Swiftcurrent at the end of Many Glacier Road, the **Swiftcurrent Campstore** (milepost 12.5 on Many Glacier Rd., 406/892-2525, mid-June–mid-Sept., 7 A.M.–9 P.M.) carries groceries, camping and hiking supplies, T-shirts, gift items, newspapers, beer, wine, firewood, and ice. Hikers can put together a hiker lunch. The camp store sits handily right across the parking lot from Many Glacier Campground and adjacent to Swiftcurrent Motor Inn.

In St. Mary, you can stock up on supplies at two grocery stores on Highway 89. The largest grocery store, but by no means a supermarket as its sign says, the **Country Market** (mid-May–mid-Oct., 8 A.M.–8 P.M.) is just south of the Going-to-the-Sun Road junction. It has a post office, fresh produce, bakery, butcher shop, beer, and wine. The **Park Grocery and Gift Shop** (0.2 mile north of Hwy. 89 and Going-to-the-Sun Rd. junction, 406/732-4482, late May–Sept.) carries

a great selection of Montana microbrews along with convenience store items and some groceries. During high season, hours are usually 7:30 A.M.–10 P.M., but the store will open a half hour later and close one hour earlier in early June and after Labor Day. Neither shop sells alcohol during Indian Days celebrations (second Thurs.–Sun. in July).

Located in Babb, **Thronson's General Store** (0.2 mile north of Hwy. 89 and Many Glacier Rd. junction, 9 A.M.–6 P.M. daily in summer, weekdays only in winter) stocks convenience store items but no beer or wine.

PICNIC AREAS

Many Glacier's small picnic area (milepost 12.2 on Many Glacier Rd.) is a great place to sit with binoculars and scan for bears on Altyn Peak—even if you aren't picnicking. It's a popular picnic site and can be crowded in high season at lunchtime. If you want to roast marshmallows on one of the fire pits, bring your own firewood because gathering wood is prohibited. The picnic area is also one of the trailheads for hiking to Lake Josephine, Grinnell Lake, Piegan Pass, and Grinnell Glacier.

Travel Rest cabins!

Serranos african

TWO MEDICINE AND EAST GLACIER

Quiet and removed, Glacier's southeast corner harbors a lesser-traveled park away from the harried corridor of Going-to-the-Sun Road. There's no hotel in Two Medicine, so even on day hikes the backcountry is not as crowded as at Many Glacier. A string of three lakes curves through the Two Medicine Valley below Rising Wolf, the peak with the largest mass in the park. Even though glaciers vacated this area years ago, their footprints left evidence of their passing in carved valleys and cirques. Today visitors can drive to the shore of the park's highest road-accessible lake or take a short half-day hike into alpine tundra.

Around the corner, the tiny burg of East Glacier buzzes in summer. Great Northern Railway's historic headliner hotel, Glacier Park Lodge, dominates the town with its garden walkway and immense log buildings. Framing the hotel, the mountains of Dancing Lady and Henry almost get lost in the long range of peaks parading west toward the Continental Divide. For those coming in historic style by train, the town launches excursions into Glacier with plenty to do: from hiking to golf, historic red bus tours to horseback riding. Yet at night, quiet stretches across the sky, broken only by the rumble of trains rolling by.

HISTORY

Two Medicine acquired its name from Blackfeet legends. According to one story, two Piegan tribes planned to meet for a medicine ceremony in the valley. Failing to find each other, they both celebrated independently. In

© BECKY LOMAX

TWO MEDICINE

HIGHLIGHTS

((Boat Tour: There's no better way to see Two Medicine Lake than on the historic *Sinopah* tour boat. It has plied the waters here since 1927 and knows its way around (page 144).

((Looking Glass Hill-Browning Loop: For the most dramatic and sometimes scary driving tour, climb up Highway 49, the first leg of Browning Loop. The narrow, windy road is a feat to drive, and the views of Two Medicine Valley stupendous (page 147).

((Running Eagle Falls: Named for a Blackfeet woman warrior, Pitamakin, this is also known as Trick Falls, because part of its waters cascade from underground chutes (page 148).

((Glacier Park Lodge: The lodge in East Glacier greets visitors as the headliner hotel for the historic chain of Great Northern hostelries built throughout Glacier. Walk its gardens leading up to the front door and lounge in its massive lobby held up by three-story Douglas firs (page 149).

((Museum of the Plains Indian: In Browning, this is one of the best places around to sample Blackfeet history and culture. Amazing beadwork and craft work of local artisans fills the gift shop (page 149).

((Scenic Point: High above the valley floor lies a top-of-the-world view, but you have to hike to get there. You'll look across the plains to the Sweet Grass Hills, see the tiny towns of East Glacier and Browning out on the prairie, and maybe if it's clear enough you'll see Minneapolis (page 151).

((Dawson-Pitamakin Loop: One of the top hikes in the park skitters high on a narrow goat trail along the Continental Divide thousands of feet above the valley floor (page 151).

((North American Indian Days: The Blackfeet celebrate for four days in early July. Visitors are welcome to attend the colorful festival in Browning (page 156).

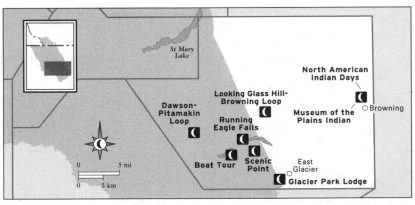

LOOK FOR ((TO FIND RECOMMENDED SIGHTS, ACTIVITIES, DINING, AND LODGING.

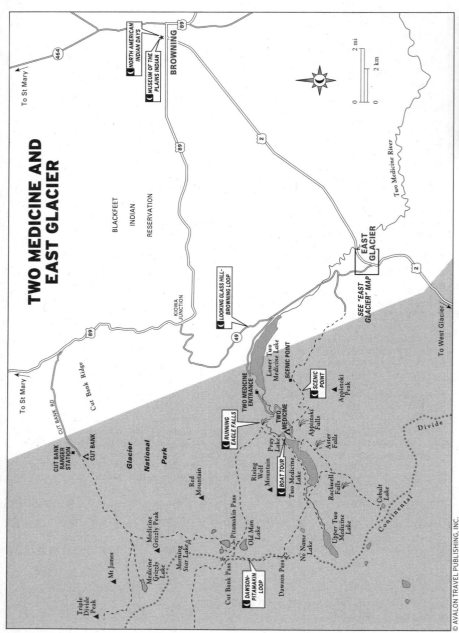

TWO MEDICINE AND EAST GLACIER

BLACKFEET INDIAN RESERVATION

THE BLACKFEET NATION

Bordering Glacier National Park on the east side, Blackfeet tribal lands extend from the Canadian border to East Glacier, covering 1.5 million acres. Around half of the tribe's 15,000 members live on the reservation.

Originally from north of the Great Lakes – perhaps as far as Labrador – the Blackfeet are related by language to the Algonquin tribes. As Europeans landed on North America's east coast in the 1600s, the Blackfeet were one of the first tribes to move westward, taking up the nomadic lifestyle of buffalo hunting in Saskatchewan, Alberta, and Montana. Bands of 20-30, each led by a chief, met for medicine lodge or sun dance rituals and separated for winter. "Siksika," or Blackfeet, may have referred to the color of moccasins, darkened by ash from prairie fires used to herd bison into an area for killing.

The loose Blackfeet Confederacy contained three tribes: the North Blackfeet and Bloods gravitated north of the Canadian border, and the Piegan settled south of the 49th parallel. All three hunted buffalo by using buffalo jumps, lighting fires to herd the large mammals into a stampede over a cliff. In the 1700s, the Blackfeet acquired horses from the Kootenai, Flathead, and Nez Perce and guns from French fur traders, altering their methods of hunting buffalo.

In the 1800s, the Blackfeet suffered devastating losses. A smallpox epidemic in 1837 killed 6,000 people, wiping out two-thirds of the population. Buffalo numbers declined and disappeared entirely, leading to Starvation Winter in 1884, in which 600 Blackfeet starved to death. By 1855, the first treaty with the

U.S. government defined Blackfeet territory, which covered almost two-thirds of eastern Montana starting at the Continental Divide. White settlers arrived, rankling the Blackfeet, who raided settlements. To squelch the hostilities, the U.S. Army sent Colonel E. M. Baker in 1870 to eradicate Mountain Chief, who led the raids. However, Baker mistakenly attacked Heavy Runner's peaceful tribe, slaughtering 200 and capturing 140 women and children.

Tribal leaders, desperate to help their destitute people, bargained with the U.S. government for their survival. They sold off portions of the reservation in trade for tools, equipment, and cattle. Glacier Park lands from the Continental Divide to the eastern boundary were one of these trades: the U.S. government paid the Blackfeet $1.5 million in 1896 for lands with potential minerals. When mineral prospecting yielded nothing, the lands became part of Glacier National Park in 1910.

Today, the Blackfeet economy is based on some cattle ranching, but 90 percent of the tribe's income comes from oil and gas extraction.

The center of Blackfeet culture is Browning, where the small but outstanding **Museum of the Plains Indian** chronicles their history and displays amazing beadwork. The tribe celebrates North American Indian Days, which traditionally begins the second Thursday of July and runs through Sunday. The four-day Heart Butte Indian Days begins the second Thursday of August. Both celebrations have rodeos and powwows with dancing, singing, and drumming open to visitors (406/338-7521, www.blackfeetnation.com).

another version, two lodges for the Sun Dance sat on either side of Two Medicine Creek. Either way, the name stuck.

The Two Medicine area was part of the 1896 land sale between the Blackfeet and the federal government. Starving and nearly decimated as a tribe, the Blackfeet swapped part of their reservation land from the Continental Divide to the current reservation boundary

for $1.5 million—a mere pittance considering what the parklands are worth.

In April 1891, Great Northern Railway began laying tracks from Cut Bank to Midvale (East Glacier) and over Marias Pass toward West Glacier. As railroad developer James J. Hill sought means to increase ridership on his new line, he spawned a grand plan for a lodge to greet guests first arriving to Midvale and

East Glacier Train Depot, across from Glacier Park Lodge and gardens

© BECKY LOMAX

several chalets sprinkled in the park's most scenic spots. For early visitors in 1911 debarking the train in Midvale, Two Medicine Lake was the first stop in Glacier's backcountry after a bumpy wagon ride. Originally a tipi enclave with canvas walls and wooden floors, the camp was hugely successful, prompting the railroad to add two log chalets—a dormitory and a din-

ing hall. By 1915, guests arrived on horseback via trail, the first leg on the Inside Trail connecting to Cut Bank and St. Mary Chalets on Park Saddle Horse Company tours—a three-day trip costing $13.25.

In 1913, Great Northern's headliner hotel—the Glacier Park Lodge—finally welcomed arriving train guests, awed at the first glimpse of Glacier. Built on reservation land purchased from the Blackfeet, the posh lodge with a plunge pool in the basement erected its elegantly large lobby with 500–800-year-old Douglas firs sent from western Washington and Oregon. Rooms touted such high-class amenities as electric lights and steam heat. The nine-hole golf course followed 14 years later—on which employees were not allowed to play for fear of upsetting high-class tourists.

In 1929, Great Northern introduced the Empire Builder, named after J. J. Hill, as its modern train for the 2,200-mile Chicago–Seattle trip that packaged Glacier Park travel for its passengers. This is still the name for the Amtrak line here. It's the only U.S. train outside Alaska that stops regularly at a major national park.

In the wake of the Depression, World War II closures, and increasing auto traffic, the Two Medicine chalets met their demise and were torn down building by building until only the dining hall remained.

Exploring Two Medicine and East Glacier

ENTRANCE STATION

East Glacier sits outside park boundaries, but Two Medicine is within the park with an entrance station location approximately four miles up Two Medicine Road. It is staffed during daylight hours seven days a week in the summer. During shoulder seasons, staffing reduces to weekends only or not at all. However, a cash-only self-pay kiosk sits on the right just past the station. Maps and the *Waterton-Glacier Guide* are available here.

Even though the Cut Bank Road enters the park, it lacks both an entrance station and self-pay kiosk. Entrance is free.

TOURS AND SHUTTLES
Red Bus

Glacier Park, Inc. (406/892-2525, www.glacierparkinc.com, adults $25–65, kids 11 and under half price) runs three tours on historic red buses, which begin at Glacier Park Lodge in East Glacier. Driven by story-telling jammer drivers who roll the canvas tops back when the weather permits, the vintage buses are not just a treat for their historic ambience, but for the whole-sky views you can get out the top. The 8.5-hour **Circle Tour** (late May–Sept.) packs in the best of the park for those who have limited time to explore all its corners. Departing daily at 9 A.M., the tour travels over Marias Pass to Lake McDonald Lodge, then crosses Logan Pass (when it is open) on Going-to-the-Sun Road to St. Mary, and then loops south over Looking Glass Hill to the Lodge. The 3-hour **Two Medicine Great Northern Tour** (late May–Sept.) departs daily at 1 P.M. for Marias Pass and Two Medicine Lake. For an excursion to Many Glacier and Waterton, the 8-hour **International Peace Park Tour** (early June–mid-Sept.) departs daily at 9:30 A.M. Prices do not include meals or park entrance fees. Reservations are required and can be made by phone or at the hotel front desk.

◖ Boat Tour

The *Sinopah* (Glacier Park Boat Company, 406/226-4467 summers only, 406/257-2426, www.glacierparkboats.com, mid-June–early Sept., adults $10.50 round-trip, kids half price) started service on Two Medicine Lake in 1927 and has never left its waters. The 45-foot, 49-passenger wooden boat cruises uplake four times daily for 45-minute tours (10:30 A.M. and 1, 3, and 5 P.M.) while the captain narrates a little history, trivia, and natural phenomenon. Two launches daily also incorporate a short guided hike to Twin Falls (0.9 mile one-way). In July, the boat company adds on the 9 A.M. hiker express. Purchase tickets (cash only) at the boat dock. To shorten the Upper Two Medicine Lake hike to four miles round-trip, catch the boat both directions, chopping off six miles. For a three-mile jaunt, hike one way along the northern lakeshore through avalanche gullies under Rising Wolf's flanks and hop the boat back. In high season, the boat returns to the upper dock to collect all hikers waiting, even if it means extra trips. For one-way rides ($5.25), buy your tickets (cash only) on board.

Sun Tours

Departing East Glacier daily at 8 A.M., Sun Tours (406/226-9220 or 800/786-9220, www.glaciersuntours.com; mid-May–mid-Oct., adults $35–55, kids ages 12 and under $15, kids under 5 free, park entrance fees not included) drives 25-passenger air-conditioned buses with extra-large windows over historic Going-to-the-Sun Road to Lake McDonald and back. Led by local guides who live on the reservation, the tours highlight Glacier's historical and present-day connection with the Blackfeet. This is one tour on which you can get the background of peak names as well as the traditional cultural meaning of park features. The guides, most of whom are excellent storytellers, also narrate natural history. Although you can call for reservations on the day of the tour, you're better off planning at least 24 hours in advance.

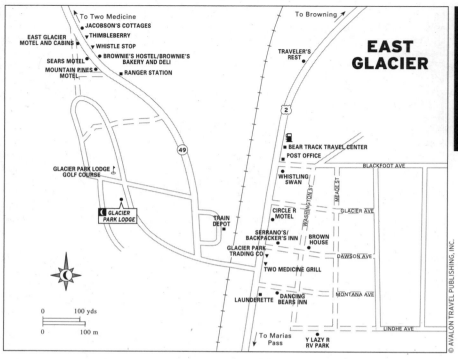

EAST GLACIER

To Two Medicine
JACOBSON'S COTTAGES
THIMBLEBERRY
EAST GLACIER MOTEL AND CABINS
WHISTLE STOP
BROWNIE'S HOSTEL/BROWNIE'S BAKERY AND DELI
SEARS MOTEL
MOUNTAIN PINES MOTEL
RANGER STATION

To Browning
TRAVELER'S REST

2

BEAR TRACK TRAVEL CENTER
POST OFFICE
BLACKFOOT AVE

GLACIER PARK LODGE
GOLF COURSE

49

WHISTLING SWAN

MEADE ST
WASHINGTON ST

GLACIER AVE

CIRCLE R MOTEL

GLACIER PARK LODGE

TRAIN DEPOT

SERRANO'S/BACKPACKER'S INN
BROWN HOUSE

GLACIER PARK TRADING CO

DAWSON AVE

TWO MEDICINE GRILL

DANCING BEARS INN
LAUNDERETTE

MONTANA AVE

LINDHE AVE

0   100 yds
0   100 m

To Marias Pass

Y LAZY R RV PARK

Shuttles

The hiker shuttle operated by Glacier Park, Inc. (406/892-2525, www.glacierparkinc.com, $8–40 depending on distance, kids half price) makes getting to trailheads easy. The east-side shuttle runs late May–September connecting points from East Glacier and Two Medicine to St. Mary, Many Glacier, and Waterton. At St. Mary Visitor Center, riders can link into Going-to-the-Sun Road shuttles running July–Labor Day. No shuttle runs directly from East Glacier to West Glacier via Highway 2. For trailheads at Marias Pass, for instance, you must drive yourself or hitchhike, which is legal in Montana. From Glacier Park Lodge, daily shuttles ($11 round-trip) hook up with Two Medicine boat departure times. Ask for schedules at the hotel front desk.

While in theory the shuttle is a good idea to access trailheads, consider where you are and how long it will take you to get to Logan Pass, for instance. That's three hours. And you won't start hiking until 11:30 A.M.. For the most efficient use of your time while staying in East Glacier, you're better off hiking in Two Medicine. Then move north to St. Mary or Many Glacier to hike trails in the central part of the park.

SERVICES

Two Medicine has no gas stations, but East Glacier has two: an Exxon at the Bear Track Travel Center at the east end of town on Highway 2 and Grizzly Gas on Highway 49 at the Sears Motel. There are ATMs at Glacier Park Trading Company and Glacier Park Lodge. The post office is in East Glacier at 15 Blackfoot Avenue (8:30 A.M.–noon and 1:30–5 P.M. weekdays only). The area's daily newspaper is the *Great Falls Tribune*.

A launderette (open 7 A.M.–9 P.M. daily) is in

East Glacier at the west end of town on Highway 2. Another laundry is at Y Lazy R RV Park on Lindhe and Meade, and it offers coin-op showers available to drop-ins.

Some cell phones have reception in East Glacier. Internet access is available at Brownie's and Bear Track Travel Center. As of 2005, high-speed Internet hasn't hit here; most connections are 56K.

Rental Cars

East Glacier offers seasonal (May–Sept.) car rentals through Dollar Rent-A-Car at **Sears Motel** (1023 Hwy. 49, 406/226-4432 or 800/800-4000, www.dollar.com). During the summer season when Amtrak stops at East Glacier, **Glacier Park Trading Company** (314 Hwy. 2, 406/226-4433, summer 8 A.M.–9 P.M., winter 9 A.M.–8 P.M.) rents Avis cars (800/230-4898, www.avis.com).

Water

Since East Glacier draws its water from surface sources, both East Glacier and Browning struggle with water quality. When bacteria get into the water, all water must be boiled (five minutes) before drinking. To be safe, it's best just to drink bottled water in East Glacier, rather than tap water. All restaurants serve bottled water, so you don't have to worry—but ask just to be sure. Glacier Park Lodge heavily chlorinates its water (you'll taste it) to eliminate the bacteria.

Emergencies

In Glacier Park, contact a park ranger for emergencies (406/888-7800). The nearest hospital is in Cut Bank—the Northern Rockies Medical Center (802 2nd St. E., 406/873-2251).

The **Two Medicine Ranger Station** (406/888-7800, summers only, 8 A.M.–4:30 P.M. daily), at the terminus of Two Medicine Road at the campground junction, has current trail information and issues backcountry campsite permits. You can also pick up copies of *The Glacier Explorer* for park naturalist programs, fishing information, free non-topographical maps of trails in the area, and bear sightings. The ranger station plots bear sightings on a

Lower Two Medicine Lake leads up valley to Rising Wolf Mountain.

© BECKY LOMAX

large wall map worth a look just for bear trivia. Rangers like to receive reports of bear sightings along trails or in the campground. The ranger station sells Tribal conservation permits ($10 per person per year) for those hiking over Scenic Point to East Glacier.

The **East Glacier Ranger Station** (824 Hwy. 49, 406/888-7800) houses a small year-round staff, but the station doesn't maintain consistent public hours. Rangers are often out working in the backcountry.

DRIVING TOURS
Two Medicine Road
Four miles north of East Glacier off Highway 49, Two Medicine Road heads up the Two Medicine Valley for 7.5 miles. It begins on the Blackfeet Reservation and winds through quaking aspen above Lower Two Medicine Lake into the park. In September, the aspens turn bright yellow, almost emitting a light of their own. **Scenic Point** rises across the lake, and the red flanks of Rising Wolf hog the valley head. You'll enter the park at 2.9 miles, crossing over a cattle guard, but you won't reach the entrance station until 4.1 miles. A few minutes past the entrance station (5.2 miles), stop for the short nature walk heading to **Running Eagle Falls.** As the road climbs into the Two Medicine Basin, look for blue camas, fleabane, paintbrush, and lupine. Once you cross the apex, the peaks of Two Medicine pop out: Sinopah, Lone Walker, and Rising Wolf. After passing the campground and picnic area entrance (7.1 miles), the road terminates in the parking lot at **Two Medicine Lake** where you can catch a boat tour on the lake or stop in the historic chalet, now a camp store selling ice-cream cones.

[Looking Glass Hill-Browning Loop
From East Glacier, this 49-mile scenic loop on the Blackfeet Reservation ties together grand views of Two Medicine Valley and peak panoramas seen from the plains. From East Glacier, the tour starts up Looking Glass Hill Highway, otherwise known as Highway 49 and

an original part of the Blackfeet Highway. Because Looking Glass Hill (Two Medicine Rd. to Kiowa Jct.) is closed in winter (Nov.–Apr.), this tour is a summer drive only. The shoulderless road with more curves than a snake is not ideal for trailers and large RVs, but they are permitted. Be aware, however, that wet downpours cause landslides on Looking Glass; the road frequently closes for repairs, and you'll hit rough sections where landslides have removed pavement. As the road climbs to a high vantage point above **Lower Two Medicine Lake,** it twists through aspen groves. Three miles past the Two Medicine junction you'll find unmarked pullouts overlooking the valley—great photo ops.

Drive slowly, for open range means no fences. Cattle may wander willy-nilly where they please here. Often, you'll round a corner into cows standing smack in the middle of the road and may have to wait for them to move. They are not particularly speedy creatures, but they can dent your car with a good kick, so give them room. Because the road is narrow and curvy, take it slow. You'll have less chance of putting a cow imprint across the front of your car.

Wind around the summit and drop to Kiowa Junction, where Highway 49 meets Highway 89 and the driving marginally improves. From here, the Blackfeet Highway continues north on Highway 89 along the Rocky Mountain Front to St. Mary. At Kiowa, turn right toward Browning, the center of the Blackfeet Reservation. Stop at the **Museum of the Plains Indians** for a look into the Blackfeet culture and history before turning onto Highway 2 for an easy cruise back to East Glacier. In front of you, the Rocky Mountains rise straight up off the plains.

SIGHTS
Two Medicine Lake
The largest of three lakes, Two Medicine Lake is the highest road-accessible lake in Glacier, sitting almost one mile high in elevation. Its waters collect from snowmelt on peaks over 8,000 feet high, but devoid of glaciers. The

lakes are all that remain of the monster thousand-foot-thick icefield that covered nearly 500,000 acres, flowing well out onto the prairie past Browning. To explore Two Medicine Lake, jump on the historic *Sinopah* tour boat for some good storytelling by Glacier Park Boat Company's captains. If waters are calm, rent a canoe to paddle its shoreline. Hike to Paradise Point for a swim in its chilly clear waters or fish for brook trout.

Family Peaks

Rich with Blackfeet history, the peaks in Two Medicine Valley tell a story. **Rising Wolf,** climbing straight out of the north shoreline to 9,573 feet, was named for Hugh Monroe, a Hudson Bay Company fur trapper who came to the Glacier area in the early 1800s. After living with the Piegans, he bargained with **Lone Walker,** the tribal chief, to marry his daughter. To see Lone Walker Mountain, look upvalley between Helen and Sinopah for what appears to be a low-angled pyramid but is actually 8,502 feet high. From Upper Two Medicine Lake, this peak sits above the lake's head. Rising Wolf married Lone Walker's daughter— **Sinopah,** the dramatic eroded pyramid directly across Two Medicine Lake at 8,271 feet.

Two Medicine Chalets

All that remains of historic Two Medicine Chalets is the dining hall, now operating as the Two Medicine Campstore and designated in 1987 as a National Historic Landmark. Built 1912–1913, the chalets replaced the original tipi camp for visitors. The log two-story chalet was once the hub of the small colony, the first stop on the Inside Trail horse trip with Park Saddle Company in the 1920s. The dining hall's most famous guest was Franklin Delano Roosevelt, who addressed the nation from here in an unofficial fireside chat in 1934.

◖ Running Eagle Falls

A short nature trail (0.6 mile round-trip) leads to Running Eagle Falls, also known as Trick Falls. In high runoff, water gushes over the top of the falls, spraying those standing nearby. But

RISING WOLF

Without a doubt, the most prominent feature in Two Medicine Valley is the hulk of 9,513-foot Rising Wolf Mountain. It's named for the first white man to set foot on the east side of Glacier Park. Born Hugh Monroe in Quebec, Canada, in 1798, the young man traveled west at age 16 as an apprentice for the Hudson Bay Company.

With an intense interest in the Indians, he was sent to live with the Small Robes band of Piegans (one group of Blackfeet) to learn all he could of their language and find beaver-trapping territory. The tribe's chief, Lone Walker, took a liking to the congenial Monroe. After several seasons with the Piegans, Monroe married Sinopah, Lone Walker's daughter, and lived permanently with them. (His father-in-law's peak sits at the head of Upper Two Medicine Lake, and his wife's peak rises straight out of Two Medicine Lake's waters just opposite Rising Wolf.)

Admitted as a member to the tribe, he was ascribed the name Rising Wolf. Although no written record exists, it is presumed that Monroe was the first white man to set eyes on St. Mary Lakes and much of Glacier's eastern lands. He served as a guide and interpreter for territorial survey teams and early reconnaissance of Glacier Park. He later abandoned Hudson Bay Company for the American Fur Company, who finally pushed to establish trading posts on the Marias River in the middle of Blackfeet country. Rising Wolf died in 1892, the same year Great Northern Railway laid tracks over Marias Pass.

While there is some discrepancy on Monroe's birthdate, it is apparent he lived to a ripe old age, in spite of the fact that he lost eyesight in one eye in a fight with a Sioux. Many of Monroe's descendants still live on the Blackfeet Reservation.

in lower flows, you can see the trick. Part of the falls runs underground and spits out through a cavern halfway down the falls' face. Running Eagle, the Blackfeet name for the falls, honors a female warrior named Pitamakin who

had her vision quest here. She was renowned for stealing horses from the Kootenai but was eventually killed on a raid.

Glacier Park Lodge

In East Glacier, Glacier Park Lodge stands as the headliner hotel for the historic chain of Great Northern hostelries built throughout Glacier. Set within the Blackfeet Reservation, the 155-room hotel built in 1915 started its life as a grand hotel providing visitors the first taste of Glacier. Since the advent of Going-to-the-Sun Road, some of the lodge's thunder has been stolen by additional avenues into the park. Today, the hotel is listed on the National Register of Historic Places. Even if you are not staying here, plan to walk its gardens leading up to the front door and lounge in its massive lobby held up by three-story Douglas firs. In the lobby, an excellent historic photo display chronicles the hotel's history.

© BECKY LOMAX

Blackfeet Sentries, Jay Laber's "rez wreck" sculptures, outside East Glacier

Blackfeet Sentries

Blackfeet artist Jay Laber gives new life to garbage in what he calls "Reborn Rez Wrecks." Using farm tools, jewelry, hubcaps, and barbwire, he sculpted a not-to-be-missed sculpture series—Blackfeet Reservation Sentries—posted on the reservation's four boundaries. Each pair of life-size sentries rides atop horses. Posted in East Glacier, one pair guards the reservation's western entrance (0.2 mile west of town on Hwy. 2). For information on Laber's work, check www.jaylaber.com.

Museum of the Plains Indian

Located in Browning, 12 miles from East Glacier, the Museum of the Plains Indian (junction of Hwy. 2 and 83, 406/338-2230, June–Sept. daily 9 A.M.–4:45 P.M., Oct.–May Mon.–Fri. 10 A.M.–4:30 P.M., adults $4, kids 6–12 $1, under 6 free, all ages free in winter) is a small but very informative center for Blackfeet culture and history. A multimedia five-screen show narrated by Vincent Price tells the story of the Blackfeet people, well worth the 20 minutes it takes to watch it. Displays cluster phenomenal beadwork, leather, tools, and clothing to tell the story the Northern Plains Indians. The life-size beaded ceremonial costumes alone are worth the price of admission.

TWO MEDICINE

Recreation

HIKING

Hiking at Two Medicine is in a class by itself. Except for a few short hikes at the lake's upper end, hikers can find solitude even on the most crowded of warm summer days. For hikes on reservation land (those leaving directly from East Glacier or the latter half of the Scenic Point trail), a Tribal recreation label is required. You can purchase the $10 annual permit at the Two Medicine Ranger Station or Bear Track Travel Center (Exxon gas station) in East Glacier.

Because quite a few junctions break off of the north and south shore Two Medicine Lake trails, you'll find one of the park's non-topographical trail maps helpful. These are available at the ranger station. For longer hikes, such as the Dawson-Pitamakin Loop, tote a good topographical map: You can buy one in the Two Medicine Campstore.

© BECKY LOMAX

Scenic Point trail, with Two Medicine Lake and Rising Wolf Mountain in the background

Aster Park

- Distance: 3.8 miles round-trip
- Duration: 2 hours
- Elevation gain: 670 feet
- Effort: easy
- Trailhead: adjacent to Two Medicine boat dock

Beginning on the south shore trail, Aster Park is reached via a spur trail just past Aster Creek. About 1.2 miles up the trail, turn left at the signed junction and follow the trail past Aster Falls as it switchbacks up to a knoll. This overlook provides the best view of Two Medicine Lake and its northern peaks.

Twin Falls and Upper Two Medicine Lake

- Distance: 1.8–10 miles round-trip
- Duration: 1–5 hours
- Elevation gain: 0–350 feet
- Effort: easy
- Trailhead: Two Medicine Lake west boat dock or Pray Lake Bridge in Two Medicine Campground

Set in a subalpine bowl, Upper Two Medicine Lake is reached by a trail passing Twin Falls—a double flume of cascades. Taking the boat both ways on Two Medicine Lake makes the shortest hikes: Twin Falls, 1.8 miles round-trip; the lake, 4.4 miles. Taking the boat one way and hiking the remaining distance shortens the hike to 7.2 miles. For the longest route, you can hike both up and back on the north shore trail or loop around Two Medicine Lake.

The trail climbs gently, passing the short spur trail to Twin Falls. After crossing avalanche gullies thick with huckleberries, you'll crest a prominent rock ledge to the lake. If

you are eating lunch at the lake, help maintain the safety of those sleeping in the backcountry campground here by not eating in the sleeping sites. Sit in the cooking area to eat or hike up the north shoreline (which is impossible to do with high water in early season).

Scenic Point

- Distance: 6.2 miles round-trip
- Duration: 3–4 hours
- Elevation gain: 2,350 feet
- Effort: moderately strenuous
- Trailhead: milepost 6.9 on Two Medicine Road

Scenic Point is one short climb with big scenery. The trail launches up through a thick subalpine fir forest. A short side jaunt en route sneaks a peek at Appistoki Falls. As switchbacks line up like dominoes, stunted firs give way to dead silver, twisted limber pines. Broaching the ridge, the trail enters alpine tundra, a seemingly barren area. Only alpine bluebells and mats of several-hundred-year-old moss campion cower in crags.

The trail traverses across a scree slope, covered in early season with steep snows to be avoided, and descends. To reach Scenic Point proper, cut off at the sign, stepping on rocks to avoid crushing fragile alpine plants. Atop, you can swan dive several thousand feet straight down into Lower Two Medicine Lake. From here, return the way you came. Or, a seven-mile drop continues to East Glacier passing outside the park boundary, where cow pies buzz with flies on the trail. Tribal recreation labels are required for hiking this option, available at the ranger station.

Rockwell Falls and Cobalt Lake

- Distance: 6.8–11.4 miles round-trip
- Duration: 4–5.5 hours
- Elevation gain: minimal to 1,400 feet
- Effort: easy to moderate

- Trailhead: adjacent to the Two Medicine boat dock

Follow the gentle south shore trail along Two Medicine Lake past beaver ponds and bear-scratched trees to Paradise Creek, where a swinging bridge makes you think of Indiana Jones movies, but it's not as scary. At 2.3 miles, turn left at the signed junction. The trail wanders through avalanche paths with uprooted trees shredded like toothpicks. At 3.4 miles, you reach Rockwell Falls. Spur trails explore the falls.

Continuing on to Cobalt Lake, the trail climbs up several switchbacks into an upper basin, where it crosses back and forth over the creek. The trail packs all of its elevation gain in the last two miles. Tucked in the uppermost corner of the basin, Cobalt Lake sits below talus slopes covered with mountain goats.

Dawson-Pitamakin Loop

- Distance: 16.9 or 18.8 miles
- Duration: 7–9 hours
- Elevation gain: 2,935 feet
- Effort: strenuous
- Trailhead: Two Medicine Lake west boat dock or Pray Lake Bridge in Two Medicine Campground

Although this loop can be done from either direction, both with the same elevation gain up to 8,000 feet, the approach to Dawson Pass is much steeper than to Pitamakin Pass. It crams all of its elevation gain within three miles, while Pitamakin Pass sprawls it less steeply out over several miles more. So pick your poison based on your preference for uphill climbs and knee-pounding descents. If you catch the Two Medicine boat one direction or the other, you'll chop off 1.9 miles.

In its loop around Rising Wolf peak, the route actually crosses three passes: Pitamakin, Cut Bank, and Dawson, the latter two passes seeing frequent winds raging enough to force crawling. Starting toward Pitamakin,

© BECKY LOMAX

Pitamakin Pass trail drops to Old Man Lake on the Dawson-Pitamakin Loop.

the trail crosses Dry Fork and follows it up to Old Man Lake (6.8 miles), a good fishing lake, before climbing to the pass (8.8 miles). With the narrow trail exposed high on a goat traverse between Cut Bank and Dawson (12.1 miles) passes, those with a fear of heights will not be comfortable. Nevertheless, the hike is a stunner!

Medicine Grizzly Lake and Triple Divide Pass

- Distance: 12 or 14.4 miles round-trip
- Duration: 6–7.5 hours
- Elevation gain: 540 or 2,380 feet
- Effort: easy to strenuous
- Trailhead: terminus of Cut Bank Road
- Directions: Locate the signed Cut Bank Road 6 miles north of Kiowa Junction on Highway 89. Follow the narrow dirt road

over cattle grates into the park and past the ranger station. The trailhead is about 4 miles up just before the campground.

Due to its location up the Cut Bank Road, no shuttle accesses this trailhead, but it's a popular trail for anglers as Medicine Grizzly Lake harbors 12-inch rainbows. Check with the ranger station before leaving, as bear activity frequently closes the lake and its spur trail. The trail follows Atlantic Creek up a forested drainage to a signed junction at 4 miles. Turn right, climbing (0.6 mile) past the Atlantic Creek campground to a second junction. To head to Medicine Grizzly Lake, continue straight for 1.4 miles.

Heading to Triple Divide Pass, the other trail bursts out of the trees, climbing up a rocky face below Mount James as it looks down on the lake. After winding into a large bowl, look for bighorn sheep, frequently browsing here. Tucked at the base of Triple Divide Peak, the pass actually stands on the split between the Saskatchewan and Missouri River drainages, beginning here with Hudson Bay Creek and Atlantic Creek.

Guides

The National Park Service guides free hikes mid-June through mid-September to a variety of destinations in Two Medicine: Upper Two Medicine Lake, Scenic Point, Dawson Pass, Rockwell Falls, and Cobalt Lake as well as a daily boat ride and hike to Twin Falls. (The hike is free, but you still need to pay for the boat ride.) Grab a copy of *The Glacier Explorer* from the ranger station for the current schedule.

Glacier Guides (406/387-5555 or 800/321-7238, www.glacierguides.com) leads day hikes for a minimum of five people ($65 per person) and custom day hikes ($400 flat fee) throughout Glacier. Guides will pick you up at the lodge, transport you to the trailhead, and bring along a deli lunch and snacks. Park entrance and boat fees are included: you just need to bring your pack, sunscreen, bug juice, and extra clothes. Reservations are mandatory. Solo hikers can sometimes hook up with a group; call to see what's on the schedule.

LEAVE NO TRACE

To be a part of keeping Glacier pristine, visitors to this unique park need to take an active role in maintaining its well-being.

- **Plan ahead and prepare.** Hiking in Glacier's backcountry is inherently risky. Three miles here may be much harder than three miles through your neighborhood park back home. Choose appropriate routes for mileage and elevation gain with this in mind, and carry hiking essentials.

- **Travel and camp on durable surfaces.** In both frontcountry and backcountry campgrounds, camp in designated sites only. Protect fragile trail-side plants by staying on the trail, refusing to cut switchbacks, and walking single file on trails – even in the mud. If you must walk off the trail, step on rocks, snow, or dry grasses rather than wet soil and fragile plants.

- **Leave what you find.** Flowers, rocks, and goat fur tufts on shrubs are protected park resources, as are historical cultural items. For lunch stops and camping, sit on rocks or logs where you find them rather than moving them to accommodate your camp.

- **Properly dispose of waste.** Whatever you bring in, you must pack out. Pack out all garbage, including toilet paper. If toilets are not available, urinate on rocks, logs, gravel, or snow to protect fragile soils and plants from salt-starved wildlife, and bury feces 6-8 inches deep at least 200 feet from water.

- **Minimize campfire impacts.** Make fires in designated fire pits only, not on beaches. Use small wrist-size dead and downed wood, not live branches. Be aware that fires and firewood collecting is not permitted in many places in the park.

- **Respect wildlife.** Bring along binoculars, spotting scopes, and telephoto lenses to aid in watching wildlife. Keep your distance. Do not feed any wildlife, even ground squirrels. Once fed, they become more aggressive.

- **Be considerate of other visitors.**

For more Leave No Trace Center for Outdoor Ethics information or materials, please visit www.LNT.org or call 303/442.8222.

Shuttles

In Two Medicine, hikers use the tour boat as a shuttle uplake to prune miles off hikes and get farther into the backcountry faster. (See *Tours and Shuttles.*) Glacier Park, Inc. also runs a shuttle from Glacier Park Lodge to Two Medicine for hiking; the shuttles arrive in time to catch the boat across Two Medicine Lake. To access other routes in the park, you'll have to hop the east-side hiker shuttle heading up to St. Mary.

BIKING

Bicycling around the park's southeast corner is usually restricted to narrow, curvy, shoulderless roadways. Although most drivers are fairly courteous toward bicyclists here, be prepared to have large RVs nearly shove you off the road, simply due to their size in comparison to the skimpy pavement. It's an area where you may encounter bears on the roadway, especially on Two Medicine Road. Particularly on Highway 49, you can round a corner into a small herd of cows, since the area is open range. And for some reason, no matter which direction you're riding, a strong headwind always blasts. Mountain biking is not permitted on trails within Glacier, so riding is restricted to roadways. Families with youngsters should stick to the campground loops at Two Medicine Campground rather than riding the roadways. Most bicyclists out for a day trip ride from East Glacier to Two Medicine Lake and back.

For bicyclists, Two Medicine Campground has shared hiker-biker campsites for $5 per person. These are reserved until 9 P.M. for bikers

Two Medicine Lake, framed by Lone Walker and Helen Mountains

and have bear-resistant food storage containers on-site.

Bicycle rentals—at least a few 10-speed, wide-tired bikes—are available at **John L. Clarke Western Art Gallery** (900 Hwy. 49, East Glacier, 406/226-9238, May–Sept. Mon.–Sat. 10 A.M.–8 P.M., on Sunday closes at 5 P.M., $3.50 per hour, $15 for 5 hours). There are a few smaller bikes to accommodate older kids. Helmets are included. Call ahead to check on availability.

TRAIL RIDING

Across the street from Glacier Park Lodge on Highway 49, **Glacier Gateway Outfitters** (0.4 mile north of Hwy. 2 and 49 junction, 406/226-4408, late May–Sept.) leads trail rides and cowboy-style horseback rides that tour cross-country rather than riding in a single-file line. The tours are outside Glacier Park on adjacent reservation land. Rides wander along Looking Glass Hill and Two Medicine River Gorge through aspens and blooms of early-season shooting stars and late-summer lupine with views of the park's front range.

Full-day ($175, bring your own lunch) and half-day rides ($94–100) depart at 9 A.M. Half-day rides depart again at 1 and 2 P.M. Two-hour rides ($50) depart three times daily. Wear long pants and sturdy shoes, such as hiking boots or tennis shoes. Kids must be at least seven years old and have some experience riding, but no special children's rates are offered. Reservations are recommended, especially in high season.

BOATING

Two Medicine may be the highest lake you can drive to in the park; it may also very well be one of the windiest. Boaters need to keep an eye on the winds; if whitecaps pop up, consider getting off the lake. The public boat ramp is right at the end of Two Medicine Road. Hand-powered craft and motorized boats are allowed with 10 horsepower or less, but no jet skis, so the lake maintains a nice quiet. On calm days, kayakers and canoers tour the lake's shore; each of the lake's sides varies the view of surrounding peaks. On Lower Two Medicine Lake, you won't see many boats. Lack of a boat ramp and

no access trails preclude most people; it's hard to bushwhack carrying a kayak.

Glacier Park Boat Company (406/226-4467 summers only, 406/257-2426, www.glacierparkboats.com) rents canoes, kayaks, and small motorboats at the Two Medicine Boat Dock for $10–15 per hour. Take cash, because Glacier Park Boat Company does not take credit cards.

FISHING

Two Medicine River links together the three lakes by the same name with brook trout populating much of the waters. For fishing **Upper Two Medicine Lake,** hike two miles after taking the boat shuttle across Two Medicine Lake. It's an attractive lake to fish, but its shoreline is brushy and the outlet clogged with downed timbers. Anglers in **Two Medicine Lake** may have more success tossing in a line from a boat rather than fishing from shore—especially because much of the shoreline is heavily timbered and brushy. On the valley's south side, Paradise Creek harbors some trout, but Aster and Apistoki Creeks are void, so don't bother dropping a line in here. On the dam-controlled **Lower Two Medicine Lake,** which is half in the park, half on the Blackfeet Reservation, only a few anglers go after the 10- to 12-inch rainbows and brookies here; difficult access with no trails or official boat ramp keeps most anglers away. Other area lakes—No Name and Old Man—support trout, but Cobalt is barren.

Licenses and Regulations

No fishing license is required in the park, but pick up park fishing regulations at the ranger station in Two Medicine. Outside the park on Lower Two Medicine Lake or Two Medicine River, you will need a Tribal fishing permit. (See the *Background* chapter for details.) Purchase fishing licenses at Bear Track Travel Center (Exxon station in East Glacier, 20958 Hwy. 2, 406/226-5504, winter 7 A.M.– 8 P.M., summer 7 A.M.–10 P.M.).

GOLF

Built in 1927, the **Glacier Park Lodge Golf Course** (406/892-2525, www.glacierpark-inc.com, late May–early Oct.) is the oldest grass greens in Montana. The nine-hole course wanders through aspen groves with views of Dancing Lady, Henry, Calf Robe, and Summit peaks. Don't be surprised if bears (or more commonly stray dogs) roam across the course. Because the course is on Blackfeet tribal lands, each of the nine holes is named after former Blackfeet Nation chiefs—Rising Wolf, Bad Marriage, Long Time Sleeps, and Stabs-By-Mistake, to name a few. An 18-round costs $24. Clubs rent for $10–12 and power carts for $15–20. For tee times, call 406/226-5342 or the hotel front desk. The lodge often offers special spring and fall rates for golf-lodging packages; call or check on the website for details.

A public, nine-hole pitch-and-putt miniature golf course covers half of the front lawn of Glacier Park Lodge. Pick up clubs for $5 per person at the front desk. Ground squirrel holes make the course slightly challenging.

CROSS-COUNTRY SKIING

Late December–April, **Two Medicine Road** (15 miles round-trip) makes a delightfully easy but long ski, with frozen Two Medicine Lake as the destination, where snows pile up enough to bury the restrooms. While the going is not tough and the gentle terrain undulates except for one long hill, winds can scour the road free of snow in places, requiring skiers to take skis off and on, and headwinds frequently blow both directions. Nevertheless, it's a stunning trip, with relatively little avalanche danger.

When snow permits, skiing **Looking Glass Hill** on Highway 49 is also popular. An eight-mile round-trip tour leads from the junction with Two Medicine Road to spectacular overlooks of Two Medicine Valley and Lake Creek drainage with views on a clear day to Divide Mountain by St. Mary. Do not forget the camera on this trip! Sometimes winds blow the pavement bare, so be prepared to take skis off and put them on again.

No equipment rental is available in East Glacier; the nearest rentals are at the Izaak Walton Inn on the Theodore Roosevelt Highway and at Glacier Outdoor Center in West Glacier. Winter

shuts down East Glacier and much of the park, so be prepared for trips here. Do not venture out without a complete pack full of emergency gear, and be prepared to self-rescue.

ENTERTAINMENT

On selected summer evenings National Park Service naturalists present free 45-minute talks on natural history and wildlife in the Two Medicine Amphitheater, usually at 8 P.M. Once a week, the Native America Speaks program features storytellers who bring to life the history of local tribes and their involvement in Glacier. For a current schedule, pick up a copy of *The Glacier Explorer* at visitors centers and ranger stations.

Glacier Park Lodge sponsors entertainment from time to time—Native American speakers and entertainers as well as musicians, such as the Trapp Family Singers. Check the sign in the lobby near the front desk for the current schedule.

◖ North American Indian Days

Held over four days beginning the second Thursday in July, North American Indian Days is a celebration of Blackfeet culture. Located behind the Museum of the Plains Indian, the powwow grounds (4th Ave. NW and Boundary St.) in Browning become home to tipis. Dancing, drumming, singing, games, and sporting events draw tribes from the U.S. and Canada. Traditional costumes—especially those worn for fancy dances—are spectacular with feathered headdresses and beadwork. Non-native people are welcome to attend. It's one of the best ways around to learn about the Blackfeet and their culture, and watching is free. For details on the powwow, call the Blackfeet Nation Planning Department (406/338-7406).

Accommodations

East Glacier is divided in half by the railroad tracks. On one side, historic Glacier Park Lodge and the golf course sit on Highway 49 followed by a compact motel strip—think very rustic here, not a highway mega-strip—which ends abruptly within one mile. On the south side of the tracks along Highway 2, East Glacier tucks several motels within a few-block radius of restaurants. All of these fill to the brim in high season, so reservations are highly recommended. Two Medicine has no lodging available, only a campground.

EAST GLACIER
Lodges and Cabins

Historic ◖ **Glacier Park Lodge** (0.1 mile north on Hwy. 49, 406/892-2525, www.glacierparkinc.com, open late May–early Oct., until mid-June $129–179, after mid-June $140–299, chalet $349–449), right across from the train depot, is actually outside the park boundary on Blackfeet tribal land. It's the only historic lodge with a heated outdoor swimming pool, golf course, and pitch-and-putt. Rooms are in the main hotel or the west wing, connected by a scenic enclosed walkway. Although the rooms tend to be larger than in the other historic park hotels, the bathrooms are still small—tiny sinks and elbow-bonking shower stalls—many converted from closets. Get a room facing the mountains: You'll enjoy the sunrises and sunsets casting orange glows. You may want to bring earplugs; the lodge catches the rumble and clatter of passing trains.

Lodge rooms, suites, and family rooms are available, along with a chalet—all nonsmoking. Rooms have phones but no television air-conditioning, or elevator access. A restaurant, lounge, snack shop, and gift shop are off the lobby, and Remedies Day Spa offers massages for trail-weary muscles. Red bus tours depart from the hotel, and trail riding is across the street. Trails to Scenic Point and Firebrand Pass depart nearby, crossing reservation land before entering park boundaries. In the eve-

ning Native American speakers often give fireside talks. Reservations are highly recommended in June and September, an absolute must in July and August.

The newest addition to East Glacier in 2004 is **《 Traveler's Rest Lodge** (0.3 mile east of Exxon station on Hwy. 2, 406/226-9143, www.glacierinfo.com, May–Sept., $85–95), which has very clean, roomy nonsmoking log mortise and tenon cabins with gas fireplaces and fully equipped kitchenettes on eight acres amid aspen trees. Each is positioned for its deck to gain privacy and views of the Bob Marshall Wilderness. The nicely decorated cabins sleeping 2–4 people in log-hewn beds have televisions and CD players but no phones. (One is available in the office.) Because of East Glacier's frequent "boil orders" for water, each cabin is equipped with five gallons of drinking water. The owners, Diane and Bob Scalese, have their engraving workshop in one of the cabins—they are well-known artisans who design, craft, and engrave spurs, bits, belt buckles, and saddle silver. They'll gladly show you their work.

Motels

East Glacier has seven small motels, some with cabins, all with convenient access to restaurants and stores. Four small seasonal (May–Sept.) ones line Highway 49's motel strip north of Glacier Park Lodge. The area hops in high summer, but highway traffic virtually disappears at night. You can hear a bit of train noise although the motels are shielded from the tracks by trees. Three other year-round motels sit in "downtown" East Glacier. While highway noise dwindles at night, train noise here does not. Advance reservations in high season are a wise idea.

Sitting right on Highway 2 across from the train depot, **Glacier Park Circle R Motel** (402 Hwy. 2 E., 406/226-9331, www.circlermotel.com, open year-round, summer $43–112; late Sept.–June $50–60) opens its older motel units in which smoking is permitted only in summer. Year-round, however, the newer non-smoking units with cable television and Inter-

net hookups offer great second-floor views of Dancing Lady peak. One suite has a full kitchen and air-conditioning.

A half block off of Highway 2, **Dancing Bears Inn** (40 Montana Ave., 406/226-4402, open year-round, summer $75–99; winter $50–55) is a bit more sheltered from train and highway clamor. Rooms offer Internet access, air-conditioning, and cable television, and some have kitchenettes.

Guesthouses

Artists may enjoy renting a room from a professional potter and sculptor at **The Brown House** (402 Washington St., 406/226-9385, www.glacierinfo.com, June–Sept., $55–60), which has two remodeled rooms for three people, each with private entrance and bath. The upstairs room has a view of the park's peaks, while the downstairs room is furnished with antiques. Originally a 1920s store, the building still has some of the fixtures from that era.

Timber Frame Guest Houses (1017 4th Ave., 406/226-9119, www.glacierinfo.com, year-round, $600–800 per week) often books up early. Near the golf course and within walking distance to restaurants, both modern homes have fully equipped kitchens, bedding, televisions, VCRs, picnic tables, large yards, and a couple of bicycles. The two-bedroom Morning Star unit has queen beds, 1.5 baths, a gas fireplace, and a barbecue grill. The one-bedroom Sinopah has a queen bed, a loft with two twin beds, and one bathroom.

Hostels

For the budget-minded, East Glacier has two hostels open May–September. **《 Backpacker's Inn** (29 Dawson Ave., 406/226-9392) has three dorms, plus two cabins located in the back yard of Serrano's Mexican Restaurant—a little oasis in the middle of town. The buildings are the renovated original pre-fab cedar Sears and Roebuck 1920 homes. Beds in the dorm rooms are $10 per person per night; bring your own sleeping bag ($1 to rent a bag). The cabins with one queen bed with linens rent for $20–30.

TWO MEDICINE

On the Highway 49 motel strip, **Brownie's Hostel** (1020 Hwy. 49, 406/226-4426) is in an old renovated two-story 1920s building. An easy six-block walk from the train station and adjacent to restaurants, the hostel has three dorms with beds at $13 per night and a fully equipped communal kitchen. Private bedrooms are also available ($26–38). The hostel sits above a bakery, deli, and convenience store with Internet access.

CAMPING

RVers requiring hookups will need to stay in East Glacier, for the park service campgrounds in Two Medicine and Cut Bank have no hookups. If these are full, check the *Theodore Roosevelt Highway* chapter for alternatives, such as Summit (11 miles) or Glacier Meadow RV Park (17 miles).

Cut Bank

Located 19 miles north of East Glacier off Highway 89, **Cut Bank Campground** (406/888-7800, late May–late Sept., $12 per night) sits at the end of a four-mile potholed dirt road inside Glacier Park. To locate the access road, look for the campground sign six miles north of Kiowa Junction. The campground is rustic with only pit toilets, pump water, and fire grates. Bring your own firewood; gathering is prohibited. With only 19 sites set in deep shade under large firs, it's a great place to escape crowds and large RVs that shouldn't attempt the rough access road. The campground has fishing in Atlantic Creek and the trailhead to Medicine Grizzly Lake and Triple Divide Pass nearby.

Two Medicine

Inside Glacier, **(Two Medicine Campground** (406/888-7800, late May–mid-Sept., $15) has great views of bears foraging on Rising Wolf Mountain, especially from the A and C loops. The campground is set back from Two Medicine Lake, surrounding the calmer waters of small Pray Lake, a good place for swimming and fishing. With 99 sites, the campground fills up in high season, but often not as early in the day as those on Going-to-the-Sun Road;

try to claim a campsite by early afternoon as they are first-come, first-serve. Flush toilets, a dump station, picnic tables, and fire grates are provided—bring your own firewood. (Gathering it is prohibited.) The north shore trail departs right from the campground. A seven-minute walk or few-minute drive puts you at the boat tour and rental dock, and the Two Medicine Campstore can cover what you've forgotten. Only 13 sites can handle RVs up to 32 feet. In late September and October, the campground allows primitive camping ($6) with no running water and pit toilets.

East Glacier

A small campground set in East Glacier, **Y Lazy R RV Park** (corner of Lindhe Ave. and Meade St., 406/226-5505, June–mid-Sept., tents $14, hookups $18) is two blocks off Highway 2. With grassy sites and a few aspen trees, its open setting affords great views of surrounding mountains. Amenities include flush toilets, picnic tables, coin-op showers, and a large laundry. The campground is an easy few-blocks walk to restaurants.

Browning

Located 2.25 miles west of Browning on a prairie wildflower knoll staring at Glacier's peaks, the **(Lodgepole Gallery and Tipi Village** (look for sign on Hwy. 89, 406/338-2787, www.blackfeetculturecamp.com, May–mid-Sept.) is strikingly different—and not just because a small herd of nearly extinct Spanish mustangs, the original Indian horse, runs free on the property (they're not for riding, just for watching). Ten traditional double-walled canvas tipis with a fire pit inside each serve as tents. Supplied wood heats the tipis on cooler nights. You bring your sleeping bag, air mattress, and flashlight; if you don't have them, you can rent them for $6 (the sleeping bags come with linen). A central bathhouse with flush toilets and hot showers services all the tipis. Overnight rates ($45 for first person in tipi, $15 each additional person, $10 for kids under 12) include a continental breakfast.

For guests staying at the tipi village, meals

by reservation are also available in the dining hall (full American breakfast $10–12, lunch $10–12, dinner $15–30). Traditional southern Blackfeet cuisine—gourmet buffalo, deer, and elk—puts a different delicious twist on dinner.

Owner Darrell Norman, a native Blackfeet artist, singer, and dancer, also teaches art classes in the adjacent gallery; you can learn to make your own drum or fetish. He also guides tours to buffalo jumps and medicine rocks.

Food

Because Two Medicine has no restaurants, you'll have to hit East Glacier to go out to eat. However, the drive between the two is short, and in the evening, driving back into Two Medicine can be a good time to spot wildlife. During special days like graduation and North American Indian Days on the Blackfeet Reservation, none of the restaurants or bars serve alcohol. The four-day celebration is usually scheduled beginning the second Thursday in July. During that time, all alcohol sales in restaurants, lounges, and grocery stores are banned on tribal lands—including all restaurants in East Glacier.

RESTAURANTS
East Glacier
In the historic Glacier Park Lodge, the **Great Northern Steak and Rib House** (on Hwy. 49 across from train depot, 406/892-2525, late May–early Oct.) is known more for its views than its cuisine. Ask to be seated near the west windows facing Dancing Lady Mountain: The sunrise smears it with pink and the sunset sky lights up overhead. The restaurant serves up three meals per day in a nonsmoking atmosphere. Like all the historic park lodges, breakfast (6:30–9:30 A.M., $5–9) is a large buffet with fruit, pastries, and entrees such as eggs, sausage, bacon, French toast, and pancakes. While selections are broad and you won't walk away hungry, the mass-produced entrees are sometimes only lukewarm. Order à la carte, if you prefer. Lunch is served 11:30 A.M.–2 P.M. ($6–9). Dinners (5–9:30 P.M., $15–24) specialize in steak, chicken, and ribs. No reservations are taken for groups smaller than 12 people, so sometimes you'll need to wait in

high season for a table. The restaurant also makes hiker lunches ($7–10); order these one day in advance.

Adjacent to the restaurant, the **The Sunset Lounge** serves up Montana microbrews along with wines and cocktails with a terrific view of Dancing Lady and Mount Henry. If you need to watch a television, this is the place to go. For a quick, light meal in a nonsmoking atmosphere, the appetizers and sandwiches ($6–9) are served 2–10 P.M., but the bar is open 11:30 A.M.–midnight.

Waiting lines on the front porch of **Serrano's Mexican Restaurant** (29 Dawson Ave., 406/226-9293, May–Sept., daily 5–10 P.M.) attest to its good food. Most dinners run $8–12 with the made-from-scratch Veggie Delight (yes, there's great vegetarian Mexican food) and Colorado Plates topping the choices, and the chiles rellenos use freshly roasted chiles. Huge plate-loads of food pacify hungry hikers. The smoke-free building is the oldest house in East Glacier; you can eat inside in its cozy dining room with wooden booths or sit on the deck out back while watching sunset. Either way, the margaritas here are easy to down.

Inexpensive **Two Medicine Grill** (316 Hwy. 2, 406/226-5572, open year-round, daily 6:30 A.M.–9 P.M., but closes Oct.–April at 7 P.M.) is a good place to grab a bagel breakfast sandwich ($4), an espresso, or a buffalo burger ($5). This small hole-in-the-wall diner was built in 1935 in Choteau and moved to East Glacier. They bake their own cinnamon rolls and serve hard ice cream and a wild huckleberry milkshake. To jaw with the cook, sit at one of the eight stools at the bar in front of

TWO MEDICINE

the grill. Dinners feature all your favorite good greasy spoon foods and run up to $14.

Offering outdoor seating when the weather permits, **(The Restaurant Thimbleberry** (1112 Hwy. 49, 406/226-5523, mid May–Sept., daily 6:30 A.M.–10 P.M.) warns diners by calling itself a "slow food restaurant." This doesn't mean the service is slow, just that the food isn't precooked. The nonsmoking restaurant is a cozy place with split log booths. Breakfast pancakes (huckleberry pancakes $6) come in one size—huge! Only two people in the history of the restaurant have completely finished their full stack. Sandwiches for lunch or dinner run $4–7. The specialty dinner is boneless melt-in-your-mouth St. Mary whitefish ($15) served with Indian frybread. Although the restaurant does not serve beer and wine, you may bring your own to accompany dinner.

Run by the same owners of Brownie's (see *Groceries*), the **(Whistle Stop Restaurant** (0.5 mile north on Hwy. 49, 406/226-9292, June–Sept., 7 A.M.–9 P.M.) sits in a funky rickety-looking old building with outside seating in good weather. The breakfast specialty is stuffed French toast, which is crammed with huckleberries or hazelnut-vanilla filling ($6). For kids, the Grizzly Paw French toast is served with chocolate sauce. Sandwiches for lunch or dinner run $5–7. The house dinner features barbecue ribs and chicken in different styles and portions ($12–19). Beer and wine are available.

GROCERIES

On the shore of Two Medicine Lake at the terminus of Two Medicine Road, **Two Medicine Campstore** (406/892-2525, mid-June–mid-Sept. 7 A.M.–9 P.M.) now operates in what used to be the historic dining hall for Two Medicine Chalets. It sells limited groceries, camping and hiking supplies, newspapers, maps, gifts, books, beer, wine, ice, and ice cream. Hikers

can build a trail lunch from convenience items sold here.

In East Glacier, three small stores sell groceries; don't expect them to carry every brand available. Open year-round, **Glacier Park Trading Company** (314 Hwy. 2, 406/226-4433, summer 8 A.M.–9 P.M., winter 9 A.M.–8 P.M.) sells fresh veggies, dairy products, wine, meat, and staples. It also carries a broad selection of Montana microbrews. The deli makes sandwiches ($5–6), good for hiker lunches, and pizzas to go. On the east end of East Glacier and also open year-round, **Bear Track Travel Center** (Exxon station, 20958 Hwy. 2, 406/226-5504, winter 7 A.M.–8 P.M., summer 7 A.M.–10 P.M.) sells convenience store foods, ice, firewood, camping and fishing supplies, beer and wine, propane, and fishing licenses.

In the same building that houses a hostel and a grocery, **Brownie's Bakery and Deli** (0.5 mile north on Hwy. 49, 406/226-4426, 7 A.M.–9 P.M. June–Sept.) is an everything place—a bakery, a deli, a convenience store, an ice cream shop, an espresso stand, and an Internet cafe ($3.50 for 30 minutes). It's a great place to pick up a deli sandwich ($5, a PBJ is only $3) for hiking or grab a light breakfast of muffins or bagels. Daily, the bakery churns out freshly baked cookies and brownies.

If you need a larger grocery store, you'll have to head to Browning, 12 miles east of East Glacier on Highway 2.

PICNIC AREA

Two Medicine has the only picnic area, adjacent to the campground. It sits in a great spot right on the shore of Two Medicine Lake amid cottonwoods with running water and flush toilets. Most the sites have some trees, which provide a good windbreak on howling days and shade on hot days. Sites include a picnic table and fire grate, but bring your own firewood. (It's illegal to gather firewood here.)

THEODORE ROOSEVELT HIGHWAY

Located on a highway that runs 2,119 miles from Minnesota to Washington, Marias Pass and Essex get lost in the parade of towns and cities that speckle U.S. Highway 2, otherwise known as Theodore Roosevelt Highway. Small mountain cabin enclaves are part of the charm of this 57-mile road, which runs through John F. Stevens Canyon between East Glacier and West Glacier. Both Marias Pass and Essex gained their notoriety through the railroad: Marias Pass as the pass the railroad chose to cross the Continental Divide; Essex as a train community to work the tracks. The history of this Rocky Mountain corridor, as much as its scenery, adds to its appeal.

The highway, open year-round, accesses some of the wildest country around. With 1.5 million acres of the Bob Marshall Wilderness Complex to the south and Glacier's 1 million acres to the north, the road passes through the largest grizzly bear habitat in the Lower 48. The Wild and Scenic Middle Fork of the Flathead River races through its canyon, where mountain goats mass in search of minerals and where bighorn sheep and elk winter. From this passageway, hikers and horseback riders depart on adventures both north and south of the canyon into the heart of the wild interior of northwest Montana.

HISTORY
Marias Pass

When Lewis and Clark passed through Montana in 1805, they failed to find Marias Pass. They came within 25 miles, but swung south on the Missouri River to cross the Continental

© BECKY LOMAX

HIGHLIGHTS

◖ Marias Pass: Too bad Lewis and Clark didn't discover one of the lowest passes through the Continental Divide. Their trip might have been much easier (page 166)!

◖ Lewis Overthrust Fault: Glacier's geology is remarkable, with the 65-million-year-old Lewis Overthrust pushing older rock on top of much younger layers. See this stone story in the cliff face along Summit and Little Dog mountains (page 166).

◖ Goat Lick: During spring and early summer, mountain goats congregate here for its minerals. Bring your binoculars to see the shaggy white beasts strutting across death-defying cliffs (page 167).

◖ Izaak Walton Inn: Far from its original mission housing Great Northern Railway workers, the historic hotel now attracts train aficionados, cross-country skiers, and those looking for something a bit different (page 168).

◖ Firebrand Pass: A gentle uphill climb through wildflowers makes you want to break out in songs from *The Sound of Music* (page 170).

◖ Stanton Lake and Grant Ridge Loop: In the Great Bear Wilderness, this hike gives one of the best panoramic views of the park's southern monoliths—Stimson, Jackson, and St. Nicholas (page 172).

◖ Rafting and Kayaking: This is one of the best ways to see the Middle Fork of the Flathead River, especially the Goat Lick, as you stare up at the nimble creatures cavorting along the cliffs (page 173).

◖ Autumn Creek Trail: With easy winter accessibility, cross-country skiing launches onto trails where few people are. This trail carries you beneath the ramparts of Marias Pass (page 175).

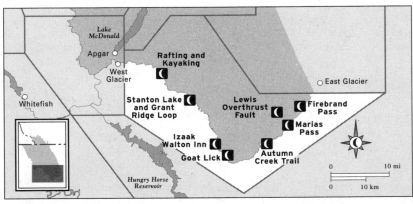

LOOK FOR ◖ TO FIND RECOMMENDED SIGHTS, ACTIVITIES, DINING, AND LODGING.

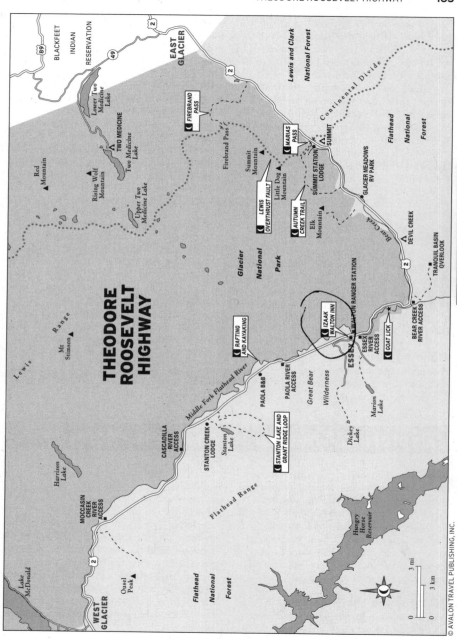

Divide on a much higher and more difficult pass. Lewis named the Marias River, christening it "Maria's River" after his cousin. The apostrophe got lost through history, much like the pass with the same name.

Reports of a "lost" pass filtered through the ranks of fur traders and mountain men. Government-funded expeditions went looking, but to no avail. But, mountain men and Native Americans wandered through the real Marias Pass—yet "undiscovered." Rumors of the pass reached Great Northern Railroad developer J. J. Hill, prompting him to dispatch a railroad engineer named John F. Stevens and his Flathead guide Coonsa to see if the fable was true. While temperatures plummeted to 40 degrees below zero in December 1889, the pair traveled on rawhide snowshoes through deep snow. Unable to slog on, Coonsa stayed behind with a fire as Stevens ventured on alone. He found the lost pass and deemed it appropriate for the railroad crossing. Within two years, Hill pushed the railroad across the Continental Divide at Marias Pass in his press to complete his transcontinental railway.

Building a Highway

As auto travel claimed Americans, the demand for a road through John F. Stevens Canyon rose to a clamor. To transport an auto over the Con-

tinental Divide, you had to cough up $12.50 to put your car on a Great Northern Railway flatbed. While building Going-to-the-Sun Road dragged on for 20 years, the road over Marias Pass went through in a jiffy. Finished in 1930, the Theodore Roosevelt Highway over Marias Pass was simply much easier than the trek through cliffs over Logan Pass.

Lodges

In 1906 as one of its early depots, Great Northern Railway built Summit Station at Marias Pass. When Glacier Park Lodge and its depot in East Glacier attracted more tourists, Summit was vacant. In 1985, it was moved to its current location and converted into the Summit Station Lodge.

In 1939, Great Northern Railway constructed Izaak Walton Inn to house railroad workers who cleared the tracks of snow in winter. The railroad planned to convert it to guest lodging when the park service built a southern road entrance into Glacier. When the Depression and World War II sent park visitation plummeting, the park scrapped the south entrance. Today, Glacier's southern valleys remain remote bastions of wilderness, accessible only by trail. The building eventually became an inn, but not under Great Northern Railway's umbrella.

Exploring Theodore Roosevelt Highway

With 2.5 million acres of public lands surrounding U.S. Highway 2—Glacier National Park, Lewis and Clark National Forest, Flathead National Forest, and the Bob Marshall Wilderness Complex—only small strips of private parcels line the valley floor. The result is a necklace of tiny mountain communities, none barely large enough to warrant the title of "town." Truly, if you blink, you will miss them.

Maintaining the Highway

The Theodore Roosevelt Highway is considerably easier to maintain than Going-to-the-Sun

Road. It is wider, more gradual, and for the most part, follows a fairly long, gentle 2,000-foot ascent from West Glacier to Marias Pass. However, even though Marias Pass is 1,500 feet lower than Logan Pass, the road still has its share of winter difficulties. While plows clear and sand the road frequently to keep it passable for winter travel, cornices thousands of feet above break loose, sending avalanches pelting down across its path. Some winters the highway is closed for several days while road crews clear a path through ice, rock, and tree debris.

TOURS AND SHUTTLES

Glacier's historic red buses run by **Glacier Park, Inc.** (406/892-2525 www.glacierparkinc.com, May–Sept.) tour Marias Pass from Glacier Park Lodge. For details on these tours, check the *Two Medicine and East Glacier* chapter.

No hiker shuttles run across Highway 2. You either have to drive yourself to trailheads or use your thumb (which is legal in Montana). To set up a point-to-point hike, **Flathead-Glacier Transportation** (406/892-3390 or 800/829-7039, www.fgtrans.com) can accommodate backpackers by reservation, dropping you off at one trailhead and picking you up at another several days later. Rates ($32–110 one-way) can be split among all people in your party. However, it's rather pricey for a round-trip day-hike shuttle.

SERVICES

Gas stations have all closed down on Highway 2 between East Glacier and West Glacier. Fill up in either of those towns before you leave.

This is not a road where the usual expectancies of civilization are readily available, nor where you'll find newspaper stands on every corner. In fact, you won't find any. For newspapers, ATMs, a post office, laundry, and anything resembling espresso, you'll need to head to East or West Glacier. For hot showers ($5), you can pop in to Glacier Meadow RV Park.

The nearest Internet services are also in East and West Glacier. In between the two towns, Internet services are just making in-roads. Campers at Glacier Meadow RV Park have access to wireless Internet, but as of 2005, other campgrounds and lodges did not. Because of John F. Stevens Canyon and surrounding steep mountains, you won't find much cell reception on Theodore Roosevelt Highway, but you can stop to use old-fashioned public pay telephones at Stanton Creek Lodge, Izaak Walton Inn, and Snow Slip Inn.

Emergencies

On the west side of the Continental Divide, the nearest hospitals are in Flathead Valley

25 minutes from West Glacier—Kalispell Regional Medical Center (310 Sunny View Ln, Kalispell, 406/752-5111) and North Valley Hospital (6575 Hwy. 93 S., Whitefish, 406/863-2501). On the east side, the nearest hospital is the Northern Rockies Medical Center (802 2nd St. E., Cut Bank, 406/873-2251) 46 miles from East Glacier. In an emergency, especially along the Middle Fork of the Flathead River, just get to a phone and call 911.

The **Walton Ranger Station** (milepost 180.5, 406/888-7800), at Walton on the southernmost tip of Glacier National Park, is adjacent to the Walton Picnic Area and the trailheads to Scalplock, Ole Creek, and the wild Nyack Loop. The station is staffed only in summer, and not full time, as the rangers here patrol miles of backcountry trails. If you need assistance, use the pay phone at Izaak Walton Inn 0.8 mile west to call Glacier Park Headquarters (406/888-7800).

The **Hungry Horse Ranger Station** (milepost 143.1 on Hwy. 2, 406/387-3800) nine miles west of West Glacier has maps, guidebooks, and information on rafting and floating in the Great Bear Wilderness.

DRIVING TOUR
Theodore Roosevelt Highway

After driving the dramatic Going-to-the-Sun Road, most visitors are less than impressed with Theodore Roosevelt Highway. You can drive the highway (Hwy. 2) from East Glacier to West Glacier in a little over an hour. Locals use the road as a faster route across the Continental Divide when too many cars clog Going-to-the-Sun Road. All large RVs and trailers use it as they are precluded from driving Going-to-the-Sun Road. In spite of its use as a year-round thoroughfare, it still is a scenic highway. Drive it from either direction: from East or West Glacier.

Public restrooms with flush toilets are few and far between on this highway. Pit and vault toilets, however, are available at Marias Pass, the Goat Lick, Walton Picnic Area, and all river accesses. Usually, these are open late

PUBLIC LANDS: WHAT'S THE DIFFERENCE?

Many people are confused by the various types of public lands. In the greater Glacier ecosystem, national park lands border national forest and wilderness area. So what do these mean?

National parks, national forests, and wilderness areas are each managed differently with different purposes:

National parks fall under the U.S. Department of the Interior. Parks are predominantly set aside for their historical, geological, cultural, or biological significance, and geared toward public recreation. Hunting is not permitted, nor is picking wildflowers or berries for commercial use. Mining and logging are also taboo. Leases for developing recreational lands are not available. Dogs are not allowed on trails, and neither are mountain bikes. Permits are needed for backcountry camping.

National forests come under the jurisdiction of the U.S. Department of Agriculture. Their purpose is different. Under permit, hunting, timber harvesting, and commercial berry picking are generally allowed. National forest land is leased for recreational development, such as ski areas. Your pooch can go with you on hikes, and you can mountain bike as long as no special designation says otherwise. Permits are not needed for backcountry camping.

Wilderness areas are administered usually by the national forest that contains the wilderness boundaries. Two concepts set wilderness apart: no mechanical transports and no permanent human inhabitants. Wilderness areas do not have roads inside them. While hunting is permitted and Fido can go along on the trail, mountain biking is not allowed. Permits are not needed for backcountry camping.

---

spring through fall; in winter, you're out of luck, unless you stop at Izaak Walton Inn.

Montana has an oddity on its highways—white crosses. And as you may guess, these mark fatalities. One cross equals one traffic fatality. Begun in 1953, the American Legion–sponsored program operates in conjunction with the Montana Department of Transportation to use the crosses as safety reminders. An estimated 2,000 sobering crosses line the state's highways, several on this highway.

SIGHTS

Theodore Roosevelt Highway sights are listed here from East Glacier to West Glacier.

Lewis and Clark National Forest

From just south of East Glacier to the Continental Divide, the Theodore Roosevelt Highway passes through the Lewis and Clark National Forest. Its 1.7 million acres serve as the headwaters for the mighty Missouri River. High prairies at 4,500 feet in elevation climb up to Rocky Mountain Peak at 9,362 feet along the Rocky Mountain Front in an extremely di-

verse ecosystem that harbors species of concern like lynx and grizzly bears.

◖ Marias Pass

At 5,220 feet, Marias Pass (milepost 197.9) is the lowest Continental Divide saddle north of New Mexico. Two monuments mark the pass: A statue of John F. Stevens commemorates his discovery of the passage, and a tall obelisk stands in memory of Theodore Roosevelt for whom the highway is named. Legend has it that he visited Many Glacier in 1910, but no official records indicate so. The 3,100-mile Continental Divide Trail crosses into Glacier National Park here where hikers and skiers launch onto Autumn Creek Trail. If signs and the monuments weren't here, you'd be hard pressed to realize you were crossing the Continental Divide, what with the area's broad flat forest.

◖ Lewis Overthrust Fault

Opposite Marias Pass, the Lewis Overthrust Fault shoved older 1.6-billion-year-old rocks on top of 80-million-year-old stones. This

© BECKY LOMAX

The Lewis Overthrust Fault is visible on Summit Mountain at Marias Pass.

fault exposed some of the oldest sediments in the world—ancient Precambrian rocks that formed as Belt Sea sediments solidified. On the face of Summit and Little Dog Peaks, look for an obvious upward line where the younger Cretaceous rock from the dinosaur age shows up as black or brown. This is the site where in the 1890s geologists discovered the Lewis Overthrust Fault, which extends into Canada and sets Glacier apart as a World Heritage Site.

Silver Stairs Falls

Tumbling thousands of feet from Tranquil Basin, an unmarked and unsigned pullout on the highway's south side stares up at Silver Stairs Falls (milepost 188.2). The waterfall cascades down a series of stairsteps created from eroding sedimentary layers. In June and July, water rages down in torrents, but by late August it slows to a trickle. You can catch quick views in a drive-by, but with alder and brush surrounding the falls, you'll get a better view by stopping.

C Goat Lick

Much of Glacier National Park's wildlife tends to be mineral deficient. Because their bodies crave minerals from their winter-deprived condition, during spring and early summer mountain goats congregate at the Goat Lick (milepost 182.6). The lick is actually a huge mass of gray rock cliffs, an exposed fault containing salts like calcium, magnesium, and potassium. Goats hop sure-footed along the steep cliff faces as if they were on flat land to slurp the minerals. Located approximately three miles south of Essex, the well-marked overlook has a couple of viewing areas with interpretive signs. Bring your binoculars or scopes for better viewing.

Bob Marshall Wilderness Complex

While Glacier rises to the north of the highway, to the south the Bob Marshall Wilderness Complex spans nearly 1.5 million acres. It actually comprises three wilderness areas: The Bob (as locals call it), the Great Bear, and the Scapegoat. The Great Bear is the section bordering

BOB MARSHALL WILDERNESS COMPLEX

The largest wilderness area in Montana, the Bob Marshall Wilderness straddles one million acres along 60 miles of the Continental Divide. With peaks reaching to 9,000 feet high, the wilderness's remote valleys are home to predators like lynx, grizzlies, black bears, mountain lions, and wolves and a huge ungulate population of deer, elk, moose, mountain goats, and bighorn sheep. Over 1,000 miles of trails crisscross its ranges. Its largest feature is the 1,000-foot-high Chinese Wall, a 22-mile-long escarpment on the Continental Divide.

It's named for Bob Marshall, a young forester who became a local legend in 1925 with marathon 30-mile mountain treks around the Missoula area. Later, he penned *The Problem of Wilderness*, a treatise defining principles that would shape the movement to preserve America's wilds, and in a one-man crusade as the Forest Service's Lands Division chief, he placed 5.4 million acres of vulnerable lands under wilderness protection. Along with Aldo Leopold and others, he launched the Wilderness Society in 1935 but died at age 38 four years later.

In 1941, the South Fork, Pentagon, and Sun River areas were set aside as primitive zones. But finally in 1964, after 10 years and 66 drafts, the Wilderness Act defined wilderness as "untrammeled lands" and protected them from development. As part of the act, the three primitive zone areas combined to create the **Bob Marshall Wilderness.**

Adding 239,936 acres to the complex, the **Scapegoat Wilderness** was recognized in 1972 after an unprecedented citizen lobby started by a hardware store owner from Lincoln. Ajoining the Bob Marshall's south end, Scapegoat houses 50 miles of the 3,100-mile-long Continental Divide Trail.

Six years later, a third wilderness was added to the complex – the **Great Bear Wilderness,** adjoining its 286,700 acres of land to the Bob Marshall. Tucked between Hungry Horse Reservoir and Glacier National Park, the Great Bear houses 300 miles of trail and tops out at 8,700 feet on Great Northern, the sweeping peak seen from the north Flathead Valley.

Together these three wilderness areas comprise 1.5 million acres of roadless lands. Along with Glacier Park's one million acres, the areas create a corridor for threatened species such as grizzly bears, lynx, and wolves. As the wilderness complex falls in four national forests, it is managed jointly by Flathead, Lewis and Clark, Lolo, and Helena National Forests.

Highway 2. The Bob Marshall was one of the country's first wilderness areas, dedicated in 1964 concurrent with the Wilderness Act. Scapegoat was added in 1972 and Great Bear six years later. While roads do not enter the wilderness areas and mechanized vehicles are prohibited (no mountain bikes or snowmobiles), a plethora of trails lead off Highway 2. Short day hikes access the Great Bear, while longer overnight treks reach The Bob, a world-class area for horse packing, fishing, and big-game hunting.

◖ Izaak Walton Inn

Historic Izaak Walton Inn (milepost 179.7) sits opposite the southernmost point of Glacier National Park at Essex. The hotel stands adjacent to the train tracks just off Highway 2. It attracts train aficionados, cross-country skiers, and those looking for something a bit different, like sleeping in a renovated caboose. Loaded with historical photos and memorabilia, the inn makes you feel almost like you've been transported back to a different era. In the downstairs bar, check out photos of avalanches burying the railroad tracks. Eat lunch on Great Northern Railway plates in the small dining room, and cozy up to the warm lobby fire.

John F. Stevens Canyon

Named for the Great Northern Railway engineer who verified the feasibility of Marias Pass as a railroad route, John F. Stevens Canyon begins just west of the pass and follows Bear Creek and the Middle Fork of the Flathead

until its terminus near West Glacier. Highway 2 and the railroad traverse the canyon's entire 40-mile distance. In places, the canyon broadens into wide valleys; in others it tightens up into narrow channels, frothing with wild waters. Although its more dramatic sections are seen best from a raft or kayak on the river, several highway pullouts still offer good photo ops.

Flathead National Forest

From the Continental Divide west past Flathead Valley and extending 120 miles south of the Canadian border, Flathead National Forest is broken up by state and private land but still tallies up a healthy 2.3 million acres. Within its glaciated mountains, it has 2,600 miles of trails. Over 46 percent of the forest is designated wilderness area. Spruce, Douglas fir, lodgepole, larch, and pine cover its slopes—home to wolverines, grizzly bears, and wolves.

Middle Fork of the Flathead River

Draining Glacier National Park and the Bob Marshall Wilderness Complex, the Middle Fork of the Flathead River is no small tributary. Designated a Wild and Scenic River, its 95-mile length is known for some of the best white-water rafting and kayaking in Montana. Dropping at 35 feet per mile, the Great Bear section teems with Class III and IV rapids; the lower waters break up long scenic floats with Class II and III rapids with such names as Jaws and Bonecrusher. Hook up with one of the four West Glacier rafting companies to explore its waves.

Wintering Range

Belton Mountain, to the road's north, is quite a different ecosystem from the heavily forested slopes on the south side. Fires, winds, and a dry exposure have minimized forest growth. Winds create a lower snowpack and south-facing slopes melt off early—both keys to making the area a prime wintering range (milepost 155–157) for ungulates such as deer, elk, and bighorn sheep. Grizzly and black bears also forage on its slopes. Even in summer, pull over at one of the several pullouts to scan the slopes with binoculars.

ROOSEVELT HIGHWAY

© BECKY LOMAX

historic Izaak Walton Inn in Essex, between Glacier National Park and Great Bear Wilderness

Recreation

HIKING

The Theodore Roosevelt Highway is one road where hiker shuttles are not available; you must get to trailheads on your own! Most of Glacier's trails on the south end are long valley hikes accessing little used areas. Additional short hikes, mostly in the Great Bear Wilderness, fill out the options—especially for hikers with Fido. While trails within Glacier do not allow dogs, your canine friend can tag along on a leash in the wilderness areas. Be aware, however, that hiking with pets in bear country poses certain dilemmas; a dog will not protect you from a bear encounter.

While trails within Glacier National Park are well-signed and frequently maintained, trails in the wilderness areas are not; signs, if any, may be just a wooden trail number or name nailed to a tree—no mileages. Take a good topographical map, which you can purchase from the Hungry Horse Ranger Station (milepost 143.1 on Hwy. 2, 406/387-3800), and know how to read it! Be prepared to encounter deadfall, downed trees, and heavy brush. Trail crews in the national forests do not have the staff numbers of the national park trail crews; it takes them longer to get to damaged or buried trails. Contrary to Glacier, bear warning signage does not exist except in extreme cases. Make noise and take precautions in bear country.

Hikes are listed here from east to west on Highway 2.

◖ Firebrand Pass

- Distance: 9.6 miles round-trip
- Duration: 4.5 hours
- Elevation gain: 2,210 feet
- Effort: moderate
- Trailhead: at milepost 203 on Highway 2

From the trailhead, the path wanders by beaver ponds, crosses into Glacier Park, passes the old Lubec ranger station site, and follows Coonsa Creek northward. At 1.4 miles, turn right at the Autumn Creek Trail junction and ascend gently through aspens and meadows thick in July with valerian, lupine, paintbrush, and penstemon to another junction about one mile later. Take a left here, gaining elevation as the trail circumvents Calf Robe's lower slopes. Make noise, for this is great bear country.

As the trail breaks completely out of the trees, you'll have views of Dancing Lady and East Glacier. The trail rounds Calf Robe into a hanging basin and then ascends to the pass, where you can look down Ole Creek and into Glacier's remote southern peaks. Scrambles up Calf Robe or Red Crow lend even better views, but don't go off trail unless you're ready to deal with steep scree hillsides.

Elk Mountain

- Distance: 7 miles round-trip
- Duration: 4 hours
- Elevation gain: 3,355 feet
- Effort: strenuous
- Trailhead: Turn north off Highway 2 at Fielding (milepost 192) and follow the dirt road #1066 about 0.5 mile to the trailhead.

Hike up through private logged land to the railroad tracks and cross into Glacier Park. The trail starts off deceptively easy enough, but shortly after turning right at the junction near a ranger cabin, the trail climbs and climbs. Steep does come close to describing the pitch as it ascends to an open saddle. No wonder you have so much solitude here. From here, you can see the remainder of the trail, climbing sharply again across a talus slope to the summit.

From the top, among debris from what was once the lookout, the views make the grunt worthwhile. Panoramas both north and south line up peak tops for miles into Glacier's re-

mote southern sector and the Bob Marshall Wilderness Complex. A knife ridge leads east toward the Continental Divide, and the view down Autumn Creek is dizzying.

Scalplock Lookout

- Distance: 9.4 miles round-trip
- Duration: 4.5 hours
- Elevation gain: 3,079 feet
- Effort: strenuous
- Trailhead: Walton Picnic Area (milepost 180.5)

This can be a gorgeous July hike, with bluebells in the high meadows, but be prepared for snow on top in June. Beginning in the Walton Picnic Area, the trail wanders along the Middle Fork of the Flathead in the first mile, crossing Ole Creek on a swinging bridge over a small gorge and ascending to the Ole Creek trail. Turn west on this trail for 0.4 mile to a second junction where the climb begins. In the remaining three miles, the trail ascends switchbacks at nearly 1,000 feet per mile.

The only respites from the relentless ascent are periodic peek-a-boo views of the Middle Fork of the Flathead River. Near the top, the trail breaks out of the trees to climb up a ridge flanked with wildflower meadows. At the top, Scalplock Lookout has a commanding view of the entire Middle Fork drainage, and the Mount St. Nicholas spire is in your face.

Marion Lake

- Distance: 3.4 miles round-trip
- Duration: 2 hours
- Elevation gain: 1,810 feet
- Effort: short, but strenuous
- Trailhead: Turn south on the Dickey Lake Road (milepost 178.7) at Essex and follow the left fork 2.3 miles to the Flathead National Forest signed trailhead.

COAL-NYACK LOOP

Remote doesn't come close to describing the Coal-Nyack Loop, an ancient Kootenai trail. A 38-mile trail encircles Mount Stimson, one of the six highest peaks in the park at 10,142 feet, but it's a rough trail. Where other trails require camping in designated sites, the Coal-Nyack Loop is wild, with wilderness camping at large the modus operandi; i.e., wherever you can find a flat place to sleep and abide by Leave No Trace principles. Without bridges, creeks require fording, and there are plenty of them, for the valley spews water in spring. Frequent avalanches splinter trees across trails. Thick brush cloaks routes. And the only access is via more trail or fording the Middle Fork of the Flathead River.

It's not a place for the faint of heart. Only those with experienced backcountry savvy should tackle the primitive conditions here. But for those heading out on foot or horseback, wilderness solitude awaits, for few intrepid souls tackle the loop.

Permits are required for backcountry camping in the Coal-Nyack Loop. Call 406/888-7800 or check for details online: www.nps.gov/glac.

Due to the trail's popularity, it sees quite of bit of summer traffic, making it well worn and quite obvious to follow. It climbs up into Marion Creek Valley fairly steeply, so be prepared for taxing your lungs a bit. You will encounter thick, heavy brush in the trail's midsection. Cowparsnip, nettles, elderberry, and false huckleberry crowd the trail—some over head high. Make noise here to avoid surprising a bear.

You know you're nearing the lake when the trail assumes a more moderate pitch, leveling out somewhat. Marion Lake sits in a photoworthy glacial cirque surrounded by cliffs and the outlet congested with logs. Anglers should bring rods, for the lake harbors westslope cutthroat trout up to 12 inches.

Dickey Lake

- Distance: 4.8 miles round-trip
- Duration: 2.5 hours
- Elevation gain: 1,460 feet
- Effort: moderate
- Trailhead: Turn south on Dickey Lake Road (milepost 178.7) at Essex and follow the right fork 3 miles to an unmarked spur where the Flathead National Forest trail begins.

This short trail in the Great Bear Wilderness gives rather decent rewards for its efforts, and anglers will want to tote a fishing rod. After wading Dickey Creek, the forested trail climbs up a large bowl riddled with avalanche paths (translate into deadfall, limbs, or uprooted and downed trees). In places, thick brush chokes the path, but you can still follow it to the headwall near the basin's end. From here, a rock cairn, which may be buried in snow that hangs late in the season, marks the trail ascending steeply through false huckleberry bushes dangling with pale apricot blossoms into a hanging valley.

Upon reaching the upper basin, the trail pops out on the edge of Dickey Lake. The shallow tarn flanked by meadows and steep talus slopes is a scenic lunch spot. You'll most likely find solitude here as the trail is not well-traveled. Anglers will enjoy fishing for cutthroats in the small lake.

Grant Ridge Loop trail in Great Bear Wilderness, with Glacier Park in the distance

❰ Stanton Lake and Grant Ridge Loop

- Distance: 2 miles round-trip or 10.2-mile loop
- Duration: 1 or 5 hours
- Elevation gain: 600 or 3,605 feet
- Effort: easy or moderate
- Trailhead: Stanton Lake Trailhead on Highway 2 at mile marker 169.9 in the Flathead National Forest

A short hike plops hikers and anglers on the shores of Stanton Lake, or a longer loop explores the ultra-scenic Grant Ridge, both in the Great Bear Wilderness. From the trailhead, a steep grunt heads straight uphill. But never fear, for it levels out soon into a nice forested walk that leads into the basin cradling Stanton Lake. For a short hike to a well-traveled destination, stop here. Anglers should bring rods to fish for westslope cutthroat, rainbows, and mountain whitefish. Some maps show the trail continuing above Stanton Lake; however, that trail peters out promptly in willow bogs.

For the Grant Ridge Loop, take the left fork before the lake and ford the outlet creek. The trail climbs a forested hillside with peek-a-boo views of Great Northern, the highest peak in the Great Bear Wilderness. At the ridge top, follow a faint, intermittent trail 0.25 mile south to a rocky outcrop overlooking Grant Peak and the waterfall springing from the glacier's snout. With views of Glacier's southern monoliths, the trail wanders north below the

ridgeline before descending switchbacks to the highway a half mile from the starting point. Many hikers prefer to do this loop clockwise, staring at Grant and Great Northern during the ridgeline walk.

Ousel Peak

- Distance: 5.2 miles round-trip
- Duration: 3.5 hours
- Elevation gain: 3,260 feet
- Effort: very strenuous
- Trailhead: mile marker 159.6 on Highway 2 in the Flathead National Forest

Do the math: This trail gains well over 1,000 feet per mile and from the first minute makes no bones about heading straight up-hill. If the uphill doesn't tax your lungs, the downhill will pound your knees. Nevertheless, the view from the top is outstanding and well worth the effort or pain. Sitting on the northern edge of the Great Bear Wilderness, the trail climbs through a forest canopy littered with various microclimates from wet seeps to dry, arid slopes. The path finally breaks out of the forest with glimpses of Glacier's peaks. At the top, remnants of the old lookout scatter across the hillside amid tiny yellow stonecrop. Look into Glacier to see Mounts Jackson and Stimson along with Harrison Glacier.

BIKING
Road Biking

Cross-country bicyclists use the Theodore Roosevelt Highway to cross the Continental Divide when Going-to-the-Sun Road is not open. However, many use Highway 2 to make a big loop through and around Glacier (Going-to-the-Sun Road and Highways 89, 49, and 2). Compared to the rest of Glacier's roads, Highway 2 is definitely an easier ride, for it has shoulders in some sections and is a bit wider and less curvy. However, due to heavy traffic in summer, it can be downright dangerous with large rigs that nearly blow cyclists off the road. Tackle it only if you can handle riding

with semis and RVs whipping by your elbows at 60 mph.

Be prepared for winds, especially at Marias Pass. They are usually blowing eastward, so those riding toward West Glacier encounter substantial headwinds. Also, be extra cautious in the five curvy miles east of West Glacier as severe turns reduce the visibility of drivers on the road. Even though no law requires a helmet, think twice about leaving your brain bucket off. Most drivers here are gawking at scenery or trying to spot wildlife rather than keeping their attention totally on the road.

Mountain Biking

Mountain bikes are not permitted on trails in the wilderness areas nor in Glacier Park. **Izaak Walton Inn** (290 Izaak Walton Inn Road, 406/888-5700, www.izaakwaltoninn.com, $20–25 per day) rents mountain bikes, which can be ridden on several of their own trails—cross-country ski trails that convert to biking trails in summer.

◖ RAFTING AND KAYAKING
The **Middle Fork of the Flathead River** is the local hotspot for rafting and kayaking. No permits are needed; however, you'll need to take care about where you set up camp. In the Great Bear Wilderness, sites are not restricted, but in the lower section, private lands abut national forest land, much of it unmarked. To know where you can camp without infringing on private landowners, take a good river or topographical map along (contact Flathead National Forest, 406/755-5401; nearest ranger station is in Hungry Horse nine miles west of West Glacier, 406/387-3800). Also, Glacier National Park requires backcountry permits for camping; no camping is permitted on the north shore.

To access Great Bear Wilderness sections of the river (Class III and IV), you'll need to fly in to Schaeffer Meadows or pack in on a horse. Contact the U.S. Forest Service Hungry Horse Ranger Station (406/387-3800) for details on rafting and floating this upper wild section.

The normal float season is mid-May through mid-July. During peak runoff in May, the trip can often be more difficult with several rapids becoming Class V and spring dumps of snow chilling the air.

From the Bear Creek confluence to the confluence with the North Fork of the Flathead, river put-ins allow easy access from Highway 2 at Bear Creek (milepost 185), Essex (milepost 180), Paola (milepost 175.2), Cascadilla (milepost 166), Moccasin Creek (milepost 160.5), and West Glacier (follow signs to the golf course). Between Bear Creek and Cascadilla, rapids rate Class III and IV. Waters flatten to a float trip from Cascadilla to Moccasin Creek, but be aware of deadly log jams. From Moccasin to West Glacier, rapids range mostly in Class II and III, with some IVs during June high water. To gauge your average float time in July, from Bear Creek to Cascadilla usually takes 6.5 hours and from Moccasin Creek to West Glacier 2.5 hours. If you're planning on rafting on your own, stop at the Hungry Horse Ranger Station nine miles west of West Glacier for maps, guidebooks, and information.

Rentals and Guides

Four local river companies operate out of West Glacier, all guiding half-day, full-day, and overnight trips on the Middle Fork of the Flathead: **Glacier Raft Company** (6 Going-to-the-Sun Road, 406/888-5454 or 800/235-6781, www.glacierraftco.com), **Great Northern Whitewater** (12127 Hwy. 2 E., 406/387-5340 or 800/735-7897, www.gnwhitewater.com), **Montana Raft Company** (11970 Hwy. 2 E., 406/387-5555, 800/521-RAFT, or 800/521-7238, www.glacierguides.com), and **Wild River Adventures** (11900 Hwy. 2 E., 406/387-9453 or 800/700-7056, www.riverwild.com). Some rent rafts and kayaks as well.

FISHING
Rivers and Streams

In Glacier Park, Ole, Park, Muir, Coal, and Nyack Creeks are closed to fishing, which leaves Summit, Railroad and Badger Creeks,

which flow from Marias Pass east through Lewis and Clark National Forest and onto the Blackfeet Reservation. **Badger Creek,** in particular, has a good reputation for rainbow trout. **Bear Creek,** good for trout fishing, drops west from Marias to its confluence with the Middle Fork of the Flathead River with westslope cutthroat, mountain whitefish, and some rainbow trout. The **Middle Fork** has plenty of river accesses for fishing: Bear Creek, Essex, Paola, Cascadilla, and Moccasin.

Lakes

Inside the southern park, good cutthroat trout fishing lakes such as Ole, Harrison, or Isabel usually require backpacking or fording the Middle Fork of the Flathead. It's actually easier to get to lakes in the Great Bear Wilderness on the south side of the highway. **Stanton Lake** is a quick destination with westslope cutthroat trout, mountain whitefish, and rainbow trout, but it's somewhat overfished because of its ease of access. Dickey and Marion Lakes also harbor cutthroat.

Guides

Four fishing companies in West Glacier guide fly-fishing trips on the Middle Fork of the Flathead River: **Glacier Anglers** (Glacier Outdoor Center, 11957 Hwy. 2 E., 406/888-5454 or 800/235-6781, www.glacierraftco.com), **Glacier Guides** (11970 Hwy. 2 E., 406/387-5555 or 800/521-7238, www.glacierguides.com), **Montana Fly-fishing Guides** (Great Northern Whitewater, 12127 Hwy. 2 E., 406/387-5340 or 800/735-7897, www.gnwhitewater.com), and **Wild River Adventures** (11900 Hwy. 2 E., 406/387-9453 or 800/700-7056, www.riverwild.com, July–early Sept.).

Summit Station Lodge (milepost 197.3 on Hwy. 2, 406/226-4428, early June–late Sept.) offers guided two- to seven-day fly-fishing packages ($795–3,221) on Glacier's east side. Using guides experienced in local waters, the lodge provides all-in-one pricing for fly-fishing vacations: food, lodging, guide service, fly-fishing school,

and transportation to fishing on the Blackfeet Reservation, in high mountain lakes, and along local creeks.

Licenses and Regulations

Fishing regulations along Highway 2 vary depending on land stewardship. Check carefully where you are before dropping a line into waters. The road passes through Blackfeet tribal lands, Glacier National Park, and national forests. For details on each of these permits, see the *Background* chapter. You can purchase Tribal fishing permits at Bear Track Travel Center (Exxon station in East Glacier, 20958 Hwy. 2, 406/226-5504, winter 7 A.M.– 8 P.M., summer 7 A.M.–10 P.M.). For Montana State licenses, go to Glacier Outdoor Center in West Glacier (11957 Hwy. 2 East, 406/888-5454 or 800/235-6781, www.glacierraftco.com).

CROSS-COUNTRY SKIING

In winter, ski routes off Highway 2 are popular for their ease of access. You'll find everything from groomed skate and classic skiing trails to snowmobile tracks and off-piste break-your-own trail treks.

Skyland Road (milepost 195.8) on Highway 2 is groomed intermittently for snowmobiling, although cross-country skiers use it too, especially to access Challenge Cabin. Ski up the road seven miles to reach the upper basin; the ski back down is a fast zing in good conditions. Likewise, several of the roads around Summit and Marias Pass in the Lewis and Clark National Forest (406/453-6157) are groomed for snowmobiling. On weekends, do not expect a quiet meander. You'll be passed by lots of snowmobilers: Although the machines are loud and smelly, most of the drivers are very courteous to skiers. Some of these roads even make good loops, but do not head off without a good topographical map. Call the national forest for maps.

Izaak Walton Inn

With 20 miles of track groomed for skate and classic skiing usually December–March,

Izaak Walton Inn (290 Izaak Walton Inn Road, 406/888-5700, www.izaakwaltoninn. com) makes a nice cross-country skiing destination at milepost 179.7 on Highway 2. At the inn, trails range from easy meanders to steep grunts. Trail passes for skiing are $10 per day and are available to day visitors as well as inn guests. Although the area never feels crowded, its most popular time is Christmas through President's Day. Lessons ($20–40 per hour) are available from the lodge as well as rentals ($20 for adults, $10 for kids), and the rentals can be taken elsewhere to use. The inn also rents snowshoes ($15), but snowshoers should get directions on where to go because snowshoe tracks trash set ski trails. One short section of trail is lit for night skiing. With rates varying depending on the number of people, the inn also guides half-day snowshoe tours ($50–105) and full-day ski tours ($85–200) in Glacier.

【 Autumn Creek Trail

One of the most popular ski trails in Glacier is Autumn Creek Trail at Marias Pass, which can be skied point-to-point if you want to set up a car shuttle or hitchhike, which is legal in Montana. The west trailhead sits at milepost 193.8 on Highway 2. Park across the highway, then ski up the access road and across the railroad tracks. The other trailhead is at Marias Pass, across Highway 2 from the parking lot (milepost 197.9). Orange markers on trees denote the six-mile trail. Beginners will find more success in the Marias Pass section rather than the steep Autumn Creek section. Those seeking to avoid the narrow, steep 660-foot elevation drop downhill should begin on the west end and finish at Summit.

SNOWMOBILING

Snowmobilers gravitate to groomed and ungroomed roads in Lewis and Clark National Forest (406/791-7700) and Flathead National Forest (406/758-5204). The most popular snowmobiling is in the Marias Pass and Skyland/Challenge complex, both straddling the

Continental Divide south of Highway 2. The Cut Bank Snowgoers and Flathead Snowmobile Association groom about 45 miles of trail here, which are open for snowmobiling December 1–May 15. Contact both local snowmobile associations via the Montana Snowmobile Association (406/788-2399, www.snowtana.com). Snow depths in both of these snowmobiling areas vary 150–250 inches. Some restrictions apply to the designated connecting trails, so get a good snowmobile map through Montana Snowmobile Association. The nearest rentals are in Flathead Valley.

ENTERTAINMENT

Every Labor Day Weekend, spiffed up and spit-shined classic cars descend on Stanton Creek Lodge for the annual **Show and Shine.** The event, now well into its second decade, goes on Friday through Monday with evening parking lot dances, barbecues, live bands, and the car show. The event used to feature a burnout race down Highway 2's straightaway in front of the lodge, but that may be a thing of the past due to safety. Call the Stanton Creek Lodge (406/888-5040 or 866/883-5040) for the current schedule and entry info.

Accommodations

Lodging spans all spectrums along Theodore Roosevelt Highway—you'll find historic inns, rustic cabins, and dude ranches. Lodging is listed here by type, then location from east to west along the highway. That 7 percent Montana State bed tax will find your bill here.

Lodges and Inns

Just west of Marias Pass on Highway 2, the **◖ Summit Station Lodge** (197.3 on Hwy. 2, 406/226-4428, www.summitstationlodge. com, early June–late Sept.) is a historic 1906 train station converted into a lodge with views of the Continental Divide's Summit and Little Dog peaks. The Summit Station offers two- to seven-day fishing packages ($795–3,221) and horseback-riding packages ($619–2,779), which include lodging, three meals per day, and guided riding or fishing. You can also rent upscale cabins ($175) nightly without the fly-fishing or horseback riding; the cozy log cabins decorated in wilderness motifs each have two queen log beds, air-conditioning, and private bathrooms, and come with a continental breakfast. The lodge also has a fine-dining restaurant and bar on the premises.

Located at Essex and open year-round, **◖ Izaak Walton Inn** (290 Izaak Walton Inn Rd., 406/888-5700, www.izaakwaltoninn. com, mid-June–mid-Sept. and mid-Dec.–Mar.

$148–242, off-season rates drop to $107–222) is a cozy place to be. From the fireplace in the lobby to the Dining Car Restaurant or the swinging seat on the porch, the inn makes you feel comfortable and at ease in its nonsmoking premises. Rooms come with continental breakfast and vary in sizes, although most bathrooms are fairly small. The inn maintains its historic ambience with no televisions or phones in the rooms; a pay phone is off the lobby. You'll have to walk the stairs here as no elevator services the building, but there is a sauna for aching muscles. To get good deals, check the inn's packages, which pair up skiing or rafting and meals with rooms. It also hosts special weekends, from photography workshops to railway fan events. You can also arrive and depart by train; it's an Amtrak stop. With railroad tracks right outside the back door, you may sleep better with earplugs, for quite a few trains pass by each night.

For something quite different, stay in one of the cabooses. A short walk over a footbridge above the railroad tracks leads to three cabooses, set alone in the trees. A three-night minimum ($675) is required (only two nights in winter) for the heated cabooses, which sleep four and have kitchenettes and full bathrooms. The inn grooms 20 miles of ski trails for skate and classic skiing in winter; in summer, they

St. Nicholas marks the southernmost peak in Glacier National Park.

ROOSEVELT HIGHWAY

are hiking and mountain-biking trails. You can rent a car ($65 per day), skis, mountain bikes, snowshoes, and kiddie sleds.

At milepost 173.8, **Glacier Haven Inn** (14305 Hwy. 2, 406/888-5720, www.glacier haveninn.com, open year-round) was taken over by new owners in May 2005, who changed the name from its long-held Middle Fork River Inn. Small clean motel rooms ($55–70) come with two double beds and satellite television. They also rent one three-bedroom cabin ($225 per night) with one bathroom, laundry facilities, a full kitchen, and satellite television. Here, pets are okay. A restaurant on the premises serves homestyle meals. During the off-season when the restaurant is closed, it still offers meals to inn guests.

Cabins

Flathead National Forest (www.fs.fed.us/r1/ flathead/, 406/387-3809) rents two cabins with three-night maximums accessible from Highway 2. These are popular destinations for skiers, snowshoers, and snowmobilers in win-

ter, and in summer one is an easy dirt road drive. Decked out with propane, mattresses, and kitchen utensils, the cabins are reasonably well equipped and warm with either propane heat or woodstoves (wood is supplied). A seven-mile ski or snowmobile ride up Skyland Road (milepost 195.8 on Hwy. 2), tiny one-room **Challenge Cabin** (Dec.–Mar., $30 per night) sleeps six people stacked like sardines. A much larger two-bedroom cabin sleeping eight, **Zip's Place** (June–Mar., $50 per night) is found by turning off Highway 2 (milepost 191.9) and driving two miles, following signs. In winter, it requires a two-mile ski or snowshoe trip to reach the front door.

Reservations are mandatory for the cabins; the Forest Service opens reservations for the following year on the first Monday in November. Once full payment is made and the contract is signed, the Forest Service sends the cabin combination for entrance.

A small set of simple rustic cabins, a restaurant, a bar, and a campground make up **Stanton Creek Lodge** (milepost 170 on Hwy.

2, 406/888-5040 or 866/883-5040, www. stantoncreeklodge.com, open year-round). Six heated cabins vary in size ($49–89), and all include linens and towels. The deluxe cabins, those open year-round, have satellite television and private bathrooms; other cabins share a bathhouse, which is closed in winter. Trails to Stanton Lake and Grant Loop depart from here, and fishing on the Middle Fork River is easily accessible.

Removed from the highway and its rumbling, **Glacier Wilderness Resort** (milepost 163 on Hwy. 2, 406/888/5664, www.glacierwildernessresort.com, open year-round) sits its individual log homes back in a woodsy setting abutting the Great Bear Wilderness. With an indoor heated pool open year-round, homes come with fireplaces, satellite televisions, DVD/VCR, fully equipped kitchens, and private hot tubs. One-bedroom homes ($145 in winter, $175 in summer) sleep up to four people; two-bedroom homes ($155 in winter, $200 in summer) sleep up to six. In summer, you can use an outdoor picnic pavilion and walking trails. In winter, cross-country skiing and snowshoeing trails tour the property.

Dude Ranch

Located in Flathead National Forest adjacent to Glacier, **Bear Creek Ranch** (milepost 192, 406/226-4489, www.bearcreekranch.com, May–Sept.) is a dude ranch specializing in western horsemanship with lessons, rides, and cattle drives. In dude ranch fashion, only six-day packages are offered, rather than single-night stays, with lodging, three meals per day, and all ranch activities—horseback riding, hiking, and fishing—for one lump rate (adults $1,795, kids 5–15 $995). Accommodations are in five cabins with private baths or in the main lodge. The dining room serves buffet meals indoors and chuck-wagon picnics outdoors.

Bed-and-Breakfasts

Located 1.5 miles from East Glacier, **Bison Creek Ranch B & B** (milepost 207.4, 20722 Hwy. 2, 406/226-4482 or 888/226-4482, mid-May–Sept., $45–75 for two people, $10

for each additional person) combines cabin stays with a continental breakfast. Rustic remodeled one- and two-bedroom Gandy Dancer cabins (built as bunkhouses for railroad repairmen) and two-bedroom A-frame chalets spread among firs and meadows. It appeals to those who want real quiet without phones or televisions (but with electricity and private baths), and the hot water may take a bit to get to your cabin. The inexpensive rates include the Montana bed tax, making them even a better deal. A small fishing stream runs nearby, and a restaurant on-site serves western dinners.

Located at milepost 172 halfway between Essex and West Glacier, **Paola Creek Bed and Breakfast** (0.25 mile up Paola Creek Road, 406/888-5061 or 888/311-5061, www. paolacreek.com, year-round, $140–170 double, $90 single with a two-night minimum) has four rooms with private baths in a larch log home sitting on the edge of the Great Bear Wilderness under large firs. The dining room—where you'll eat a huge breakfast—stares right into Glacier at St. Nicholas's toothy spire. In summer, you can sit and enjoy the serene outdoor setting. Cross-country ski trails lead outside the back door, and fishing and hiking are quickly accessible. The B&B is nonsmoking and does not allow pets.

CAMPING

Along Highway 2, no national park campgrounds are present, but you can find two Forest Service campgrounds and several private campgrounds (which will add on a 7 percent Montana bed tax).

National Forest
Service Campgrounds

A U.S. Forest Service campground at Marias Pass, the **Summit Campground** (Lewis and Clark National Forest, 406/791-7700, summers only, $10) is a typical small Forest Service campground, watched over by campground hosts. The 17 sites, which are fairly close to the highway and in heavy timber, have picnic tables (some wheelchair accessible) and fire pits, but no hookups. Drinking water is available,

and so are pit toilets, but you must pack your own garbage away with you. It's first-come, first-serve, so get there by early afternoon in high season, especially if you want to nab one of the campsites farthest from the highway. Firewood is not available; you can collect it in the woods here.

A Forest Service campground on Highway 2 (milepost 190), **Devil Creek Campground** (Flathead National Forest, 406/387-3800, summers only, $10) has 14 sites, a few of which can handle up to 40-foot RVs. Amenities are minimal: drinking water, vault toilets, fire pits, and picnic tables, but no hookups. The campground usually has a host on-site. It's near the highway, so don't expect total wilderness here, but at least it's set back in the trees and shady with a woodsy feel. Sites are first-come, first-serve, so you'll need to have a campsite by early afternoon in high season, especially if you want one farther away from the highway. Pack out your own garbage. You can gather firewood in the woods. From the campground, a trail leads 5.9 miles up to Elk Lake or 8.2 miles to Moose Lake.

Private Campgrounds

Located 16 miles west of East Glacier between milepost 191 and 192, **(Glacier Meadow RV Park** (406/226-4479, www.glaciermead-owrvpark.com, mid-May–mid-Sept.) has 41 sites on a 58-acre meadow and forest setting with dump station, laundry, playground, full hookups, flush toilets, hot showers, and wireless Internet. The campground sits in full view of the highway, and all the sites are open, providing good satellite dish reception for those so inclined, but you'll not get much privacy from your neighbors. Rates range $24–26 cash ($2 extra to pay with credit card), depending on whether you have electricity and water hookup or just electricity, with access to a central water source. Kids under 10 are free. In the evening and early morning, elk sometimes browse in the meadow here.

Located 16 miles from West Glacier and 10 miles from Essex, **Stanton Creek Lodge** (milepost 170 on Hwy. 2, 406/888-5040 or 866/883-5040, www.stantoncreeklodge.com, open year-round) has tent ($12.50) and eight full-hookup RV ($24.50) sites right on the highway. Amenities include flush toilets, hot showers, picnic tables, and fire pits. A full-service bar and restaurant is on-site with the trailhead to Stanton Lake and Grant Loop a few minutes' walk away and fishing 10 minutes away. While you can camp here in winter, the water is turned off—no flush toilets or hot showers.

Food

Restaurants along Highway 2 vary from old dives to fine dining. They are listed here in order of location from east to west along the highway. Don't be surprised if one is closed when its hours say otherwise—if fish are biting, owners will close.

RESTAURANTS

Located 1.5 miles from East Glacier at milepost 207.4, **Bison Creek Ranch** (20722 Hwy. 2, 406/226-4482, www.angelfire.com, mid-May–Sept., daily 5–9 P.M., $8–17) has served up the Schauf family's western home cooking since the 1950s. House favorites include Edna's fried chicken and St. Mary Lake whitefish. Come hungry, for dinners are large, complete with salad bar, soups, rolls, veggie, potato, and ice cream. If anglers, bring their own catch along, they'll cook it up for you.

The **(Summit Station Lodge** (milepost 197.5, 406/226-4428, www.summitstation-lodge.com, early June–late Sept., 5–9 P.M. daily, $12–26) opens its dining room nightly to the public for fine dining by Chef Xavier Simental. The menu changes weekly but has a smattering of Northern Italian pastas, steak, fish, chicken, and at least one vegetarian entree. Regional cuisine features Montana-raised

bison and elk, sometimes prepared in traditional Blackfeet style. A fairly extensive wine list carries worldwide selections. Sip an after-dinner cocktail in the lounge, which stays open until 11 P.M.

For a real taste of old funky Montana, stop at the **Snow Slip Inn** (milepost 191 on Hwy. 2, 406/226-9381, open year-round, 7 A.M.–midnight), six miles west of Marias Pass. The door may fall off its hinges, and whomever is tending the bar may cuss at you, but you're in real Montana here, not a hybridized tourist place. The tiny bar and restaurant are permanently filled with smoke. You can shoot pool while you wait for a hamburger ($6) or other bar food.

The **Dining Car Restaurant** (290 Izaak Walton Inn Rd., Essex, 406/888-5700, www.izaakwaltoninn.com, year-round, 7:30 A.M.–8 P.M. daily) serves up scrumptious meals on replicas of Great Northern Railway's historic dinnerware. (The gift shop sells the dishes, too!) The cozy restaurant is a great place to stop for a huckleberry pancake or corn flake–crusted French toast breakfast ($7). Lunch favorites include a portabello mushroom burger or chicken and dumplings ($8–9). Enjoy a leisurely dinner ($11–23) of wild mushroom ravioli, chicken with huckleberry-orange sauce, or pork tenderloin with red onion marmalade over a glass of wine as trains rumble past your window.

Located at milepost 173.8, **Healthy Haven Cafe** (14305 Hwy. 2, 406/888-5720, www.glacierhaveninn.com, open Memorial weekend through Labor Day weekend, Tues.–Sun., 9 A.M.–2 P.M. and 5–9 P.M.), formerly known as the Middle Fork River Inn, serves inexpensive home-style meals ($5–13). Until July 4, it's only open from Thursday dinner through Sunday lunch. For breakfast, you can go light with the homemade granola or pack on the calories with the house crepes topped with a three-cream mix and seasonal fresh fruit. Lunches and dinners serve traditional cafe sandwiches or a made-to-order deli sandwich on homemade bread ($6). Dinner specials change nightly, too.

Stanton Lodge (milepost 170 on Hwy. 2, 406/888-5040 or 866/883-5040, www.stantoncreeklodge.com, open daily, Wed.–Mon. 11 A.M.–7 P.M., closes at 6 P.M. in winter, $5–10) has a tiny lunch and dinner restaurant with a full service bar—a good place to grab a sandwich or buffalo burger. Adorned with photos and T-shirts of their car rally winners, the restaurant is one of those funky, dark, but comfy places; you can also sit outside on the small deck, but the views are the parking lot and highway. You won't be able to get near the place on Labor Day weekend during their annual Show and Shine classic car rally.

GROCERIES

Highway 2 is lacking in grocery stores, even in convenience stores. The Half Way House near Essex (milepost 178) used to be a place you could grab chips, pop, and other convenience store items, but the store burned down in 2004. Owners are rebuilding and should be back open sometime in 2006. To stock up for camping, you'll find seasonal grocery stores in East and West Glacier. Larger food markets are in Browning on the east side and Hungry Horse and Columbia Falls on the west.

PICNIC AREA

Only one designated picnic area is set aside on the Theodore Roosevelt Highway, and that is **Walton** (milepost 180.5). Behind the Walton Ranger Station, the small picnic area clusters under thick trees with little view. Picnic tables, pit toilets, and fire pits are available, but you'll need to bring your own firewood; gathering wood is prohibited. It is, however, the trailhead for the Ole Creek Trail and Scalplock Lookout.

But with six river accesses along the Middle Fork of the Flathead, there are plenty of places sans picnic tables at which to pull off to eat lunch at a scenic spot.

WATERTON

For such a small park, Waterton Lakes National Park packs a punch. It houses rare plants found nowhere else and a plethora of wildlife that rivals its large northern sisters of Banff and Jasper. Hanging on the Continental Divide's east side, mountains abut prairies where geological overthrusts exposed the oldest sedimentary rock in the Canadian Rockies. Although active glaciers vacated its borders years ago, the results of ice gnawing on its landscape left lake pockets strewn through the park—lakes that frequently kick up with winds, making it the second windiest place in Alberta.

Dominated by the Prince of Wales Hotel and Waterton Lake, the deepest lake in the Canadian Rockies, the park serves as a destination in itself as well as an entrance to Glacier's remote north country. On any summer day, the Waterton Townsite bustles with shoppers, bicyclists, backpackers, boaters, and campers. The MV *International* shuttles hikers and sightseers across Waterton Lake and the international boundary to Goat Haunt, U.S.A. Only two roads pierce the park's remarkable interior, both gateways to lakes, waterfalls, canyons, and wildlife.

HISTORY
In 1858, Lieutenant Thomas Blakiston, a European explorer, came to southern Alberta searching for a railroad route through the Canadian Rockies. He traveled to the large chain of Waterton Lakes, naming them for the British naturalist Charles Waterton, who never visited the area.

When the area became Kootenay Lakes

© BECKY LOMAX

HIGHLIGHTS

◖ Boat Tour: The deepest lake in the Canadian Rockies and clearly the central feature in Waterton, Upper Waterton Lake spans the international boundary, and there's no better way to see it than on the historic MV *International* (page 185).

◖ Chief Mountain: Actually in Glacier Park rather than Waterton, the 9,080-foot Chief Mountain sits prominently above Chief Mountain Highway and is historically a sacred Blackfeet site. Look carefully to see Ninaki (the mother) and Papoose peaks spiking up behind it (page 191).

◖ Prince of Wales Hotel: The historic 1927 hotel sits regally atop a knoll above the Waterton Townsite. Part of the chain of Swiss-style hotels and chalets built by Great Northern Railway, the hotel maintains a decidedly British ambience with kilt-wearing bellhops and high tea served in the afternoon (page 191).

◖ Goat Haunt, U.S.A.: Accessible only by boat or on foot, Goat Haunt rests at Waterton Lake's southern end in Glacier Park—home of the International Peace Park Pavilion and launchpad to Glacier's remote northern trails (page 191).

◖ Cameron Lake: The glacially fed lake at the end of Akamina Parkway receives snowmelt from Herbst Glacier across the international boundary. Rent a boat to row its shoreline or walk the pathway along the west shore (page 192).

◖ Red Rock Canyon: Argillites in striking reds and greens layer atop one another in a colorful mosaic—sedimentary layers that are evidence of the ancient Belt Sea. A short walk is required to see all its splendors (page 192).

◖ Maskinonge Lake: Located on the axis of two migration flyways, Waterton is home to trumpeter swans, yellow-headed blackbirds, and Vaux's swifts. Take your binoculars for unusual bird sightings (page 192).

◖ Bison Paddock: Bison once roamed the prairies in vast numbers, but today wild bison no longer range through northwestern Montana. In a tribute to the great herds that once fed on Waterton's grasslands, Parks Canada maintains a drive-through grazing land where you can view these majestic creatures (page 192).

◖ Bear's Hump: A bit of a grunt, but well worth the climb for its view, the trail gives you an eagle's-eye view of Waterton Townsite and Waterton Lake (page 194).

◖ Carthew-Alderson: A scenic point-to-point trail crosses a high, windswept alpine pass and descends past blue icy jewels en route back to the Townsite (page 195).

WATERTON

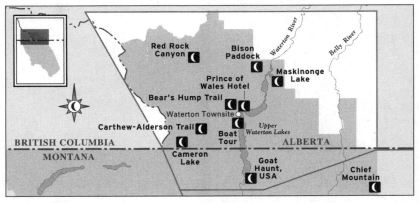

LOOK FOR ◖ TO FIND RECOMMENDED SIGHTS, ACTIVITIES, DINING, AND LODGING.

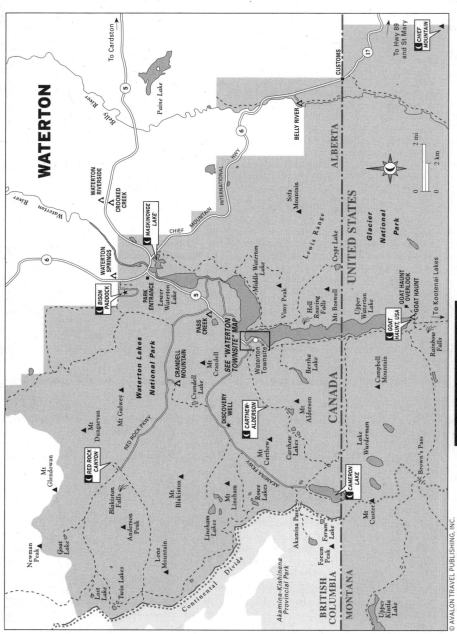

WATERTON

To Cardston →

Belly River

Paine Lake

Waterton River

5

6 HWY

5

6

CUSTOMS

17

To Hwy 89
and St Mary

CHIEF
MOUNTAIN

BELLY RIVER

ALBERTA

WATERTON
RIVERSIDE

CROOKED
CREEK

MASKINONGE
LAKE

CHIEF MOUNTAIN

INTERNATIONAL

WATERTON
SPRINGS

BISON
PADDOCK

PARK
ENTRANCE

Lower
Waterton
Lake

PASS
CREEK

CRANDELL
MOUNTAIN

Mt
Crandell

Crandell
Lake

SEE "WATERTON
TOWNSITE" MAP

Waterton
Townsite

Middle Waterton
Lake

Vimy Peak

Hell
Roaring
Falls

Mt Boswell

Sofa
Mountain

Lewis Range

Crypt Lake

UNITED STATES

Glacier
National
Park

Upper
Waterton
Lake

GOAT
HAUNT USA

GOAT HAUNT
OVERLOOK

GOAT HAUNT

Rainbow
Falls

To Kootenai Lakes

2 mi

2 km

0

0

Waterton Lakes

National Park

Mt Galwey

Mt
Dungarvan

RED ROCK PKWY

RED ROCK
CANYON

Mt
Glendowan

Blakiston
Falls

Anderson
Peak

Mt
Blakiston

DISCOVERY
WELL

CARTHEW-
ALDERSON

Mt
Carthew

Carthew
Lakes

Mt
Alderson

Bertha
Lake

Campbell
Mountain

CANADA

Lake
Wurdeman

Brown's Pass

Newman
Peak

Goat
Lake

Lost
Lake

Twin Lakes

Lone
Mountain

Lineham
Lakes

Mt
Lineham

Rowe
Lakes

AKAMINA PKWY

Akamina Pass

Forum
Peak

Forum
Lake

CAMERON
LAKE

Mt
Custer

BRITISH
COLUMBIA

MONTANA

Akamina-Kishinena
Provincial Park

Continental Divide

Upper
Kintla
Lake

WATERTON

KOOTENAI BROWN

John George "Kootenai" Brown was not only influential in the formation of Waterton Lakes National Park, but became the stuff of legends. Born in Ireland in 1839, he served with the British Army in India before coming to North America in 1861. With no money, he landed in Barkerville, British Columbia, in the Cariboo Gold Rush. What gold he mined, he spent, for he left with nothing several years later.

At 26 years old, he crossed the Continental Divide at South Kootenay Pass to Kootenay Lakes (Waterton Lakes), falling in love with the country. He inherited his name through his close ties to the Kootenai Indians. His adventures, however, took him away from the area. Blackfeet attacked and shot him in the back with an arrow. Reputedly, he pulled the arrow out himself and cleaned the wound with turpentine.

Venturing into Montana, he spent 12 years as a trader, a pony express rider, a scout for Custer, and buffalo hunter. When buffalo became scarce, he moved on to wolves. While he was riding pony express for the U.S. Army,

Chief Sitting Bull and the Sioux took him prisoner, stripping and tying him to a stake while they debated his fate. He escaped in the middle of the night.

In 1869, he married a Métis woman, Olivia Lyonnais, and started a family. Finally, after being hauled into a Fort Benton court on murder charges and acquitted, he and his family packed off to Alberta. He built a cabin by Upper Waterton Lake, working as a guide, commercial fisherman, hunter, rancher, trader, and scout for the Rocky Mountain Rangers during the 1885 North-West Rebellion, the same year Olivia died. He later married Isabella, a Cree.

When Canada established the Kootenay Lake Forest Reserve in 1885, Brown became its first game warden and fisheries officer. In 1910, he was promoted to Forest Ranger in Charge. A year later, when Kootenay Lakes officially became Waterton Lakes, he stepped in as its first superintendent.

Kootenai Brown died in 1916 and is buried with his two wives along the entrance road to Waterton.

Forest Park in 1895—Canada's fourth national park, the brainchild of Pincher Creek rancher F. W. Godsal—the legendary Kootenai Brown took the reins as its first game guardian and fisheries inspector. In 1911, he became Waterton's first superintendent, and the park's name officially changed to Waterton Lakes National Park.

Waterton produced Western Canada's first oil well in 1902. But within four years, the site closed down, the yield having trickled to nothing. Meanwhile, an oil well near Cameron Falls produced one barrel a day and prompted building the Waterton Townsite. When oil riches dissipated in 1910, tourists arrived, fueled in part by Great Northern Railway's Glacier development. The Townsite sprouted cottages, a hotel, tennis courts, a golf course, packhorse outfitters, and boating.

In 1913, Great Northern scouted Waterton for an appropriate hotel site, but World War I and a proposed dam in Waterton tabled its construction. Ironically, the Prohibition in America prompted it to be built. Alcohol, after all, was still legal in Alberta, attracting scads of Montanans for thirst quenching. In 1927, the Prince of Wales Hotel finally opened on the wind-battered knoll above town and the 72-foot MV *International* launched its first sightseers up Waterton Lake.

Ecological Significance

For such a tiny park, Waterton is a nexus. The park sits on a narrow north–south wildlife corridor and the axis of two major bird migratory highways. Over 250 species of birds nest here or use the park's rich habitats for migration stopovers. In one of the last places in North America, grizzly bears roam into the fringes of their original grassland habitat. Over 45 dif-

ferent habitats provide harbor for 10 species of amphibians and reptiles, 24 species of fish, and 60 species of mammals. Rare trumpeter swans nest here, as do Vaux's swifts.

Because Arctic and Pacific weather systems collide here, a breadth of vegetation abounds. With more than 1,370 plants, mosses, and lichens, Waterton houses more than half of Alberta's plant species, 179 which are considered rare, 22 found nowhere else in the province. Moon-worts, a small fern, come in eight varieties here: one is found in only Waterton. The park's diminutive acreage has more plant diversity than the much larger Banff, Jasper, Kootenay, and Yoho parks combined! For such extremes and such rarities likewise contained in its sister park Glacier, the United Nations Educational, Scientific and Cultural Organization (UNESCO) named Waterton-Glacier a **Biosphere Reserve** and a **World Heritage Site.**

Exploring Waterton

Waterton's 52 square miles is tiny compared to Glacier. The Townsite sits at 4,200 feet in elevation, but surrounding peaks climb to 9,000 feet. While the Townsite houses about 100 people in winter, in summer it burgeons to nearly 2,000 residents. The park sees less than 400,000 annual visitors—about 20 percent of Glacier's crowds.

Waterton and Glacier span the 49th parallel (the international border), yet the parks are one connected system. Humans use one to access the other via Waterton Lake, and grizzly bears cross back and forth. In 1932 **Waterton-Glacier International Peace Park** was established, the world's first peace park. It celebrates the longest undefended border in the world—5,525 miles.

PARK ENTRANCE

The 5-mile (8-kilometer) road connecting the park entrance station with Waterton Townsite is worth a drive with a pair of binoculars. The park entrance road turns south off Highway 6, reaching the entrance station in less than half a mile. Because Linnet, Maskinonge, and Lower Waterton Lakes attract scads of birds as well as moose, bear, elk, and smaller wildlife, you should stop at a picnic area along its route for wildlife-watching: Knight's Lake (0.6 mile, 0.9 kilometer), Hay Barn (2.5 miles, 4 km), and Marquis (4.1 miles, 6.5 km). The Waterton Lakes Visitor Information Center is 4.8 miles (7.7 km) from the entrance station.

U.S. park passes are not valid in this Canadian park, although many Americans expect them to be. Even though Waterton-Glacier is an International Peace Park, no combined park pass is sold to date. To enter Waterton, you must purchase a separate Parks Canada day pass (adults CDN$6, kids CDN$3, and seniors CDN$4.50, maximum per vehicle CDN$12) valid until 4 P.M. the following day. You can also purchase year-long passes good for all Canadian National Parks (adults CDN$38, seniors CDN$29, maximum per vehicle CDN$75).

VISITOR CENTER

The **Waterton Lakes Visitor Information Center** (4.6 miles, 7.6 km south of the park entrance station on the park entrance road, 403/859-5133, May and Sept. daily 9 A.M.–5 P.M., June–Aug. 9 A.M.–8 P.M.) sits across from the entrance road to Prince of Wales Hotel. It is the best stop for information, wilderness use permits, road conditions, fishing licenses, and maps. The trail to Bear's Hump departs from here. During months when the center is closed, you can get the same information, licenses, and permits from the Parks Canada office (215 Mount View Rd., 403/859-2224, open year-round weekdays 8 A.M.–4 P.M.).

TOURS AND SHUTTLES
◖ Boat Tour
Waterton Shoreline Cruises (at the marina at the junction of Mount View Rd. and

WATERTON

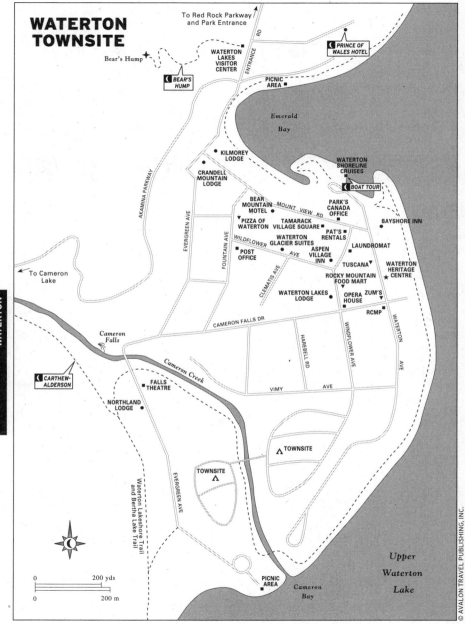

WATERTON TOWNSITE

To Red Rock Parkway and Park Entrance

Bear's Hump

PRINCE OF WALES HOTEL

WATERTON LAKES VISITOR CENTER

ENTRANCE RD

BEAR'S HUMP

PICNIC AREA

Emerald Bay

KILMOREY LODGE

AKAMINA PARKWAY

CRANDELL MOUNTAIN LODGE

WATERTON SHORELINE CRUISES

BOAT TOUR

BEAR MOUNTAIN MOTEL

MOUNT VIEW RD

PARK'S CANADA OFFICE

EVERGREEN AVE

PIZZA OF WATERTON

TAMARACK VILLAGE SQUARE

BAYSHORE INN

PAT'S RENTALS

FOUNTAIN AVE

WATERTON GLACIER SUITES

WILDFLOWER

LAUNDROMAT

POST OFFICE

AVE

ASPEN VILLAGE INN

TUSCANA

WATERTON HERITAGE CENTRE

To Cameron Lake

CLEMATIS AVE

ROCKY MOUNTAIN FOOD MART

WATERTON LAKES LODGE

OPERA HOUSE

ZUM'S

Cameron Falls

CAMERON FALLS DR

RCMP

HAREBELL RD

WINDFLOWER AVE

WATERTON AVE

CARTHEW-ALDERSON

Cameron Creek

FALLS THEATRE

NORTHLAND LODGE

VIMY

AVE

TOWNSITE

Waterton Lakeshore Trail and Bertha Lake Trail

EVERGREEN AVE

TOWNSITE

Upper Waterton Lake

0   200 yds

0   200 m

PICNIC AREA

Cameron Bay

© AVALON TRAVEL PUBLISHING, INC.

WATERTON

the MV *International* on Waterton Lake at Goat Haunt, U.S.A.

Waterton Ave., 403/859-2362, www.watertoncruise.com, May–early Oct., daily, adults round-trip CDN$27, kids CDN$10–14, kids 3 and under free) operates the historic MV *International* on Upper Waterton Lake. During the two-hour tour on the wooden 200-passenger boat cruising here since 1927, knowledgeable guides punctuate their patter with humor. From June to mid-September, the boat docks for 30 minutes at Goat Haunt—time enough to walk to the International Peace Park Pavilion. For the best views, go for a sunny seat on the top deck. If the weather is brisk, just bundle up. From early June to late September, trips depart at 10 A.M. and 1 and 4 P.M. In July and August a 7 P.M. boat stops in Goat Haunt for only 10 minutes. In shoulder seasons, two boats per day launch at 10 A.M. and 2:30 P.M. Hikers may catch an early boat and return on a later boat; just notify the ticket agent of your return intentions. Because advanced reservations are only taken for large groups, in high season you should get to the dock early.

Canadian Wilderness Tours

Offering evening wildlife watching programs, Canadian Wilderness Tours (403/859-2058 July–Aug. only, 800/408-0005, www.whitemountainadventures.com, end of June–mid-Aug. daily, adults CDN$40, kids CDN$30, two people minimum) takes visitors to prime wildlife spots for watching bears, mountain goats, elk, and birds. Naturalist guides pick you up at your hotel at 7 P.M. and supply spotting scopes and binoculars for the two-hour tour full of tidbits on habitat, nesting, behavior, feeding, and wildlife trivia. Reservations by phone are required.

Shuttles

Hikers can access Waterton trailheads via shuttles—by land or water. The **Crypt Lake Water Shuttle Service** (Waterton Shoreline Cruises, 403/859-2362, www.watertoncruise.com, July–Aug., daily, adults CDN$14 round-trip, kids CDN$7) departs from the marina at 9 and 10 A.M. for a 15-minute ride crosses Upper Waterton Lake to Crypt Landing, where the

© BECKY LOMAX

10-mile (17.2-kilometer) round-trip trail begins. Watch your hiking time, for the return boats depart Crypt Landing at 4 and 5:30 P.M. No reservations are taken for this shuttle, so arrive at least 20 minutes before departure.

Departing daily at 8:30 A.M. from Tamarack Village, the **Cameron Express** (Tamarack Village Square, 214 Mount View Rd., 403/859-2378, www.watertonvisitorservices.com, late May–early Oct., CDN$10) shuttles hikers to the popular Carthew-Alderson trailhead for a point-to-point 11-mile (18-kilometer) hike back to the Townsite. Reservations are a good idea, especially in high season; you can make them with a credit card by phone. They'll also provide custom shuttles to other trailheads; ask for rates and details. To access Glacier's east-side shuttle run by Glacier Park, Inc., the Tamarack provides transportation (CDN$55 minimum or CDN$20 per person) on demand to Chief Mountain Customs departing at 3:45 P.M. from Waterton. Walk through customs to the Chief Mountain parking lot, where you catch the shuttle to Many Glacier, St. Mary, Two Medicine, and East Glacier.

SERVICES

Gas up before you head north across the border—gas in Canada is more expensive than in the United States, usually around $0.50 per gallon more. Also, be aware that gas is sold by the liter in Canada rather than the gallon, so the price on the pump will look pretty darn good. To convert the price, calculate 3.7 liters equals one gallon.

Pat's Gas Station (224 Mount View Road, 403/859-2266, www.watertoninfo.ab.ca) is much more than a place to gas up or buy propane for the RV. While Pat can magically perform minor car repairs, its claim to fame is its rental line: surrey bikes (CDN$20 per hour), binoculars (CDN$10), mountain bikes (CDN$8–11 per hour), baby backpacks (CDN$10), and tennis rackets ($3 per hour). You can even rent a scooter (CDN$70 per day). Pat's also sells food and convenience items as well as Cuban cigars, fishing tackle, park permits, and newspapers. Gas is also available at

Tamarack Village Square (214 Mount View Rd., 403/859-2378, www.watertonvisitorservices.com), another multi-service business with a convenience store, hiking guide service, hiker shuttle, and outdoor shop.

A launderette (301 Windflower Ave., 403/859-2460) is open during summer months daily 10 A.M.–8 P.M. The Townsite post office (102 Windflower Ave.) is open year-round Monday–Friday 8 A.M.–4:30 P.M. Remember: You must use Canadian postage stamps rather than U.S. stamps to post mail from Canada! ATMs are located at Pat's Gas Station, Tamarack Village Square, Rocky Mountain Food Mart, and the Prince of Wales Hotel. While plugging in the amount, remember that the ATM gives Canadian currency! *The Calgary Sun* carries regional, national, and international news, and a free newspaper, The Boundary (www.watertonboundary.com), published weekly mid-May through early September, carries the local Waterton news.

Shopping

Shopping in Waterton is a different experience. While a certain British flair marks some of the shops with bone china and Irish linens, souvenirs are decidedly Canadian with moose and traditional Royal Canadian Mounted Police decorating T-shirts. Most shops are open from late May through late September seven days a week, but almost none are open in winter. During shoulder seasons, hours are short, often 10 A.M.–5 P.M., but in high season, shops stay open into the evening (7–8 P.M.). Many stores and restaurants sell specialty Cuban cigars, unavailable in the United States. But remember, these cannot go back over the border into the United States.

If you need outdoor gear, **Waterton Outdoor Adventures** (Tamarack Village Square, 214 Mount View Rd., 403/859-2378) can outfit you from head to toe with hiking, backpacking, and camping gear. The shop carries good reputable brands, too, at reasonable prices. This is the best place to buy topographic maps for hiking. Chocoholics gravitate toward **Welch's Chocolate Shop** (corner of Cameron Falls Dr.

and Windflower Ave., 403/859-2363), which stocks all kinds of international chocolate treats and makes its own fudge and candy.

Currency Exchange

In Waterton, most businesses, including restaurants, shops, and lodges will accept U.S. currency; however, any change will always be given back in Canadian currency. For conversions, most businesses use the bank exchange rate, but some have their own policies. For the best exchange rates, use a credit card as much as possible. Waterton has no banks; the nearest banking services are in Cardston and Pincher Creek, but the Tamarack Village Square, also known as **Waterton Visitor Services** (214 Mount View Rd., late May–early Oct., shoulder seasons 8 A.M.–6 P.M., high season 8 A.M.–8 P.M.), offers currency exchange.

Emergencies

For emergencies, contact the RCMP (202 Waterton Ave., 403/859-2244 or 403/653-4931) during summer months or Parks Canada Wardens (215 Mount View Rd., 403/859-2224) year-round. The nearest hospitals are 30 miles (50 km) away

in Pincher Creek (403/627-3333) and Cardston (403/653-4411). To contact the park's one emergency ambulance, call 403/859-2636.

DRIVING TOURS
Chief Mountain Highway

The Chief Mountain International Highway provides a summer-only connection between Glacier and Waterton Parks. Its season and hours operate around the Canadian and U.S. customs stations at the border (open mid-May–Sept.; May and after Labor Day 9 A.M.–6 P.M., June–Labor Day 7 A.M.–10 P.M.). You may want to top off on gas in the United States since gas is generally more expensive in Canada. (The nearest gas is in Babb or Waterton Townsite.) The 30-mile road undulates over rolling aspen hills and beaver ponds as it curves around Chief Mountain, imposing alone on Glacier's northwest corner. A few unmarked pullouts offer good photo ops. Drive this open range carefully, for cows wander the road. Your car also may need a good cleaning if wet cow pies litter the road!

As the road rounds Chief Mountain, it enters Glacier Park—no entrance station is here;

WATERTON

AKAMINA-KISHINENA PROVINCIAL PARK

Where Waterton Lakes National Park ends at the Continental Divide, Akamina-Kishinena Provincial Park picks up following the boundary of Montana's Glacier National Park to the North Fork of the Flathead River. This 27,000-acre park is remote, accessible only on foot from Akamina Parkway in Waterton Lakes or trails from the end of a 68-mile (109-kilometer) dirt road that takes off 10 miles (16 km) south of Fernie, British Columbia.

Akamina-Kishinena is part of the same narrow Rocky Mountain ecosystem that provides corridors for grizzly bears and other wildlife. Geologic wonders display themselves in Forum Peak's 1.3-billion-year-old sedimentary rocks, and rare plants like the pygmy poppy grow here.

From Waterton, hikers and mountain bikers can access the park via an old circa 1920

trail that connects the Cameron Valley to the North Fork of the Flathead Valley. To access Akamina-Kishinena, hike to Akamina Pass, the boundary between Waterton Park and Akamina-Kishinena. From there, you can mountain bike to Wall Lake (6.7 miles, 11.2 km round-trip from Akamina Parkway) or hike to Forum Lake (4.8 miles, 8 km round-trip from Akamina Parkway).

Some Canadians want to expand Waterton Lakes to include Akamina-Kishinena, which would increase the size of Waterton and complete the "Crown of the Continent" ecosystem. It is, after all, part of the Rocky Mountain grizzly bear corridor.

For more information, contact British Columbia Parks (205/489-8540, www.gov.bc.ca/bcparks).

no payment is required—and reaches Chief Mountain Customs at 18.6 miles. After customs, the road enters Alberta and Waterton Lakes National Park, but you won't reach an entrance station until nearly at the Townsite. After the road crosses the Belly River, it briefly exits the park, crossing the Blood Indian Reserve (part of the Blackfoot family) before re-entering the park. Burn from the 1998 Sofa Mountain Fire lines both sides of the road. As you crest a big rise, stop at the overlook (28 miles, 45 km) to gaze at the Waterton Valley. For the descent, shift into second gear to avoid burning your brakes.

Akamina Parkway

A 10-mile (16-kilometer) paved drive climbs above Waterton Townsite along the base of Crandell Mountain on Akamina Parkway. The road is open all year, although in winter only to Little Prairie. Just west of the Waterton Visitor Information Center, the signed Akamina Parkway turns off and begins climbing steeply from Waterton Townsite as it curves up above the Cameron Creek Gorge. It passes the **Oil City Historic Site** as well as trailheads to Crandell Lake, Lineham Falls, Rowe Lakes, Akamina Pass, and Forum Lake. For those looking to picnic along Cameron Creek, picnic tables, toilets, and shelters are at McNeally's (4 miles, 6.4 km) and Little Prairie (8.1 miles, 13 km). The road ends at **Cameron Lake.** On the return trip, shift into second gear for the steep descent back to the Townsite; you can always smell the brakes of those who forget.

Red Rocks Parkway

Red Rocks Parkway (May–Oct.) is rather self-descriptive, for the paved road ends at a red-rock canyon. Locate the signed turnoff on the park entrance road (2.2 miles, 3.5 km from the Townsite; 2.8 miles, 3.9 km from park entrance station). The 9.3-mile (15-kilometer) narrow road climbs through grasslands, squeezes through a canyon, and opens up into meadows along Blakiston Creek. Through the canyon, the road is quite narrow but passable for trailers and RVs. Bring your binocu-

historic Prince of Wales Hotel in Waterton

lars for wildlife-watching of bears and bighorn sheep. Crandell Mountain Campground (4.6 miles, 7.5 km) is accessed via this road. The parkway ends where a self-guided trail leads around **Red Rock Canyon.** To picnic along Red Rocks, you'll find tables, pit toilets, and shelters at three spots: Coppermine Creek (5 miles, 8 km), Dungarvan (8 miles, 13 km), and Red Rocks (9.3 miles, 15 km).

SIGHTS
◖ Chief Mountain

Located along Chief Mountain Highway, Chief Mountain rises up 9,080 feet abruptly from aspen parklands and prairies. It marks the northeasternmost peak in Glacier National Park. Legend tells of a young Flathead Brave who carried a bison skull to its summit and remained there for four nights wrestling the Spirit of the Mountain. When he finally prevailed, the Spirit gave him a protection totem to keep him safe in battle and hunting.

◖ Prince of Wales Hotel

Designated a Canadian National Historic Site, the 122-foot-tall five-story 90-room Prince of Wales Hotel took more than a year to build. Constructed by Great Northern Railway as a link for the Glacier chain, the hotel opened its doors in 1927. Even if you are not staying here, drop in to see its massive lobby with floor-to-ceiling windows looking down Waterton Lake. Kilt-wearing bellhops haul luggage, and the lobby serves high tea in the afternoon. Walk out on the bluff for the best photographic views of Waterton Lake. But hold onto your hat, for howling winds frequently rage!

Waterton Lake

Set in a north–south trough gouged by Pleistocene ice age glaciers, Waterton Lake is the deepest lake in the Canadian Rockies. (It's actually Upper Waterton Lake, which feeds Middle and Lower Waterton Lakes, but no one calls it that.) Its 487-foot depths hold 50-pound lake trout and tiny ice age relics—the opossum shrimp. Spanning the international boundary, the half-mile-wide and nearly seven-mile-long lake conveys visitors over its waters in the 1927 wooden MV *International.*

The U.S.-Canadian Border

For Waterton visitors, the border inside the park is an attraction. The boat tour down Waterton Lake crosses the international boundary. Visitors can debark in Goat Haunt and walk to the Peace Park Pavilion without going through customs, or hike over the border to Goat Haunt on the Waterton Lake Trail (but you must go through customs when you arrive at Goat Haunt Ranger Station).

◖ Goat Haunt, U.S.A.

A tiny seasonal enclave housing rangers, Goat Haunt, U.S.A., rests at Waterton Lake's southern end in Glacier Park. Accessed only by boat or on foot, Goat Haunt sees hundreds of visitors per day in high season. Most arrive via the MV *International.* Walk the paved pathway to the International Peace Park Pavilion, where displays tell the story of the peace park. Trailheads depart

International Peace Park Pavilion at Goat Haunt, U.S.A.

© BECKY LOMAX

WATERTON

to Goat Haunt Overlook, Kootenai Lakes, and Rainbow Falls.

🅒 Cameron Lake

Tucked in a glacial cirque at the terminus of Akamina Parkway, Cameron Lake reflects the steep slopes of Mount Custer. Look across the glacially-fed lake to Herbst Glacier: you're looking across the international boundary into Montana. Avalanches preen the slopes into good bear habitat. Rent a rowboat or canoe to paddle around the lake's shoreline, or saunter the pathway along the west shore watching for moose, shorebirds, and bears. The Carthew-Alderson trail departs from here.

Waterton Heritage Centre

Waterton Heritage Centre (117 Waterton Ave., 403/859-2267, mid-May–Sept., 10 A.M.–6 P.M.) is a small museum with displays on Waterton's natural and cultural history. Books—from hiking guides to coffee table picture books—are also sold here. Run by the Waterton Natural History Association, the center also hosts geology, botany, wildlife, photography, and birding field courses (one-day course CDN$50–75; two- or three-day program CDN$100–175) taught by local experts.

Cameron Falls

On the edge of the Waterton Townsite on Evergreen Avenue, Cameron Falls is a picturesque falls. In June, water roars through its slots, but substantially drops by August. Several benches allow for gazing. Here, Cameron Creek has eroded a massive fold of the Waterton Formation, a 600-million-year-old rock layer. Short, steep 10-minute trails on both sides of the creek access viewpoints. Opt for the north side switchback trail for better views.

🅒 Red Rock Canyon

Red Rocks Parkway begins at Blakiston Creek and terminates at Red Rock Canyon, a colorful narrow canyon. Walk the 0.4-mile (0.7-kilometer) pathway up one side and down the other to take in all its hues. Iron-rich argillite sediments layer on top of each other, some

turning red from oxidization, others remaining green. Evidence of the ancient Belt Sea, these rocks are some of the oldest exposed rock in the world, created between 800 million and 1.6 billion years ago. Look for sea evidence of mud cracks and ripple marks.

🅒 Maskinonge Lake

Birders and wildlife watchers migrate to Maskinonge Lake for its rich diversity. Located east of the park entrance, the aspen-rimmed lake attracts waterfowl, osprey, trumpeter swans, yellow-headed blackbirds, and kingfishers. Because Waterton is on the axis of two migration flyways, it sees over 250 species of birds. The lake also attracts everything from huge Shiras moose weighing 1,500 pounds to muskrats, mink, and tiny vagrant shrews. When rare trumpeter swans nest in July and early August, some of the area is closed to protect their offspring. Don't forget to take your binoculars and spotting scopes!

🅒 Bison Paddock

Once roaming the plains in vast numbers 150 years ago, wild bison have all but vanished from North America. On Highway 6, 1.2 miles (2 km) west of the park entrance road, the Bison Paddock contains a small herd. Bison weigh close to 2,000 pounds and look like shaggy cows. But don't be lured into thinking they are docile: They may look big, lunky, and dumb, but they are extremely unpredictable and aggressive. Drive on the narrow, roughly paved 2.5-mile loop through the grassland paddock; for safety, stay inside the vehicle.

Discovery Well and Oil City

Located on the Akamina Parkway, two stops mark the sight of the Discovery Well, western Canada's first oil well, and its accompanying townsite. The first is at 4.8 miles (8 km) up the road; it's the actual site of the first well from 1902. Continue on a bit to the original townsite for **Oil City.** A short five-minute walk through the trees leads to the hotel foundation—all that remains of the 20-block city that was plotted out. Closed within four years, Oil City soon became a ghost town.

Recreation

HIKING

Waterton has well over 124 miles (200 km) of trails. Paved and dirt walking trails (1.9 miles, 3.2 km) in Waterton Townsite connect many of the sights, restaurants, lodging facilities, the campground, and picnic areas. From the marina to Cameron Bay, the trail follows the shoreline. Trails also connect to the Falls Theater, Cameron Falls, Bertha Lake and Waterton Lake trailheads, Emerald Bay, and Prince of Wales Hotel. Contrary to Glacier's backcountry rules, Waterton's trails permit dogs on a leash, but keep your pet under control and away from wildlife.

For those planning to camp in the backcountry, wilderness permits are necessary ($8 per person per night, ages 16 and under free) for all of the nine designated backcountry campsites. Reservations are available for $12 per trip 90 days in advance beginning April 1 each year. You can get permits and reservations at the Waterton Visitor Information Center or Waterton's Parks Canada office.

Shuttles by water and land make for easy trailhead access. Waterton Shoreline Cruises (403/859-2362, www.watertoncruise.com) operates the Crypt Lake and Goat Haunt boats. The Tamarack Village (214 Mount View Rd., 403/859-2378, www.watertonvisitorservices.com) operates the land shuttles.

Bertha Lake

- Distance: 7 miles (11.4 km) round-trip
- Duration: 3–4 hours
- Elevation gain: 1,480 feet
- Effort: 2 miles moderate, remainder strenuous
- Trailhead: southwest corner of Waterton Townsite off Evergreen Avenue

The trail is a signed interpretive path to Lower Bertha Falls. The path climbs gradually along the western shore of Waterton Lake to an overlook with views of Mount Cleveland, the highest peak in Glacier. At the junction, take the right fork and head across the dry open hillside to Lower Bertha Falls, where pounding waters crash through bedrock. For a destination, the falls is 4 miles (6.4 km) round-trip.

Those continuing farther should cross the bridge below the falls and begin incessant switchbacks up through a forested hillside beside Upper Bertha Falls, a larger sister of the lower falls. Soon, the trail crests a timbered knoll high above narrow Bertha Lake. The best view of the lake is here. To reach the shore, descend 0.1 mile to the campground near its outlet.

Waterton Lake Trail

- Distance: 8.7 miles (13 km) one-way
- Duration: 4–5 hours
- Elevation gain: minimal
- Effort: easy by elevation gain, moderate by length
- Trailhead: southwest corner of Waterton Townsite off Evergreen Avenue

Bordering the west lakeshore of Waterton Lake, the trail begins at the Bertha Lake Trailhead. After 1 mile (0.6 kilometer), the trails diverge, with the Waterton Lake Trail dropping in a quick steep descent to Bertha Bay Campground on the lakeshore. From here, the trail wanders through cottonwoods, subalpine firs, lodgepoles, and aspen. A few overlooks offer views of the lake.

The trail crosses the international boundary at 3.8 miles (6.1 km) before connecting to a well-signed maze of trails at the end of Waterton Lake. Follow signs to Goat Haunt and catch the MV *International* back to the Townsite. Before you leave in the morning, book your return trip with Waterton Shoreline Cruises. Bring your passport; you'll need it for customs in Goat Haunt.

WATERTON

Crypt Lake

- Distance: 11.2 miles (17 km) round-trip
- Duration: 5–6 hours
- Elevation gain: 2,300 feet
- Effort: moderately strenuous
- Trailhead: Crypt Landing, accessible by boat from Waterton

Catch the water taxi operated daily by Waterton Shoreline Cruises to reach Crypt Landing. From Crypt Landing, the climb begins immediately working its way up through a wooded hillside along Hellroaring Creek Valley. An alternate route leads to the edge of Hellroaring Creek and its waterfalls; you can take one route up and one down this short section. Soon, the trail passes Twin Falls and lodgepole pines give way to open meadows and boulder fields.

The trail appears to dead-end in a headwall. But, an iron ladder climbs up to a four-foot-high tunnel with an awkward walk or crawl. The tunnel emerges on a cliff with a steel cable for assistance in crossing. The trail breaks into a tight cirque housing Crypt Lake, which drains from an underwater channel. The international boundary crosses the lake's southern end. In a mad dash, hikers suddenly check their watches and all jump up to speed down the trail en masse to catch the return boat.

◖ Bear's Hump

- Distance: 1.7 miles (2.8 km) round-trip
- Duration: 1.25 hours
- Elevation gain: 550 feet
- Effort: strenuous, but short
- Trailhead: Waterton Visitor Information Centre parking lot

The trail heads uphill immediately—piling on switchback after switchback in a vertical thighmaster. At least it offers two benches en route for rest. Although partially forested and thick with thimbleberry and virgin's bower, the hike is cool in early morning or late afternoon after the hump shades the east slope from the sun. The visitor center has a free interpretive guide to accompany the trail.

Topping out on the Bear's Hump, a rocky outcropping on Mount Crandell's ridge, the trail offers one of the best views of the Waterton Townsite, Prince of Wales Hotel, Waterton Lake, Glacier National Park, and prairielands heading eastward. On top, three benches offer good spots to scenery gaze before you tackle the knee-pounding descent.

Lineham Falls

- Distance: 5.2 miles (8.4 km) round-trip
- Duration: 2.5 hours
- Elevation gain: 1,290 feet
- Effort: moderate
- Trailhead: on Akamina Parkway, look for a marked pullout on the right at 5.6 miles (9.3 km)

In early July, this trail bursts with wildflowers: arrowleaf balsamroot, paintbrush, and lupine. Beginning as an old dirt road, the trail soon narrows and climbs through a pine forest and open dry meadows above Lineham Creek. Within a half mile, the trail re-enters a fir forest. As the canyon narrows, the trail drops to Lineham Creek and a meadow. From here, you'll have to poke around for two unmarked spur trails: One leads toward the creek, the other higher up. Both spurs give different views of the 410-foot falls tumbling down the cliffs.

Cameron Lakeshore

- Distance: 1.9 miles (3.2 km) round-trip
- Duration: 1 hour
- Elevation gain: none
- Effort: easy
- Trailhead: at the day-use facility at Cameron Lake

© BECKY LOMAX

Grizzly Gardens at Cameron Lake

This short trail follows the lake's west shoreline to a wooden platform and small interpretive display called Grizzly Gardens, where trees are starting to cut the view. Although the trail is flat, watch your footing on tree roots in the trail. Several points reach the shoreline for photos of Mount Custer and Herbst Glacier. At the trail's terminus, glass the avalanche slopes for grizzly bears feeding on glacier lilies. Do not continue farther; bears depend on quiet here for denning, feeding, and cub rearing.

Carthew-Alderson

- Distance: 11.8 miles (18 km) one-way
- Duration: 6 hours
- Elevation gain: 1,440 feet
- Effort: moderately strenuous
- Trailhead: behind day-use facility at Cameron Lake

Catch the 8:30 A.M. Cameron Express hiker shuttle to Cameron Lake. One of the most popular hikes in Waterton, the trail climbs 4.5 miles to Carthew Summit, where alpine tundra stretches along a windswept ridge. Be prepared for strong winds here, even on a sunny summer day. Some winds may even force you to crawl over the pass. Views span deep into Glacier's interior.

The descent is a knee-pounder, dropping over 3,000 feet in elevation. From the summit, the trail passes by several high tarns, sometimes flanked with snowfields well into July. As the path drops along a cliff wall, it reaches a ridge above Alderson Lake. Once you depart the lake, only peek-a-boo views of avalanche chutes break out from the thick timber en route to Waterton Townsite.

Blakiston Falls

- Distance: 1.2 miles (2 km) round-trip
- Duration: 45 minutes
- Elevation gain: minimal
- Effort: easy
- Trailhead: end of Red Rocks Parkway

Turn left just after you cross Red Rocks Creek. Then across Bauerman Creek, look for the hiker trailhead and walk through a coniferous forest. Blakiston Creek tumbles below the trail, and Mount Blakiston peeks into view from time to time. At Blakiston Falls, a wooden deck conveniently makes for easy observation of the tumbling falls.

Goat Lake

- Distance: 7.8 miles (12.6 km) round-trip
- Duration: 4 hours
- Elevation gain: 1,750 feet
- Effort: moderately strenuous
- Trailhead: at end of Red Rocks Parkway

Pack along your fishing rod, for rainbow trout populate Goat Lake. Begin the hike by crossing Red Rocks Creek and continue along the heavily traveled Snowshoe Trail following

WATERTON

Bauerman Creek up valley. The trail climbs gently through a timbered canyon with not much to offer in the way of views except a few glimpses of the creek. At 2.5 miles (4 km), you'll reach the junction heading to Goat Lake.

The trail climbs abruptly here, gaining all of its elevation in an endless ascent, eventually opening onto wildflower meadows as it aims for the cliffs of Avion Ridge. As the trail reaches Goat Lake's outlet, it pops through a narrow opening into the upper cirque. When you reach the lake, be sure to scan the cliffs above for its namesake mountain goats.

Rainbow Falls

- Distance: 1.4 miles round-trip

- Duration: 1 hour

- Elevation gain: minimal

- Effort: easy

- Trailhead: behind ranger station at Goat Haunt in Glacier National Park

Rainbow Falls is one option for a short hike from the boat tour on Waterton Lake. (Check with Waterton Shoreline Cruises for a schedule and book a return boat that allows enough time to complete your hike. Take passports and ID, for you will also need to pass through customs in Goat Haunt.)

Follow the paved trail to the first junction, taking the right fork onto dirt. The trail wanders through thick forests, which are quite full of mosquitoes in early summer. Just before reaching Waterton River, take a left turn at the signed junction, heading up the east bank toward Rainbow Falls. The falls is actually a series of cascades cutting troughs in bedrock, but a great place to sit for a snack or lunch.

Goat Haunt Overlook

- Distance: 2 miles (3.2 km) round-trip

- Duration: 2 hours

- Elevation gain: 844 feet

- Effort: very strenuous

- Trailhead: behind ranger station at Goat Haunt in Glacier National Park

Goat Haunt Overlook is another option for a short hike from the boat tour on Waterton Lake. (Check with Waterton Shoreline Cruises for a schedule and book a return boat that allows enough time to complete your hike. Take passports and ID, for you need to pass through customs in Goat Haunt to hike the trail.)

Follow the paved trail past the first right-hand turn to dirt trail and hike 0.1 mile on the Continental Divide Trail heading south toward Fifty Mountain. At the signed junction, turn left. The trail climbs gently for a few hundred feet before it turns steeply straight up hill. It's a grunt, but the view is well worth the climb. At the overlook, you can flop on a conveniently placed log to eat lunch and gander down lake to the Waterton Townsite and Prince of Wales Hotel.

Kootenai Lakes

- Distance: 5.6 miles (9 km) round-trip

- Duration: 3–3.5 hours

- Elevation gain: minimal

- Effort: easy

- Trailhead: behind ranger station at Goat Haunt in Glacier National Park

Kootenai Lakes attracts hikers for its often-seen moose and sometimes-seen nesting trumpeter swans. Access is via the tour boat. (Check with Waterton Shoreline Cruises for a schedule and book a return boat that allows enough time to complete your hike. Take passports and ID, in order to pass through customs in Goat Haunt.)

At Goat Haunt, follow the paved trail past the first right-hand turn and hike on the Continental Divide Trail heading south toward Fifty Mountain. The trail wanders through old growth forest. At 2.5 miles (4 km), take the right junction toward the campground.

If you eat lunch here, do so on the beach or in the cook area and protect the cleanliness of the tenting sites for those sleeping in bear country.

International Peace Park Guided Hike

At least once a week during July and August, National Park Service interpretive rangers from Waterton and Glacier jointly lead the International Peace Park Hike. The 14-kilometer (8.7 mile) hike leaves at 10 A.M. from the Bertha Lake Trailhead. Bring a sack lunch, water, and extra clothes, and wear sturdy walking shoes. You'll stop at the boundary for a hands-across-the-border ceremony and photos before hiking to Goat Haunt and returning by boat to the Townsite by 6 P.M. Group size is limited to 35, so you'll need to pre-register at the Waterton Lakes Visitor Information Center (403/859-5133) or Glacier's St. Mary Visitor Center (406/732-7750). It's free, but you'll need to pay for the boat ride and make reservations through Waterton Shoreline Tours.

Guides

Several guide companies operate in Waterton, all offering custom half-day (CDN$40–100 per person) and full-day (CDN$90–150 per person) hikes with interpretive services. Rates are usually based on having a two-person minimum and may or may not include transportation depending on the trailhead's location. Boat shuttle costs are extra. When flat rates are used, they run $150–300 per day, depending on length, difficulty, and expectations; this cost is divided between the number of participants. Bring your own trail snacks, lunches, and water.

Brian and Lauren Baker, long-time Waterton folks who run the outdoor gear shop, primarily guide groups through **Waterton Outdoor Adventures** (Tamarack Village Square, 214 Mount View Rd., 403/859-2379, www.watertonvisitorservices.com, late May–early Oct.). While they may end up referring single hikers or couples to another guide service, they also happily offer trail advice to hikers going on their own.

Beth Russell offers guiding services through her shop, **Trail of the Great Bear** (114 Waterton Ave., 403/859-2663 or 800/215-2395, www.trailofthegreatbear.com). Using local expert naturalists, she puts together everything from introductory hikes to trips specializing in geology, botany, or wildlife—whatever interests you have.

Canadian Wilderness Tours (403/859-2058 July–Aug., 800/408-0005, www.whitemountainadventures.com) guides treks from nature walks to strenuous scrambles. The company is in Canmore and staffs a guide in Waterton late June through August. You'll need to make your reservations by phone.

BIKING

All roadways in Waterton offer good bicycling. Particular favorites are Akamina and Red Rocks Parkways. Neither have big shoulders, and both narrow up tightly in spots, so be prepared to ride with cars at your elbows. Be prepared to encounter bears on both roads.

Waterton offers ample places for both mountain bikers and roadies to ride. In addition to roadways, four trails in Waterton National Park permit bicycles. Parks Canada levies heavy fines up to CDN$2,000 for riding on sidewalks, grass, or walking trails. For campers traveling by bicycle, both the Townsite and Crandell Mountain Campgrounds have bear-resistant food storage facilities.

Alberta law requires kids under 18 to wear a helmet while bicycling. Given the narrow roads and the fact that most drivers are gaping at the scenery or looking for bears, it's a wise idea for all ages to wear helmets. Wind, here, can be strong enough to knock you off your bike.

Bike Trails

Four trails in Waterton permit bikes. For these, mountain bikes will handle terrain rubble better than road bikes. For current trail conditions, check with the visitor center.

Departing from 8.4 miles (14 km) up the Akamina Parkway, **Akamina Pass Trail** is a wide, but stiff and steep 0.8-mile (1.3-kilometer) climb on a forested trail. Even though the pass offers no great scenery, it's the Continental Divide and marks the boundary of Waterton National Park and Akamina-Kishinena Provincial Park as well as Alberta and British Columbia. After crossing the pass, you can continue riding to Wall Lake—adding another 4.8 miles (8 km) round-trip.

Beginning at the end of Red Rocks Parkway, the **Snowshoe Trail** rides 9.8 miles (16.4 km) round-trip along Bauerman Creek to the Snowshoe Warden Cabin. An abandoned fire road, with a fairly wide berth, the trail has some steep sections and creek fords for spice. Bikes are prohibited on the side trails. Hikers with a little savvy here do biking-hiking trips—bicycling for quicker backcountry access.

Leaving Chief Mountain Highway less than half a mile from the Highway 5 junction, the 12.6-mile (21-kilometer) round-trip **Wishbone Trail** starts off wide and easy on an old wagon road through aspen parklands, but about halfway it soon becomes narrow and overgrown. At 4.9 miles (8.2 km), you'll reach the Vimy Trail (hiking only) junction just before traversing above the Lower Waterton Lake shoreline.

The most challenging ride is the 12.6 mile (21-kilometer) **Crandell Mountain Loop**, combining trails to circle the mountain. Be prepared to encounter rough terrain and washouts. You can start at three different trailheads: Crandell Lake Trailhead 3.6 miles (6 km) up Akamina Parkway, 3.6 miles (6 km) up Red Rocks Parkway on the Crandell Campground turnoff, or Waterton Townsite.

Rentals

Pat's Gas Station (224 Mount View Rd., 403/859-2266, www.watertoninfo.ab.ca) rents mountain bikes by the hour (CDN$8) or full day (CDN$34). The shop also carries full suspension mountain bikes (CDN$45), helmets (free with rentals; otherwise CDN$10), and cycle trailers (CDN$25) for baby hauling.

You'll see Pat's famous two-person four-wheel surrey bikes tootling around the Townsite (CDN$20 per hour); they're fun for a spin, but stick to the Townsite roads!

TRAIL RIDING

Horseback riding is available daily through **Alpine Stables** (2.4 miles, 4 km from park entrance on park entrance road, 403/859-2462, www.alpinestables.com, May–Sept., 9 A.M.– 5 P.M.). Guided hourly rides (CDN$25) leave daily at 10 A.M. to 4 P.M., touring on open grasslands with big views of surrounding Waterton peaks. During July and August, rides depart every hour. With small saddles, the stables can take kids as young as four years old. You can either reserve a spot or simply show up about 20 minutes early. Wear long pants and tennis shoes or boots. For 90-minute rides (CDN$34), departures are at 3:30 and 5 P.M. Two-hour rides (CDN$42) leave at 10 A.M. and 1 and 5 P.M. Three- and four-hour rides (CDN$58–74) depart twice daily at 9:30 A.M. and 1:30 P.M. For longer rides of up to eight hours (CDN$119), you'll need to bring your own lunch and be ready to leave at 9 or 10 A.M.

If you're traveling with your own equine, Alpine Stables will board your horse (CDN$9 per night, including feed).

BOATING

Motorized boats are permitted on only two lakes: **Upper and Middle Waterton Lakes.** Jet skis are banned. You can launch boats on ramps at Linnet Lake Picnic Area (0.7 mile, 1.1 kilometer from the Townsite on the park entrance road) on Middle Waterton Lake or the marina on Upper Waterton Lake. The marina sells gas and also has overnight mooring services operated by Waterton Shoreline Cruises (403/859-2362).

Boaters are not permitted to camp in their watercraft, but several wilderness campsites are accessible by boat. Permits are required for these (CDN$8 per person per night; kids 16 and under free). Reservations are available for CDN$12 per trip 90 days in advance begin-

ning April 1 each year. Both permits and reservations are available at the Waterton Visitor Information Center or Waterton's Parks Canada office.

KAYAKING AND CANOEING

Canoeing, kayaking, and rowing are perfect activities for many of Waterton's road-accessible lakes. However, be aware that winds are common here with an average speed of 20 mph on Waterton Lake.

Waterton Lakes

A few paddlers tackle Upper Waterton Lake; those who do stick close to the shoreline because of the wind. With less hefty gales, more kayakers and canoers gravitate toward Middle Waterton Lake, the Dardanelles (the waterway connecting the two lakes), and Lower Waterton Lake for exceptional wildlife-watching and birding. Hay Barn and Marquis Picnic Areas are the most popular put-ins for paddling these sections.

Cameron Lake

Cameron Lake is an ideal spot for sea kayaking, canoeing, and rowing. Winds are often less cantankerous here than at Waterton Lakes and the views equally as tantalizing. Do not land or hike on the slopes surrounding the southern half of the lake; this is prime grizzly bear habitat. Canoes, paddleboats, and rowboat rentals (403/859-2396, mid-June–Aug., 7:30 A.M.–7:30 P.M., CDN$20–25 per hour, cash only) are available at the lakeshore. Lifejackets and paddles are included in the rates.

FISHING

As in Glacier, fish are no longer stocked in Waterton Lakes National Park; however, introduced species still populate waterways: arctic grayling, British Columbia and Yellowstone cutthroat, and rainbow, eastern brook, and brown trout. Seventeen species of native fish—bull trout, ling, lake chub, deepwater sculpin, northern pike, pygmy whitefish, and spottail shiner, to name a few—still harbor here.

In **Waterton Lake,** catch rainbow trout, whitefish, and pike. Fish feed here on the tiny opossum shrimp, a crustacean that is a relic descended from pre-ice age days. The record lake trout caught in Waterton Lake was 51 pounds. Some hiking destinations, like **Goat Lake,** have good rainbow trout fishing.

Season

Four waterways are open year-round for fishing: the Dardanelles, Lower Waterton Lake, Waterton River, and Maskinonge Lake. One river is closed year-round—the North Fork of the Belly River. From late May through early September, anglers may fish Upper and Middle Waterton Lakes, Crandell Lake, Cameron Lake, Cameron Creek, and Akamina Lake. Blakiston Creek limits fishing to late June through early September. Beyond that, the general fishing season is late June through the end of October.

Regulations

Waterton Park requires a Tribal fishing permit (seven days CDN$7, annual CDN$20) to fish within park boundaries. Purchase one at the visitor center, Parks Canada office, campground kiosks, Cameron Lake boat rentals, or Pat's Gas Station. The license is valid in all Canadian mountain parks. Kids under 16 can either purchase their own permit to catch a full limit or share limits with an adult. Check for species limits when you purchase fishing licenses. In general, native species—bull trout, kokanee, and cutthroat (those caught in the three Waterton Lakes)—are catch-and-release only. You may, however, keep two fish of introduced species: arctic grayling, rainbows, brown trout, brookies, lake trout, northern pike, mountain whitefish, lake whitefish, and cutthroat caught elsewhere than the three Waterton lakes.

Lead weights less than 50 grams (1.75 oz.) are not permitted due to contamination of waterfowl. As in Glacier, bull trout are a protected species in Waterton. Follow the adage, "No black, put it back."

WATERTON

WATERSKIING

Waterskiing is permitted only on Upper and Middle Waterton Lakes; however, most water-skiers gravitate to the middle lake. It's more sheltered and less windy than its upper sister. You'll find boat ramps at Linnet Lake Picnic Area (0.7 mile, 1.1 km from the Townsite on the park entrance road) on Middle Waterton Lake or the marina on Upper Waterton Lake. Because the water is extremely cold, water-skiers wear dry suits or full wetsuits here. Floating debris—logs, sticks, and branches—is common; keep your eyes open for these hazards. Waterton has no water-ski boat or ski rental service.

WINDSURFING

It's a rare day when Waterton doesn't see wind. Winds don't just blow here; they gust and howl. For traveling windsurfers with their own gear (no rental gear is available in Waterton), Upper and Middle Waterton Lakes are good places to catch some waves. The glacier-fed lakes, however, are freezing cold. Wear a wet or dry suit to prevent hypothermia. To windsurf here, you should know how to water start and self-rescue; it's not a place for beginners. For the best launching on the upper lake, head to the picnic shelters on Waterton Avenue one block west of Vimy Avenue. For safety, check the current weather report at the Waterton Visitor Information Center before launching into a big wind.

SCUBA DIVING

Scuba divers go after a spot in Emerald Bay, where a sunken circa 1900 paddle steamer, *The Gertrude,* provides exploration at a 65-foot (20-meter) depth. For the clearest waters, early spring and fall are best for scuba diving here. Just remember that historic artifacts, which include anything on the wreck, are protected by the park; leave all things where you find them. Bring your own gear, as the nearest scuba shop for rentals and repairs is 78 miles (130 km) east in Lethbridge.

GOLF

Focusing on your putting can be difficult with huge scenery. Not only are sandtraps a hazard, but sometimes grizzly bears are too. Located 1.7 miles (3 km) from the Townsite, the 18-hole **Waterton Golf Course** is an original Stanley Thompson design like the Banff Springs and Jasper courses—rolling fairways bordered with aspens. The dawn-to-dusk course charges CDN$33 for 18 holes. A full pro shop rents golf carts (CDN$27) and clubs (CDN$7–11), and a licensed clubhouse keeps guests fed and watered on its patio with outstanding views. For tee times, call 403/859-2114. Many of Waterton's hotels offer golf packages in May and after mid-September.

TENNIS

Four hard-surface public tennis courts are smack in the Townsite Center on Cameron Falls Drive between Harebell Drive and Windflower Avenue. **Pat's Gas Station** (224 Mount View Rd., 403/859-2266) rents tennis rackets for $3 per hour. The free courts are available on a first-come, first-serve basis. Limit playing time to 30 minutes when other players are waiting. The outdoor courts are unlit at night and covered in snow in winter.

CROSS-COUNTRY SKIING AND SNOWSHOEING

In winter, when heavy snows render many of the roads impassable by vehicle, the parkways become ideal cross-country ski trails. Alternatively, ski along Waterton Lake or on the lake after it freezes. With less than 100 residents wintering in Waterton, services are minimal, so plan on bringing skis and snowshoes. The park does not permit snowmobiles, so a quiet backcountry winter experience is guaranteed. Also, dogs are not permitted on the park's groomed ski trails, which helps maintain the tracks in good condition for gliding.

Waterton is a land of winter extremes. It records the highest precipitation levels in Alberta, much of it in snowfall. It also records winter winds over 60 miles per hour, which can plummet wind chills. With winter chinooks, the park is also one of Alberta's warmest areas with an average of 28 days above freezing. With this diversity, you can expect all types of

snow—from dry, light powder to heavy, wet glop—and conditions that change within an hour. Most cross-country skiers here sacrifice a bit of speed for reliable glide by using waxless skis

Two designated ski trails are marked and track-set for weekends: **Cameron** and **Dipper Ski Trails,** both off Akamina Parkway, which is plowed to the trailheads at Little Prairie. Other trails such as Crandell Lake, Rowe Trail, and Akamina Pass are popular trails, but skiers should be prepared with pieps (avalanche rescue beacons) for avalanche travel. Contact the Waterton Parks Canada office (403/859-2224) for details.

ENTERTAINMENT

During summer months, Parks Canada offers evening slide shows and indoor programs at the Townsite Falls Theater (across Evergreen Ave. from Cameron Falls) and Crandell Mountain Campground. Programs vary, but cover wildlife, ecology, and geology. Contact 403/859-2445 for current schedule.

The **Waterton Opera House** (309 Windflower Ave., 403/859-2466), which shows movies rather than staging operas, opens during summer months only. Shows change regularly, but don't expect to see world premieres at this tiny outpost. In mid-June, the opera house hosts the three-day **Waterton International French Film Festival** (www.watertoninternationalfrenchfilmfest.com, CDN$6 per show, CDN$35 for all show pass) with eight full-length features plus short films with English subtitles.

For 10 days in late June, the **Waterton Wildflower Festival** (800/215-2395, www.watertonwildflowers.com) pulls together hikes, art shows, photography courses, watercolor painting workshops, drawing classes, slide shows, and free evening lectures in a tribute to the park's rare and diverse wildflowers. Some events are single-day programs lasting two hours; others are multiday. All are taught by regional experts. Course fees range CDN$25–150, but several are free. You can register with a credit card by phone or online; or stop in Trail of the Great Bear shop on Waterton Avenue.

Accommodations

In Waterton, everything is within walking distance, with the compact town less than a mile across. You're not far from restaurants, shopping, boat tours, hiking, tennis, or movies no matter where you stay. While the town bustles in summer, in winter only a few services and hotels remain open. All accommodations add a 5 percent provincial tax and 7 percent Goods and Services Tax on to your rates; together, those add up, so don't be surprised that your final room bill tallies higher than you might have expected.

Lodges and Inns

Located on a bluff above Waterton Lake and the Townsite, historic 【 **Prince of Wales Hotel** (4.6 miles, 7.6 km south of park entrance station across from the visitor center, 406/892-2525, www.glacierparkinc.com, early

June–mid-Sept., CDN$179–599 until mid-June; after mid-June CDN$259–799, rates for two people, additional CDN$15 each) is a four-storied wonder, and yes, it is named for Prince Edward. Its lobby with floor to ceiling windows swings with large rustic chandeliers. Lake-view rooms and suites allow you to shower with a view into Glacier Park while mountain-view rooms lend to spying bighorn sheep on Crandell Mountain. But in spite of its grand facade, the building is old, creaky, and thin walled, and the upper stories seem to sway in high winds. Be prepared for tiny sinks and small bathrooms—many installed in what were once closets. All nonsmoking, rooms have phones, but no television nor air-conditioning. An elevator accesses upper floors but requires a bellhop to run, so it is not available at all hours—nor does it always work. If

WATERTON

WHAT IS GST?

In Canada, a GST/HST (Goods and Services Tax/ Harmonized Sales Tax) is applied to lodging, restaurants, souvenirs, and services. Visitors from outside Canada can claim a refund of the GST on certain goods and services and under certain conditions. You'll need to keep your receipts to apply for your refund. (Credit card slips and photocopies are not acceptable.) To qualify for a tax refund, you must:

• not be a Canadian resident

• purchase eligible goods for personal use

• purchase eligible short-term accommodations

• have paid GST/HST on your purchases

• have Proof of Export for the eligible goods you purchased in Canada (receipts must be validated by customs officials at border crossings or airports)

• have a total purchase amount (before taxes) of at least CDN$200

• have each receipt for eligible goods showing a minimum total purchase amount (before taxes) of CDN$50

• remove the goods from Canada within 60 days of the date you bought them.

In short, taxes paid on camping fees and hotel rooms can be refunded, provided your stay was less than one month and criteria listed above are satisfied. However, taxes paid on RV or trailer rentals are not eligible. Taxes paid on meals and beverages consumed in Canada are not refundable, but taxes paid on hard goods (souvenirs, books, gifts, clothing) taken home are eligible. In general, the following are not eligible for a tax refund: tobacco products, entertainment, transportation, gas, rentals, parking, services (dry cleaning, car repairs, guiding), and medical expenses.

For more details, call 800/668-4748 (in Canada) or 902/432-5608 (from outside Canada). You can also check online and download a refund application: www.cra-arc.gc.ca/tax/non-residents/visitors/tax-e.html. While in Waterton, pick up tax refund forms at Tamarack Village Square (214 Mount View Rd.).

you're on one of the top floors, you'll get a workout climbing to your room. A restaurant, gift shop selling English bone china and Waterford crystal, and lounge surround the lobby. A 5-minute drive or 20-minute walk down a trail accesses the town for boat tours, shopping, bicycle rentals, and restaurants. Reservations are required.

Tucked under the trees on Emerald Bay, **[** **Kilmorey Lodge** (117 Mount View Rd., 403/859-2334 or 888/859-8669, www.kilmoreylodge.com, mid-May–mid-Oct. CDN$123–240, winter rates CDN$24–44 less) may be small, but the log inn is loaded with country ambience and cozy romance. Open year-round, its 23 unique rooms furnished with antiques and down comforters match the 1920s era of the lodge's narrow hallways lined with historic photos. With no in-room phones nor televi-

sions, the atmosphere is quiet and relaxed. With no air-conditioning, rooms are equipped with fans, but with cool evening temperatures in Waterton, they mostly go unused. The lodge also houses the best restaurant in Waterton—the Lamp Post Dining Room—as well as a small outdoor cafe in summer. In winter, a fire blazes in the Ram's Head Lounge's river rock fireplace; in summer, its deck opens for shaded seating.

The 17-room year-round country-style **Crandell Mountain Lodge** (102 Mount View Rd., 403/859-2288 or 866/859-2288, www.crandellmountainlodge.com, June–mid-Sept. CDN$129–199, mid-Sept.–May CDN$40 less per night) almost gets lost beneath the monolith of its namesake peak. The two-story circa 1940 inn has a variety of country theme rooms—all nonsmoking—from

standards to three-room suites with full kitchens and fireplaces. In a private garden area, a huge deck with a barbecue and lounge chairs begs for afternoon relaxation. Plates of chocolate chip cookies on the patio are additional treats. In May, early June, and late September, the lodge offers special activity packages; check on the website for current offerings.

Modern, large, and loaded with amenities such as free use of the Waterton Spa and Recreation Center's salt-water pool and facilities, **Waterton Lakes Lodge** (end of Clematis Ave., 403/859-2151 or 888/985-6343, www.watertonlakeslodge.com, open late April–Nov.; mid-June–mid-Sept. CDN$205–315) has 80 air-conditioned all nonsmoking standard and deluxe rooms as well as kitchenettes and suites. Accommodations are spread throughout nine two-story buildings sitting adjacent to each other. While some rooms have fireplaces and jetted tubs, all rooms have televisions, dataport hookups, and phones. A restaurant, lounge, and cafe complete the scene. Shoulder season rates drop 30–50 percent in spring before mid-June and in fall after mid-September.

Motels and Cabins

Right on Waterton Lake, **The Bayshore** (junction of Mount View Rd. and Waterton Ave., summers 403/859-2211 or 888/527-9555, winters 604/708-9965, www.bayshoreinn.com, mid-April through mid-October, CDN$144–225) lakeshore rooms have prime views from private balconies that make up for its room decor reminiscent of chain hotels. The complex has restaurants, a lounge, a saloon, a hot tub, gift shop, and ice cream shop on site and sits adjacent to the marina, shopping, and additional restaurants. The Townsite Loop trail system passes between the inn and the lake. For the best deal, room rates drop CDN$25–40 in the shoulder seasons from opening until mid-June and from mid-September to closing.

The **Aspen Village Inn** (111 Windflower Ave., 403/859-2255 or 888/859-8669, www.aspenvillageinn.com, mid-May–mid-Sept. CDN$146–257) has both comfortable standard hotel rooms and suites with kitchens

in its modern two-story Windflower and Aspen buildings, where decks hang with colorful flower boxes. Rooms have satellite televisions. Bright cottages accommodating 2–8 people are great for families (summer rates CDN$154–230), and extras especially appealing to families include a playground, outdoor barbecue picnic area, and Jacuzzi. Surrounded by mowed lawns, the large red-metal roofed complex (you won't get lost trying to find it!) is centrally located right in the heart of the Townsite. Early May and mid-September through mid-October see a drop in rates around 30 percent.

Open year-round, the (**Waterton Glacier Suites** (107 Windflower Ave., 403/859-2004 or 866/621-3330, www.watertonsuites.com, early May–mid-Sept., CDN$169–259; winter rates drop by CDN$40–80) has 26 modern clean and spacious units with balconies, refrigerators, microwaves, televisions, air-conditioning, dataports, and whirlpool tubs. Some rooms have fireplaces, and all have mountain views. Most guests rave about friendly service here. A quick two-block walk reaches restaurants, shopping, and the tour boat.

If you're looking for really affordable, your answer is the **Bear Mountain Motel** (208 Mount View Rd., 403/859-2366, www.bearmountainmotel.com, late May–early Oct., CDN$80–120). In 2004, new owners purchased the circa 1960 wood-and-masonry El Cortez Motel. The 36 bedrooms with small bathrooms are the same, but new carpets, beds, linens, and paint in 2005 have upgraded the accommodations of the one-, two-, and three-bedroom suites, several with small kitchenettes. Rooms have small televisions but no phones. Pay phones are near the office.

Bed-and-Breakfast

For park history buffs, the **Northland Lodge** (408 Evergreen Ave., 403/859-2353, www.northlandlodgecanada.com, mid-May–mid-October, CDN$99–175) carries a certain attraction. Louis Hill, builder of the Prince of Wales Hotel and many of Glacier Park's historic hotels, constructed the Swiss-style lodge as his private residence circa 1948, although

he never had time to live there. The lodge only has nine rooms (two with a shared bath and the rest with private baths), split between three levels. A large balcony is great for soaking up views with complimentary coffee and muffins in the morning. Cameron Falls is a short half-block walk away, as is the trailhead to Bertha Falls and Lake. A 10-minute walk puts you in the heart of shopping and restaurants, or you can hop on the 20-minute more scenic Townsite Loop trail just across the street. Room rates see a 30 percent drop in May and late September through October.

Hostel

For a hostel, the **Hostelling International Waterton Alpine Centre** (corner Cameron Falls and Windflower Ave., 403/859-2151 or 888/985-6343, www.hihostels.ca) seems entirely upscale. Since it is connected to Waterton Lake Lodge, hostelers can lounge in the saltwater pool, hot tub, sauna, and steam room—all included in the price! Internet access is available as well as laundry facilities and shared kitchen. The year-round hostel has 21 beds in six rooms; dorm beds are CDN$35 per non-member, but Hostelling International Members (CDN$35 memberships, www.hihostels.com) get about a 10 percent discount in rates.

CAMPING
Inside the Park

Smack in the middle of the Waterton Townsite, it's hard to feel like you're camping here with mowed lawn sites; however, the **Waterton Townsite Campground** (403/859-2224, www.pc.gc.ca, mid-Apr.–mid-Oct., unserviced sites CDN$19–22, full hookups CDN$30) sits on prime real estate with gorgeous views. The 238-site campground borders the Townsite Loop trail and the beach. A few trees shade some sites, but most are open, offering little privacy. Go for the most scenic unserviced spots in the G loop—sites 26–46, but be prepared for strong winds. For more sheltered scenery, go for the Cameron Creek E loop sites (even numbers 2–16). It includes hot showers, flush toilets, drinking water, kitchen shelters (the

only place where fires are permitted), a dump station, and the trailheads to Bertha Lake and Waterton Lakeshore are within a few minutes' walk. In July and August, the campground fills early; plan on arriving by noon to claim a site, or make reservations (CDN$11 processing fee) through the National Parks Canada Campground Reservation Service (877/737-3783, www.pccamping.ca). In early or late season, you'll have your pick of sites, with the campground virtually empty.

On the opposite side of Crandell Mountain from the Townsite and 3.8 miles (6 km) up the Red Rocks Parkway, **Crandell Mountain Campground** (403/859-2224 www.pc.gc.ca, mid-May–mid-Sept., CDN$17) nestles in the woods along Blakiston Creek. With its sites deep in trees, the campground has a remote feel with trees and brush providing some privacy between sites. Sometimes you can see bear and moose nearby on Blakiston Creek. Its 129 sites offer no hookups; however, running water is available as well as flush toilets, a dump station, fire grates, kitchen shelters, and a trailhead with an easy walk to Crandell Lake (5 km, 3.1 miles round-trip). The campground takes no reservations, so plan on claiming your site by midday in July and August. Firewood is supplied, but it costs CDN$6 per site to burn it. A quick 10-minute drive puts you at the end of Red Rocks Parkway, where trailheads lead to Blakiston Falls and Goat Lake.

On Chief Mountain Highway and 17 miles (26 km) from Waterton Townsite, the **Belly River Campground** (www.pc.gc.ca, mid-May–mid-Sept., CDN$13) has 24 pleasant sites in aspen groves with kitchen shelters, well water, fire grates, and pit toilets. Some sites are shaded; some are open, but not much in the way of views meets the eye. It is, however, a good site for wildlife-watching and birding, and the closest campground to Chief Mountain Customs for those who want to shoot across the boundary first thing in the morning. A short trail leads up the Belly River but dead-ends just before the international boundary. Firewood is available, but it costs CDN$6 per site to burn it.

In winter when all other campsites have closed, free sites are available at **Pass Creek Winter Campground** (403/859-2224, www.pc.gc.ca, late Oct.–mid-Apr.). Located on the entrance road 3.1 miles (5 km) from the Townsite, the eight sites offer primitive camping with only a pit toilet and a woodstove in the kitchen shelter. Water from the creek may be boiled or purified for use.

Outside the Park

Just outside the park boundary, three private campgrounds can handle the overload when Waterton Townsite and Crandell Mountain are full. On the Highway 6 to Pincher Creek, **Waterton Springs Campground** (1.5 miles or 2.5 km north of the park entrance road, 403/859-2247 or 866/859-2247, www.watertonsprings.com, mid-May–early Oct.) has 70 full-hookup unshaded parking lot-type sites (CDN$28) and 75 tent sites (CDN$17) set around small ponds and a creek in an aspen parkland—both away from the highway. Amenities include showers, flush toilets, picnic tables, launderette, camp store,

Internet access, outdoor pool, playground, and fire grates. Views of surrounding peaks are best from the tent sites.

Waterton Riverside Campground (3.2 miles, 5.2 km east of park entrance road, 403/653-2888, June–mid-Sept., hookups CDN$20, tents CDN$16) has 65 sites with running water, flush toilets, showers, playground, and fire pits. Locate the campground 0.6 mile (1 kilometer) down a dirt road; set far back in aspen parklands, the treed campground is very quiet. The owners do not take reservations, so an earlier arrival in high season is advisable. You can canoe and swim on the Waterton River, which runs adjacent to the campground.

Operated by Waterton Natural History Association, **Crooked Creek Campground** (3.8 miles, 6 km east of park entrance road, 403/653-1100, mid-May–early Sept., hookups CDN$18, tents CDN$11) has 52 sites in an older campground set adjacent to the highway. Amenities include pit toilets, running water, kitchen shelter, dump station, and firewood.

Food

Most restaurants in the Townsite cluster along Waterton Avenue and spill over to Windflower Avenue. While most of the hotel dining rooms cater to fine dining, the town has several worthy places to grab a meal without dropping an exorbitant pile of cash. You'll also find your final bill jacked up a bit in price by the GST (Goods and Services Tax).

RESTAURANTS

Located in the Prince of Wales Hotel, the **Royal Stewart Dining Room** (406/892-2525, early June–mid-Sept.) looks out its massive floor to ceiling windows down Waterton Lake. The nonsmoking restaurant's claim to fame is its view more than its service or culinary uniqueness. As in all of the park's historic hotels, breakfast (6:30–9:30 A.M., CDN$6–12) is a huge buffet spread of fruits, pastries, and

mass-produced hot items. If you're not hungry enough for the buffet, you can order à la carte. The dining hall is also open for lunch (11:30 A.M.–2 P.M., CDN$7–12) and dinners (5–9:30 P.M., CDN$19–30), which carry the hotel's British theme into its cuisine with English and Canadian dishes. No reservations are accepted for groups fewer than 12 people, so you may have a waiting line in high season. The restaurant also makes hiker lunches (CDN$8–13); order these one day in advance.

The British atmosphere of the Prince of Wales Hotel goes into full swing with **Valerie's Tea Room** (406/892-2525, early June–mid-Sept.) in the hotel lobby. Afternoon tea—more or less a full sugarfest meal of desserts—is served 2–5 P.M. in front of the huge lobby windows. Homemade pastries, scones, fruits, and berries stack on multi-tiered serving dishes, and

WATERTON

Devonshire cream comes on the side. You can go American with coffee rather than tea, too. It's a unique experience, but more mood than anything else for the price (CDN$35.50 adults, $8.29 kids, including tax and gratuities). If you partake in high tea, you may be too full to need evening dinner reservations.

If you're not staying at the hotel, at least drop by for a drink to enjoy the sweeping views. The tiny nonsmoking **Windsor Lounge** (406/892-2525, early June–mid-Sept.) is a gorgeous cozy place to sit in front of the window looking down Waterton Lake. You can also order drinks for the lobby if you prefer sitting by the larger windows. A bar menu (appetizers and sandwiches) is available (2–10 P.M., US$6–9). Beer, wine, and cocktails are served 11:30 A.M.–midnight.

Kilmorey Lodge houses the ◖ **Lamp Post Dining Room,** (117 Mount View Rd., 403/859-2334 or 888/859-8669, www.kilmorey lodge.com, open daily year-round, 7:30 A.M.–10 P.M.), hands down the best fine dining in Waterton. The restaurant serves up eclectic flavors from East India to coastal delights. For breakfast (CDN$6–10), try saskatoon berry jam on your toast (take a jar of jam home, too, for CDN$6). For lunch, test the wild game chili (CDN$11). Dinners (CDN$16–37) are scrumptious with triple berry elk chops or Alberta beef steaks. In case you haven't had your fill of saskatoons, save room for saskatoon berry pie (CDN$5). An extensive wine list specializes in a broad selection from British Columbia as well as imported wines from around the world. Reservations are highly recommended during summer.

For the same yummy fare but in a more relaxed setting, the **Ram's Head Lounge** (7:30 A.M.–10 P.M.) has cozy eating in front of the fieldstone fireplace in winter and alfresco on the smoke-free patio in summer. The lounge serves the same menu as the dining room and has a small, reasonably priced bar as well.

Located in the Bayshore Inn, the **Kootenai Brown Dining Room** (junction of Mount View Rd. and Waterton Ave., 403/859-2211 or 888/527-9555, daily early May–mid-Oct., 7 AM–10 P.M.) has mostly a view going for it as the restaurant sits right on Waterton Lake. Breakfast (CDN$7.50–12) features multi-grain pancakes. Order the Bayshore ($11) if you're hungry and want to try a little of everything on the menu. Salads, sandwiches, burgers, pizza, and pasta are served for lunch (CDN$6–15), and dinners feature steaks, chicken, fish, and pasta (CDN$19–33), with the menu recommending a chef's choice wine to accompany each dish. The restaurant also makes hiker lunches to go (CDN$9.50).

Also part of the Bayshore complex, but not nearly as pricey as the dining room, the **Glacier Café** (Waterton Ave., 403/859-2211, May–mid-Oct., 7 A.M.–10 P.M.) serves lighter meals for breakfast, lunch, and dinner (CDN$5–11): croissants and lattes to burgers, calzones, and a huge selection of dessert goodies. If you prefer people-watching while you eat, the cafe has a shaded sidewalk deck.

For pasta, head to ◖ **Tuscana Ristorante** (110 Waterton Ave., 403/859-2236, www.tuscana.ca, daily May–Sept., 10:30 A.M.–midnight), which used to be the Little Italian Cafe. With covered outdoor seating, the restaurant serves all the basic pastas and lasagnas as well as a few more interesting concoctions, such as lasagna with spinach and their specialty meat sauce. You can also build your own pasta. Lunch pastas range CDN$9–12, while dinner specials bump up to CDN$15–26. Wines hail from Canada, Argentina, France, Australia, and New Zealand. Reservations are highly recommended for dinner in high season.

Known for creative hand-crafted pizzas, ◖ **Pizza of Waterton** (103 Fountain Ave., 403/859-2660, May–Oct., shoulder seasons Wed.–Sun. 5–10 P.M., high season daily 11 A.M.–midnight, CDN$12–20) can satisfy that craving for the Italian pie. It also serves big salads and a good selection of Canadian microbrews to accompany pizzas, which you can feast on inside the homey restaurant or outside on the deck watching bighorn sheep browse through town. For an easy take-out dinner while camping at the Townsite, order a pizza to go.

For a buffalo burger (CDN$7) with friendly service, head to **(Zum's Eatery and Mercantile** (116 Waterton Ave., 403/859-2388, daily May–Sept.). Its broad menu makes it a great place to take the family for breakfast and lunch, where entrees range CDN$5–16. Dinners, which specialize in schnitzel, bratwurst, fish, steaks, and chicken are a little more pricey (CDN$16–33), but sometimes you can still order off the lunch menu. Shaded outside seating along the sidewalk allows for people-watching. To satisfy your sweet cravings, order the wildberry pie (CDN$5), a yummy combination of raspberries, blueberries, blackberries, rhubarb, and apple.

CAFFEINE

Over the past few years, espresso shops have boomed in Waterton. Even several of the traditional long-time restaurants have added espresso machines. Although it may be the tiniest place to order a latte, the **(Waterton Bagel & Coffee Shop** (309 Windflower Ave., 403/859-2466, May–Oct., 7:30 A.M.–10 P.M.) answers the need for a caffeine fix well! Along with a full espresso menu, it serves smoothies, juices, biscotti, bagels, and muffins. The diminutive shop only seats a couple of people on stools, but you can grab a bagel with cream cheese (CDN$3) and head one block away to the beach to eat.

GROCERIES

While several locations in town carry convenience foods (Pat's Gas Station and the Tamarack Village, both on Mount View Rd.), only one grocery store—**Rocky Mountain Food Mart** (307 Windflower Ave., May–Sept., daily 8 A.M.–8 P.M.)—stocks a full line with produce, meats, dairy, deli, and a bakery. However, it is small, so expect limited brands. It also carries ice, firewood, and camping supplies.

WATERTON

FLATHEAD VALLEY

The Flathead Valley is an outdoor paradise. Surrounded by mountains and abundant lakes, fishing, skiing, hiking, biking, and boating are right out the back door. The largest freshwater lake west of the Mississippi hosts almost every water sport imaginable. In winter, logging roads convert to ski and snowshoe trails, and two alpine ski areas rack up the vertical for skiers and snowboarders. With 2.5 million acres of wilderness and national parklands, and one of the country's largest national forests, there's no shortage of space to get away from it all.

While strip-mall culture is making some inroads into the valley, paving once pastoral farm lands while Vail-wannabes throw mansions up on hillsides, an underlying culture remains—one where ripped Carhartts and a duct-taped jacket rank as fashion. Rather than hit the nine-to-five office hours, lots of folks here work seasonally—in Glacier or Flathead National Forest in summer, and ski areas in winter. And for those skiers, many in the valley adhere to the six-inch rule: If six inches or more of snow falls, call in late for work.

HISTORY

Originally the home for the Flathead, Salish, and Kootenai Indians, the Flathead Valley saw its first white man—famed explorer David Thompson—in 1809. Within 40 years, trappers, homesteaders and ranchers edged their way into the valley. By the end of the century, Great Northern Railway laid tracks through the Flathead, prompting Kalispell to be plotted for township in 1890, in theory to become the next St. Paul.

© BECKY LOMAX

HIGHLIGHTS

◖ Flathead Lake: The largest freshwater lake west of the Mississippi draws waters from as far north as Canada. Sail its blues or drive around its perimeter (page 211).

◖ Whitefish Lake: With parks, beaches, and boat ramps this is the place to cool off on hot summer days (page 212).

◖ Mount Aeneas: No wonder the short trails are popular in Jewel Basin, achieving amazing views of the Great Bear Wilderness as well as Flathead Lake (page 214).

◖ Danny On Trail: Hands down the most popular trail in the Flathead, not just for its ease of access, but for its gorgeous wildflowers and stunning views of Glacier Park from the top (page 215).

◖ Big Mountain Resort: Winter on skis or summer on foot, the Glacier Chaser lift is worth a ride to the top for its views spanning mountains and valleys as far as the eye can see (page 219).

LOOK FOR ◖ TO FIND RECOMMENDED SIGHTS, ACTIVITIES, DINING, AND LODGING.

Growing with ranchers, farmers, and timber harvesters, the Flathead soon sprouted other towns clustered around its lakes and rivers. In 1901, Great Northern rerouted its railroad tracks from Kalispell to Whitefish to access Canadian coal, catapulting the tiny Whitefish lakefront community into a train town. The mid-1900s saw tremendous change in the Flathead with the construction of the Hungry Horse dam spawning an aluminum plant and Big Mountain Ski Resort growing. Today, while the original valley ranching, farming, and timber still support many families, part of the Flathead economy for its 82,000 residents comes from technology industries and tourism.

FLATHEAD VALLEY

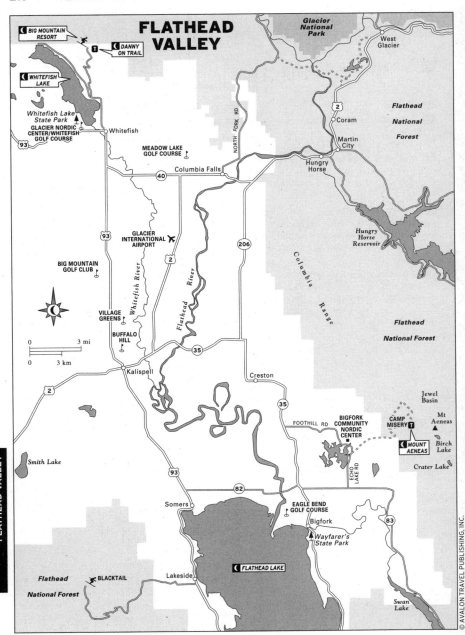

FLATHEAD VALLEY

BIG MOUNTAIN RESORT

DANNY ON TRAIL

WHITEFISH LAKE

Whitefish Lake State Park

GLACIER NORDIC CENTER/WHITEFISH GOLF COURSE

Whitefish

MEADOW LAKE GOLF COURSE

Columbia Falls

GLACIER INTERNATIONAL AIRPORT

BIG MOUNTAIN GOLF CLUB

VILLAGE GREENS

BUFFALO HILL

Whitefish River

Flathead River

NORTH FORK RD

Glacier National Park

West Glacier

Coram

Martin City

Hungry Horse

Flathead

National

Forest

Hungry Horse Reservoir

Columbia Range

Flathead

National Forest

Kalispell

Creston

Jewel Basin

Mt Aeneas

CAMP MISERY

MOUNT AENEAS

Birch Lake

FOOTHILL RD

BIGFORK COMMUNITY NORDIC CENTER

Crater Lake

ECHO LAKE RD

Smith Lake

0   3 mi

0   3 km

Somers

EAGLE BEND GOLF COURSE

Bigfork

Wayfarer's State Park

Flathead

National Forest

BLACKTAIL

Lakeside

FLATHEAD LAKE

Swan Lake

Exploring Flathead Valley

Flathead Valley centers around four main towns: Kalispell, Whitefish, Columbia Falls, and Bigfork. Each has its own draw, brought on by the seasonal recreation available in the area.

Outside the four main towns, small burgs dot the area. On the west side of Flathead Lake, the little village of Lakeside buzzes with summer water fun and serves as the launching point to reach Blacktail Mountain Ski Area in winter. Just north of Lakeside, Somers is a blink-and-miss-it town, but popular for its marina and boat tours.

Kalispell

Kalispell (9 miles from the airport, 34 miles from Glacier) is the nucleus of Flathead Valley. With more than three golf courses along with fine restaurants, the Flathead's largest town has moved beyond its cow town identity. In historic downtown Kalispell, you can check out 20 art spots identified by yellow and red banners and tour the pre-1900s Conrad Mansion. In August, catch the Northwest Montana Fair and Rodeo, and in October, join in the Glacier Jazz Stampede.

Whitefish

The recreation capital of Flathead Valley, Whitefish (11 miles from the airport, 27 from Glacier) is packed in summertime with boating in Whitefish Lake and golf at the valley's only 36-hole course. In winter, skiing becomes the passion at Big Mountain Ski Resort, just above town. Surrounded by rampant new housing developments, downtown Whitefish fits compactly into several square blocks with boutiques, restaurants, and art galleries.

Columbia Falls

The gateway to Glacier, Columbia Falls (8 miles from the airport, 18 miles from Glacier) never had a falls of its own until the town built one (behind the bank on Hwy. 2 and Nucleus Ave.). Recently, the town has boomed with new restaurants in its downtown area, upgrading its dining quality considerably. Beside its newly rebuilt public outdoor swimming pool, Columbia Falls is home to Big Sky Waterslides.

Bigfork

On Flathead Lake's northwest corner, Bigfork (26 miles from the airport, 40 miles from Glacier) combines easy access to the Swan Mountains with boating on the lake. Bigfork Summer Playhouse dominates the town, packing restaurants before nightly shows. Quaint shops and galleries fill its several-block-long village, and its one-lane steel bridge crosses the Swan River. In early June, the town hops with the Bigfork Whitewater Festival, when kayakers shoot the Swan's Wild Mile.

VISITORS CENTERS

One of the easiest ways to grab additional information on the Flathead is to contact visitors centers. Flathead Valley has six: **Flathead Valley Convention and Visitors Bureau** (15 Depot Park, Kalispell, 800/543-3105, www.montanasflatheadvalley.com), **Kalispell Chamber of Commerce** (15 Depot Park, Kalispell, 406/758-2800, www.kalispellchamber.com), **Whitefish Chamber of Commerce** (520 E. 2nd St., Whitefish, 406/862-3501, www.whitefishchamber.com), **Columbia Falls Chamber of Commerce** (233 13th St. E., 406/892-2072, www.columbiafallschamber.com), **Bigfork Chamber of Commerce** (Olde Town Center, Bigfork, 406/837-5888, www.bigfork.org), and **Lakeside Chamber of Commerce** (406/844-3715, www.lakesidechamber.com).

SIGHTS
◖ Flathead Lake

Stretching 28 miles long and 15 miles wide, Flathead Lake is the largest freshwater lake west of the Mississippi. Its 188 square miles, six state parks, islands, deep fishing waters, and wildlife refuges make it a summer playland. Highways encircle the lake, popping at

© BECKY LOMAX

Wild Horse Island in Flathead Lake

13 different points in to public lake accesses. The southern half of the lake falls in the Flathead Indian Reservation, home to the Salish and Kootenai tribes.

For boat tours on Flathead Lake, three options offer different experiences, all requiring reservations. But just a warning: If nasty weather prevails, launches will cancel. Catch a 1.5-hour midday or sunset cruise out of Somers with **Far West Excursions** (5471 Hwy. 93, 406/857-3203, mid-June–Sept., Sun.–Tues., 1 and 7 P.M., adults $15, seniors $12, kids 12 and under $9) aboard a 65-foot cruise boat with indoor and outdoor seating. In Bigfork, **Questa Sailing Charters** (150 Flathead Lake Lodge, 406/837-5569, mid-June–Sept.) launches from Flathead Lake Lodge's dock on two 51-foot 1928–1929 Q class sloops. On the beautifully restored 1928 and 1929 boats, trips depart daily at 1:30 P.M. (adults $39, seniors and kids 12 and under $32) and 7 P.M. for the popular adults-only sunset cruise ($44) that includes complimentary wine and beverages. To see bighorn sheep and wildlife, charter a **Wild Horse**

Island Boat Tour from Pointer Cruises (452 Grand Dr., Bigfork, 406/837-5617, May–Nov., $70 per hour) to visit the lake's largest island, state park, and wildlife refuge with more than 75 species of birds. The small charter holds up to nine guests; bring a lunch and spend a few hours hiking the unique island.

◖ Whitefish Lake

The 3,315-acre Whitefish Lake in Whitefish buzzes with summer activity. Anglers quietly hit the lake in early morning and evening, while midday turns into a frenzy of water-skiers, jet-skiers, party barges, kayakers, canoers, and swimmers clustered around Whitefish State Park, City Beach, and Les Mason Park. In winter when ice covers the lake, hockey players make their own rinks and ice anglers drill holes to fish.

Flathead River

Outside Hungry Horse, the South, Middle, and North Forks of the Flathead River meet. From here, the Flathead River flows 55 miles

HUCKLEBERRY MANIA

The huckleberry is a small dark purple berry about the size of your little fingertip. Resembling a blueberry, only much sweeter and more flavorful, it grows only in the wild on low deciduous bushes whose leaves turn red in fall. Huckleberries grow mostly at elevations above 4,000 feet and ripen anytime between late July and September.

The berry has yet to be successfully cultivated. Outside the park, around Hungry Horse, and in Flathead Valley, you'll find berry stands selling hucks that have been picked by commercial permit in national forests or private lands. Expect to pay about $35–40 per gallon of the precious purple gems. (Now you know why huckleberry pie is so expensive!) Be careful when purchasing berries from fruit stands early in the summer, as you may be buying frozen berries from last year rather than freshly picked berries. The frozen berries are still yummy, but a little softer when they thaw than the freshly picked ones. Fresh ones usually hit the stands in late July.

You can pick your own huckleberries to eat – no permit needed. While locals all have their secret stashes in Flathead National Forest and aren't about to divulge their prized secrets, you can usually find good huckleberry picking on Big Mountain.

Two mammals crave the berries: bears and humans. Glacier Park rules permit plucking a few berries to eat, but harvesting for commercial purposes is not allowed. You'll find them on many hikes in Flathead National Forest and the park.

High in vitamin C, the berries are not only healthy and low in fat, but they enliven any pastry, pie, sauce, or fruit concoction. They're wonderful in smoothies and delightful on pancakes. And you'll find them here in everything, from ice cream to beer.

What huckleberry products are out there? Just about anything! Syrup, jam, and jellies top everyone's favorites. But hucks flavor and scent chocolates, honey, cocoa, barbecue sauce, tea, salad dressing, ice cream topping, daiquiri mix, lotion, lip balm, bubble bath, shampoo, soap, and more.

But one word of advice: Do not use huckleberry shampoo before hiking in bear country!

---

like a snake across the valley to Flathead Lake. Seven river accesses allow places for anglers, canoers, and floaters to hop onto its meandering pace. Toward Flathead Lake, the river takes several sharp S turns in sloughs and estuaries, bird habitat for ospreys and waterfowl.

Big Moutain

Skiers and snowboarders flock to Big Mountain's 3,000 acres in winter for its 11 lifts accessing on average 300 inches of snow per year. Snow ghosts—ice encrusted bent firs—compete with the view of Glacier National Park from the mountain's 6,817-foot summit. In summer, gondola rides, mountain biking, hiking, and huckleberry picking attract visitors.

Museums

In Kalispell, the historic Victorian **Conrad** **Mansion** (between 3rd St. and 4th St. on Woodland Ave., 406/755-2166, www.conradmansion.com, May 15–Oct. 15, Tues.–Sun. 10 A.M.–5 P.M., adults $8, seniors $7, kids $3) preserves 26 rooms with their original 1895 furniture. Vintage clothing and toys recall the days of rummaging through Grandma's attic.

Also in Kalispell, the **Hockaday Museum** **of Art** (302 2nd Ave. E., 406/755-5268, www.hockadayartmuseum.org, June–Aug. Mon.–Sat. 10 A.M.–6 P.M. and Sun. noon–4 P.M., Sept.–May Tues.–Sat. 10 A.M.–5 P.M., adults $5, seniors $4, kids $1, under 6 free) features Montana artists—particularly Native Americans and Glacier Park artists. The museum shop also features pottery, jewelry, and paintings by local artists. A children's Discovery Gallery has creative hands-on exhibits for kids.

FLATHEAD VALLEY

On top of Big Mountain outside Whitefish, the **USFS Environmental Education Center** (406/862-2900, www.bigmtn.com, mid-June–mid-Sept. daily 10 A.M.–4 P.M., free) requires a hike or gondola ride up Big Mountain to reach its exhibits, but it may be the only place you can touch a grizzly bear! Rub your hands in the fur of wolverines, weasels, and mountain goats. Free guided flower walks (July–Aug.) depart daily at 10 A.M. and 3 P.M.

Recreation

The Flathead Valley is a four-season recreation mecca. Lakes draw summertime paddlers and swimmers; fall lures hunters; ski resorts cater to floating through powder snow; and spring explodes with hiking.

HIKING

Since Flathead National Forest surrounds Flathead Valley, hikers have no shortage of trails within spitting distance of their back porch. Most trails are multi-use, permitting mountain bikes and motor bikes, but a few—such as the Jewel Basin trails or the Danny On Trail on Big Mountain—limit use to hikers.

With 50 miles of hiking paths, Jewel Basin has trails for tiny tots through oldsters. Open for hiking usually June–October, depending on snow, the 15,349-acre hiker-only area is called The Jewel, for 27 alpine fishing lakes spangle its basins. Paths tromp across huckleberry meadows and high ridges with top-of-the-world views. Fido can go on a leash. It's extremely popular; July 4 weekend sees 200 people per day.

To get here, a seven-mile narrow curvy dirt road climbs up to 5,717 feet off the valley floor. Leave low-clearance vehicles and trailers behind as it's riddled with washboards, rollers, and limited turnouts. Trail signage is scanty, so maps are handy: contact Swan Lake Ranger Station at 406/837-7500. All hikes begin at the Camp Misery Trailhead, a less-than-inspiring name!

To reach Camp Misery, drive Highway 35 from either Bigfork or Kalispell and turn east onto the Swan Highway (Hwy. 83) two miles north of Bigfork. Follow 83 to Echo Lake Road and head north approximately three miles to the Jewel Basin Road (#5392).

◖ Mount Aeneas

- Distance: 5.9-mile loop

- Duration: 3 hours

- Elevation gain: 1,811 feet

- Effort: moderately strenuous

- Trailhead: Camp Misery Trailhead in Jewel Basin

Mount Aeneas, at 7,528 feet, is the highest peak in The Jewel and offers big views for little work, but don't expect solitude at the summit. Combined with Picnic Lakes, the trail loops on a ridge and through a lake basin. From the top, you'll see Flathead Lake, Glacier National Park, the Bob Marshall Wilderness Complex, and the Swan Mountains. A lot of scenery for a short hike!

Begin hiking up trail #717, a wide road-bed. In 1.5 miles, the trail reaches a four-way junction—stay on #717 heading uphill. After a few switchbacks, you'll pass an ugly microwave tower before waltzing with the mountain goats along an arête to the summit. From the summit, drop down through the Picnic Lakes Basin. At the lakes, hook onto #392, then right onto #68, and left onto #8. (At 1.7 miles from Camp Misery, Picnic Lakes makes a good tiny kid destination—just reverse the route.)

Birch Lake

- Distance: 6 miles round-trip

- Duration: 3 hours

- Elevation gain: 800 feet

- Effort: moderate

- Trailhead: Camp Misery Trailhead in Jewel Basin

A short hop over a ridge along with a skip down a trail plops hikers on the banks of Birch Lake—a great destination for kids. The lake's west end makes for good swimming, but don't expect balmy waters. This clear snowmelt pond retains its chill even in August. For those with more gumption, another 2.5 miles sets hikers astride the boulder shoreline of Crater Lake.

Begin hiking up the broad roadway of trail #717 to the four-way junction. Take the right fork on #7. The trail curves around the lower flanks of Mount Aeneas as it descends to Birch Lake. (You'll have to hike up this on the way out!) At the lake, a trail circles the lake, but the best place to plunk yourself is on the lake's obvious peninsula.

❰ Danny On Trail

- Distance: 4 miles one-way

- Duration: 2 hours

- Elevation gain: 2,400 feet

- Effort: moderate

- Trailhead: Big Mountain Village, 7 miles above Whitefish, next to Chalet

The Danny On Trail chocks up over 14,000 hikers annually. At the top, the USFS Environmental Education Center provides interpretive resources for the trail. Catch the chairlift up to hike down ($10, kids 12 and under free), or hike up and take the chair ride down free. While you can hike with your pooch on a leash here, Fido may not ride up or down the chairlift.

After beginning in Big Mountain Village, the trail switchbacks up through a forested slope and crosses ski runs as it sweeps around the mountain. Valerian and penstemon bloom in July; huckleberries scent the air in later summer. Junctions to Flower Point are well-marked: stay left at both to go directly to the top. (Or loop through Flower Point for a 5.6-mile hike.) At the East Rim junction, turn left for a gentle, scenic loop before the final steep ascent. Panoramas at the top span Glacier Park to Flathead Lake.

BIKING

For roadies, oodles of two-lane highways and paved country lanes tie into long loops around Flathead Lake or short farmland tours, while single-track and dirt-road choices swamp mountain bikers. For itineraries to suit your palate and abilities, check Glacier Cyclery's website (www.glaciercyclery.com) for popular bike routes.

For single-track mountain biking, **Big Mountain Resort** (end of Big Mountain Rd., Whitefish, 406/862-2900, www.bigmtn.com, mid-June–mid-Sept., $10) hauls bikes and riders up its chairlift. Although the grade isn't steep, hairpin turns and natural obstacles chuck the trail in the have-some-experience-first category. Rent bikes (adults $25–35, kids $15, all with helmets) and mountain scooters, a cross between a skateboard and a bike (adults $20, kids $8), at the mountain's rental shop. If you're nervous, hire a guide for a two-hour tour or lesson ($40–56 for first person, each additional person $10–28).

Rentals

For scads of information on where to bike, **Glacier Cyclery** (326 E. 2nd St., Whitefish, 406/862-6466, www.glaciercyclery.com) is one of the best places to go. The shop rents touring bikes and mountain bikes ($17.50–35 per day, $125–150 weekly), which come with helmets. They can also equip you with car racks ($15 per day), Burleys ($20 per day), and panniers ($20 per week). **Mountain Mike's** (417 Bridge St., Bigfork, 406/837-2453, mtnmikes@centurytel.com, late Apr.–early Oct. Mon.–Sat. 8 A.M.–4 P.M.) rents kid and adult mountain bikes ($20 including helmet), convenient for touring Swan Valley. You can also hire a guide ($30 per person, reservations required) for half-day dirt-road or single-track tours.

Cross your fingers that you won't need a repair shop, but if you do, you'll find several in the yellow pages. Difficult to find, but well

worth the phone call for directions, Mitch Moylan of **Sun Road Cycles** (350 Gooderich Rd., Kalispell, 406/862-BIKE or 406/862-2453) is certified for and especially adept at repairing high-end cycles.

BOATING
Flathead Lake

On Flathead Lake's north end, three communities—Bigfork, Somers, and Lakeside—service boaters with marinas (May–Oct.). For those looking to launch boats, Flathead Lake has 13 public accesses, six of which are state parks ($5 day use fee) maintained by Montana Fish, Wildlife, and Parks (406/752-5501, www.fwp.state.mt.us.).

Boat rentals are available in four locations: **Wild Wave Watercraft** (7125 Hwy. 93 S., Lakeside, 406/844-2400 or 406/257-2627), **Flathead Boat Rentals** (5417 Hwy. 93 S., Somers, 406/857-3334), **Bigfork Marina and Boat Center** (100 Parkway Ave., Bigfork,

406/837-4224), and **Marina Cay Resort** (180 Vista Ln., Bigfork, 406/837-5861, www.marinacay.com). Expect to pay $50–65 per hour for jet skis, $50–90 per hour for water-ski boats, $75–100 for pontoon fishing boats and party barges. Hand-propelled craft like canoes, kayaks, and rowboats usually run $10–20 per hour. In addition to your rental fee, you'll need to pay for the gas used.

Whitefish Lake

For launching boats, public boat ramps are located at Whitefish Lake State Park ($5 day use fee) and City Beach ($4 launch fee). For rentals, mooring, and fuel service, **Whitefish Lake Lodge Marina** (1390 Wisconsin Ave., 406/862-9283, mid-May–Sept.) is the only option. The marina also rents party barges and fishing pontoons ($75–90 per hour), jet skis ($60 per hour), water-ski boats ($85 per hour), and canoes and two-person kayaks ($15 per hour); in addition to hourly rates, you'll pay for gas, tax, and oil.

FLATHEAD VALLEY

© BECKY LOMAX

Flathead River

KAYAKING AND CANOEING

White-water kayakers gravitate to the Swan River outside Bigfork, but wear wetsuits in its freezing cold waters. For Class IV–V rapids, the **Swan River Wild Mile,** a short one-mile stretch below Bigfork Dam, sees its best water May–July. Sea kayakers and canoers head for the ambling stretches of the Flathead and Whitefish Rivers as well as the larger lakes—good any time of year.

Rentals and Guides

You can rent kayaks to take to Glacier from all of these companies. Many of Flathead's kayak rental companies operate out of their homes, without keeping "shop hours," so call to make reservations. Lifejackets and paddles are included in rates.

The staff at **Whitefish Sea Kayaking** (406/862-3513, wfseakayak@yahoo.com, year-round) rent sea kayaks (single $20 for three hours, $30 per day; double $30 for three hours, $40 per day), and for $10 they'll deliver the kayaks to Whitefish Lake. If you want to float Whitefish River, they'll pick you up down the river. They also guide half-day ($60) and full-day ($80, bring your own lunch) trips on Whitefish and Flathead Lakes.

Glacier Sea Kayaking (406/862-9010, sea kayak@digisys.net) rents sea kayaks ($55–60 per day, including car racks). The shop, open by appointment only, is outside Whitefish, so you'll need to call to get directions. Staff also guide private trips ($145–185 per person) and teach lessons ($100–145 per person).

For paddling Flathead Lake, **Bigfork Jake's Kayak Company** (406/837-4853, www.bigfork-jakeskayaks.com, May–Oct.) operates a mobile sea kayak rental company. They'll meet you at the lake or in Bigfork if you plan on taking the kayaks elsewhere. Their kayak rentals (half day $45, full day $65) include a car-top carrier.

A bit hard to locate, call for directions, **Silver Moon Kayak** (1215 N. Somers Rd., Kalispell, 406/752-3724, Wed.–Sun.) is convenient for Flathead River or Lake trips. Half-day canoe or sea-kayak rentals run $30–50; full-day rentals are $40–65. White-water kayaks are $35 per day. Rentals include foam blocks and straps for transporting. Silver Moon guides lead two-hour ($30) to full-day tours ($95–110, including lunch and rental); their specialty trip is Paddle by Moonlight (June–Sept.; call for the current schedule). Lessons for all sea-kayaking levels and beginning white-water run $30–90.

For canoe rentals, **Ski Mountain Sports** (242 Central Ave., Whitefish, 406/862-7541, $35 per day) provides the best service for paddling the Whitefish River, dropping canoes off at Whitefish Lake and picking you up down the river ($10–15).

FISHING
Flathead River

Flathead River is a giant highway for migrating fish—mostly nonnative—from the lake upstream to spawn in tributaries. Because of dam control and cold glacial water, do not expect blue-ribbon trout fishing, but the river doesn't see lots of fishing pressure. Closer to the lake, the water slows into large sloughs, where northern pike lurk. Seven river accesses offer places to fish and to launch boats downstream: Blankenship Bridge, the Highway 2 bridge at Hungry Horse, a spur road at Bad Rock Canyon's west end, Kokanee Bend, Pressentine Bar, the old Steel Bridge, and the Stillwater mouth. Most anglers hit the stretch between Columbia Falls and the Old Steel Bridge in Kalispell.

Flathead Lake

Flathead Lake teems with cutthroat, giant trophy lake trout, mountain and lake whitefish, largemouth bass, bull trout, and yellow perch. It's good for all types of fishing: bait to lure, fly-fishing to trolling. The southern half of the lake is on Salish and Kootenai tribal lands: Fishing here requires a Tribal recreation label (Flathead Indian Reservation, 406/675-2700, $10 per year) available at small town businesses surrounding the southern lake shore.

Whitefish Lake

Whitefish Lake draws anglers for its lake trout

© BECKY LOMAX

fishing for lake trout in Whitefish Lake

and whitefish. During winter, some anglers ice fish, but mostly on the lake's east end, since the west end doesn't freeze some years. Northern pike, lake trout, and kokanee are common, and it is regularly stocked with westslope cutthroat trout.

Fly Shops and Guides

Hit up fly-fishing shops in the Flathead for locally made hand-tied flies and tackle as well as advice on where fish are biting. Most of the following shops also offer guide services that range $250–350 for two people from half to full days. Rates usually do not include Montana fishing licenses. In Whitefish, **Lakestream Fly Fishing Shop** (334 Central Ave., 406/862-1298, www.lakestream.com) guides its fly-fishing trips on a private lake. **Stumptown Anglers** (5790 Hwy. 93 S., Whitefish, 406/862-4554) guides trips on five different northwest Montana rivers including the Flathead. **Arends Fly Shop** (7356 Hwy. 2 E., Columbia Falls, 406/892-2033, www.montanaflies.com) hits the South and main forks of the Flathead River

for fish. For guided fishing on Flathead Lake and Swan River, head to **Two River Gear** (603 Electric Ave., Bigfork, 406/837-3474).

Montana has no shortage of independent fly-fishing guide services operating unattached to shops. You can find them in the yellow pages or through the Internet. Check that the guide service is licensed with the state before hiring their services.

A Montana State license is required to fish in Flathead Valley. See the *Background* chapter for details.

Charter Services

Charter fishing services on Flathead Lake operate May–September. Expect rates to range $260–700 per day, depending on duration and number of people. Located at Marina Cay in Bigfork, **A Able Fishing and Tours** (406/257-5214 or 800/231-5214, www.aablefishing.com) guides fishing trips on Flathead Lake with a character named "Shorty" who guarantees fish! Several other charter services operate on Flathead Lake; locate them in the yellow pages.

GOLF

Golf Digest rated Flathead Valley as one of the world's 50 greatest golf destinations—not just because the scenery is good and the prices are reasonable, but because of nine championship courses. With over 16 hours of daylight in early summer, courses open from dawn to dusk, adjusting tee times as daylight drops. Depending on snows, most courses are open April–October.

For golfing here, expect to pay $25–71, depending on the course, season, and time of day. Rates in April, May, and October and daily after 3 P.M. run cheaper. Club rentals range $15–30 and carts $14–20 for 18 holes.

One of the best resources for Flathead golf is www.golfmontana.net, where you can get stats for all the local courses. A central number (800/392-9795) will get you guaranteed reservations. With a two-day advance reservation, you'll get the same rate the golf course offers. For guaranteed reservations with less notice, rates run $5 higher than if you call the golf courses direct and take what's available.

Courses

Six courses—all with rentals, pro shops, restaurants, and lounges—sprawl across the Flathead. **Whitefish Lake Golf Course** (1200 Hwy. 93 N., Whitefish, 406/862-4000, www.golfwhitefish.com) is Montana's only 36-hole course. The north course tours through large cedars and firs; the south course runs past Lost Loon Lake. Both have grand views of Big Mountain. **Eagle Bend Golf Course** (279 Eagle Bend Dr., Bigfork, 406/837-7310 or 800/255-5641, www.golfmt.com) is ranked in the top 50 public courses in the United States. The challenging 27-hole course is a Jack Nicklaus design with big variety in its hole layouts. From different tees, you can see Flathead Lake, Swan Mountains, and Glacier Park; osprey often fly overhead.

Meadow Lake Golf Course (490 St. Andrews Dr., Columbia Falls, 406/892-2111 or 800/321-4653, www.meadowlakegolf.com) weaves its 18 holes through the woods with some tight fairways and lots of adjacent houses.

A couple of ponds and a creek separate the fairways, and some trees shade the course. **Big Mountain Golf Club** (3230 Hwy. 93 N., Kalispell, 406/751-1950, www.golfmt.com) is a Scottish links–style course. Since its 18 holes sit midvalley with few trees, views open up to Big Mountain, Glacier Park, and Columbia Mountain. The Stillwater River runs adjacent to the back nine.

Village Greens (500 Palmer Drive, Kalispell, 406/752-4666, www.montanagolf.com) surrounds its bent-grass greens with a few trees, ponds, and some houses. The 18 holes afford a pleasant place to play on one of the easier courses here. **Buffalo Hill** (1176 N. Main St., Kalispell, 406/756-4530, www.golfbuffalo.com) combines an older course with a newer course for 27 holes. The older Cameron Nine abuts the highway; the newer 18-hole course is moderately difficult with a lot of terrain variety.

SKIING
◖ Big Mountain Resort

Located seven miles from Whitefish, Big Mountain Ski Resort (end of Big Mountain Rd., 406/862-2900, www.bigmtn.com, late Nov.–early Apr. 9 A.M.–4:30 P.M., adults $49, kids 7–18 $36, 6 and under free) lives up to its big name with 3,000 acres of skiable terrain, 2,400 feet of vertical, 11 lifts, and 91 named runs. Big bowls, glades, and long runs dominate the face. With runs heading 360 degrees off the summit, you can even find good skiing in the mountain's famous fog.

Big Mountain's village contains 10 restaurants, shops, rental gear ($15–35 per day), ski school, day care, and lodging from economy to upscale condos. The Nordic Center also has trails groomed for classic and skate skiing ($5 per day), but beware: Trails here are not easy for beginners. Nordic rentals ($15 per day) are available in the Outpost Rental Shop (406/862-2946). You can also get deals on lift tickets: early and late season rates, lodging-lift packages, and multiple day passes, some of which must be purchased before the season starts. Call or check online for these.

In summer (mid-June–mid-Sept.), the resort runs its Glacier Chaser lift for sightseeing ($10, kids 12 and under and seniors free). It also offers mountain biking, festivals, and Walk in the Treetops ($48, age 10 and 54-inch height minimum), a boardwalk tour through the tree canopy 70 feet up in the air (you're clipped in with a safety harness).

Blacktail Mountain

A 14-mile drive from Lakeside puts you at 6,676 feet atop Blacktail Mountain Ski Area (406/844-0999, www.blacktailmountain.com, Dec.–Apr. Wed.–Sun. 9:30 A.M.–4:30 P.M., adults $30, teens $20, kids $13, 7 and under free), where the weather is amazingly good compared to the fog that creeps into the north valley. In a twist from the usual ski area, you start skiing from the top. This small family-run area is perfect for beginning and intermediate skiers. Three chairs and a beginner handle-tow access 1,000 acres of terrain. You can ski for $15 on Thursdays.

cross-country skiers hit the surrounding forests

© BECKY LOMAX

The three-story day lodge with great views of beginners crashing as well as Glacier Park and Flathead Valley has a shop, rentals ($15–22 per day), cafeteria, and restaurant-bar. Free county-maintained Nordic ski trails are available just down the hill, but you must bring your own gear.

CROSS-COUNTRY SKIING

Several small cross-country ski areas dot Flathead Valley. In addition to trails at Big Mountain Resort and Blacktail Mountain Ski Area, three other areas groom trails for Nordic skiing usually between mid-December and March.

In Whitefish at Whitefish Lake Golf Course on Highway 93 North, **Glacier Nordic Center** grooms 7.5 miles daily for skate and classic skiing ($5). On-site, the Outback Ski Shack (406/892-9498) rents both skate ($15–18) and classic ($10–14) gear, and teaches lessons in both disciplines ($25).

In deep woods broken by open meadows in Flathead National Forest, you can glide gentle flats or scare yourself coming down Look-out Run at **Round Meadows** (406/863-5400). Drive 11 miles north of Whitefish on Highway 93; turn onto Farm to Market Road, then go two miles up Star Meadows Road. The area's 11 miles of trails are groomed usually on Fridays for classic and skate. Skiing is free, but donations help fund grooming.

On 6 miles of easy paths crossing creeks and meandering through timbered terrain, **Bigfork Community Nordic Center** (www.bigforknordic.org) grooms trails a couple times per week for classic skiing only. Six access points stretch along Foothills Road 8 miles north of Bigfork. Skiing is free, but donations help grooming. Check the website for details.

Rentals

In addition to Big Mountain Resort and the Outback Ski Shack, Nordic skis are rented at both **Sportsman Ski Haus** stores in Whitefish (Mountain Mall, 406/862-3111) and Kalispell (40 E. Idaho, 406/755-6484). Rentals run around $10 for skis, boots, and poles. Snowshoes are also available to rent.

SNOWMOBILING

The Flathead Valley is surrounded by 200 miles of groomed snowmobile trails (Dec.–mid-April, but some trails close April 1). Flathead Valley Snowmobile Association (406/756-3703 or www.snowtana.com for Montana Snowmobile Association) maintains the grooming on nine popular trails near Whitefish, Columbia Falls, and Bigfork. For those striking out on their own, be sure to check conditions with Glacier Country Avalanche Center (406/257-8402 or 800/526-5239, www.glacieravalanche.org).

Rentals and guide services are available at **Extreme Motorsports** (803 Spokane Ave., Whitefish, 406/862-8594) and **J & L Rentals** (5410 Hwy. 2 W., Columbia Falls, 406/892-7666, www.jandlrvrentals.com). Expect to pay around $175 per day for renting a snowmobile (helmets included); snowmobile suits, boots, and gloves are extra. To hire a guide costs $120–150 per day.

ENTERTAINMENT AND EVENTS

Theaters

In Bigfork, the **Bigfork Summer Playhouse** (526 Electric Ave., 406/837-4886, www.bigforksummerplayhouse.com, May–Sept., $18 adults, $13 kids under 12) presents five shows in repertory during each summer, from Broadway musical favorites to comedies. In Whitefish, **Whitefish Theater Company** (1 Central Ave., 406/862-5371, www.whitefishtheaterco.org) sponsors plays, concerts, speakers, films, and Alpine Theater Company productions through the year.

While we may be on the dark side of the moon regarding lots of things, you can actually catch a just-released blockbuster movie in the Flathead—but don't expect a hotbed of foreign, independent, or avant garde films. Whitefish has one movie theater, **Mountain Cinema** (Mountain Mall on Hwy. 93, 406/862-3130). Kalispell has several: **Liberty Theater** (120 1st Ave. E.), **Strand Theater** (120 2nd St. E.), and **Gateway Cinema** (1275 Hwy. 2 W.), all listed on the same Signature Theatres schedule (406/752-7800). One of three remaining drive-in theaters in Montana, **Midway Drive-in** (3115 Hwy. 40 W., Columbia Falls, 406/892-4515) is open only during summer months. In June and early July, when the skies don't darken until 11 P.M., shows do not begin until very late; by August, they can start around 9:30 P.M.

Rodeos and Fairs

Located midvalley between Whitefish and Kalispell, **Majestic Valley Arena** (3630 Hwy. 93 N., 406/755-5366, www.majesticvalleyarena.com) is the hub for big events: concerts, rodeos, equestrian competitions and expositions, and trade shows. Special attractions include calf-roping, pro-rodeos, and horse jumping. For cowpoke wannabes, the annual **Northwest Montana Fair and Rodeo** opens in mid-August at the Flathead County Fairgrounds (265 N. Meridian, Kalispell, 406/758-5810). The five-day, six-night event features PRCA Rodeos, fireworks, animal and produce exhibits, pari-mutuel horse racing, team penning, musical concerts, and livestock sales.

Events

The annual **Glacier Jazz Stampede** (406/862-3814 or 888/888-2308, www.kalispellchamber.com) is for those who love traditional jazz, swing, and big band sounds. The event crams four days of jazz from 12–14 bands from all over the U.S. and Canada pounding out nearly nonstop music in four different Kalispell venues. Bands, schedules, and ticket prices vary yearly for each event, but you can order an "all event" ticket ($50–60) online.

Attracting hundreds of spectators even in soggy weather, the **Bigfork Whitewater Festival** (406/837-5888, www.bigfork.org) runs nearly 200 kayakers down the Class V Wild Mile of the Swan River at the peak of spring runoff. Traditionally held for two days over the first weekend in June, competitions run the gamut from slalom to rodeo. Local pubs and restaurants party with nightly entertainment.

In the doldrums of winter, Whitefish celebrates its wacky **Winter Carnival,** (406/862-3501 or 877/862-3548, www.whitefishchamber.org) a three-day spree of ski races,

FLATHEAD VALLEY

ice hockey, the penguin plunge, a figure-skating show, torchlight parade, ski joring, and snow skating held the first weekend in February. Hundreds of people line the few blocks of downtown Whitefish for an old-fashioned, drive-the-old-tractor-down-main-street parade disrupted by Yetis and Viking women.

Casinos

While gambling is legal in Montana, casinos haven't rocketed to Las Vegas style—or even to the level of those found on some Native American reservations. Here, most bars have a few slot machines squirreled away in a corner; some even run a card table or two. In a twist to the usual gas station-convenience mart, some gas chains add small, dark, and smoky casinos featuring gaming machines and poker tables. And that's about it.

While gambling may be rather commonplace in Montana, you will not find gaming inside Glacier National Park or on the Blackfeet Reservation.

Accommodations

You'll find everything from motels to guest ranches for Flathead Valley through the visitors bureaus and chambers of commerce. You can also rent homes—nightly, weekly, and long-term. Two reputable companies offer property management: Hideaway Resorts (406/862-5500 or 888/836-5500, www.hideawayresorts.com) and Lakeshore Rentals (406/863-9337 or 877/817-3012, www.lakeshorerentals.net).

All accommodations listed here are open year-round unless noted otherwise. When making reservations, be sure to ask about golf or ski packages, as many places offer good deals in season—even independent motels. Rates vary according season; the ranges listed reflect the low rates of the off-season and high rates of peak seasons. However, what is considered high and low season varies with location: in summer, Flathead Lake sees high season, but in winter, it's high season at Big Mountain Resort. A 7 percent Montana State bed tax will be added to your bill. In Whitefish, an additional 2 percent resort tax will also be added.

MOTELS AND LODGES

Scattered throughout Flathead Valley, you can find most major low end to moderately priced chain hotels congregated in Kalispell, Whitefish, Columbia Falls, and Bigfork.

Bigfork

The most reasonably priced lodging is

Timbers Motel (8540 Hwy. 35 S., 406/837-6200 or 800/821-4546, www.timbersmotel.com $52–148), which puts you within a five-minute drive to Eagle Bend Golf Course and just a couple minutes from the Bigfork Summer Playhouse. It sits on a small knoll on, but above the highway; however, traffic on this highway slows substantially at night.

Right in downtown Bigfork, **Bridge Street Cottages** (309 Bridge St., 406/837-2785 or 888/264-4974, www.bridgestreetcottages.com) offers higher end lodging with a three-night minimum stay. Four of the units sit right on the Swan River. Surrounded by small perennial gardens, these well-furnished, well-kept one-bedroom cottages built in 2004 come with Internet access, cable television, air-conditioning, and come with fully equipped kitchens ($105–275 per night). Cottage suites ($75–150) are smaller with just a fridge and microwave.

Columbia Falls

Good for families on a budget, two simple motels sit conveniently near the water slide in Columbia Falls. **Glacier Inn Motel** (300 Hwy. 2 E., 406/892-4341, $39–72) has a city park next door where the kids can romp on the playground equipment. **Glacier Mountain Shadows** (7285 Hwy. 2 E., 406/892-7686, $48–115) is an older but renovated motel at the base of Columbia Mountain a two-minute drive from the water slide.

Kalispell

Right in downtown Kalispell's shopping district, the historic **((Kalispell Grand Hotel** (100 Main St., 406/755-8100 or 800/858-7422, www.kalispellgrand.com, $65–130) makes you take a leap back in time. Walking in the lobby, you're greeted by a tin ceiling, ornate pump organ, and the original wide, oak banister stairway. Rooms have smaller bathrooms with showers rather than tubs. Although the ambience harkens back to 1912, when the hotel opened with a room costing $2, its modern amenities now include an elevator, high speed Internet, air-conditioning, and televisions. The Painted Horse Grille and an art gallery sit off the lobby.

Whitefish

The Whitefish Motel (620 8th St., 406/862-3507, $25–78) has fully equipped kitchenettes, living rooms, and bedrooms two miles from City Beach and six blocks from downtown shopping and restaurants.

BED-AND-BREAKFASTS
Bigfork

Five miles outside town in a private wooded setting, **((O'Duachain Country Inn** (675 Ferndale Dr., 406/837-6851 or 800/837-7460, www.montanainn.com, $100–195) combines a three-story log home (rooms with shared baths) and a two-story guest house (private bath suites). For enjoying the peaceful garden, a large wraparound deck is cluttered with willow chairs and rockers, or you can soak in the outdoor hot tub. The multicourse breakfast is served on formal linens with china, crystal, and silver. For hiking, a seven-minute drive leads to the turnoff of Jewel Basin Road.

A short 3.5 miles south of Bigfork puts you at **Candlewycke Inn Bed & Breakfast** (311 Aero Lane, 406/837-6406 or 888/617-8805, www.candlewyckeinn.com, $95–145). On 10 acres, the nonsmoking cedar and log inn serving a full breakfast in the morning has seven folk-art-themed rooms and suites with private baths and pillow-top beds (two-night minimum stay in summer). One suite can sleep up to five

people ($200). You can walk on trails around the property, cross-country ski in winter, or lounge on the massive decks or in the hot tub.

Columbia Falls

On 10 quiet acres 10 minutes from town, **Bad Rock Bed and Breakfast** (480 Bad Rock Dr., 406/892-2829 or 888/892-2829, www.badrock.com, $99–179) opens its doors to guests with four log cabins surrounding a river-rock and log-frame house. Cabin rooms have hand-crafted log furniture, while the three house rooms are decorated in different styles. All have private baths. Breakfast is a large Montana-style affair, sometimes featuring Belgian waffles heaped with huckleberries.

Whitefish

Extremely convenient to restaurants and nightlife in downtown Whitefish, the **((Garden Wall Inn** (504 Spokane Ave., 406/862-3440 or 888/530-1700, www.gardenwallinn.com, $125–195) is furnished with antiques and oversized clawfoot tubs inside, while a perennial garden blooms outside. You'll feel like the inn is an extension of Glacier Park, with historic photos and picture books in the living room, and if the weather deteriorates, you can curl up in front of a real fire in the glazed brick fireplace. The 1920s inn has five guest rooms, each with private baths, fluffy towels, and robes. In the morning, a coffee or tea tray is delivered to your room, the wake-up notice for breakfast in the dining room, where you'll feast on treats like huckleberry-pear crepes.

A five-minute drive from downtown and 10 minutes from Big Mountain Ski Resort, **Hidden Moose Lodge** (1735 E. Lakeshore Dr., 406/862-6516 or 888/733-6667, www.hiddenmooselodge.com, $89–199) provides upscale Montana-outdoors themed rooms with private baths. A great room centers around a cozy large river rock fireplace, and decks face the woods. Amenities include wireless Internet, a hot tub, air-conditioning, and complimentary evening beverages. Breakfast is big with Hidden Moose chorizo quiche being one of the favorite entrees.

RESORTS

All resorts are open year-round. During a high season (winter for ski resorts, summer for golf and beach), premium rates are charged, but you can get great deals during low seasons or off-seasons.

Ski and Golf

Seven miles above Whitefish at the valley's north end, **Big Mountain Resort** (406/862-2900 or 800/858-5439, www.bigmtn.com) has all lodging options from motels and condos ($55–699 per night) to vacation homes ($100–2,100 per night), along with restaurants, shops, skiing, hiking, and mountain biking. While all restaurants and amenities are in full swing in winter while the ski lifts operate, summer (with lower lodging rates than winter) sees fewer restaurants and shops open during the gondola operational season. In fall and spring when the gondola is closed, restaurants and shops close, too, but that is an excellent time to find cheaper lodging and quiet.

In Whitefish one mile from downtown restaurants and nightlife, **((Grouse Mountain Lodge** (Hwy. 93 and Fairway Dr., 406/862-3000 or 800/321-8822, www.montanasfinest.com, $99–259) sits its modern hotel rooms right on a 36-hole golf course that converts in winter into groomed Nordic skiing trails. With an indoor pool and outdoor hot tubs, three eating venues, DSL and wireless Internet access, and comfortable lobby with its huge river rock fireplace, staying here is a piece of cake. Rooms come in seven configurations all with private baths—from a basic hotel room to a high-end room with oversized shower sporting multiple water heads. For accessing Whitefish, Glacier airport, or Big Mountain Ski Resort, a complimentary shuttle will bop you quickly to your destination, and Montana Adventure Company located in the lobby can book activities for you—from skiing to Glacier Park tours.

Outside Columbia Falls in among big trees, **((Meadow Lake Resort** (100 St. Andrews Dr., 406/892-8700 or 800/321-4653, www.meadowlake.com) is also a good bet, sitting right on an 18-hole golf course with a pro shop and rentals. For lodging, the resort has 24 modern hotel rooms ($95–165), one- or two-bedroom condos with fully equipped kitchens and private decks ($130–295), and vacation homes ($190–445). Amenities include a restaurant, indoor and outdoor swimming pools and spas, and tennis courts. In winter, the resort provides a ski shuttle to Big Mountain Resort. The on-site concierge books activities—whitewater rafting, scenic boat cruises, and horseback riding—and to free up time for adults, Troop Meadow Lake supervises the kids for swimming, movie night, arts and crafts, and outdoor activities.

Lakefront

On Flathead Lake, **Marina Cay Resort** (180 Vista Ln., Bigfork, 406/837-5861 or 800/433-6516, www.marinacay.com, $89–495) has suites and condos along with restaurants, seasonal outdoor pool and hot tub, and marina with boat rentals. You can easily walk seven minutes to downtown Bigfork's shops and restaurants. Eagle Bend Golf Course is a five-minute drive away, and the closest hiking trails are in Jewel Basin.

Averill's Flathead Lake Lodge (Flathead Lake Lodge Rd., Bigfork, 406/837-4391, www.averills.com, mid-July–Labor Day, adults $2,653 per week, infants–teens $112–1,981 per week, meals included) is a family-owned working dude ranch on 2,000 acres. Lodging, meals, and activities all wrap up in one big price for 7- or 14-day vacations. With horseback riding, fishing, swimming, water skiing, tennis, and sailing, the ranch centers around the classy log lodge and cabins. You can park the car and dive into vacation mode for several days, as the ranch coordinates the activities.

On Whitefish Lake, **Bay Point on The Lake** (300 Bay Point Dr., 406/862-2331 or 888/229-7646, www.baypoint.org, $79–324) has cottages and condos with 600 feet of private beachfront. All cottages and condos are privately owned; some have been renovated recently, others have not. Additional amenities include an indoor swimming pool, sauna, and hot tubs. A short five-minute drive puts you in

downtown Whitefish for restaurants and shopping. Golf and skiing are both within a 7- to 15-minute drive.

CAMPING

In Flathead Valley, state parks for camping tend to cluster around lake shores with drinking water, picnic tables, and flush toilets, but no hookups. Conversely, most private commercial campgrounds have full hookups, laundry, hot showers, dump stations, and camp stores, and will accommodate large RVs with pullouts as well as tents. Commercial campgrounds add a 7 percent Montana bed tax to your bill, and Whitefish private campgrounds add another 2 percent resort tax. Most will give 10 percent discounts to AAA, Woodall's, and Good Sam members.

Bigfork

Located on Flathead Lake, **Wayfarer's State Park** (0.5 mile south of Bigfork on Hwy. 35, 406/837-4196, www.fwp.state.mt.us, May–Sept., $13–15 per site) has quick access to boating and fishing. With 30 sites on 68 acres with a boat ramp, a swimming area, and 1.5 miles of hiking trails, the park is one of the largest on Flathead Lake. Pets are allowed on a leash. Campground amenities include firewood, fire grill, flush and vault toilets, showers, picnic tables, and drinking water.

Columbia Falls

Three private campgrounds surround Columbia Falls, all with the quickest access to Glacier Park (15–20 minutes away) compared to other campgrounds in Flathead Valley. All three are right on major four-lane highways, so be prepared for a little road noise. For all three, the closest golf course is Meadow Lake, and the closest grocery stores are in Columbia Falls.

With 35 sites in a grassy setting surrounded by trees, **Columbia Falls RV Park** (1003 Hwy. 2 E., 406/892-1122 or 888/401-7268, May–Sept., $13–28) is the closest to Glacier and one mile from both the water slides and the town's outdoor swimming pool. Restaurants and grocery stores are within one mile. Full

hookups are available, along with laundry, big bathrooms with hot showers and flush toilets, mini-store, and gift shop.

Easy to find with its flower-painted VW bug and trailer as a sign and adjacent to a summer outdoor drive-in theater, **Glacier Peaks RV Park** (3185 Hwy. 40, 406/892-2133 or 800/268-4849, open all year, $8 tents, $26 full hookup, $25–75 cabins) has 60 grassy sites in a treed setting with some shade. With its location at the junction of Montana Highway 40 and U.S. Highway 2, driving access is quick to Columbia Falls (5 minutes), Whitefish (10 minutes), and Kalispell (20 minutes). The campground has cable, phone, and computer lines available as well as a laundry, dump station, hot showers, flush toilets, and a playground.

With 35 grassy treed and partially shaded sites, **LaSalle RV Park** (5618 Hwy. 2 W., 406/892-4668 or 877/894-4178, www.lasallervpark.com, open all year, $14.50–21, seventh night free) offers free cable and wireless Internet at every site. Other amenities include flush toilets, hot showers, laundry, six log sleeping cabins ($25), and a playground. Driving access is quick to Columbia Falls (7 minutes), Whitefish (15 minutes), and Kalispell (15 minutes).

Kalispell

Quite a few commercial campgrounds scatter around Kalispell, all within 30–40 minutes from Glacier and 15–20 minutes to Flathead Lake. Several golf courses are within five miles, along with shopping and restaurants.

The nearest to Glacier, **Rocky Mountain "Hi" RV Park and Campground** (825 Helena Flats, 406/755-9573 or 800/968-5637, www.glaciercamping.com, open year-round, daily $17–22, weekly $90–125, cabins $40–55) sits adjacent to a spring-fed creek with 98 grassy sites tucked between large fir trees and a few open sites with views of the Swan Mountains. Because it is away from the highway, it's quiet; you'll hear little road noise here. With swimming, fishing, and canoeing in the wide creek and a playground on-site, it's a good campground for kids. Amenities include cable

TV hookup, hot showers, flush toilets, picnic tables, fire pits, dump station, and laundry. Shopping, restaurants, and grocery stores are 10 minutes away.

Located five minutes from downtown Kalispell, **Glacier Pines RV Park** (1850 Hwy. 35, 406/752-2760, www.glacierpines.com, open all year, $24, no tent sites) has grassy sites under large trees. Amenities include flush toilets, hot showers, laundry, dump station, picnic tables, fire pits, modem hookups, camp store, horseshoe pits, and a seasonal outdoor heated swimming pool. The campground sits on a two-lane highway, so it picks up some traffic sounds.

Sitting right on the Flathead River, **Spruce Park on the River** (1985 Hwy. 35, 406/752-6321 or 888/752-6321, www.spruceparkrv.com, open year-round, $15–25.50) accommodates 100 RVs and 60 tents in shaded sites with a five-minute drive to restaurants and grocery stores. Amenities include flush toilets, hot showers, laundry, cable TV hookup, playground, and pet walks, and you can wash your RV here. Because of its location on the riverfront, you can fish right from the campground; with its location on a two-lane highway, you'll pick up some traffic noise.

Whitefish

Within 30–35 minutes from West Glacier, campers have three options in Whitefish for campgrounds, all with extremely different environments. Whitefish Lake Golf Club is within a 5–10 minute drive as are shopping and restaurants in town; Big Mountain is a 15-minute drive up the hill.

Set in deep woods right on Whitefish Lake, **Whitefish Lake State Park** (one mile west of Whitefish on Hwy. 93, then one

mile north following signs, 406/862-3991, www.fwp.state.mt.us, May–Sept., $15 per site) is perfect for swimming and launching boats, but not particularly for sleeping as the train tracks cross through the park with nearly 30 trains per day rumbling along and tooting their horns as they enter town. With a good set of earplugs, you can survive the night. Amenities include flush toilets, picnic tables, fire pits, and running water. Grocery stores and restaurants are a seven-minute drive away, but this is the nearest campground to golf.

Located conveniently within Whitefish city limits, **Whitefish RV Park** (6400 Hwy. 93 S., 406/862-7275, www.whitefishrvpark.com, open year-round, $18–29) is a short five-minute walk to shopping, theaters, restaurants, and the winter bus to the ski area. With 57 grassy sites separated by small trees, it sits right behind the Cheap Sleep Motel, which shelters it from some of the four-lane highway noise, but not all. Amenities include flush toilets, hot showers, playground, laundry, cable TV, picnic tables, and a dump station.

Two miles south of Highway 40, **Whitefish KOA** (5121 Hwy. 93 S., 406/862-4242, www.koa.com, open year-round, RV sites $25–60, tent sites $20–36, cabins $30–60) sits on 33 secluded acres shielded from the highway by thick forest. This is quieter than the other two Whitefish campgrounds. The indoor-outdoor pool attracts kids while oldsters gravitate to the adults-only hot tub. A full-service restaurant serves nightly barbecues, sandwiches, and pizza. Other amenities include flush toilets, hot showers, modem dataports, free mini-golf, free continental breakfast, and bike rentals. Grocery stores, shopping, and restaurants are 5–10 minutes away.

Food

Dining in the Flathead Valley is a casual affair, even in the priciest restaurants. Don't bother with a suit and tie or fancy dinner dress; even in fine establishments, relaxed attire is common. Check the yellow pages for options: You'll find Mexican to Japanese, country cafes to steak houses.

BIGFORK

For a tiny town, Bigfork packs in the tasty restaurants, most of which are in downtown within two blocks walking distance of the theater. On performance nights, you won't get in a restaurant for dinner unless you make reservations.

Burgers and Beer

For the best burger and beer after hiking in Jewel Basin, stop at **Garden Bar and Grill** (451 Electric Ave., 406/837-9914, 10 A.M.–2 A.M., $6). You can eat in the bar or out back in the funky garden where live music cranks out tunes on summer evenings. You'll have trouble choosing from the 20 microbrews on tap. In Montana, kids can enter bars usually until 8 P.M.

Eclectic Cuisine

Bigfork's newest restaurant upstairs in Twin Birch Square, **Montana Bistro** (459 Electric Ave., 406/837-2786, daily 11:30 A.M.–9:30 P.M., lunch and dinner, $12–19) dabbles in Creole, Italian, Asian, and Northwest cuisine on an ever-changing menu. The open kitchen lets diners watch their meals being prepared; sit in the cozy dining room or outside in the courtyard in summer. Dinner favorites include a three-inch-thick juicy pork roast (you'll most likely need a doggy bag), or go lighter with an Asian chicken salad sporting a curry sauce. On theater nights, a special menu is served 9:30–10:30 P.M. for après show dining.

Known for exceptional food at modest prices, **C Showthyme!** (548 Electric Ave., 406/837-0707, www.showthyme.com, daily at 5 P.M., $12–31) dishes up a repertoire of fresh fish and pasta to wild game and steaks. One friend swears by the before-dinner wicked gin and tonic. Start dinner with the warm brie cheese salad ($7) or just dive straight into an entree with the chicken relleno Montana ($14)—a cheese-stuffed chile wrapped in a chicken breast and tortilla covered with shrimp sauce. An extensive wine selection features Australian and New Zealand imports as well as West Coast vintners. For dessert, try the house specialty of crème caramel ($5), or for something thematically Montanan, finish with a huckleberry ice cream crepe floating on huckleberry sauce ($5). The cozy two-story brick old bank building opens up for outside seating, too, in summer. For theater-goers, the restaurant is extremely convenient—right next door.

French

Who knows better how to cook French delicacies than a native! **La Provence** (408 Bridge St., www.bigforklaprovence.com, 406/837-2923, Mon.–Sat. 5:30–10 P.M., $15–21) features gourmet Southern French cuisine concocted by Marc Guizol, the owner-chef from Provence. Start off your evening with escargot and traditional French onion soup with Gruyère. Entrees sauced with wines come in fish, duck, rack of lamb, and venison or pork tenderloins. Finish with a traditional soufflé. An extensive wine list accompanies the menu, of course, featuring French vintages. Sit inside surrounded by the works of local artists, or in summer outside on the patio. For lunch, the restaurant operates as the **La Petite Provence Bistro** (Tues.–Sat. 10 A.M.–3 P.M., $4–8), serving gourmet French deli goodies, like homemade pastries, quiche, and Le Nicois sandwiches of ham, salami, Gruyère, and red wine vinaigrette.

COLUMBIA FALLS

Columbia Falls has never been known as a dining mecca, but recently, new restaurants have opened, giving it options beyond the fast food enterprises along the highway. However, if you

A GUIDE TO LOCAL BREWS

Northwest Montanans do like their local microbreweries. To help you navigate the mystery of the brews, here's a guide to the beers you'll find.

Bayern Brewing (Missoula): The Flathead Lake Monster is a unique mild reddish combination of five grains. For filtered golden wheat beer, go for the Trout Slayer.

Big Sky Brewing (Missoula): One of the most popular brown ales in northwest Montana, Moose Drool may have gained its notoriety through merchandising its name, but it tastes darn good, too. For a lighter English-style ale, try Scape Goat Pale Ale. In winter, the Powder Hound ale hits the taps.

Blackfoot River Brewing (Helena): Look for Woollybugger Wheat, a German Hefeweisen, and Missouri River Steamboat Lager, a light hoppy amber. Or for a full-bodied extra stout, try the Double Black Diamond Extreme Stout.

Flathead Lake Brewing (Bigfork): The youngest brewery, which opened in 2005, names its headliner light-bodied American ale after Flathead Lake's huge winter waves: White Cap Pale Ale. Also, try the California-style Flathead Lake Steamers and Scottish-style Last Train Home Amber.

Glacier Brewing (Polson): With a full line, the brewery produces three lighter beers: the German Kolsch Golden Grizzly Ale, the sweet and malty North Fork Amber Ale, and the Port Polson Pilsner. Those in search of a good wheat beer should try a Wild Wolf, while those with a yen for roasted chocolate creamy flavors should pick up a Slurry Bomber Stout.

Great Northern Brewing (Whitefish): Although the brewery changed hands a few years ago along with some of the beer flavors, the Hefeweisen called Wheatfish and the light-bodied Hell Roaring Amber are good. If you haven't overdosed on huckleberries here, you can try them in beer with the Wild Huckleberry Wheat Lager. In winter, look for Snow Ghost.

Lang Creek Brewery (Marion): The brews span the range from very light to very dark. On the lighter end, look for the golden Dutch Skydiver Blonde. For something a bit richer, try the English-style Tri-Motor Amber. On the dark end, sip the unfiltered American brown Good Medicine Brown Ale. Two of the beers add honey for a bit of sweetness – Taildragger Honey Wheat and the light-bodied Huckleberry 'N Honey.

Whitefish Brewing (Whitefish): Its one claim to fame is Montana Nut Brown Ale, a sweet and malty dark beer.

---

do crave fast food, head for the local one-of-a-kind place—**Fox's Drive In** (Hwy. 93 and 9th St., 406/892-2020, Mon.–Sat.), but expect a brief wait while they slap your burger on the grill—no precooking here!

Cafe

The newest addition to town is **Coffee Traders Pines Café** (1st Ave. W. and Hwy. 2, 406/892-7633, 7 A.M.–5 P.M. daily). Noted local coffee roasters—Montana Coffee Traders—know how to brew up an espresso ordered in "the fast lane" to go as well as great breakfasts (until 11 A.M.) and lunches (11 A.M.–3 P.M. daily, Sun. until 2 P.M.). The ambience still clings fondly to memories of the old local dive Pine Tree Cafe, with the pine tree still in the middle.

The menu, ranging $4–7, has huge breakfast omelets, deli sandwiches (to be really decadent, go for the lobster artichoke melt), and wraps, salads, and baked goodies like muffins, scones, and cookies. Given its location en route to Glacier, it's an easy place to grab a sandwich to go for the trail. Check your email here on free Internet. Montana Coffee Traders has two other valley cafes (328 W. Center St., Kalispell, 406/756-2326; 110 Central Ave., Whitefish, 406/862-7667).

Ribs

When Flathead Valley locals want down-home cooking, they head for their favorite dive, **The Back Room of the Nite Owl** (Hwy. 2, 406/892-3131, Sun. 2–9 P.M., Mon.–Thurs.

4–9 P.M., Fri. and Sat. 4–10 P.M., $6–14). The restaurant serves strictly old-time Montana feasts of gooey ribs and broasted chicken. You can order the ribs country, spare, or baby-back, or if you can't decide, a gigantic combo plate piles on all three. Don't look for commercial sauces on the ribs-only the restaurant's own concoction of secret spices. Frybread with honey, cole slaw, and homemade French fries fill the plate to overflowing. It's a place to abandon all thoughts of calories or cholesterol and just pig down. A waitress may still call you "Hon" as she delivers you a roll of paper towels instead of dainty napkins to handle the colossal mess. Just dig in, and when you're done, lick your fingers. Don't plan on dessert; you won't have room.

KALISPELL

Kalispell has most of the common national chain restaurants, but not right in the downtown core. For dinner, you should make reservations in fine establishments, but at most others you can just pop in.

Cafes

With its bright colorful interior displaying local art, the **Knead Café** (25 2nd Ave. W., 406/755-7510, www.theknead.com, Mon.–Fri. 7 A.M.–9 P.M., Sat. 8 A.M.–9 P.M., Sun. 9 A.M.–2 P.M.) can please both a vegetarian and a meat lover with its fresh and slightly different Mediterranean flavors. Breakfasts ($4–6) feature a make-your-own omelet, while lunches ($5–7) grill up a mean portabello with lemon cilantro sauce sandwich. For dinner ($10–14), start with hummus and tabouli served on greens with pita bread ($5) and follow with the spanikopita on roasted garlic cream sauce or Portuguese paella. A full line of beers, wines, and espressos complement any meal here, as do goods from its own bakery.

For burgers and shakes à la 1950s, drop in at **Norm's News** (34 Main St., 406/756-5466, Mon.–Sat. 9 A.M.–5 P.M., Sun. 11 A.M.–4 P.M., $3–6). A tradition since 1938, the soda fountain lets you munch while you browse over 2,500 magazines and newspapers. The kids will also go crazy with the candy collection, featuring over 400 different sugar treats. For nostalgia buffs, the jukebox and ornate back bar are just worth a look, and, of course, the menu features traditional soda fountain fare: hamburgers, hot dogs, sundaes, shakes, and ice-cream sodas.

Pizza

For those with beer and pizza taste buds, head to **Moose's Saloon** (173 N. Main, 406/755-2337, www.moosessaloon.com, daily 11 A.M.–1:30 A.M., $5–15), where peanut shells and sawdust cover the floor in this funky old-time bar that's been a valley staple since 1957. It will be just what you imagine a Montana bar to be—dark, smoky, and loud, loud, loud. But the pizza is darn good with one of the best crusts around. You'll get the kitchen sink on the combination pizza, and beer prices are cheap. If you want to forgo the atmosphere, you can order to go.

Fine Dining

Award-winning **Café Max** (121 Main St., 406/755-7687, www.cafemaxmontana.com, Tues.–Sat. 5:30–9 P.M.) is known for its creative cuisine. The à la carte menu rotates weekly with its elegantly presented bistro fare and whatever seasonal treat Douglas Day, the owner-chef, has concocted from Pacific Northwest ingredients: First courses ($6–9) feature crab cakes and goat cheese crepes and salads ($5–6) followed by entrees ($15–30) of duck, steaks, pork tenderloins, or fish. An extensive international wine list specializes in Washington and Oregon vintages. Day also hosts special six-course wine-tasting dinners ($30–40); call for a current schedule.

Adjacent to the historic Kalispell Grand Hotel, the **Painted Horse Grille** (110 Main St., 406/257-7035, www.paintedhorsegrille.com, lunch Mon.–Fri. 11:30 A.M.–2:30 P.M., $6–8; dinner Mon.–Sat. 5–9 P.M., $13–24) owners completely renovated the old Kalispell Bar in 1999. While the decor is somewhat bland, the food is not! Chef Brett Morris's cuisine has risen in the ranks of Flathead fine

dining and never fails to please. Not-to-miss house specialties include the fall-off-the-bone braised elk shank and fresh pine nut–crusted wild salmon. A large selection of northwest wines and a full cocktail bar are available to accompany dinner, but most notably the restaurant follows its equine theme by stocking wines from 14 Hands winery in Washington State. If you still have room for dessert, chocoholics will enjoy finishing off dinner with the triple chocolate torte ($5).

WHITEFISH

As a resort town, Whitefish is overloaded with outstanding restaurants. Because of crowds, you'll need to make reservations to avoid long waits in high summer or winter. In off-seasons (spring and fall), a few restaurants alter their hours or close for a month on a whim to go fishing; call ahead to be sure they are open.

Cafes

For breakfast and lunch ($5–8), you might have to arm wrestle a local's claim to a daily seat at **The Buffalo Cafe** (516 E. 3rd St., 406/862-2833, weekdays 6:30 A.M.–2 P.M., Sat. 7 A.M.–2 P.M., Sun. 9 A.M.–2 P.M.) to order the house Buffalo Pie with hash browns, ham, and cheese, and topped with two poached eggs.

Loula's (300 2nd Ave., 406/862-5614, daily 7:00 A.M.–4 P.M.) is the place for French toast with raspberry sauce. Before leaving, pick up one of their trademark freshly baked fruit pies to go ($17.50–23.50)

Italian

Mambo Italiano (234 E. 2nd St., 406/863-9600, Mon.–Sat. 5–10 P.M., $9–19) transports you beyond the Flathead to Italy with its cramped noisy dining room lilting to tunes of Frank Sinatra and Andrea Bocelli. Start with the Tootsie Roll appetizer, a ricotta cheese–stuffed phyllo on marinara. You can feast on the huge Dotter Gordon salad topped with eggplant or meatballs or a house pasta like fettuccine alla Lulubella, a carbonara well worth knocking your cholesterol through the roof. Order a jug of house red wine for the table—

you'll be charged by how many glasses you drink (a guess on the waitstaff's part) rather than the bottle. And it's decent wine, too.

For specialty pizzas—none of which remotely resemble a national chain pizza—try **Dire Wolf Pub** (845 Wisconsin Ave., 406/862-4500, 11 A.M.–11 P.M. daily, $7–16) for a Going-to-the-Sun Pizza laden with smoked chicken, sun-dried tomatoes, garlic, and feta, or **Truby's Wood Fired Pizza** (115 Central Ave., 406/862-4979, Mon.–Sat. 11 A.M.–midnight, Sun. 4–10 P.M., $8–17) for a Fungus Among Us mushroom pizza.

Asian

Although most people don't see sushi and Montana going together, the sushi at **Wasabi Sushi Bar and Ginger Grill** (419 2nd St., 406/863-9283, Tues.–Sun., opens at 5 P.M., $7–25) is downright unbeatable. Here sushi rolls ($7–10), sake, and grilled Asian goodies come in a relaxed, bright wasabi green-walled atmosphere. Large mirrors reflect the deft fingers of the sushi chefs in action as they make your rolls. While the menu also carries full teriyaki dinners, many make a feast of ordering several sushi rolls—traditional rolls, or with a more contemporary flare, like the Temptress, a deep fried roll, or the Black Widow, a tuna roll topped with hot Sri Racha.

Cajun and Creole

At **Tupelo Grille** (17 Central Ave., 406/862-6136, nightly at 5 P.M., $12–21), the flavors come from New Orleans. Start with a duck, chicken, and andouille gumbo ($5) followed by a tasty version of shrimp and grits, where grilled shrimp doused in a spicy tasso cream sauce smothers grilled grits. If you can't decide between the Louisiana flavors, order the Cajun Creole combo plate ($18), which piles up a platter of crawfish étouffée, shrimp Creole, and chicken and sausage jambalaya. Don't leave without your dessert: the bread pudding is a must.

Fine Dining

Whitefish also has more than its share of fine restaurants. For prime rib, Montana game, and

high-end steaks accompanied by an extensive wine list, make reservations at ◖ **Whitefish Lake Restaurant** (1200 Hwy. 93 N., 406/862-5285, www.golfwhitefish.com). At Whitefish Lake Golf Course, the 1937 log building was renovated in 1999, upgrading the facility but retaining its original historic ambience. During the golf season, the restaurant is open daily for lunch (11 A.M.–3 P.M.) and dinner (5:30–10 P.M., $15–44), but in winter, it only opens in the evening for dinner (until 9:30 P.M.). For an appetizer, try the New Zealand mussels ($11) followed by one of the restaurant's fish favorites, a halibut baked in phyllo with feta, roasted garlic, and spinach. The house specialty is roasted rack of lamb topped with a three-onion demi-glace. Dinners come will a full complement of salad or soup, grilled veggies, and potato or rice.

GROCERIES
The Flathead Valley has no shortage of supermarket chains and local grocers. But for seasonal, locally grown goodies, try one of the summer **farmers markets,** which usually congregate May–September in Whitefish (Tuesday at the north end of Central Ave., Thursday at the Super 1 parking Lot), Bigfork (Wednesday at Bigfork School), and Kalispell (Tuesday and Saturday at the Kalispell Center Mall).

Information and Services

SHOPPING
While Flathead Valley, thank goodness, has no Mall of America clone or factory outlet mall, it does have its share of small strip malls and chain stores. However, if you can, head to the few strikingly different shops worth browsing: art galleries, jewelry and gift shops, and eclectic collections. Most of the one-of-a-kind locally owned stores cluster in the few blocks of downtown Whitefish, Bigfork, and Kalispell.

For classy, high quality toys—inventive, classic, and educational—stop in **Imagination Station** (221 Central Ave., Whitefish, 406/862-5668, and 132 Main St., Kalispell, 406/755-5668). They'll even ship your toys home for you, so you don't have to haul everything on the airplane. In Kalispell, visit **Sassafras** (120 Main St., 406/752-2433, Mon.–Sat. 9:30 A.M.–6 P.M.), an artist co-op, featuring the works of 30–40 local northwest Montana artists. Pieces range from watercolors and cards to pottery, jewelry, clothing, furniture, and sculptures. You'll find works with Glacier Park themes here, too.

Outdoor Gear
For outdoor gear—camping, backpacking, skiing, snowboarding, and fishing clothing and equipment—five shops carry good brand-name selections and know how to fit equipment to individual people. **Rocky Mountain Outfitter** (135 Main St., Kalispell, 406/752-2446) specializes in hiking, backpacking, climbing, and skiing. Don Scharfe, the owner, is well known for first ascents on several of Glacier's peaks.

The folks at **Ski Mountain Sports** (242 Central Ave., Whitefish, 406/862-7541) are the local alpine ski experts, but in summer, the shop outfits hikers, backpackers, and canoers and specializes in high-end outdoor clothing. With two stores, **Sportsman Ski Haus** (junction of Hwy. 2 and Hwy. 93, Kalispell, 406/755-6484, and 6475 Hwy. 93, Whitefish, 406/862-3111) carries gear and clothing for skiers, snowboarders, hikers, backpackers, anglers, hunters, campers, tennis players, bicyclists, and ice skaters. In three locations, **Stumptown Snowboards** (128 Central Ave., Whitefish, 406/862-0955; Depot Park Square, Kalispell, 406/756-5721; and Big Mountain Village, Whitefish, 406/862-5828) are the local experts in snowboarding and skateboarding with full equipment lines and clothing.

Maps and Books
To stock up on good topographical maps of Glacier and Flathead National Forest, you'll

FLATHEAD VALLEY

MADE IN MONTANA

Looking for souvenirs to take home? Keep a lookout for the blue Made in Montana logo. Only arts, crafts, food, and other products made by Montana residents and grown or produced within the state may bear the label. More than 2,600 businesses – some producing only one item – use the distinctive label.

What products bear the Made in Montana logo? Look for foods like coffee, jams and jellies, preserves, teas, pasta, salad dressings, barbecue sauces, herbs, cheese, jerky, and cookies. Personal health care products range from soaps and shampoos to lotions and oils. Toys, games, pet goodies, furniture, and clothing also can sport the Made in Montana logo, as can arts and crafts, like photography, music, lithographs, paintings, candles, and more.

A local Flathead favorite, **Montana Coffee Traders** has been roasting beans since 1981. Local blends celebrate Montana with the light- and medium-roasted Montana Blend and the light-roasted with a bit of vanilla almond Glacier Blend. The Grizzly Blend promotes the protection of crucial grizzly bear habitat, and the Wild Rockies Blend promotes protection and restoration of wildlands habitat. Look for these products in local grocery stores or order online: www.coffeetraders.com.

If you need a Made in Montana product fix after you get home, check www.madein-montanausa.com for companies that sell Made in Montana products online.

find the widest selection at Rocky Mountain Outfitter or Sportsman Ski Haus. Likewise, both shops carry guidebooks for hiking, fishing, and cross-country skiing in the area—a few field guides, too. You can also find guidebooks, natural history, Lewis and Clark, Montana history, and field guides for flowers, birds, and animals at **Books West** (101 Main St., Kalispell, 406/752-6900) and **Bookworks** (244 Spokane Ave., Whitefish, 406/862-4980).

SERVICES

Post Offices

Each major town in Flathead Valley has one post office; Kalispell has two. Hours are generally Monday–Friday 8:30 A.M.–5:30 P.M. and Saturday 10 A.M.–2 P.M. Exceptions are noted with locations as follows: Bigfork (265 Holt Dr., 406/837-4479), Columbia Falls (65 1st Ave. E., 406/892-7621, closes at 4:30 P.M. on weekdays), Kalispell (350 N. Meridian Rd., 406/755-6450; 248 First Ave. W., 406/755-0187, closes at 1 P.M. on Sat.), and Whitefish (424 Baker Ave., 406/862-2151). Somers (150 Somers Rd., 406/857-3330, Mon.–Fri. 8 A.M.–4:45 P.M., closed Sat.) and Lakeside (7196 Hwy. 93 S., 406/844-3224, Mon.–Fri. 7:30–11 A.M. and noon–4 P.M., closed Sat.) each have a post office, too.

Banks

Banks and ATMs are common in Flathead Valley, but several have branches in more than one town. Glacier Bank (www.glacierbank.com) has offices and ATMs in Kalispell (202 Main St., 406/756-4200), Bigfork (Old Town Center, 406/837-5980), Columbia Falls (822 Nucleus Ave., 406/892-7100), and Whitefish (319 E. 2nd St., 406/863-6300). First Interstate Bank (www.firstinterstate.com) is located in Kalispell (2 Main St., 406/756-5200) and Whitefish (3rd St. and Spokane Ave., 406/863-8888). First Citizens Bank is located in Columbia Falls (540 Nucleus Ave., 406/892-6800) and Kalispell (490 W. Reserve Dr., 406/758-8200).

Internet

While Flathead Valley has DSL and wireless services, it's still not ubiquitous here. If you have a laptop, you may end up using the old-fashioned dial-up modem in many motels. You can get online in the local public county libraries on their computers for a limited amount of time in Kalispell (247 1st Ave. E., 758-5820), Columbia Falls (130 6th St. W., 406/892-5919), Bigfork (525 Electric Ave., 406/837-6976), and Whitefish (9 Spokane Ave., 406/862-6657). Each library has its own policies and hours

(mostly Mon.–Sat., but hours vary by the day and library); call for details.

You won't find large Internet cafes with oodles of terminals, but a few cafes have one computer with Internet access available for patrons. **Montana Coffee Traders Cafes** (110 Central Ave., Whitefish, 406/862-7667; 1st Ave. W. and Hwy. 2, Columbia Falls, 406/892-7633) have a free Internet computer for browsing while you drink a latte. In Bigfork, you can get on the Internet at **Wild Mile Deli** (435 Bridge St., 406/837-3354, www.wildmile-deli.com, Mon.–Sat. 8 A.M.–9 P.M. and in summer on Sun. until 8 P.M.).

INFORMATION
Newspapers and Magazines
The local valley daily news comes in the *Daily Interlake,* but you'll also find other northwestern Montana newspapers around, such as *Great Falls Tribune* and *The Missoulian.* Community weeklies, which cover everything from local events to politics, include Columbia Falls' *Hungry Horse News,* the *Whitefish Pilot,* and the *Bigfork Eagle.* For a peek into the local lifestyle, pick up a copy of *Flathead Living* magazine, found in the airport, hotels, stores, and resorts. It's heavy on advertising, but then it's free! For a look at northwestern Montana from a more down to earth approach, pick up a free copy of Missoula's *Independent.*

Emergencies
For medical, fire, or police emergencies in Flathead Valley, call 911. For medical emergencies in Whitefish and Columbia Falls, **North Valley Hospital** (6575 Hwy. 93 S., Whitefish,

406/863-2501) is closest. A new North Valley Hospital is in the building phase, which will change its location to the junction of Highways 40 and 93 sometime in 2007. For emergencies in Kalispell, Bigfork, and Lakeside, the newly upgraded **Kalispell Regional Medical Center** (310 Sunny View Ln., Kalispell, 406/752-5111) is closest.

City police stations have jurisdictions inside city limits, so much of Flathead Valley is covered by the county sheriff department. In an emergency, when you dial 911, you don't have to think about whether you are inside city boundaries or not; your emergency will be relayed to the appropriate jurisdiction. But just in case, here are the police and sheriff contacts you may need: Flathead County Sheriff (920 S. Main St., Kalispell, 406/758-5585), Columbia Falls Police (130 6th St. W., 406/892-3234), Kalispell Police (312 1st Ave. E., 406/758-7780), and Whitefish Police (2nd St. and Hwy. 93, 406/863-2420).

Ranger Stations
With Flathead National Forest surrounding the Flathead Valley you can pick up maps, current trail and camping information, forest and ski conditions, and regulations in several national forest offices and ranger stations: Flathead National Forest (1935 3rd Ave. E., Kalispell, 406/758-5200), Talley Lake Ranger Station (1335 Hwy. 93 W., Whitefish, 406/863-5400), Swan Lake Ranger Station (200 Ranger Station Rd., Bigfork, 406/837-7500), and Hungry Horse Ranger Station (8975 Hwy. 2 E., Hungry Horse, 406/387-3800).

BACKGROUND
The Land

GEOLOGY

Glacier's mountains reflect approximately 1.6 billion years of geologic history. During that time, sediment deposition, uplifts, erosion, intrusions, and glaciation all left their footprints. To sculpt Glacier and Waterton's scenery into its characteristic jagged parapets with swooping valleys, three geologic events occurred. First, sediments layered on top of each other. Then, mountains moved, and last, an ice age gouged out formations.

And ever since, erosion relentlessly continues to shape the landscape. Wind and water chip away at peaks. Freeze-melt cycles wreak havoc on cliffs, prying off slabs of rock. Over time, weather leaves its thumbprint on the land.

Ancient Belt Sea

Approximately 1.6 billion to 800 million years ago, a shallow lake formed—the ancient Belt Sea. Covering parts of Washington, Idaho, Montana, and Canada, the Belt Sea accumulated sands washing down from adjacent highlands. Through pressure and heat, dolomites, limestone, argillites, siltites, and quartzites layered like a colorful cake, one on top of the other. In a geologic feat found in very few places in North America, Glacier retained its sedimentary rock instead of watching it metamorphose over time. You can easily pick out its layers. Check at Logan Pass, where multihued sediments stripe Mount Clements.

© BECKY LOMAX

Uplift of Mountains

Between 150 and 60 million years ago, massive tectonic movement along monstrous faults created mountains. During this uplift, a several-mile-thick Belt Sea chunk slid 50 miles east and atop much younger rock. Older Precambrian (pre-oxygen life forms) rocks—1,500 million years older—moved on top of younger Cretaceous (dinosaur age) volcanic and shale rocks in a formation known as the **Lewis Overthrust Fault.** Look for its evidence where geologists originally discovered the fault in 1890: north of Marias Pass on U.S. Highway 2. In the whole Rocky Mountain range, Glacier has the oldest exposed sedimentary rock because of the uplift.

During the uplift, rock heated and became pliable like bread dough. Sometimes it simply folded. Look for evidence of folding on Waterton Lake's east shore, above the Ptarmigan Tunnel trail, and between Josephine and Bullhead Lakes on the Swiftcurrent Trail.

Glaciation

More recently, glaciation carved the landscape. Two million years ago, the Pleistocene ice age engraved the park's topography with advancing and retreating glaciers. At the ice age's largest point, only the tops of Glacier's highest peaks poked out as nunataks, a mountaintop completely surrounded by glacial ice. Thousands of feet of ice gouged out valleys.

These ancient ice rivers left their mark on the landscape. When three or more glaciers gnawed away on a peak, the result is a horn like Mount Reynolds or Triple Divide. Sometimes two glaciers chewed ridges paper thin like the Iceberg Wall, a feature known as an arête, which means "fish bone" in French. Large lakes filled in U-shaped valleys, the mark of glacial carving: Compare the rounded valley floor of the McDonald Valley with river-carving, such as Grand Canyon's V shape. As glaciers retreated, they left large piles of debris—rocks, sand, and gravel—in the form of moraines, like a big pile of dirty laundry. Large moraines like Howe Ridge remain from Pleistocene ice, whereas smaller rubble piles

in Grinnell or Sperry Glacier basins are from more recent glacial melting.

Tarns, small glacial lakes, formed in depressions where the ice carved deeper. The upper ends of glaciers often chewed out cirques, steep-walled round basins like the Avalanche Lake basin. Lower ends of glaciers plummeted off cliffs, forming hanging valleys: Bird Woman Falls dives from a hanging valley suspended between Mount Oberlin and Mount Cannon. As you hike, you may find glacial striations or large scratches on rocks where ice abraded the surface. Check the erratics—large boulders strewn about from receding glaciers—on the Avalanche Lake trail for striations.

While most of the Pleistocene ice melted in Glacier about 12,000 years ago, several miniature ice ages have since continued chewing on the land. The glaciers currently in the park are products of the last 8,000 years. During the Little ice age, 1500–1850, most glaciers grew. Tree ring studies show evidence of more than 150 glaciers in the early 1900s. Less than 25 percent of those remain in Glacier today; 37 glaciers are named, the largest of which is Blackfoot Glacier at 0.7 square miles. Sadly, Waterton no longer has active glaciers, only snowfields, but at Cameron Lake, you can look across the border to Herbst Glacier.

Glaciers and Snowfields

In Glacier Park, it's often hard to tell the difference between a glacier and a snowfield. In early summer, particularly, they look the same, covered with fresh snow from winter. But they are distinctly different.

When more snow accumulates than melts annually, glaciers form. The snow transforms into icy grains through freeze-thaw cycles. Snows build up on the upper end of glaciers and push down, compressing ice crystals. Over years, the ice compacts in layers, mounting into a huge mass with a rigid surface and supple base.

Glaciers are moving ice—moving so slow that you can't detect movement by watching them. As the ice presses down with help from gravity, it forms a thin elastic barrier that carries the

ANCIENT ROCKS

ARGILLITES

Of Glacier's colorful rock formations, the most striking is the argillite, an iron-rich mudstone formed in layers on the floor of the ancient shallow Belt Sea 800 million to 1.6 billion years ago. Its blue-green and purple-red hues leap off mountainsides and intensify under water. This clay and silt bound together by silica contains iron, which changes to red hematite when exposed to oxygen, thus giving Grinnell argillite its color. The Appekunney argillite did not oxidize, forming greenish chlorite instead. Driving down the east side of Going-to-the-Sun Road, notice the colors on Red Eagle Mountain. Also, look for both argillites on the Grinnell Glacier Trail, the Iceberg Trail, at Red Rocks Falls, and while rafting on the Middle Fork of the Flathead.

RIPPLE ROCK AND MUD CRACKS

Evidence of the Belt Sea's action remains etched in stone in the form of raindrop impressions, water ripples, and mud cracks. Ripple rocks, found most often in red, blue, or beige

© BECKY LOMAX

Ripple marks in argillite indicate formation in the Belt Sea.
layers, look like sands on a beach where waves left their marks.

As the Belt Sea dried up, sediments compacted and cracked, similar to a mud puddle drying up in a driveway. Large blocks show a web of cracks filled in with alternate sediments. The effect creates something that looks like abstract maroon or greenish tiles. Look for slabs with both ripple marks and mud cracks on the trails in Many Glacier Valley.

---

mass of ice toward the toe of the glacier where it may calve off in chunks. Sperry Glacier moves about 12–20 feet per year, while Grinnell moves much more—30–50 feet per year. When the ice travels over convex ground features, its surface cracks, forming crevasses sometimes hundreds of feet thick. Sometimes hidden, crevasses make glaciers deadly for travel.

To move, a certain amount of ice is needed—usually a surface of 25 acres and depth of 100 feet. Less than that, and the ice becomes static—just a permanent snowfield. Moving glaciers behave similar to a bulldozer, gouging out broad valleys. You'll often be able to recognize them by their tell-tale debris bands—lines of rocks on the surface. When the ice recedes, or melts, rocks and debris are left in large moraines or as erratics. Contrary to the icefields that Glacier once had, today's glaciers are considerably smaller and fast on their way to becoming snowfields.

CLIMATE

Glacier and Waterton center on a collision course for both Arctic Continental and Pacific Maritime weather. West of the divide, wet weather races in from the Pacific, with accompanying moderate temperatures. Precipitation results in an annual average 29 inches of rainfall and 157 inches of snow near West Glacier. Waterton also sees more precipitation than the rest of Alberta.

Although the east side of the divide sees just as much precipitation as the west, one factor produces more extremes—wind. While winter winds often blow snow from slopes, providing forage for ungulates, they also have been known to blow trains off their tracks near East Glacier. Several east-side high passes are notorious for raging unpredictable winds causing hikers to crawl on all fours. **Chinook** winds—warm winds with speeds reaching over 90 miles per hour—happen any time of the year, but they

MAGMA INTRUSIONS

Don't be fooled like a recent New York writer. Yes, Granite Park and its namesake chalet are dubbed for the igneous rock; however, no granite is to be found in Glacier Park. Instead, early prospectors found Purcell lava or pillow lava, rounded blue-gray formations. This lava intruded up through sediment layers and billowed out in ropey coils and bubbles. You can see these formations on the Highline Trail between Granite Park Chalet and Ahern Pass.

Various intrusions occur elsewhere in the park, but one of the most visible from a roadway is the diorite or Purcell sill. It appears from a distance like a 100-foot-thick horizontal black line sandwiched between thinner lighter layers. When the magma boiled up between limestone layers 800 million years ago, it superheated the limestone, turning it white. You can see the diorite sill from Many Glacier Road, visible along Mount Gould and Mount Wilbur as a thick dark line. Hikers will see it as black jagged teeth above Iceberg Lake or the solid line above Grinnell Glacier.

On the Highline Trail, the path passes through the sill approximately one mile beyond Haystack Saddle. Look for a crystallized green sheen covering deep black. You'll notice your footing changes abruptly when you step onto the sill; instead of broken shard slabs, you'll find something more solid – something igneous.

STROMATOLITES

The Belt Sea became habitat for blue-green algae. Six species of this petite primitive life formed there, doing what algae does best: As sunlight hit the algae, its cells removed carbon dioxide from the water and gave off oxygen. During this process, calcium carbonate formed into stromatolites, a round rock formation looking like Van Gogh's *Starry Night* swirls. You'll find stromatolites along Going-to-the-Sun Road and on the Highline Trail before climbing up to Haystack Saddle. While these are the only fossils in the park's alpine lands, their presence in the Belt Sea produced an oxygen-rich atmosphere that allowed other life forms to develop – yes, humans.

are most obvious in winter. Native Americans called them "snow eaters" for rapidly melting snow. When a chinook descends the Continental Divide's east side, it becomes warm and dry, fooling trees into thinking it's spring and catapulting their cells into their spring water absorption. When temperatures plummet again, the cold freezes the water and kills the trees. This accounts for the number of dead silver trunks dotting east-side forests, especially visible in Two Medicine and Waterton.

Glacier is a country of weather extremes. Its maximum high hit 99°F while its low kneeled to −36°F. Elevation makes a huge difference, too: While Lake McDonald beckons swimmers to sunny beaches, frigid winds can rage across Logan Pass. Sometimes, you can experience four seasons in one day, so always dress in layers and carry extra clothing, no matter what the weather looks like in the morning! Rains move in fast, and snows may fall during all months of the year.

Spring

While March, April, and May are appealing off-months to travel, in Glacier they are wet and cold, still clinging to winter. Snow buries the high country and much of the lowlands until late spring. May is rather moody: It can be extremely wet with frequent late snowstorms and avalanches in the high country.

Summer

During summer months, June habitually monsoons, but July and August usher in warmer, drier skies. Often higher elevations are substantially cooler—up to 15 degrees chillier than valley floors. While cool breezes are welcome on baking summer days, they can also bring snows in August.

Fall

Autumn begets lovely bug-free warm days and cool nights. While golds paint aspen and

AVERAGE PRECIPITATION AND TEMPERATURES

Month	Average number rainy/snowy days	Average snowfall (inches)	Average of temperature (low-high, °F)
Jan.	17	40	12-28
Feb.	13	23	18-34
Mar.	13	15	22-41
Apr.	11	4	29-52
May	13	0.4	37-64
June	13	0.2	44-71
July	9	0	47-79
Aug.	9	0	46-78
Sept.	9	0.1	39-67
Oct.	11	2	32-53
Nov.	15	17	25-37
Dec.	17	38	18-30

Temperatures are from West Glacier.

larch trees, temperatures bounce through extremes—from highs of 75–80°F during the day to below freezing at night. Seemingly schizophrenic, rains and snows descend for a few days followed by clearing and warming trends.

Winter

Winter temperatures in Glacier vary depending on elevation but mostly hang in the 10–25°F range, producing voluminous snows. Logan Pass is buried under 350–650 inches of snow per year. Temperatures can spike above freezing, with its companion rain, or below zero with an Arctic front. Because chinooks visit Waterton more than most of Alberta, it is one of the warmest places in the province in winter. While the Canadian prairies suffer below freezing temperatures, Waterton may be reveling in 30–50°F.

Daylight

Given Glacier's latitude and placement on the mountain time zone's western edge, hours of daylight fluctuate wildly during the year. In June, over 16 hours of sun leaves lots of time to wear yourself out. First light fades in around

5 A.M., and dark doesn't descend until almost 11 P.M. By late August, however, it's dark at 9 P.M. with daylight cruising on a shorter ride until December's slim 8.5 hours of daylight. Around the winter solstice, the sun rises around 8 A.M. and sets at 4:30 P.M.

FLORA

Glacier and Waterton parks are rich in floral diversity. Forests, prairies, and tundra all sprout with different vegetation specific to elevation, habitat, and weather. Glacier is home to 46 rare Montana plants, four of which are found only in the park. In addition, the park houses 1,150 vascular plants, 400 mosses, and 275 lichens. It harbors species at the edges of their distribution: Great Plains flowers to arctic bulbs. The Lake McDonald Valley shelters nearly 100 Pacific Coast species.

For a small park, Waterton has a corner on the rare plant market: 30 are found only within its borders, including the rarest plant, the Waterton moonwort. Waterton can also brag a total of 970 vascular plants, 190 mosses, and 220 lichens, ironically chalking up more diversity than its larger park neighbors, Banff and Jasper.

Grasslands

More than 100 grass species proliferate across the Glacier-Waterton bunchgrass prairies, which poke into valley drainages on the Continental Divide's east side and have been preserved by natural fires in the North Fork Valley. Waterton houses one of two prairie lands in the Canadian national park system and one of North America's last places where grizzly bears range into historic grassland habitat.

Aspen Parklands

Aspens proliferate on east-side slopes, populating the valleys of Many Glacier, Belly River, Two Medicine, St. Mary, and Waterton. Harboring elk herds in winter and broken by wildflower meadows of arrowleaf balsamroot and sticky geranium, groves of quaking aspen shake their leaves in the slightest breeze—hence their name. They mark the transition between grasslands and coniferous forests.

Montane Forests

In low to mid-elevations, dense montane forests mix poplars and firs, which vary substantially depending on moisture and winds. Cedar-hemlock forests with birch dominate wetter western valleys, while drier slopes are covered with limber pine, Douglas fir, white spruce, and lodgepole pines. The western larch, a conifer that loses its needles each winter, also inhabits lower elevation forests. Below the canopy, twinflower, foamflower, and orchids find their niche along with juniper, Pacific yew, thimbleberry, and serviceberry.

Subalpine Zone

Between 5,000 and 7,000 feet in elevation, stately forests surrender to subalpine firs, dwarfed and gnarled in their struggle to survive in a short growing season, brutal winds, frigid temperatures, and heavy snows. For survival, trees develop a bent, stunted krummholz, forming a protective mat rather than growing upright. Whitebark pine and Englemann spruce also sneak into the subalpine. Between tree islands, lush mountain meadows bloom with a colorful array of columbine, bog gentians, valerian, fleabane, and beargrass.

Alpine Tundra

Nearly 25 percent of Glacier and Waterton is alpine tundra. Above the tree line, the land appears to be barren rock. But a host of miniature plants adapt to the harsh conditions of high winds, short summers, cold temperatures, and little soil. Low-growing perennials and hairy leaves provide protection from winds and the sun's high elevation intensity. Mats of pink moss campion, delicate spotted saxifrage, purple butterworts, and Jones columbine fling their energies into showy flowers, however tiny they may be.

Huckleberries

Of all Glacier's flora, the huckleberry draws the most attention. While several varieties grow throughout the park, from lowlands to subalpine zones, they all have one thing in common: a sweet berry. Look for a low-growing shrub with

small green to reddish leaves. About the size of a small blueberry, huckleberries are ripe when they are a rich dark purple-blue. Lowland huckleberries ripen in late July, but mid-August–September is known as huckleberry season.

Wildflowers

Glacier's wildflowers peak in late June–early August, depending on snowmelt and elevation. Early season brings on fields of yellow glacier lilies and white spring beauties poking their buds up through the snowpack. In lower elevations, large white heads of cow parsnip bloom alongside roads and continue into higher elevations as summer progresses. During some summers, beargrass—a tall white lily—blooms so thickly on subalpine slopes that the hillsides still look snow-covered. Paintbrush spews fields in yellow, red, fuchsia, white, salmon, and orange. Just a reminder: Picking flowers in national parks is prohibited. Use your camera instead.

Poisonous Plants

Very few plants in Glacier are poisonous to the touch. Several can be toxic if eaten, so it's best to avoid eating plants or mushrooms unless you know what you're doing. Most of Glacier is inhospitable for poison ivy, oak, and sumac. But keep your eyes open for stinging nettles, which line many of the trails: Although not poisonous, they leave an obnoxious itchy residue on contact. A few people have allergic reactions to cow parsnip: If you have sensitive skin, wear long sleeves and long pants to avoid contact with the plant.

FAUNA

Glacier and Waterton teem with wildlife: 24 fish species, 63 mammals, and 272 birds. The Crown of the Continent remains a North American bastion of an intact ecosystem, with many animals present that were here before the human impact of the past 150 years. In the late 1980s, wolves migrated from Canada, completing more of the original members of Glacier's wildlife family. Only mountain bison and woodland caribou remain extirpated.

Bears

Two bears roam Glacier's mountains: the black bear and grizzly bear. Omnivores and opportunistic feeders, bears will eat anything that is easy pickings. Spending most of their waking time eating to gain 100–150 pounds before winter, Glacier's bears feed on a diet heavy in plant matter: bulbs, roots, berries, shoots, and flowers. Ants, insects, carrion, and ground squirrels fill in proteins. Contrary to popular opinion, humans are not on their list of favorite foods.

Because bears are extremely fast learners, they adapt quickly to new food sources, be it a pack dropped by the side of the trail or dog food left out in a campground. For this reason, Glacier imposes strict rules for handling food and garbage in picnic sites, campgrounds, and backcountry areas. All garbage cans and dumpsters are bear resistant. Bears that eat human foods and garbage find themselves in the bear management game—moved to a new habitat, or worse, destroyed.

A grizzly bear leaves a hind footprint in mud.

© BECKY LOMAX

Because grizzly and black bears are integral to Glacier's ecosystem, the National Park Service employs several bear rangers whose jobs entail monitoring and deterring bears from trouble. For bruins who hang near roadways and front country campgrounds, the bear team usually employs hazing methods—loud noises, gunshots, pellet bean bags, and sometimes Karelian bear dogs—in an attempt to teach the bear to stay away. Nuisance bears will be transplanted to remote park drainages or destroyed if their offenses warrant.

Bears are one of the least productive mammals, giving birth once every two or three years. While black bears have a gestation of 220 days, for grizzlies spring mating season is followed with delayed implantation, where the fertilized eggs simply "hang" until winter. Pending the sow's health, the egg or eggs implant, resulting in one, two, or three cubs born during winter's deep sleep. If her health is severely threatened, she may abort the egg instead.

Bears don't actually hibernate, for their respiration and pulse remain close to normal. Instead, they enter a deep sleep in which their body temperature drops slightly. Before they crawl into their dens for winter, they eat mountain ash berries, rough grasses, and twigs to form an anal plug; then they will not eat, urinate, or defecate for the winter. When bears emerge in the spring ravenously hungry, they head for avalanche chutes to rummage for carcasses buried in the snow.

Megafauna

Megafauna are the big animals everyone wants to see, like bears. Glacier and Waterton harbor three elusive members of the cat family: mountain lions, bobcats, and Canadian lynx. Quiet hunters and mostly nocturnal, cats may see you while you have no idea that they linger nearby. Deer make up the biggest part of the mountain lion's diet, with the cat populations rising and falling with deer numbers. With keen eyesight and hearing, these three cats stalk their prey, the lynx with the help of large "snowshoe" feet.

Gray wolf packs usually inhabit fairly large ranges, 100–300 square miles, so chances of seeing a wolf are fairly rare in spite of the fact that they have the relatively high reproductive potential of 4–7 pups per year. Coyotes, foxes, wolverines, and badgers round out the large carnivore list. Although wolverines are supposedly the most obscure of creatures, many hikers have been lucky to spot them along the Highline Trail. High remote terrain, snowfields, and plentiful ground squirrels provide a good habitat.

Ungulates populate Glacier's high and low country. Moose frequently browse in stream beds and along lakes. Keep your eyes open in the Swiftcurrent Valley, especially around bogs and willow thickets. Elk, mule deer, and white-tailed deer inhabit areas park-wide at tree line and below, while mountain goats and bighorn sheep cling to rocky alpine slopes. During late spring, goats congregate at the Goat Lick on U.S. Highway 2 looking for minerals for their depleted systems. They also are a regal staple at Logan Pass.

In Waterton, a small bison herd grazes in a paddock—a tiny remnant of what once roamed the prairies here by the thousands. Visitors may drive the viewing road and hike a short overlook trail to see the bison.

Small Mammals

Members of the weasel family—fishers, pine martens, minks, and weasels—inhabit forests and waterways. The short-tailed weasel changes color in winter: Its fur becomes white, except for the small black tip of its tail. Snowshoe hares also change to white in winter, their large namesake feet providing extra flotation on snow. In subalpine country, a chorus of eeks, screams, and squeaks bounce through rockfalls. The noisemakers are most often pikas and the ubiquitous Columbian ground squirrel, easily recognized by its reddish tint. Looking like fat furballs, hoary marmots splay on rocks sunning themselves. Scampering between rocks in the alpine zone, golden-mantled ground squirrels look like oversized chipmunks with their tell-tale white stripes.

© BECKY LOMAX

Hoary marmots frequent the subalpine terrain along the Continental Divide.

Fish

With 750 lakes and 1,500 miles of streams, Glacier provides abundant habitat for fish, both native and nonnative species. Bull trout, westslope cutthroat, and whitefish are among the 17 species of native fish. To promote recreational fishing, lakes were stocked with nonnative fish such as rainbow trout, arctic grayling, and kokanee salmon. Introduced species flourished, threatening native fish whose populations are now waning. Since the 1970s, fish are no longer stocked in Glacier or Waterton.

Fish in Waterton Lakes feed on a tiny crustacean, the opossum shrimp—a relic species that inhabited the area prior to the Pleistocene Ice Age. As glaciers melted, the tiny shrimp returned through the Missouri-Mississippi watersheds. Spending its entire life in darkness, it lingers on the lake bottom during the day, surfacing only at night.

Birds

More than 200 species of birds inhabit the

area, so every park visitor can see wildlife. Bird checklists are available at visitor centers in both parks to assist with identification. In summer, trees teem with songbirds—cedar waxwings, thrushes, chickadees, vireos, sparrows, dark-eyed juncos, and finches, to name a few. Brilliantly colored western tanagers and striking mountain bluebirds flit between treetops. Woodpeckers, including the large, red-capped pileated woodpecker, tap at bark in search of bugs. Ground birds such as the chicken-sized grouse surprise hikers on trails, while smaller ptarmigans—whose plumage turns white in winter—blend with summer coloration into rockfalls. Steller's jays and Clark's nutcrackers add to the cacophony, as do common sightings of rufous and calliope hummingbirds.

Because of Glacier's abundant rivers, streams, and lakes, waterfowl finds plentiful habitat. Loons, grebes, mergansers, and goldeneyes fill almost every lake, while harlequin ducks migrate to rapidly flowing streams in spring for nesting. Tundra swans use Glacier's lakes as a stopping ground during their annual migra-

tion to and from their arctic breeding grounds. American dippers, or water ouzels, nest near waterfalls: The dark bird's obvious bobbing action is a dead giveaway as to species.

Raptors

Nothing is more dramatic than sighting a golden eagle soaring along a cliff face. Common nesters in remote spots, goldens often return yearly to the same location. Glacier also boasts about 10 nesting pairs of bald eagles, who can be seen along waterways any month of the year. Above lakes, ospreys dive for fish from impressive heights while red-tailed hawks and American kestrels hover over field mice. Listen carefully, for nights are haunted by the "whew" of the small pygmy owl as well as the six deep hoots of the great horned owl.

Snakes and Insects

For the most part, Glacier and Waterton are devoid of poisonous snakes and spiders. The climate is simply too harsh for rattlesnakes. However, you will find garter and bull snakes on some trails. Due to colder conditions, spiders here are small, although a bite may produce swelling or an allergic reaction.

ENVIRONMENTAL ISSUES
Global Warming

Although earth's temperatures have spiked tropically and dropped icily several times, the current increase in global temperatures affects Glacier Park. While glaciers have shrunk since 1850, climatologists predict that the park's namesakes will melt by 2030. It's not just a loss of ice, but a shift in flora and fauna. As temperatures warm, the tree line advances up in elevation, encroaching on alpine zones. Basins scoured clean by ice and open wildflower meadows became heavily forested with spruce, fir, pines, shrubs, and bushes.

While Glacier's tree line was once 3,200 feet lower, the extent of change expected in the future is unknown. Plants at the fringes of their distribution may disappear as their habitat changes. Shifts in habitat may force

wildlife to change elevation or latitude in search of food sources. Because of Glacier's easily accessed alpine areas, scientists are monitoring melt rates of Grinnell and Sperry Glaciers to help predict future impacts on the park's biodiversity.

Grizzly Bears

In the 1800s, more than 100,000 grizzly bears roamed grasslands and foothills in the Lower 48. Today, in less than one percent of their historic range, fewer than 1,000 grizzlies forage for food. In 1975, grizzly bears were listed as threatened on the Endangered Species List. Since then, a bear management plan assisted recovery in Glacier, Flathead National Forest, and the Bob Marshall Wilderness Complex.

In a multiyear effort to count the grizzly population, Kate Kendall of the U.S. Geological Survey conducted two studies in Glacier and surrounding lands. Collecting scat and bear hairs via barbwire stapled to rub trees and surrounding scent lures, field assistants used tweezers to bag the hairs for DNA genotyping of species, sex, and individual. Finished in 2000, the first study resulted in a count of 437 grizzly bears in the greater Glacier area. While hiking in the park, you may see barbwire attached to trees; look carefully, but do not contaminate bear hairs with human DNA by touching them.

Grizzlies require a large range; many travel outside the park and across international boundaries. Human pressures from road and house building, agriculture and livestock, timber harvesting, and mineral, oil, and gas mining severely impact grizzly bear habitat. Just outside Waterton, legal Canadian hunting and predator-control programs subject bears to high mortality rates. In 2004, northwest Montana saw 31 grizzlies killed from poaching, management actions, and private landowners—30 percent higher than the previous record. While bad berry crops and encroaching rural developments may contribute to bears getting into trouble, clearly inappropriate attractants—garbage, livestock grain, and bird feeders—led to many of the deaths.

Endangered and Threatened Species

Gray wolves once ranged throughout most of North America. By 1920, predator-control programs extirpated them from Glacier and Waterton, in 1973 they were placed on the Endangered Species List. In 1986, following the natural migration of the Magic Pack from Canada, Glacier saw its first litter of pups born in over 50 years. While the recovery goal of 100 wolves in the Northern Rockies has not been met, wolf populations have grown to several packs throughout northwest Montana. While wolf hunting or trapping is prohibited in the United States, hunting and trapping are legal in Canada, and ranchers on both sides of the border may kill wolves for livestock protection.

Of all the ungulates, **bighorn sheep** face the greatest risk. Once widely scattered across most western mountain ranges, the sheep today live in fragmented pockets. Hunting, disease, agriculture, mining, competition for food, fire suppression policies, and habitat destruction forced this grassland forager into the more rugged fringes of its historic range. Today, 250–400 bighorn sheep graze in Glacier, with an additional population in Waterton. Current studies use GPS radio collars to track the sheep.

The **Canada lynx,** a rarely seen cat, was listed as threatened in 2000. Recorded sightings of the feline have declined substantially in the past 40 years. It usually follows its chief prey, the snowshoe hare, in coniferous forests. Ongoing studies follow tracks in winter to ascertain the lynx's status.

Two indigenous trout descended from Arctic lakes formed as the ice age retreated: **westslope cutthroat trout** and **bull trout.** Glacier provides a stronghold for these fish; while bull trout populations have declined 90 percent (it's been listed since 1998 as an endangered species), pure cutthroat have yet to be placed on the list. While habitat degradation and overfishing contributed to the demise, the biggest menace came from nonnative species stocked for recreational fishing, turning them into fast cuisine for lake trout. But the species sees the most danger through hybridization with other trout, like rainbows. Removing nonnative species is impractical; the park uses fishing regulations to protect pure populations.

Fire

Like snow, wind, or rain, lightning-caused fire is a natural process. It is healthy for the ecosystem, for it removes bug infestations, reduces deadfall and nonnative plants, releases nutrients into the soil like a good fertilizer, and maintains a natural mix of vegetation. Following years of heavy fire suppression policy, forest fuels built up to high levels in the park. Each summer, Glacier averages 13 fires with 5,000 acres burned; some summers, like 2003 when 150,000 acres blazed, see more. Most fires burn unevenly, creating a mosaic of charred timber amid greenery. That patchwork ultimately leads to more vegetation and wildlife diversity. In the natural process of regrowth, the burns flourish rapidly with wildflowers, birds, and wildlife.

Historical Protection

Glacier has amassed substantial cultural and historical resources, but to date, Glacier has no full time archaeologist to oversee protection of archaeological and historic assets. At 50 years old, something can be considered historic, according to federal law—even garbage dumps. To date, Glacier has identified 429 archaeological sites and Waterton 358. But many have not been cataloged. While the park does all it can to protect its cultural and historical resources, more funding is needed to extend adequate protection.

Nonnative Plants

Sometimes the prettiest flowers can be the most noxious. Such is the case with exotic weeds such as spotted knapweed, St. John's wort, and the oxeye daisy, introduced through horses, cars, livestock, and railroads. With their broad roots, high seed production, and chemicals that inhibit growth of native plants, these exotics infest grasslands, lessening diversity and reducing wildlife habitat. Both Parks Canada and Glacier's National Park Service curb the spread of nonnative plants through mowing, herbicides, or natural means.

History

Human use of the Crown of the Continent dates back 10,000 years. Evidence of fishing in Upper Waterton Lake and driving bison across the Blakiston Valley prairies most likely belonged to the ancestors of native peoples living near Glacier and Waterton today.

Native Americans

Spanning what became the U.S.-Canadian border, the **Blackfeet** or Nitsitapii (meaning "real people") included three nomadic groups who based much of their livelihood on hunting bison in the vast prairies on the Continental Divide's east side. The most northerly group, the Sitsika or Blackfoot, were the first to meet European traders. (To refer to the collective, Canada prefers Blackfoot, but Blackfeet is in use the United States.) The other two—the Blood or Kainai and Piegan or Piikani—made up the southern groups. For thousands of years, according to the Blackfeet, their lands ran between the Saskatchewan and Yellowstone Rivers.

During summers, Blackfeet groups convened for the Sun Dance, a ceremony held on the plains. But during the rest of the spring and summer, efforts focused individually on stocking food: hunting, digging roots, and collecting berries. As bison moved northwest to their wintering ranges, groups met again for hunts—sometimes buffalo jumps, where hunters funneled bison over a cliff. Afterward, they returned to their winter camps sheltered in deep mountain forests.

For the Blackfeet, the Glacier Park area was known as the "Backbone of the World." Used for spiritual sanctuary, the mountains provided places for prayer and sacred ceremonies. A place to gather guidance, the mountains also yielded holy plants and roots used for their healing properties. Some of Glacier's peaks, lakes, and rivers still use Blackfeet names today: Going-to-the-Sun Mountain, Two Medicine Lake, Pitamakin Pass, and Running Eagle Falls.

On the Continental Divide's west side,

the **Salish** and **Kootenai** hunted, trapped, and fished, ranging east over the mountains on annual bison hunts. Known as the Ktunaxa, the Kootenai (variously spelled Kootenay, Cootenay, or Kutenai) comprised seven bands spanning the western Rockies from southern Alberta to Missoula, Montana. The Kootenai typically used mountain passes like Marias, Cut Bank, Red Eagle, and Brown to cross through Glacier and Waterton to hunt as the Blackfeet used the same passes for raiding parties. For the Kootenai, the Lake McDonald area was a place for sacred dances, hence its original name of Sacred Dancing Waters.

Two other native people lived in the Glacier-Waterton vicinity: the Assiniboines or Stoney Indians and the Gros Ventres. Both of these tribes find namesakes in the park, with a lake, a pass, and three peaks named for the Stoney. In the park's northeast corner, the Gros Ventres, which means Big Belly, left their names on the Belly River and Mokowanis (which means "Big Belly") drainages with Gros Ventre Falls. Little evidence remains in the park of the presence of the Flathead and Kalispel tribes.

As westward expansion brought more people, Native Americans moved within government reservation boundaries: The Sitsikas settled near Calgary. The Blood moved onto a reserve adjacent to Waterton, while the Piegans, the largest of the three Blackfeet groups, split into two, with the North Piikani settling near Pincher Creek and the South Piikani on the Continental Divide's west side in Montana. The Salish and Kootenai moved to the Flathead Reservation southwest of Glacier. Smallpox and whiskey took their toll on the tribes.

Development

In 1803, when Lewis and Clark came west, they bypassed Glacier. Coming within 25 miles at Camp Disappointment, located today on the Blackfeet Reservation, they never found Marias Pass, one of the lowest passes through the treacherous Rocky Mountains. But throughout

the century, French, Spanish, and English fur trappers entered the Glacier-Waterton area.

Westward expansion also brought miners looking for copper and gold. But lands between the Continental Divide and the plains belonged to the Blackfeet. In 1895, the federal government negotiated a settlement with the Blackfeet to purchase the land. During the turn of the 20th century, mining boomed in Many Glacier and Rising Sun, while Waterton spewed Western Canada's first oil well and Kintla Lake Montana's first. Neither oil nor mining paid off, both easily supplanted by burgeoning tourism.

Building a Park

Pressure to find rail passages through the northern Rockies began in the mid-1800s. When Great Northern Railway finally succeeded in 1891 to lay track over the Continental Divide, the face of Glacier changed. To counter travel to Europe, train riders needed a destination. The railroad's economic needs and pressure from preservationists spawned the idea of Glacier National Park, which finally took shape on May 11, 1910.

William Logan—for whom Logan Pass is named—took the reins as the first superintendent of the nation's 10th park. Charged with building a headquarters, hiring rangers, constructing trails, and surveying for a road through the park's interior, Logan did little his first year but put out fires. Literally. Over 100,000 acres went up in flames. His second summer finally saw steps toward readying Glacier for visitors.

Great Northern Railway created many of the park's attractions: hotels, tent camps, chalets, roads, trails, and boats. Competing for travel time and dollars from wealthy Americans taking steamships to Europe, the railroad pitched a slogan "See America First" to lure vacationers to Glacier, which became known as "America's Switzerland."

Horse concessionaires operating from every hotel and chalet in the park merged into the Park Saddle Horse Company. By the mid-1920s, on horseback was the way to see the park. At its peak, the Park Saddle Horse Company operated more than 1,000 horses and led more than 10,000 visitors through the park each summer.

The demand for a road bisecting Glacier's interior increased. Although its western portion began in 1919, the 52-mile project was not completed until 1932. Opening of Going-to-the-Sun Road ushered in a new era of park visitation. A fleet of 32 red buses hit Glacier's roads for touring. With increased motorized travel, camping gaining popularity, and budget motor inns added to Great Northern's property collections, saddle trips and the chalets met their demise.

During World War II and the Depression, travel curtailment and fuel conservation dropped visitation significantly, forcing hotels and chalets to close. Several fell into massive disrepair and had to be razed. Bus tour business began to usurp rail travel, the Park Saddle Horse Company folded, private car travel increased, and the railroad lost $500,000 annually, which it offset with ridership profits. Finally, in 1954, Great Northern unloaded the remaining chalets on the National Park Service for $1. In 1957, the company sold the rest of the hotel chain to a Minneapolis hotel corporation, which subsequently sold three years later to Glacier Park, Inc., which would sell again 21 years later to Dial Corporation.

International Peace Park

In 1932, Glacier and Waterton took to front headlines as the world's first peace park. Due to the brainchild and work of Alberta and Montana chapters of Rotary International, lobbying efforts paid off, as the Canadian Parliament and U.S. Congress officially recognized the continuity between the parks. With credit to the longest undefended border in the world, they dedicated the parks together as **Waterton-Glacier International Peace Park.**

Biosphere Reserve and World Heritage Site

In 1976, UNESCO (United Nations Educational, Scientific, and Cultural Organization)

designated Glacier Park as a Biosphere Reserve. Three years later, Waterton Lakes received the same recognition. As a Biosphere Reserve, the parks are recognized for their huge diversity of wildlife, plants, and habitats. In 1995, UNESCO followed the biosphere designation with declaring the parks a World Heritage Site for natural beauty and unique geological features, such as Triple Divide Peak and the continent's oldest exposed sedimentary rock.

Recreation

BACKPACKING

Glacier National Park's backpacking is rivaled nowhere else. Designated and permitted backcountry campsites spread campers out, so you never feel crowded. You can hit the popular trails in the Belly River or head for something really remote, like the Nyack-Coal Loop. Backpacking information, permit applications, trail status reports, and backcountry campsite availability are online: www.nps.gov/glac. Call a permit office or 406/888-7800 to speak with someone in person regarding conditions and routes. Use hiker shuttles to create easy point-to-point routes.

Guides

Glacier Park allows only one backpacking concessionaire, and that's **Glacier Guides** (406/387-5555 or 800/521-7238, www.glacier-guides.com), a company that has been guiding in Glacier for over 20 years. Guide services, shuttles, food, group equipment, park entrance fees, and permits are included for roughly $115 per day on trips that depart weekly for 3, 4, and 6 days. Custom trips ($140 per person per day with four people; more with fewer people) and one 10-day Continental Divide trip are also available. If you want the backpacking experience but don't want to carry more than a day pack, you can hire a Sherpa to haul up to 40 pounds of your gear ($150 per day). You can also rent gear—packs, tents, sleeping bags, and pads. Reservations are required.

Climbing

Glacier's peaks and off-trail scrambles are irresistible; however, the park's crumbly sedimentary rock makes climbing risky. Loose handholds, wobbly footholds, rockfall, and unstable scree and talus slopes are hazardous. For this reason, most ascents are actually scrambles, but still not for the inexperienced. For routes, J. Gordon Edwards's *A Climber's Guide to Glacier National Park* is the undisputed bible.

For those looking to hook up with climbers, **Glacier Mountaineering Society** offers volunteer-led climbs for members usually on weekends, and each summer they pack one week in July full of climbs for their Mountaineering Week. Only $15 buys an annual

backpacking on Pitamakin Pass, near Two Medicine

© BECKY LOMAX

GETTING INTO THE BACKCOUNTRY

Glacier rates high with backpackers. Miles of well-marked scenic trails take backpackers to remote, rugged traverses and over high alpine passes. It's truly a place to get away from it all.

Backcountry camping is by permit only. Each campground has 2-7 sites with four people permitted per site. All backcountry campgrounds have pit toilets — some with amazing views — community cook sites, and tent sites. No food, garbage, toiletries, or cookware should ever be kept in the tent sites. Near the cook sites, a bear pole or bar makes hanging food easy. Some campsites have food storage boxes.

Many backcountry campsites do not allow fires, so carry a lightweight stove for cooking. Take low-odor foods to avoid attracting bears, and practice Leave No Trace principles religiously.

In addition to regular backpacking gear (tent, sleeping bag, pad, clothing, rain gear, topographical maps, compass or GPS device, first-aid kit, bug juice, sunscreen, fuel, cook gear, and stove), bring a 25-foot rope for hanging food, a small screen or strainer for sifting food particles out of gray water, a one-micron or smaller filter for purifying water (tablets and boiling can do the job, too), and a small trowel for emergency human waste disposal when a pit toilet is unavailable.

Permits may be acquired two ways: by mail, permits may be reserved for $20 (a limited number of sites are assigned this way, and you still have to pay your per person fee when you pick up the actual permit); or stop by a permit office (8 A.M.-4:30 P.M., May-Nov.; some permit offices stay open later in the evening) no more than 24 hours in advance. Advance reservations and walk-in permits cost $4 per person per night. Permits are available at Apgar Permit Office (406/888-7859), St. Mary Visitor Center (406/732-7751), Many Glacier Ranger Station (406/732-7740), Two Medicine Ranger Station (406/226-4484), and Polebridge Ranger Station (406/888-7742). In winter, call 406/888-7800.

SUGGESTED ROUTES: 3-4 DAYS

- **Gunsight Pass Trail:** Shorter backpacking favorites zip into the high country for spectacular views. Beginning at Jackson Glacier Overlook, this 20-mile trail grabs views of Jackson and Blackfoot Glaciers before crossing the Continental Divide at Gunsight Pass and dropping to Sperry Chalet and Lake McDonald Lodge.

- **Highline Trail:** For an international hike, begin at Logan Pass and finish 30 miles later at Goat Haunt to catch the boat across Waterton Lake.

- **St. Mary to Two Medicine:** A 35-mile trail passes prime fishing lakes and bighorn sheep along several high passes. Most notably, the trail crosses below Triple Divide Peak, the apex of three continental waterways heading to the Pacific, Atlantic, and Hudson Bay.

SUGGESTED ROUTES: 5-10 DAYS

- **Continental Divide National Scenic Trail:** The trail runs 110 miles from Marias Pass to Waterton, stringing together high passes and valley lakes in a stunning conclusion to the 3,100-mile trail.

- **Northern Traverse:** Beginning at Chief Mountain Customs, the 58-mile trail follows the Mokowanis Valley over Stoney Indian Pass to Goat Haunt and then the Olson Creek Valley to Browns Pass and Hole-in-the-Wall before cresting Boulder Pass and dropping to Kintla Lake, all just south of the Canadian border.

- **North Circle Tour:** Following in the footsteps of the historic horseback tours through Glacier, this 54-mile trail begins in Many Glacier, tours the Belly River and Mokowanis Valleys, crosses Stoney Indian Pass, then heads south to Fifty Mountain and Granite Park on the Highline Trail before crossing Swiftcurrent Pass back to Many Glacier.

membership! Their website is loaded with climbing info, too: www.glaciermountaineers. com. No commercial guiding outfitters operate climbing trips in Glacier.

Safety while climbing is imperative. Each year, accidents and fatalities occur from falling while climbing. Glacier's sedimentary rock is crumbly, loose, and prone to give way. Rocks cause people to fall as well as take people out that they drop on. Only venture off the trail for climbing if aware of the terrain and inherent risks.

Begin all off-trail adventures by registering at a ranger station or visitor center and go prepared. Be aware of closures for bears and fragile vegetation, especially around Logan Pass. (Check with visitors centers or ranger stations for status or call 406/888-7800.) Do not attempt climbing in Glacier alone or without experience; do not take unnecessary risks. Always practice Leave No Trace principles. For emergencies, carry a cell phone along, but do not depend on its ability to work everywhere in the park. Instead, be ready to self-rescue.

WALKING TRAILS

Glacier is known as a "hiker's park," and no wonder! With 732 miles of trails, everything from a short, leisurely amble to a multiday top-of-the-world Continental Divide backpack trip crams in its borders. Ranger stations and visitors centers have small brochures describing hikes in their locales; the same information is also available online as well (www.nps.gov/glac).

Trail Status

Conditions on Glacier's trails vary significantly depending on the season, elevation, recent severe weather, and bear closures. Swinging and plank bridges across rivers and creeks are not installed until late May–June. Those at higher elevations may not be put in until early July. Some years, bridges have been installed, only to be removed a few weeks later to wait for swollen rivers high with runoff to subside. Ptarmigan Tunnel's doors—closed for the winter—open in July. Steep snowfields inhibit early hiking on the Highline Trail until July.

In some years, large drifts across trails must be blasted to open the paths even late in July. To find out about trail conditions before hiking, you can stop at ranger stations and visitor centers for updates or consult Trail Status Reports on the park's website.

Signage

All park trailheads and junctions have excellent signage. Be prepared, however, to convert kilometers to miles in your head to understand distances. Some signs show both kilometers and miles, others simply kilometers. This is, after all, the International Peace Park, and kilometers are definitely more international. If you hike in Waterton, all trail sign distances use kilometers. Just pull out your math skills: To convert kilometers to miles, multiply the kilometers listed by 0.6. (Example: Multiply 3 kilometers by 0.6 to get 1.8 miles.) To convert miles to kilometers, multiply the miles by 1.6. (Example: Multiply 2 miles by 1.6 to get 3.2 kilometers.) These calculations are simple,

Yellow warning signs indicate frequent bear sightings, thus caution.

EDUCATION

One of the best ways to learn about Glacier's wildlife, geology, photography, birds, and cultural history is to join the regionally and nationally recognized experts from **Glacier Institute** (406/756-1211, www.glacierinstitute.org, $50–1,750). Offered year-round, the courses use in-the-field, hands-on learning at field camps or out in the field throughout the Crown of the Continent Ecosystem. You can join a sea-kayaking trip to Wild Horse Island in Flathead Lake, track animals on snowshoes, hike to Ptarmigan Tunnel to look at Glacier's amazing geology, or take a night walk to look for owls. College credit is available for some of the workshops and classes. Seminars range from wilderness first aid to art, from science to ecology. Kids' programs range from single-day to week-long ($95–320). Single-day courses average $50–60; most multiday courses range $150–320, including lodging and meals

at either the Big Creek Camp in the North Fork or Glacier Field Camp near the west park entrance. Most courses are not classroom studies, but take to the wilds on rafts, kayaks, bikes, or foot. Instructors are regional experts, some noted nationally for their skills.

For those looking for an intimate experience in Glacier, **Glacier National Park Associates** (406/387-4299, www.nps.gov/glac) looks for volunteers each summer for backcountry projects. Some tasks restore historic log structures, reconstruct damaged trails and backcountry campsites, and transplant seedlings from the park's native-plant nursery. Past projects have included work at Sperry Chalet and backcountry patrol cabins. Led by a backcountry ranger intern, participants usually work on one project during a three- to five-day stay in the backcountry. No special skills are required – just a desire to help.

easy approximations you can remember for the trail. Some hikers enjoy kilometers—the number is always higher, so the accomplishment is greater! (Note that for longer distances, such as while driving, more accurate conversion factors are needed: To convert kilometers to miles, multiply by 0.62; to convert miles to kilometers, multiply by 1.61.)

Trailheads may also display **bear warnings** or **bear closure** signs to alert hikers to frequent bear activity. Heavily traveled areas may have a **footprint with a red slash**—universally recognized as "Don't walk here." Obey these signs: They are protecting fragile alpine meadows from abuse or protecting an area replanted with native plants.

Solo Travelers

Even though solo hiking in bear country is not recommended, some hikers do venture into the backcountry alone. If you're one of them, make tons of noise while hiking and brush up on your bear country hiking skills. Solo travelers looking for trail companionship should

hook up with park naturalist hikes (check *The Glacier Explorer* for times and dates) or sign on with a guided hike through Glacier Guides (406/387-5555 or 800/521-7238, www.glacierguides.com).

Hitchhiking to Trailheads

You may see hitchhikers sticking a thumb out, especially along Going-to-the-Sun Road. Several point-to-point hikes require getting back to a vehicle at another trailhead, and hitchhiking is an easy, common, and legal way to do it, especially if you miss the shuttle. If hitchhiking, be cautious of where you stand on the road. Choose a spot where a car can get completely off the narrow road to pick you up. Don't bother hitchhiking where no pullout is available; no one will stop.

FISHING
Licenses

Glacier National Park does not require fishing licenses, but fishing outside the park does. Outside Glacier, anglers must possess a

Montana State Fishing License (residents pay $11.25–19.25 for 2 days to full season; resident seniors pay $6.25; and nonresidents can purchase 2-day, 10-day, or seasonal licenses $24.25–69.25), which can be purchased in sporting-goods stores and fly shops across Montana. You can also order one online from Montana Fish, Wildlife, and Parks at www.fwp.state.mt.us.

On the Blackfeet Reservation, you'll need a Blackfeet Tribal fishing permit (Blackfeet Fish and Game Department, 406/338-7207, www.blackfeetnation.com, $20 per day, $30 for 3 days, or $65 per season). Permits are also required for boats and float tubes ($20 per year), but the season-long fishing permit includes tags for those in the price. If you plan on fishing more than 1 day with a boat or float tube, the season-long permit is the better deal.

Regulations

Fishing regulations vary substantially by area; anglers are required to know the rules and know their fish. You can pick up regulations when and where you buy your license. In general, the fishing season begins the third Saturday in May and ends November 30, but lake fishing is permitted year-round. While strict daily fishing limits regulate catches in Glacier (5) and the Bob Marshall Wilderness Complex (3), many fish have higher limits depending on species or no limit at all. Bull trout are a protected species and must be thrown back into the water immediately. Look for the lack of black on the dorsal fin: No black, throw it back.

Inside the park, lead is prohibited in weights, lures, and jigs; outside the park, it's recommended to use weights made of non-lead materials. To dispose of entrails in the front country, use a bear-resistant garbage container. In the backcountry, puncture the air bladder and throw entrails 200 feet out into the water away from trails and campsites.

For Glacier's regulations, stop by a ranger station or visitors center or check the park website (www.nps.gov/glac) for a complete list. For a complete list of the State of Montana (www.fwp.state.mt.us) and Blackfeet Reservation (www.blackfeetnation.com) regulations, check the websites. For Waterton's fishing licenses and regulations, see the *Waterton* chapter.

BOATING

Out-of-state boats over 12 feet in length must have a home state registration and cannot be used in Montana more than 90 consecutive days. In-state boats must have Montana registration and decals on the boat ($2.50 annual fee, paid to the county of residence). Special restrictions apply to rental boats; ask for boating rules when you rent. For a complete list of Montana boating regulations, see www.fwp.state.mt.us.

Tips for Travelers

FOREIGN TRAVELERS
Entering the United States

International travelers entering the United States must be aware that border requirements are rapidly changing. In addition to passports, many travelers will need a visa to visit the United States and Canada. Those visiting the United States from selected countries in the Visa Waiver Program don't need visas but must have machine-readable passports and limit their stay to 90 days. These countries are Andorra, Australia, Austria, Belgium, Brunei, Denmark, Finland, France, Germany, Iceland, Ireland, Italy, Japan, Liechtenstein, Luxembourg, Monaco, Netherlands, New Zealand, Norway, Portugal, San Marino, Singapore, Slovenia, Spain, Sweden, Switzerland, and United Kingdom. If you are from a country not recognized in the Visa Waiver Program, give yourself plenty of time to apply for your visa. For additional information, check the Customs and Border Protection website: www.cbp.gov.

Travel requirements are also changing for international visitors from the western hemisphere, no longer permitting simply driver's licenses and birth certificates for entry. From 2005 to 2007, the Western Hemisphere Travel Initiative will require all travelers to the United States from the Americas, Caribbean, and Bermuda to have a passport. By December 2005, air and sea travel visitors from the Caribbean, Bermuda, and Central and South America need a passport. By December 2006, the list includes Mexico and Canada. By December 2007, the requirement affects all land borders, too.

Citizens from countries other than the United States and Canada must fill out an I94 form to enter the United States. You can pick up this form at any port of entry (except Goat Haunt) for $6. Only U.S. currency is accepted; U.S. border guards will not take credit cards or Canadian currency.

Entering Canada

For international travelers beginning their trip in Canada, visas are not required from the same countries recognized by the United States for visa waivers, plus Antigua and Barbuda, Bahamas, Barbados, Botswana, Cyprus, Greece, Israel (National Passport holders only), Malta, Mexico, Namibia, Papua New Guinea, Republic of Korea, St. Kitts and Nevis, St. Lucia, St. Vincent, Solomon Islands, Swaziland, United States, and Western Samoa. For more information on Canadian entry, check www.cic.gc.ca.

CROSSING THE U.S.-CANADIAN BORDER
Identification

Canadian and U.S. citizens should bring proof of citizenship when crossing the international border either way between Canada and Montana. Until December 2007, one item should be a picture ID (such as a driver's license) issued by federal, provincial, or state governments; another should be a birth certificate or passport. After 2007, you'll need a passport. Single parents must have proof of child custody. Resident aliens must possess a permanent resident card.

Passports and visas (if required) are proof of identification for international visitors.

Road Ports of Entry

Chief Mountain Customs (9 A.M.–6 P.M. May and after Labor Day, 7 A.M.–10 P.M. June–Labor Day) is a seasonal east-side port of entry on Chief Mountain International Highway. A year-round port of entry on Waterton-Glacier's east side, **Piegan/Carway** (7 A.M.–11 P.M.) sits on U.S. Highway 89/Canada Highway 2. Because Trail Creek Customs closed several years ago during flooding up the North Fork Valley, the only west side port of entry now is **Roosville** on U.S. Highway 93, north of Eureka. It's open 24 hours 365 days per year, but is also 90 miles from West Glacier.

Goat Haunt

Even though Goat Haunt, U.S.A., is out in the middle of nowhere, the tightening of border policies has affected the small seasonal port of entry. Because of its relationship in the International Peace Park, special regulations are in effect here. For visitors in Canada traveling down Waterton Lake in private boats or touring on the MV *International,* clearing customs is not required, even though you cross the border partway down the lake. At Goat Haunt, you can get off the boat and wander around freely along the beach and walkway between the International Peace Park Pavilion and the boat dock. That is not considered seeking admission into the United States, even though you have stepped on to U.S. soil from Canada. Hikers crossing the international boundary from Canada into the United States by trail or boat (private or tour) must report to the National Park Service rangers at Goat Haunt for inspection. Only Canadian and U.S. citizens (legal resident aliens of the United States included) are permitted to hike beyond Goat Haunt, after passing inspection. For further information on crossing from Canada into the United States, call 406/889-3865.

For day hikers to return to Canadian soil, a customs inspection is not required; however, backpackers hiking into Canada or catching

the Waterton boat must call into Canadian customs upon reaching the Waterton Townsite. For information in advance of your trip, call the Canada Customs and Revenue Agency at 403/653-3535.

Foreign visitors (non-Canadian and non-U.S.) may not use the Goat Haunt port of entry, but rather must enter the United States through Chief Mountain, Piegan/Carway, or Roosville. They may, however, visit Goat Haunt briefly and return on the next boat to Waterton. Foreign visitors already in the United States may hike across the border into Canada or take the boat, but they must report to customs by phone upon reaching the Waterton Townsite.

Border No-Nos
In general, Canada and the United States have similar border laws: no fruits, vegetables, plants, drugs, firearms, firewood, fresh meat, or poultry products. Pets are permitted across the border only with a certificate of rabies vaccination within 30 days prior to your crossing. Pepper sprays are considered firearms in Canada; they must have a USEPA-approved label to go across the border. For clarification, call 250/887-3413. If you purchase Cuban cigars in Waterton, they are not permitted back across the U.S. border.

Money and Currency Exchange
Those popping into Waterton for a day or two may not even want to exchange money. Waterton has no bank, but the Tamarack Village (214 Mount View Rd., 403/859-2378, www.watertonvisitorservices.com, late May–early Oct.) does offer money-exchange services. Most stores and businesses in Waterton accept U.S. currency, but expect Canadian currency as change. Although it's convenient to use U.S. currency, stores will vary slightly on the exchange rates honored. To receive the best exchange rates, use credit cards; banks always give a better rate than the stores.

There will also be some Canadian coins floating in your change in Montana. These are treated at par; loonies, toonies, and dollars are not. For Canadians visiting the Glacier and Flathead Valley area, some businesses accept Canadian currency. They are used to converting it, but sadly, the days of Canadian at par are mostly gone. If you're traveling farther south in the state where cashiers may be unfamiliar with loonies, convert into U.S. currency. Credit cards will receive the most accurate exchange rate. On Glacier's east side, you'll find no banks to exchange currency—only on the park's west side in Flathead Valley.

For both Canada and the United States, travelers checks in smaller amounts ($50 and under) work best for short trips on either side of the border; then you're not left dragging around scads of foreign currency. International travelers should exchange currency at their major port of entry (Seattle, Vancouver, Calgary).

TRAVELING WITH CHILDREN
Junior Ranger Program
Kids can earn a Junior Ranger Badge by completing self-guided activities in the Junior Ranger Newspaper, available at all visitors centers. Most activities target ages 6–12 and coincide with a trip over Going-to-the-Sun Road. When kids return the completed newspaper to any visitor center, they are sworn in as Junior Rangers and receive Glacier Park badges.

Discovery Cabin
The Discovery Cabin in Apgar serves up educational kid-fun during summer. Hands-on activities guided by interpretive rangers teach children about wildlife, geology, and habitats. Check with Apgar Visitor Center for directions and hours.

Hikes
For kids, short hikes work best. On Going-to-the-Sun Road, go for Avalanche Lake, Hidden Lake Overlook, and St. Mary and Virginia Falls. In Many Glacier, hike to Red Rocks Lake or hop the boat across Swiftcurrent and Josephine Lakes to hike to Grinnell Lake. In Two Medicine, take the boat uplake to hike to Twin Falls or Upper Two Medicine Lake.

When hiking with children, always take snacks and water along. If toting a wee one who still needs to be carried, Glacier Outdoor Center (11957 Hwy. 2 E., West Glacier, 406/888-5454 or 800/235-6781, www.glacierraftco.com) rents kiddie packs at $20 per day.

TRAVELING WITH PETS

Pets are allowed in Glacier Park, but only in limited areas: campgrounds, parking lots, and roadsides. Pets are also not allowed on beaches, off-trail in the backcountry, nor at any park lodges or motor inns. When outside a vehicle, pets must be on a six-foot or shorter leash or be caged. In a campground, pets must be leashed or caged. Be kind enough to not leave it unattended in a car anywhere. Be considerate of wildlife and other visitors by keeping your pet under control and disposing of waste in garbage cans.

If you prefer to kennel your pet while you are in Glacier, Flathead Valley has the only options. Two of the closest are in Columbia Falls—**Stage Stop Farm and Kennels** (1892 Columbia Falls Stage, 406/892-5719) and **Triple R Kennels** (636 Kelley Rd., 406/892-3695)—but you can check the yellow pages for Kalispell, Whitefish, and Bigfork choices.

Trail Restrictions

No pets are allowed on Glacier Park trails, with the exception of the paved 2.6-mile Apgar Bike Trail, where they are allowed on a leash. (The trail is okay for hikers, too.) Protection of fragile vegetation and preventing conflicts with wildlife are two main reasons; bears stand alone in their own class of reasons to leave poochie home. If you must hike with Fido, head to Flathead National Forest where pets are permitted on a leash. Contrary to Glacier, Waterton does permit dogs on its trails, but bring a leash along and use it.

SENIORS
Golden Age Passport

National parks (as well as lands run by the U.S. Fish and Wildlife Service, U.S. Forest Service, and Bureau of Land Management) have a great deal for seniors age 62 and older who are U.S. citizens or permanent residents: $10 buys a Golden Age Passport, good for life. To purchase, bring proof of age (state driver's license, birth certificate, or passport) in person to any national park entrance station (cash only). In a private vehicle, the card admits all passengers within a vehicle; for single entries (such as on a bus tour), it admits accompanying spouse and kids.

Senior Discounts

A Golden Age Passport grants 50 percent discount on fees for federally run tours, campgrounds, parking, and boat launching; however, discounts do not apply to park concessionaire services—like hotels, boat tours, and bus tours. Also, park hotels do not give discounts to seniors, but some private lodging establishments surrounding the park do. Ask to be sure.

ACCESSIBILITY

Visitors with special needs should pick up an *Accessible Facilities and Services* brochure from visitors centers (Logan Pass, St. Mary, or Apgar), all of which are accessible by wheelchair, or entrance stations. Park information is available also by TDD: 406/888-7806.

Park Entrance

The Golden Access Passport is available free for any blind or permanently disabled U.S. citizen or permanent resident. The lifetime pass permits free access to all national parks and sites run by the U.S. Fish and Wildlife Service, U.S. Forest Service, and Bureau of Land Management. The pass admits the person who signs for the pass as well as family members in a private vehicle. With single entries (on a bus, for instance), it admits the cardholder, spouse, and kids. This pass also grants a 50 percent discount on fees for federally run tours, campgrounds, parking, and boat launching, but discounts do not apply to concessionaire services. Passes may only be purchased in person at entrance stations with proof of medical disability or eligibility for receiving federal benefits.

Park Facilities

Five campgrounds in Glacier reserve 1–2 sites each for wheelchair needs: Apgar, Fish Creek, Rising Sun, Sprague Creek, and Two Medicine. Picnic Areas at Apgar, Rising Sun, and Sun Point also have wheelchair access. So do all lodges within the park boundaries, although they have a limited number of ADAAG rooms. Other wheelchair-accessible sites include boat docks at Lake McDonald, Many Glacier, and Two Medicine as well as evening naturalist programs in Apgar Amphitheater, Lake McDonald Lodge Auditorium, Many Glacier Hotel Auditorium, Rising Sun Campground, and Two Medicine Campground. Most parking lots offer designated parking.

Trails

Glacier and Waterton both offer wheelchair-accessible trails. In Glacier, the Apgar Bike Trail, Trail of the Cedars at Avalanche, Running Eagle Falls Nature Trail in Two Medicine, Goat Lick Overlook, Oberlin Bend Trail, and the International Peace Park Pavilion at Goat Haunt are all wheelchair-accessible. Admittedly, some of the pavement can be a little rough in places; just be prepared for it. In Waterton, wheelchairs may access Linnet Lake Trail, Waterton Townsite Trail, and Cameron Lake Day Use Area.

While pet dogs are not permitted on backcountry trails, aid dogs are allowed—although, due to bears, they are discouraged. If you choose to hike with an aid dog, for safety stick to well-traveled trails during midday.

Interpretive Services

Special programs and sign-language interpretation may be available with a two-week notice. Call 406/888-7930 to schedule.

HEALTH AND SAFETY
Bears

Safety in bear country starts from knowledge and behaving appropriately. With the exception of Alaska and Canada, Glacier beats out any other North American location for the highest density of grizzly bears, and black bears find likable habitat here, too. Regardless of bruin species, one caveat affects the safety of humans and bears: food. Proper use, storage, and handling of food and garbage keeps bears from being conditioned or habituated to situations in which they may become aggressive. With strict food and garbage rules, Glacier has minimized aggressive bear encounters, attacks, and deaths—both of humans and bears.

Camp safely. Use low-odor foods, keep food and cooking gear out of sleeping sites in the backcountry, and store it inside your vehicle in front-country campgrounds. In front-country campgrounds, you'll find detailed explanations of how to safely camp in bear country stapled to your picnic table. For information on camping in bear country, pick up a copy of *Waterton-Glacier Guide* and Glacier's *Backcountry Guide* at entrance stations, visitors centers, ranger stations, permit offices, or online: www.nps.gov/glac.

Hike safely. When taking your first hike, you'll hear jingle bells. When entering your first gift shop, you'll see them—**bear bells.** They're everywhere. And so are the jokes, calling them "dinner bells." While making noise while hiking is the best safety assurance in bear country, bells are not the best way to do it. And many hikers hate them. To check their effectiveness, see how close you come to hikers before you hear their ringing. Sometimes, it's too close! Bear bells are best as a souvenir, not as a substitution for human noise on the trail. Human noise is best; so talk, sing, hoot, and holler. You'll feel silly at first, but after a while, you'll realize it's something everyone does here.

While firearms are not permitted in national parks, **pepper sprays** are. Many hikers carry pepper sprays for deterring aggressive, attacking bears; however, they are not repellents like bug sprays to be sprayed on the human body, tents, or gear. Instead, you spray the capsicum derivative directly into a bear's face, aiming for the eyes and nose. While pepper sprays have repelled some attacking bears, wind and rain may reduce effectiveness, as will the product's age. Small purse-sized pepper sprays are not

BEAR TIPS

HIKING IN BEAR COUNTRY

Some of Glacier's most heavily tromped trails march smack through prime bear habitat, where a surprise encounter on the trail with a grizzly can turn one's insides to Jell-O. With a few precautions, you can eliminate scares from surprise meetings.

- Make noise. Glacier is one park where peace and quiet on the trail could lead to dangerous situations. To avoid surprising a bear, use your voice – sing loudly, hoot, or holler – and clap your hands. Bears tend to recognize human sounds as ones to avoid; they'll usually wander off if they hear people approaching. Consciously make loud noise in thick brushy areas, around blind corners, near babbling streams, and against the wind. You'll often hear hikers just hooting out nonsense; it's okay. They're not crazed. It's just their particular bear noise.

- Hike with other people. Avoid hiking alone. Keep children near.

- Avoid bear feeding areas. Since bears must gain weight before winter, feeding is their prime directive. Often, bears will pack in 20,000 calories in a day. In early season, glacier lily bulbs attract grizzlies because of their high nutritional value. By midseason, cow parsnip patches provide sustenance, in between high-protein carrion. If you stumble across an animal carcass, leave the area immediately and notify a ranger. Toward summer's end, huckleberry patches provide high sugars. Detour widely around feeding bears.

- Hike in broad daylight, avoiding early mornings, late evenings, and night.

- Never approach a bear. Watch the body language. A bear who stands on hind legs may just be trying to get a good smell or better viewpoint. On the other hand, head swaying, teeth clacking, laid-back ears, a lowered head, and huffing or woofing are signs of agitation: Clear out!

- If you do surprise a bear, take care of yourself. Contrary to all inclinations, do not run! Instead, back away slowly, talking quietly and turning sideways or bending your knees to appear smaller and nonthreatening. Avoid direct eye contact, as the animal kingdom interprets eye contact as a challenge; instead, avert your eyes. Leave your pack on; it can protect you if the bear attacks.

- In case of an attack by a bear you surprised, use pepper spray if you have it. Protect yourself and your vulnerable parts by assuming a fetal position on the ground with your hands around the back of your neck. Play "dead." Move again only when you are sure the bear has vacated the area.

- If a bear stalks you as food, or attacks

adequate for bears—only an eight-ounce can will do. Practice how to use it. Pepper spray is not protection: Carrying it does not lessen the need for making noise. Be aware that pepper sprays are not allowed by airlines unless checked in luggage, and only brands with USEPA labels may cross through Canadian customs.

Bears are dangerous around food, be it a carcass in the woods, a pack left on a trail, or a cooler left in a campsite. Protecting bears and protecting yourself starts with being conscious of food—including wrappers and crumbs. Gorp tidbits dropped along the trail attract wildlife, as do "biodegradable" apple cores chucked into the forest. Pick up what you drop and pack out all garbage; don't leave a Hansel and Gretel trail for bears. Bear attacks can be avoided.

Mountain Lion Encounters

These large cats rarely prey on humans, but they can—especially smaller two-legged munchkins. Making bear noise will help you avoid surprising a lion. Hiking with others and keeping kids close is also a good idea. If you do stumble upon a lion, above all, do not run. Be

at night, fight back, using any means at hand – pepper spray, shouting, sticks, or rocks – to tell the bear you are not an easy food source. Try to escape up something, like a building or tree. While bears stalking humans as prey is rare, it's good to be prepared anyway.

- Special bear signage is used at trailheads to inform hikers of exceptional trail concerns. Yellow **bear warning** signs indicate bears are frequenting the trail, and you should use extra caution. Make more noise than usual on these trails. Orange **bear closure** signs indicate a trail is closed, usually because one has been aggressive or is defending a carcass. If a trailhead has no sign, hikers still need to be cautious, for Glacier is a bear's park.

- Two books are plump with accurate information on bears: Bill Schneider's *Bear Aware* and Stephen Herrero's *Bear Attacks: Their Causes and Avoidances.*

BLACK BEARS VS. GRIZZLY BEARS

While neither black nor grizzly bears are safer, it's good to know what the bear is when you see one. Even though colors are used to name the bears ("grizzly" means "silver-haired"), bears appear with a variety of fur hues regardless of species. A reddish black bear can give birth to three cubs of different colors: blond, black, and brown. And grizzly bears appear in all colors of the spectrum. Don't be fooled by color; look instead for body size and shape.

Although hard to assess through binoculars, the bears are two different sizes. Grizzlies are bigger than black bears, standing on all fours at 3-4 feet tall. They weigh in at 300-600 pounds. Black bears average 12-18 inches shorter on all fours. Adult females weigh around 140 pounds, while males bulk up to 220 pounds.

In profile, the grizzly has one notable feature: a hump on its shoulders. The solid muscle mass provides the grizzly's arms with power for digging and running. Black bears lack this hump. Face profiles are also different. On the grizzly, look for a scooped or dished forehead-to-nose silhouette; the black bear's nose will appear straighter in line with its forehead. Note the ears, for the grizzly's will look a little too small for its head while a black bear's ears seem big, standing straight up. While you don't want to get close enough to check the real thing, paw prints in mud reveal a difference in claws and foot structure. Grizzly claws are 4 inches long with pads in a relatively straight line, while black bear claws are 1.5 inches with pads arced across the top of the foot.

Although both bears have mediocre vision, they are fast runners. In three seconds, a grizzly bear can cover 180 feet. And contrary to popular lore, humans are not a food source. In fact, both bears are omnivores, feeding primarily on vegetation and carrion.

calm. Group together to appear big. Look at the cat with peripheral vision rather than staring straight on as you back slowly away. If the lion attacks, fight back with everything: rocks, sticks, or kicking.

Water Hazards

Contrary to popular opinion, bears are not the number one cause of death and accidents in Glacier, but rather drowning. Be extremely cautious around lakes, fast-moving streams, and waterfalls where moss and clear algae cover the rocks, making them slippery. Waters here are swift, frigid, plumb-full of submerged obstacles, unforgiving, and sometimes lethal.

Giardia

Lakes and streams can carry parasites like *Giardia lamblia.* If ingested, it causes cramping, nausea, and severe diarrhea for a long period of time. It's easy to avoid giardia by boiling water (for one minute plus one minute for each 1,000 feet of elevation above sea level) or using a one-micron filter. Bleach also works (add two drops per quart and then let it sit for 30 minutes). Tap water in the park campgrounds and

© BECKY LOMAX

The trail to Sperry Glacier crosses falls spilling out of Feather Woman Lake.

radiation: You might feel cool, but your skin will still burn. To prevent sunburn, use a strong sunscreen and wear sunglasses and a hat.

Crevasses and Snow Bridges

While ice often looks solid to step on, it harbors unseen caverns beneath. Crevasses (large vertical cracks) are difficult to see, and snow bridges can collapse as a person crosses. You're safer just staying off the ice; even Glacier's tiny icefields have caused fatalities. Also, steep slopes can run into rocks or trees; if sliding for fun, slide only where you have a safe runout.

Hypothermia

Hypothermia is insidious and subtle, and especially targets exhausted and physically unprepared hikers. The body's inner core loses heat, reducing mental and physical functions. Watch for uncontrolled shivering, incoherence, poor judgment, fumbling, mumbling, and slurred speech. Avoid becoming hypothermic by staying dry, donning rain gear and warm moisture-wicking layers. Leave the cotton clothing back in the car! If someone in your party is hypothermic, get him or her sheltered and into dry clothing. Give warm liquids, but be sure they're nonalcoholic and decaffeinated. If the victim cannot regain body heat, get into a sleeping bag, with you and the victim stripped for skin-to-skin contact.

Blisters

Ill-fitting shoes and incorrect socks cause most blisters. Although cotton socks feel good, they are not the best choice for hiking because they absorb water from the feet and hold it, providing a surface for friction. Synthetic or wool-blend socks wick water away from the skin. To prevent blisters, recognize "hot spots" or rubs, applying Moleskin or New Skin to the sensitive area. In a pinch, duct tape can be slapped on trouble spots. Once a blister occurs, apply special blister Band-Aid bandages or Second Skin, a product developed for burns that cools the blister off and cushions it. Cover Second Skin with Moleskin to absorb future rubbing and hold the Second Skin in place.

picnic areas has been treated, and you'll definitely taste the strong chlorine in the hotel water systems.

Dehydration

Many first-time hikers to Glacier are surprised to find they drink substantially more water here than at home. Glacier's winds, altitude, and lower humidity can add up to a fast case of dehydration—which often manifests first as a headache. If you are hiking, drink lots of water—more than you normally would. If you hike with children, monitor their fluid intake.

Altitude

Some visitors from the lowlands may feel the effects of altitude—a lightheadedness, headache, or shortness of breath—in high zones like Logan Pass. Slowing down a hiking pace helps, as does drinking lots of fluids and giving the body time to acclimatize. If symptoms are more dramatic, descend in elevation as soon as possible. Altitude also increases the effects of UV

Hantavirus

The Hantavirus infection, which causes flu-like symptoms, is contracted by inhaling the dust from deer mice urine and droppings. If you suspect you have the virus, get immediate medical attention. To protect yourself, avoid areas thick with rodents—burrows and woodpiles. Store all food in rodent-proof containers. If you find rodent dust in your gear, disinfect with water and bleach (1.5 cups of bleach to one gallon of water).

Mosquitoes and Ticks

Bugs carry diseases such as West Nile virus and Rocky Mountain spotted fever. Protect yourself by wearing long sleeves and pants as well as using bug repellents in spring and summer when mosquitoes and ticks are common. If you are bitten by a tick, remove it and disinfect the bite; see a doctor if lesions or a rash appears.

Hospitals and Emergencies

For emergencies inside the park, call 406/888-7800. For emergencies outside the park, call 911. On Glacier's west side, the nearest hospitals are in Flathead Valley. Kalispell Regional Medical Center (310 Sunny View Ln., 406/752-5111) and North Valley Hospital (6575 Hwy. 93 S., Whitefish, 406/863-2501) are 35 minutes from West Glacier and can be up to 90 minutes from Logan Pass depending on traffic. North Valley begins ground breaking on its new hospital in 2006; the new facility will be one mile south of the current one on Highway 93. On Glacier's east side, Northern Rockies Medical Center (802 2nd St. E., Cut Bank, 406/873-2251) is approximately an hour from East Glacier and just under two hours from St. Mary.

ESSENTIALS

Getting There

ORIENTATION

Getting your bearings in Glacier is not difficult; the park splits along the Continental Divide into an east and west side, each with several entrances following valley drainages. Two Medicine, St. Mary, and Many Glacier dominate the east, while Lake McDonald and the North Fork cover the west. Although Highway 2 passes briefly through the park's southern tip en route between Washington State and Michigan, southern entrances into the park's core are all via foot or horseback trails. On the north side, Waterton Lakes National Park provides access via boat, foot, or horseback across the Canadian-U.S. border into Glacier's interior.

Only one route bisects the entire park: Going-to-the-Sun Road. If there is a rush hour in Glacier, it's on this road 11 A.M.–4 P.M. But rush hour is not restricted to weekdays; it's seven days per week mid-July–mid-August.

Most summer visitors love the park's east side, where tiny seasonal towns fall away into miles and miles of open prairie. On a clear day, not much is there to obstruct a view to Ohio. And by autumn, not much remains open to take the Rocky Mountain Front's brutal winds.

The park's west side—with its own remote corners—all drains through the gateway of Flathead Valley into Flathead Lake. Mixed with farmland, rural pockets, and re-

© BECKY LOMAX

sort towns, the valley—anchored in winter by recreational skiing—is a year-round enclave for 80,000 people.

SUGGESTED ROUTES
I-90 to West Glacier

From I-90 about 9 miles west of downtown Missoula, U.S. Highway 93 North/Montana Highway 200 (Exit 96) leads straight north 103 miles to Flathead Valley. This scenic route passes below the craggy Mission Mountains and along Flathead Lake, the largest freshwater lake west of the Mississippi.

In downtown Kalispell, you'll turn east onto Highway 2 for the remainder of the trek to the park, but as you turn onto Highway 2, you'll begin a confusing maze through Flathead Valley as the highway jogs and turns onto different streets. To help, follow signs to Glacier Park or West Glacier. When you turn right onto U.S. Highway 2 East, you're also on East Idaho Street. Travel for 2 miles past easily recognizable box stores and car dealerships. Highway 2 will turn left at LaSalle (LaSalle and Highway 2 are the same road), which runs north 12 miles toward Columbia Falls. At an intersection with Montana Highway 40, the highway turns right; follow it through Columbia Falls, continuing another 16 miles on Highway 2 northeast to West Glacier. Total mileage from I-90 to West Glacier is 145 miles; driving time is usually less than 3.5 hours on the mostly two-lane highway but can be as much as 4 hours with heavy traffic, snow, or road-construction delays.

I-90 to East Glacier

This long but extremely scenic approach follows the Rocky Mountain Front, a highway for golden eagle migrations and the buttress for the Bob Marshall Wilderness Complex. This is also the route for those stitching together a visit to both Yellowstone National Park and Glacier. Leave I-90 in Butte, turning north toward Helena onto I-15 (Exit 129/227). Drive 101 miles, about 1.5 hours, from I-90 to Exit 228 2 miles north of Wolf Creek. Turn north here onto U.S. Highway 287.

From here north, high sideways winds can slow travel, gusts strong enough to rock RVs and trailers. Follow the narrow two-lane Highway 287 north 66 miles through Augusta to Choteau (pronounced "SHOW-toe"), turning left onto U.S. Highway 89, also Choteau's Main Street for a bit. From Choteau, head north 72 miles to Browning. Again, narrow curves slow driving time, but you will soon see Glacier's peaks jutting up from the plains. Just before Browning, you'll join U.S. Highway 2. At Browning's west end, turn left as Highway 2 leaves town. It leads 13 miles to East Glacier. Total driving time from I-90 is about 5 hours to cover 253 miles. High winds and traffic will slow your travel, but the scenery is worth the drive.

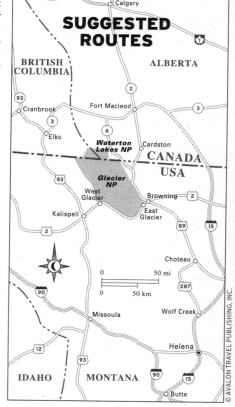

From the Canadian Rockies

Many travelers link Glacier into an extended trip in the Canadian Rockies national parks—Jasper, Banff, Yoho, and Kootenay. The Flathead Valley connects directly to the Canadian Rockies via Highway 93, which runs north–south through Jasper, Banff, and Kootenay. To get to Glacier, travel south on Highway 93 through British Columbia toward Cranbrook. Four miles (6 km) before Cranbrook, merge with Canada 3 heading 36 miles (58 km) east toward Elko. At Elko, one option is to head directly toward Waterton, staying on Canada 3 for 60 miles (96 km) over Crow's Nest Pass and turning south onto Highway 6 at Pincher to drive 19 miles (30 km) to Waterton Lakes National Park. Or at Elko, turn south with Highway 93 as it separates from Canada 3, driving 24 miles (39 km) toward Roosville on the Canadian-U.S. border. After crossing through customs, continue south 63 miles on Highway 93 through Eureka to Whitefish. Drive cautiously: Deer frequently cross this road between Eureka and Whitefish, earning it the nickname "Deer Alley."

In downtown Whitefish (just 25 miles left to go to West Glacier), Highway 93 turns south again at the third stoplight. Drive 2 miles to a junction with Montana Highway 40, where you will see signs to Glacier Park. Turn left, driving toward Columbia Falls. At 4.5 miles, the highway merges with U.S. Highway 2. Follow the signs to Glacier Park. Expect total driving time from Banff to West Glacier to be about 5 hours. For an alternate route from the Canadian Rockies, head to Calgary.

From Calgary

From Calgary, Canada, head south for 113 miles (181 km) on Canada Highway 2 toward Fort Macleod. Just before town, the highway merges with Canada 3 for a few miles heading east. If you are starting your Glacier adventure in Waterton Lakes National Park, turn west instead onto Canada 3 toward Pincher Creek (17 miles, 27 km). At Pincher, turn south onto Canada Highway 6 for 20 miles (32 km) to the park entrance. From Calgary to Waterton is 149 miles (240 km) via Pincher Creek and 153 miles (246 kilometers) via Cardston. With speed limits in Canada being slightly slower than in the United States, the distance can be covered in 2.75 hours.

To head straight to Glacier, continue from Fort Macleod south through Cardston to Carway. The 165 miles (266 km) from Calgary to the border at Carway should take about three hours. Remember, speed limits are posted in kilometers (80 kph is 50 mph) As a general rule, Canadian highway speed limits tend to be a little lower than U.S. speed limits, especially compared to Montana's rural narrow two-laners, which can hit 70 mph.

From Carway, drop over the Canadian-U.S. border 19 miles on U.S. Highway 89 toward St. Mary for Going-to-the-Sun Road's east entrance, 25 minutes from the border. To enter the park instead at Many Glacier, drive 10 miles south from the border on Highway 89 to Babb and turn right for another 12 miles (40 minutes total) to Many Glacier Hotel and Swiftcurrent.

FLATHEAD VALLEY

The closest and easiest access to Glacier National Park is Flathead Valley. If flights arrive before evening, you can catch a shuttle and be at Lake McDonald inside Glacier Park in time to catch the sunset. Because the airport has no lodging options in the immediate vicinity, those coming in on late flights (or wishing to explore Flathead Valley a bit) will need to stay in Kalispell, Whitefish, or Columbia Falls. While many choose Columbia Falls for its proximity between the airport and the park, Whitefish lures others for its shopping, nightlife, nearby Whitefish Lake, and Big Mountain Resort.

Airport

The closest airport to Glacier National Park—**Glacier Park International Airport**—services only a few airlines coming from a handful of locations: Skywest/Delta from Salt Lake City, Northwest from Minneapolis, America West from Phoenix, Horizon Air from Seattle, and

Big Sky from Montana cities. But don't ask travel agents for a flight to Glacier airport; they won't know what you are talking about. Known with the airlines as Kalispell Airport or **Flathead County Airport (FCA)**, the airport's "international" reputation comes from a few charter flights from Canada. With only a couple of gates, this tiny airport is easy for meeting up with people, walking to the baggage claim just a few hundred feet from your gate, or finding the car rental desk. The entire arrival and departure schedule (under 20 of each) is listed online: www.glacierairport.com.

Because the airport is almost midway between Kalispell, Columbia Falls, and Whitefish, late arriving flights can speed you to a local Flathead Valley hotel in minutes. In the terminal, the **Kindred Spirit Gift Shop** (10 A.M.–4:30 P.M. daily in winter and till 5:30 P.M. in summer) carries local arts, crafts, and, of course, huckleberry products, and **The Glacier Grille** (5 A.M.–6 P.M. daily) serves cafeteria food, espresso, beer, and wine. The airport is 25 miles from West Glacier.

Although Spokane, Washington, can be an alternative airport, it requires a longer drive to get to the park—about 4.5 hours; however, it may fit better in a travel itinerary. Spokane is 271 miles from West Glacier with travelers passing through Flathead Valley to get there. Travelers from Spokane should shortcut the route from I-90 by turning north at St. Regis and following the signs to Glacier Park (north on Hwy. 135, northwest on Hwy. 200, east on Hwy. 28). You'll pass the funky little towns of Paradise and Hot Springs, shooting back several decades, before joining Highway 93 heading north at Flathead Lake.

Train

Amtrak's Empire Builder service (800/USA-RAIL or 800/872-7245, www.amtrak.com) from Chicago and Seattle or Portland runs twice daily. From Seattle ($92 one-way), the eastbound train lands riders conveniently in West Glacier in early morning; both the east- and westbound trains stop in Whitefish, West Glacier, Essex, and East Glacier (summers

only). Between Seattle and Shelby, Montana, National Park Service guides offer educational services aboard. Many travelers to Glacier opt for the rail approach to follow the route of early park tourists. For those arriving by train, station stops in West and East Glacier make for a no-brainer arrival directly adjacent to the park. Eastbound trains, if they are running on time, hit Whitefish at 7:26 A.M. and arrive in West Glacier at 8:16 A.M., Essex at 8:55 A.M., and East Glacier at 9:54 A.M. Westbound arrivals run between 6:45 P.M. (East Glacier) and 8:56 P.M. (Whitefish).

Special Amtrak deals are available. Kids ages 2–15 are half price, and seniors can usually get 15 percent discounts. Veterans, AAA and NARP members, military personnel, and students can also get 10–15 percent discounts: check Amtrak's website for details.

Amtrak's federal funding frequently goes in and out of limbo, with the route bypassing Glacier being high on the chopping block list. Check with Amtrak for changes to schedules and service.

Bus

Trailways' **Rimrock Stages** (800/255-7655, www.rimrocktrailways.com) runs daily service between Missoula and Whitefish ($27 one-way). No bus service connects directly with East or West Glacier. For that reason, many bus travelers head to Whitefish, where they can catch Amtrak to the park. However, only one bus runs daily, leaving Missoula at 8:20 P.M. and arriving at midnight in Whitefish, where you need to grab a place to sleep until morning when the train ($5–7 one-way) to West Glacier departs at 7:46. Return connections are more time consuming: The westbound train arrives in Whitefish at 8:56 P.M., but you won't be able to catch your bus to Missoula until 4:35 P.M. the next day. But if you have to hang out in a town, Whitefish is a good one to explore.

Taxis and Shuttles

Headquartered one mile north of the airport, **Flathead-Glacier Transportation** (406/892-3390 or 800/829-7039, www.fgtrans.com)

provides shuttles and transportation to all east- and west-side hubs in Glacier, Big Mountain Ski Resort, and all towns in Flathead Valley. Drivers will meet any airport flights, as well as pick you up at any of the park lodges, at some trailheads, or surrounding towns to transport you back to the airport. Sample rates from the airport are $32 to West Glacier, $44 to Lake McDonald Lodge, $110 to East Glacier. Call ahead for reservations.

Tours

With **Glacier Park, Inc.** (406/892-2525, www.glacierparkinc.com), you can leave the driving to someone else on the Great Lodges of Glacier tour, a six-day romp through all four of the park's historic lodges offered almost weekly July–August. The tour begins and ends in East Glacier, but the package includes pickup at Glacier Park International Airport in Flathead Valley. Traveling by historic red jammer buses, the tour stays at Glacier Park Lodge, Prince of Wales Hotel, Many Glacier Hotel, and Lake McDonald Lodge. Rates start at $1,409 for adults, $688 for kids, and include lodging, some meals, and transportation around Glacier.

For something a bit more rustic, **Glacier Guides** (406/387-5555 or 800/321-7238, www.glacierguides.com) offers several six-day camping and hiking trips mid-July–August. Beginning and ending in Whitefish, the group tours Glacier, staying in front-country campgrounds where the guides cook up home-style meals. Options for guided long or short hikes give daily choices for different energy levels; the trip finale is rafting on the Middle Fork of the Flathead River. Equipment, guide service, transportation in Glacier, park entrance fees, and meals are also included. Rates start at $997 per person.

Car Rental

Glacier Park International Airport terminal has four rental-car agencies with desks in the airport: Hertz (U.S. 406/758-2220 or 800/654-3131, www.hertz.com), National (406/257-7144 or 800/CAR-RENT,

www.nationalcar.com), Avis (406/257-2727 or 800/230-4898, www.avis.com), and Budget (406/755-7500 or 800/527-0700, www.budget.com). Kalispell and Whitefish also have rental-car agencies (see the *Flathead Valley* chapter), which will deliver a car to the airport or pick you up.

RV Rental

Gardner RV and Trailer Center (3100 Hwy. 93 S., Kalispell, 406/752-7683 or 800/473-0682, www.gardnerrv.com) and **J and L RV Rentals/Sales, Inc.** (1805 Hwy. 2 West, Columbia Falls, 406/892-7666, www.jandl-rvrentals.com) rent motor homes and trailers. Although somewhat expensive, RVing is an easy way to tour national parks with the good parts of camping but without the hassle of tents. Be aware, however, of Going-to-the-Sun Road's vehicle length restrictions (21 feet). Only the smallest RVs will be able to cross the highway. In larger RVs, you must use shuttles or red bus tours to see the historic road, or rent a car.

Equipment Rental

Glacier Outdoor Center (11957 Hwy. 2 East, West Glacier, 406/888-5454 or 800/235-6781, www.glacierraftco.com) has the most comprehensive collection of rental gear. The center rents outdoor gear for rafting, bicycling, camping, backpacking, fishing, snowshoeing, and cross country skiing—everything from sleeping bags to stoves, lifejackets to rods and waders, headlamps to rain gear, tents to coolers. Complete rafting setups ($150 plus) and car camping packages ($125 plus) are available as well as all items singly. Mountain bikes range $15–30; bike racks for cars also available. Fishing gear ranges $5–50 plus.

Two other companies rent some camping and backpacking gear: **Glacier Guides** (11970 Hwy. 2 East, West Glacier, 406/387-5555 or 800/521-7238, www.glacierguides.com) rents backpacks, sleeping bags, tents, and sleeping pads as a package at $15 per day, but items are also available singly. **Great Northern Whitewater** (12127 Hwy. 2 East, West Gla-

cier, 406/387-5340 or 800/735-7897, www.gn-whitewater.com) rents camping gear (tents, sleeping bags, stoves), canoes, and kayaks. Camping items are available singly or in a full set; rates vary around $70 per person for a complete package.

Food and Accommodations

For airport arrivals, travel directly into the park on the same day. Flathead-Glacier Transportation will even shuttle late flight arrivals to park locations. If you want to stay in Flathead Valley, lodging options range from dirt cheap to high end, several offering complimentary airport shuttles. No lodging exists in the immediate airport vicinity, but Flathead Valley accommodations span Columbia Falls, Kalispell, and Whitefish (check the *Flathead Valley* chapter for accommodations and rates). En route to the park, Columbia Falls—9 miles and 12 minutes away—is between the airport and Glacier with options running the gamut from a budget motel to a golf resort. Farther away, Kalispell (9 miles, 12 minutes from the airport) and Whitefish (11 miles, 15 minutes from the airport) offer all lodging price ranges. Although these towns are the opposite direction from Glacier, they still easily access the park; both are approximately a 45-minute drive from West Glacier.

Other than the cafeteria inside the airport, no restaurants are close. En route to Glacier, Columbia Falls has everything from fast food to sandwiches, gooey ribs, and Mexican fare. Those looking instead for fine dining experiences should gravitate to Whitefish or Kalispell. Check the *Flathead Valley* chapter for restaurant options.

GREAT FALLS

Straddling the mighty Missouri River, Great Falls, Montana, is an east-side access to Glacier Park, but from there plan on renting a car. Because connections with the train are non-existent and no bus service reaches East Glacier, most travelers flying into Great Falls rent a vehicle to drive the 143 miles to Glacier National Park. With a flight arriving by late af-ternoon, you can be lounging at Glacier Park Hotel in East Glacier to watch the sunset that same day.

However, there's one reason to spend a wee bit of time in Great Falls—the bicentennial of Lewis and Clark's exploration of the northwest. The intrepid pair followed the Missouri through Great Falls and wandered around on the Blackfeet Reservation, coming within 25 miles of Marias Pass, one of the easiest passes over the Continental Divide. They missed it, along with Glacier Park, and instead crossed farther south on a much more difficult pass in much more difficult conditions. The bicentennial is celebrated through 2006, with events and exhibits. Regardless of the year of your visit, you should squeeze in the **Lewis and Clark National Historic Trail Interpretive Center** (4201 Giant Springs Rd., 406/727-8733, 9 A.M.–6 P.M. daily late May–Sept., 9 A.M.–5 P.M. Tues.–Sat. and Sun. noon–5 P.M. Oct.–May, adults $5, youths $2). The Forest Service–operated center is well worth a stop with its displays, live demonstrations, and multimedia shows.

If you have time to kill in Great Falls, take in the **C.M. Russell Museum** (400 13th St. N., 406/727-8787, www.cmrussell.org, 9 A.M.–6 P.M. daily May–Sept., 10 A.M.–5 P.M. Tues.–Sat. Oct.–Apr., adults $8, students $3). The museum collection celebrates the work of the famous western painter Charlie Russell (1864–1926), known for his depictions of cowboys, mountains, hunters, and horses, and who summered in his cabin on Glacier's Lake McDonald.

For travelers coming fairly prepared, Great Falls can work as a travel hub. But for those requiring camping equipment or RV rentals, none are available in the city itself nor on Glacier's east side. The nearest equipment and RV rentals are on the park's west side in West Glacier and Flathead Valley, both a convoluted detour out of the way from Great Falls.

Airport

Great Falls International Airport (GTF) (406/727-3404, www.gtfairport.com) receives air service from Delta/Sky West, Northwest,

Big Sky, and Horizon Air with arrivals from Seattle, Spokane, Minneapolis, Salt Lake City, and various Montana locations. Like the Kalispell airport, its international label comes from a couple charter flights from Canada. Located outside town, the airport is convenient for picking up on-site rental cars but requires hotel-provided shuttles or a taxi ride to access hotels and restaurants in town 10 minutes away.

Train

Amtrak's Empire Builder (800/USA-RAIL or 800/872-7245, www.amtrak.com) runs from Chicago westbound once daily past Glacier. (Chicago to East Glacier starts at $204.) From Great Falls, the closest westbound train depot is Shelby, 87 miles north. However, bus service no longer connects Great Falls to Shelby. If you want to hitchhike, which is legal in Montana, to Shelby, you can nab a really cheap ticket to East Glacier ($9–12 one-way) on the train that leaves daily at 5:22 P.M. From Shelby, the train arrives in East Glacier at 6:45 P.M., Essex at 7:41 P.M., West Glacier at 8:23 P.M., and Whitefish at 8:56 P.M. On this route, Amtrak tends to run late at least one-third of the time. Not just five minutes late, but up to several hours behind schedule, especially in winter. So, be prepared to contend with waiting and arriving in the middle of the night.

Special Amtrak deals are available. Kids ages 2–15 are half price, and seniors can usually get 15 percent discounts. Veterans, AAA and NARP members, military personnel, and students can also get 10–15 percent discounts: check Amtrak's website for details.

Amtrak is frequently threatened to have its federal funding yanked. If funding is cut, service on this route will be disrupted. Check with Amtrak for any changes to schedules and service.

Bus

As of summer 2005, Trailways' Rimrock Stages (800/255-7655, www.rimrocktrailways.com) discontinued its bus service from Great Falls to Shelby to connect with Amtrak, effectively stranding travelers seeking train connections. To make matters worse, no bus service runs between Great Falls and East Glacier. If you happen to get as far as Great Falls by one of the Rimrock Stage buses, you're stuck. You'll have to either hitchhike from here or rent a car.

Taxis and City Buses

Some hotels provide airport shuttle service. Otherwise, **Diamond Cab** (406/453-3241) is the only option to hop into town from the airport. Although you can bop around town on the city buses running 6:30 A.M. to 6:30 P.M. daily except for Saturday (9:30 A.M.–5:30 P.M. only) and Sunday (no service), the buses do not connect with the airport.

Car Rental

Great Falls has most national rental car chains. Alamo, Hertz, and Avis are right in the airport terminal. The airport's website (www.gtfairport.com) lists all local car-rental agencies in addition to those housed in the terminal. Most rental-car agencies with offices elsewhere than the airport terminal will either pick you up by shuttle or deliver your car to you.

After renting a car, two routes lead to East Glacier, both with spectacular views of the Rocky Mountain Front as it pops up off the plains. For easy interstate and highway driving, hop on I-15 heading north to Shelby and then U.S. Highway 2 westward to East Glacier (143 miles). Because of the straight and wide roads, folks who just want to get to Glacier quickly take this route. Usually driving time is 2.5 hours.

A much more interesting approach with a few less miles, however, strikes off through small rural Rocky Mountain Front towns. From Great Falls, head 10 miles north on I-15 to catch Highway 89 north toward Browning. The route travels past Freezeout Lake, known for its snow goose migration, and through Choteau, the epitome of a Rocky Mountain Front town with 1,700 residents, hunting, and grain elevators. In Browning, turn onto U.S. Highway 2 heading west to East Glacier. While this 139-mile route is a few miles shorter, the narrow road makes for

a little slower driving, so it can take about 2.75 hours to get to East Glacier.

Food and Accommodations

Great Falls has hotels and motels ranging from low end to moderately priced accommodations, but nothing too upscale. Most national hotel chains are downtown. For hotels offering airport shuttles, check the Great Falls Airport website (www.gtfairport.com) or the Great Falls Convention and Visitors Bureau (800/735-8535, www.greatfallscvb.visitmt.com).

For a taste of old Great Falls, two historic bed-and-breakfasts offer five rooms each, starting at $75–85. Neither allows young kids, inside smoking, or pets inside the building. **Charlie Russell Manor** (825 4th Ave. N., 406/455-1400 or 877/207-6131, www.charlie-russell.com) is a 7,000-foot restored 1916 manor house. The **Collins Mansion** (1003 2nd Ave. NW, 406/452-6798 or 877/452-6798, www.collinsmansion.com) is a renovated 1891 Queen Anne mansion listed on the National Register of Historic Places.

For a filling meal at a reasonable price, head for **MacKenzie River Pizza Company** (500 River Dr. S., 406/761-0085, open 11 A.M.–9 P.M. daily, until 10 P.M. Fri. and Sat. nights, closing time one hour later in summer, $7–20), Montana's creative answer to pizza chains. The restaurant serves cowboy nachos, giant salads and sandwiches, and of course eclectic pizzas. If you're out on the town, try one of Montana's microbrews—a Moose Drool Brown Ale if you like dark beers, or a Scape Goat Pale Ale, both from Big Sky Brewing.

CALGARY

Calgary, Alberta, may provide the perfect hub for some travelers depending on the city of origin, and if you schedule your trip in mid-July, you can take in one of the biggest rodeos around—the Calgary Stampede. However, travel from Calgary to Glacier or Waterton can be a challenge. No train connection is available. No bus route goes all the way to Waterton or Glacier. Most visitors traveling from Calgary

simply rent a vehicle. With an early afternoon flight arrival, you can be walking the beach at Waterton Lake in the evening.

Airport

Calgary International Airport (403/735-1200, www.calgaryairport.com) is a truly international airport with flights from Tokyo, London, and Frankfurt. It's a bustle of activity with restaurants, shopping, and over 25 airlines servicing the area. Airport shuttles connect with downtown, hotels, rental-car agencies, and the Greyhound Bus Terminal.

Because Calgary is still 149 miles (240 km) from Waterton, some visitors chop off part of the distance by flying via Air Canada (888/247-2262, www.aircanada.com) on to Lethbridge (www.lethbridgecountyairport.com), where they rent a car to drive the 87 miles (140 km) farther to Waterton.

Train

If you're traveling by **VIA Rail Canada** (800/VIA-RAIL or 800/842-7245, www.viarail.ca), you'll see lots of Canada, but have a difficult time getting to Waterton and Glacier. While Canadian trains hit Winnipeg and Vancouver, which are roughly the same latitude as Waterton, the railroad bypasses entirely Calgary, southern Alberta, and southeastern British Columbia. Instead, from Winnipeg, the railway cuts north to Edmonton and Jasper, before dropping south to Vancouver—essentially going about as far north of Waterton and Glacier as you can get. No trains connect anywhere near Waterton! The closest you can get is Edmonton, 183 miles (294 km) north of Calgary, which still puts you 332 miles (534 km) from Waterton. To get to Waterton, you can switch to bus or air transportation, but eventually you'll need to rent a car to get all the way here.

Bus

Greyhound Canada (403/265-9111 or 800/661-8747, www.greyhound.ca, no reservations accepted) services cities in southern Alberta, but not Waterton. Bus service runs several

times daily from Calgary International Airport to Lethbridge (CDN$70 round-trip). From here, you'll have to pick up a rental car at Lethbridge Airport to drive 87 miles (140 km) to Waterton Lakes National Park. Greyhound also runs daily buses from Calgary to Pincher Creek, but no farther: in Pincher Creek, you're stuck 30 miles from the park with no car rentals available. For VIA Rail Canada riders debarking in Edmonton, daily bus service runs to Calgary and then on to Lethbridge or Pincher Creek, but no closer.

Car Rental

Most major car-rental chains have desks inside the Calgary Airport terminal or within a shuttle hop down the road. Vehicles can be booked from home through American sister companies. Rates range CDN$60–90 per day, depending on the vehicle's size.

RV Rental

Two RV rental companies are within three kilometers (less than two miles) from the Calgary Airport and offer transfers from the airport and airport hotels: **Canada RV Rentals** (250/814-0251 or 866/814-0253, www.canada-rv-rentals.com) and **CanaDream** (403/291-1000 or 800/461-7368, www.canadream.com). Two larger chains also rent campers and RVs in Calgary: **Cruise Canada** (403/291-4963 or 800/327-7799, U.S. 800/327-7778, www.cruise-canada.com) and **Go West** (604/987-5288 or 800/661-8813, www.go-west.com).

RVing is a fun but somewhat pricey way (small rigs start at CDN$150 per day) to tour national parks without having to put tents up and down each day; however, be aware of Going-to-the-Sun Road's vehicle-length restrictions (21 feet). You may have to supplement your RV tour with shuttles or red bus tours to see the historic road. Only the smallest RVs will be able to cross the highway.

Equipment Rental

For those needing outdoor gear, **Calgary Outdoor Centre** (2500 University Dr. NW, 403/220-5038, www.calgaryoutdoorcentre.ca)

rents equipment for reasonable rates. It has gear for camping, backpacking, boating, fishing, snowshoeing, and skiing. Tents start at CDN$8, day packs CDN$3, GPS units CDN$7, stoves CDN$3, and sleeping bags CDN$5.50. Rafts, kayaks, canoes, mountain bikes, and car racks are also available as well as clothing, rain gear, and hiking boots. Call to reserve your gear ahead of time, a must during midsummer; a half-day nonrefundable deposit by credit card is required. When you pick up your gear, try it on to be sure it fits, and have the staff demonstrate how to use equipment you are unfamiliar with. You'll also need a driver's license or photo ID to rent gear.

Food and Accommodations

The airport terminal itself houses the pricey but extremely convenient **Delta Calgary Airport Hotel** (403/250-8722 or 877/814-7706, www.deltahotels.com, CDN$189–314). Within a few miles of the airport, major chain hotels range in rates from lower end (Travelodge, 403/291-1260 or 800/578-7878, www.travelodge.com, CDN$108 and up) to higher end (Hilton Garden Inn, 403/717-1999 or 877/782-9444, www.hiltongardeninn.com, CDN$179 and up). Some offer airport shuttles. For additional hotel information and reservations, check http://calgary.airporthotelguide.com or contact Tourism Calgary (403/263-8510, www.tourismcalgary.com).

The real budget-minded may want to head for a hostel. Hostelling International operates the **Calgary City Centre Hostel** (403/670-7580, www.hihostels.ca), with dorm beds costing CDN$30 per night. If you are planning on staying in hostels across Canada as part of your Glacier-Waterton trip, consider purchasing a Hostelling International $35 membership, which gives 10–15 percent discounts on nightly rates. Waterton Lakes National Park also offers lodging in a Hostelling International lodge, but Glacier National Park does not.

Canadian cuisine is somewhat bland, but a few Alberta specialties merit a taste test. Calgary is in the heart of cattle country; grass-fed Alberta beef graces menus in all forms. Buf-

falo, too. At the high end, it's amazingly good; at the lower end, it's still decent. Here a burger and fries may be different: Your fries may come with gravy on top. And contrary to many towns east of the Rocky Mountains where steak and

potato fare reigns, Calgary is much more internationally cosmopolitan with a good share of ethnic restaurants. Don't forget: Canada's 7 percent GST (Goods and Services Tax) will be added on lodging and food bills.

Getting Around

DRIVING

Driving in Glacier National Park is not particularly easy. Narrow roads built for cars in the 1930s barely fit today's SUVs, much less RVs and trailers. With no shoulders and sharp curves, roads require reduced speeds and shifting into second gear on extended descents to avoid that burning brake smell. Two roads cross the Continental Divide: Going-to-the-Sun Road bisects the park, while U.S. Highway 2 hugs Glacier's southern border. Both are two-laners; however, Going-to-the-Sun Road is the more difficult drive, climbing 1,500 feet higher on a skinnier and windier road than Highway 2. Going-to-the-Sun Road is open summers for about five months, while Highway 2 is open year-round.

Paved two-lane roads also lead to Two Medicine, St. Mary, Many Glacier, and Waterton. But don't have fantasies here: Just because roads are paved doesn't mean that they are smooth. Frost heaves and sinkholes pockmark them, bouncing passengers and slowing travel. Two nasty dirt roads lead up the North Fork Valley; on the east side, a dirt road leads into the Cut Bank Valley. Don't have illusions here either: There is no talk of paving these roads. In some places they are decent; in others they are as bad as they can be without requiring a four-wheel drive.

Service Stations

Gas up before you go! You won't find service stations on every corner here. Gas is available in West Glacier, East Glacier, St. Mary, Babb, and Waterton, but few of the stations can mend severely broken down vehicles. For big vehicle work, you'll need to hit Browning or Flathead Valley.

MAPS AND PLANNERS

Park maps that include both Glacier and Waterton are handed out at every entrance station and available at visitors centers, ranger stations, and online (www.nps.gov/glac). These maps are perfect for driving tours and perhaps a short walk or two. However, for those heading into the backcountry on day hikes and backpacking trips, a topographical map is more useful. Glacier's *Trails Illustrated* (includes Waterton) and the *USGS Glacier Park* (not including Waterton) topographical maps are both available through **Glacier Natural History Association** (406/888-5756, www.glacierassociation.org). For more detailed maps, USGS maps are available in the 7.5 Minute Series at Flathead Valley sporting goods store or through USGS (888/ASK-USGS or 888/275-8747, http://store.usgs.gov).

For hiking trails, area brochure maps (Many Glacier, Lake McDonald, Two Medicine, Logan Pass, and St. Mary) are available at ranger stations, visitors centers, hotel activity desks, and online. These do not have as much detail as topographical maps but can work in a pinch for day hikes on well-signed trails.

Yearly, the park service updates its *Glacier Vacation Planner,* a newspaper listing current campground, road, park, visitors center, border, trail, and safety concerns. Call the park for a mailed copy (406/888-7800) or the current edition is also online (www.nps.gov/glac).

SHUTTLES
Van Shuttles

Within Glacier, the park service recognizes one company to provide hiker shuttles: **Glacier Park, Inc.** (406/892-2525, www.glacierparkinc.com,

CELL PHONES

Probably one of the best inventions for emergencies, cell phones allow immediate access to help. However, in an area as mountainous as northwest Montana, they do not always work.

When driving, you may find dealing with a flat tire up the North Fork Valley requires more than a cell phone call to AAA. Depending on your location, your phone may not get service. Throughout much of Going-to-the-Sun Road and Glacier Park, cell-phone reception is sporadic to nonexistent.

Hikers and backpackers should carry the cell phone for emergencies, but do not rely on it as the sole means of rescue. High mountains and deep valleys often prevent reception. Be prepared to deal with emergencies and self-rescue, if possible.

When phones do work in Glacier, use of cell phones in the backcountry requires etiquette:

- Turn off ringers because phone noise catapults hikers and campers from a natural experience back into the hubbub of modern life.

- If you must make a call (and the phone does work), move away from campsites and other hikers to avoid disrupting their experience.

- In backcountry chalets, go outside and away from people.

- On trails, refrain from using phones in the presence of other hikers.

- Be considerate of other people in the backcountry and their desire to "get away from it all."

$8–40 depending on distance, kids half price, cash only). Hiker shuttles operate July–Labor Day between West Glacier and Many Glacier across Going-to-the-Sun Road and late May–late September on the east side connecting East Glacier, St. Mary, Many Glacier, and Waterton. Call or check online for current schedules. No reservations are taken, and you pay when you board.

For points adjacent to the park, **Flathead-** Glacier Transportation (406/892-3390 or 800/829-7039, www.fgtrans.com) offers shuttle services any time of the year provided roads are open ($70–220): Polebridge, Chief Mountain Customs, Two Medicine, St. Mary, or Many Glacier and Highway 2; the cost of the drop-off or pickup can be split between all the people in your group.

In Waterton, **Waterton Visitor Services** (Tamarack Village Square, 214 Mount View Rd., 403/859-2378, www.watertonvisitorservices.com, late May–early Oct., CDN$10–55) shuttles hikers to the popular Carthew-Alderson trailhead or to Chief Mountain Customs to catch Glacier's east-side shuttle.

Boat Shuttles

Hikers and backpackers also use tour boats as hiking shuttles to cut off several miles. In Glacier, **Glacier Park Boat Company** (406/257-2426, www.glacierparkboats.com, June–Sept., $5.25–6.75 one-way, kids 4–12 half price) carts hikers across Two Medicine Lake and in Many Glacier across Swiftcurrent and Josephine Lakes. Pay with cash at the docks; you do not need reservations for catching a return boat. If the last boat back is full, the boat company continues to run shuttles until all hikers are accommodated.

In Waterton, **Waterton Shoreline Cruises** (403/859-2362, www.watertoninfo.ab.ca, May–Sept., adults CDN$13–26, kids 4–12 CDN$6.50–9) accesses Crypt Lake Trailhead and trailheads at Goat Haunt.

TOURS
Bus Tours

Two bus-tour companies operate in Glacier Park, both traveling the scenic Going-to-the-Sun Road. The historic red buses with roll-back canvas tops are operated by **Glacier Park, Inc.** (406/892-2525, www.glacierparkinc.com, late May–late Sept., adults $28–70, kids half price, park entrance fees and meals not included). Tours depart from park lodges for Going-to-the-Sun Road or Waterton. The six-day Great Lodges of Glacier tour (adults $1,409, kids $688) runs weekly July–August.

Reservations are highly recommended for daily tours and required for the six-day Great Lodges tour.

Departing from East Glacier, St. Mary, or Rising Sun, **Sun Tours** (406/226-9220 or 800/786-9220, www.glaciersuntours.com, mid-May–mid-Oct., adults $35–55, kids ages 12 and under $15, kids under 5 free, park entrance fees not included) leads daily tours over Going-to-the-Sun Road in 25-passenger air-conditioned buses with huge windows. Interpretation is steeped in Blackfeet cultural history and park lore. In July and August, Sun Tours adds a tour from West Glacier.

Boat Tours

Five lakes in Waterton-Glacier International Peace Park have scenic boat tours. In Glacier, **Glacier Park Boat Company** (406/257-2426, www.glacierparkboats.com, June–Sept., $10.50–15, kids half price) operates daily boat tours on Lake McDonald, Two Medicine Lake, St. Mary Lake, and in Many Glacier on Swiftcurrent and Josephine Lakes. Departure times vary. Buy tickets (cash only) early at the docks in high season, for tour boats fill up. In Waterton, scenic boat tours travel down Waterton Lake across the international border. **Waterton Shoreline Cruises** (403/859-2362, www.watertoninfo.ab.ca, May–early Oct., adults CDN$26, teens CDN$13, kids 4–12 CDN$9, under 4 free) departs several times daily with a stop at Goat Haunt, U.S.A. (except in October). Purchase tickets at the dock.

BY RV
Road Restrictions

Going-to-the-Sun Road restricts RVs and trailers. From bumper to bumper, vehicles must be 21 feet or shorter to drive the road between Avalanche Campground on the west and Sun Point on the east. A truck or car and trailer combination must also be under 21 feet. The maximum width allowed, including mirrors, is 8 feet; maximum height is 10 feet. In spite of meeting width and height requirements, camper drivers will still feel pinched as they navigate the skinny lanes hemmed in by a ver-

tical 1,000-foot wall and a 3-foot-tall guardrail in construction zones.

Don't lose heart here, just because you travel by RV. You can still see the dramatic Going-to-the-Sun Road. Several options can still get you up the scenic highway: red bus tours, Sun Tours, and hiker shuttles, or rent a car in West Glacier, East Glacier, or St. Mary.

Camping

Several campgrounds inside the park can accommodate larger RVs and fifth wheels. Apgar can handle the largest RVs, up to 40 feet. Fish Creek, Many Glacier, and St. Mary have sites that can fit RVs up to 35 feet. Two Medicine can accommodate RVs up to 32 feet. Only the shorter RVs can fit into sites at Rising Sun (up to 25 feet), Avalanche (up to 26 feet), and Sprague Creek (up to 21 feet, but no towed units). Large units are not recommended at Bowman Lake, Cut Bank, Kintla Lake, Logging Creek, and Quartz Creek.

Campgrounds inside the park do not have hookups, nor do campgrounds in adjacent national forests or the North Fork. Waterton Lakes National Park, however, is an exception, for the Townsite Campground has hookups. If hookups are essential, plan on camping outside the park where most commercial campgrounds offer them. Hookups are available at West Glacier, East Glacier, St. Mary, Flathead Valley, outside Waterton Park, and along the Theodore Roosevelt Highway.

Disposal Stations

Seven locations inside park boundaries have disposal stations: Apgar, Fish Creek, Many Glacier, Rising Sun, St. Mary, Two Medicine, and Waterton. Many private campgrounds adjacent to the park have disposal stations at West Glacier, St. Mary, and East Glacier. Be aware that no disposal facilities are up the North Fork Valley.

Repairs

Should you need repair services, you'll need to drive to the Flathead Valley, where your best bet is to consult RV repairs in the yellow pages

and start calling to find who can fit you in to their repair schedule the soonest. If you cannot drive to the Flathead, try **Rocky Mountain Repair** (406/253-9694) or **On the Road RV** (406/755-1510 or 406/250-0175); both offer mobile services and can repair many things where you are, but you'll definitely pay more to have them come to Glacier.

BY BICYCLE

Glacier is a tough place to bicycle. No shoulders, narrow roads, curves, and drivers gawking at scenery instead of the road all shove the biker into a precarious position. With that caveat said, for a cyclist nothing competes with bicycling Going-to-the-Sun Road! It's the premier bicycling route here. Other roads surrounding Glacier also make good rides, particularly the 142-mile loop linking Going-to-the-Sun Road and Highways 89, 49, and 2. Roadie racers do it in one day; tourers ride the loop in two or three days.

Bike Trails

Designated bike trails are few and far between in Waterton-Glacier. In fact, Glacier has only two trails, both in the Apgar area—one paved, one dirt. No bicycles are allowed on any other backcountry trails in Glacier. In Waterton, however, four trails permit bicycles.

Campsites

Several of Glacier's campgrounds maintain campsites specifically for bikers and hikers: Apgar, Fish Creek, Sprague Creek, Avalanche, Rising Sun, St. Mary, Many Glacier, and Two Medicine. Held until 9 P.M., the sites are shared, holding up to eight people who pay $5 per person. If these sites are full, you must find a regular designated unoccupied tent site (which during high season late at night is impossible). Hiker-biker sites have special bear-resistant food storage containers.

Safety

Because of narrow, shoulderless roads, bikers should have some riding ability before hitting Glacier's roads. Although bicyclists on Going-to-the-Sun Road are fairly commonplace, many drivers are so agog at the view that they may not be fully conscious of your presence—which is a good reason to wear a helmet. For safe riding, put a flag on your bike and wear bright colors. Drainage grates, ice, and debris can throw bikes off balance quickly, so always wear a helmet, even when slogging up Going-to-the-Sun Road. Always ride on the right side of the road in single file. For added protection, be sure your bike has reflectors on both ends, and use lights in low light or early morning and late evening.

Restrictions

Because of high traffic and narrow lanes, Glacier enforces bicycling restrictions on Going-to-the-Sun Road's west side. Between June 15 and Labor Day, two sections of the road are closed 11 A.M.–4 P.M.: Apgar turnoff at the Lake McDonald's south end and Sprague Creek Campground; eastbound (going uphill only) from Logan Creek to Logan Pass. For planning, the ride from Sprague to Logan Creek takes about 45 minutes; the climb from Logan Creek to Logan Pass usually takes about three hours.

Repairs

For any bicycle repairs, you'll have to go to Flathead Valley where all the bike shops are. (See the *Flathead Valley* chapter for suggestions.) In a pinch, check with **Glacier Outdoor Center** (406/888-5454) in West Glacier, which rents bikes and may be able to help with a minor repair.

BY MOTORCYCLE

Motorcyclists relish riding Going-to-the-Sun Road. On sunny days, the ride is unparalleled; on inclement days, it can be bone-chilling. Many motorcyclists enjoy riding in Montana because the state requires helmets only for those 17 years old and younger. However, riding helmetless is something you may want to think twice about—most drivers on Going-to-the-Sun Road find their attention severely divided between the scenery and the road.

Motorcyclists are also allowed to use the shared biker-hiker campsites ($5 per person) at the park's major campgrounds. These are first-come, first-serve and held until 9 P.M.

If you need repairs, the Flathead Valley has several motorcycle shops. Some specialize in one brand over another, including Harley-Davidsons. Your best bet is to check under motorcycle repair in the yellow pages of the phone book to pick the appropriate service for your machine.

RESOURCES
Suggested Reading

DRIVING GUIDES

Peterson, Chris, ed. *Glacier National Park Auto Tours.* Columbia Falls, MT: Hungry Horse News, 2000. This large 16-page guide describes four auto tours in the park: Going-to-the-Sun Road and Many Glacier Road, Two Medicine and East Glacier, Waterton, and the North Fork. Each road details specific stops and what to see there.

Schmidt, Thomas. *Glacier-Waterton Lakes National Park Road Guide.* Washington, DC: National Geographic, 2004. A handy 93-page guide to driving the park's roads. Each section is complete with a map, nature notes, landscape features, and stops.

GEOLOGY

Alt, David, and Donald W. Hyndman. *Roadside Geology of Montana.* Missoula, MT: Mountain Press, 1986. Although Glacier's roads are treated minimally here, the diagrams and descriptions are useful even to non-geologists. It is the best resource for geology on roads outside the park.

Raup, Omar B., Robert L. Earhart, James W. Whipple, Paul E. Carrara. *Geology Along Going-to-the-Sun Road.* West Glacier, MT: Glacier Natural History Association, 1983. An easy-to-read 63-page geology guide for folks with no science background. Maps, 21 stops, and diagrams describe the geologic phenomenon on the historic highway along with great photos showing rock formations.

GRIZZLY BEARS

Chadwick, Doug. *True Griz.* San Francisco, CA: Sierra Club Books, 2003. True stories of four grizzly bears—their survival and deaths. Chadwick is a very reputable bear biologist.

Herrero, Stephen. *Bear Attacks: Their Causes and Avoidance.* Guilford, CT: The Lyons Press, 2002. Somewhat sensationalized with attention to gory detail, Herrero's book paints a picture of the myriad reasons for bear attacks while also covering safety and how to avoid attacks. Not for light sleepers who plan to go into the backcountry, but Herrero is one of the leading authorities on bear research.

McMillion, Scott. *Mark of the Grizzly.* Helena, MT: Falcon Press Publishing Company, 1998. McMillion tells the stories behind 18 different grizzly bear attacks. He doesn't shy away from the gore, nor does he become preachy or judgmental, but he does examine each attack in detail to determine what we learn about bears.

Schneider, Bill. *Bear Aware.* Helena, MT: Falcon Press Publishing Co., 2004. This handy little 96-page book is packed with advice on how to hike safely in bear country. One section tackles bear myths, debunking them with facts.

HISTORY

Buchholtz, C.W. *Men in Glacier.* West Glacier, MT: Glacier Natural History Association, 1976. It's a hard book to read because of its large size with small print (it would be much better as a regular-sized paperback), but it's thick with information on Glacier's human history, from early Native Americans to park rangers.

Djuff, Ray, and Chris Morrison. *Glacier's Historic Hotels and Chalets: View with a Room.* Helena, MT: Farcountry Press, 2001. Loaded with historical photos, this quasi-coffee-table book tells the story behind each of Glacier Park's lodges and chalets, including chalets no longer existing. A great background read for anyone who falls in love with Glacier's historic lodges.

Hanna, Warren L. *Montana's Many-Splendored Glacierland.* Grand Forks, ND: University of North Dakota Foundation, 1987. The fact that Hanna's book is somewhat outdated doesn't matter here; he covers historical detail that no one else does—from Marias Pass to Native Americans, dude-wranglers, and celebrity visitors. Historical photos are also included.

Holterman, Jack. *Let the Mountains Sing: Place Names of the Waterton-Glacier International Peace Park.* Kalispell, MT: Jack Holterman, 2003. A list of how peaks, passes, lakes, rivers, and valleys in Glacier acquired their names.

Houk, Rose. *Going-to-the-Sun: The Story of the Highway Across Glacier National Park.* Del Mar, CA: Woodland Press in conjunction with Glacier Natural History Association, 1984. In this small 48-page book, historical photos accompany a short narration of building the park's most famous road.

Lawrence, Tom. *Pictures, a Park, and a Pulitzer: Mel Ruder and the Hungry Horse News.* Helena, MT: Farcountry Press, 2000. Photos and stories from Lawrence, a Pulitzer Prize—winning journalist and editor for 32 years at the *Hungry Horse News.* Much of the history covers Glacier.

Schultz, James Willard. *Blackfeet Tales of Glacier National Park.* Helena, MT: Riverbend Publishing, 1916. Original Blackfeet stories collected by Schultz in the late 1800s, including the history of Two Medicine, Cut Bank, St. Mary, Swiftcurrent, and Chief Mountain.

NATURAL HISTORY

DeSanto, Jerry. *Logan Pass.* Guilford, CT: Globe Pequot Press, 1995. Gorgeous photos and short, easy-to-read whys of the Logan Pass environment, from grizzly bears to bikes, red buses, hiking, climbing, winter, wildflowers, and geology.

Fisher, Chris. *Birds of the Rocky Mountains.* Edmonton, AB: Lone Pine Publishing, 1997. A Lone Pine Field Guide for birds found in the Rocky Mountains—every species from raptors to waterfowl, songbirds to woodpeckers. Large drawings help with identification, and descriptions include details on size, range, habitat, nesting, and feeding. Details point out differences between similar species.

Fisher, Chris, Don Pattie, and Tamara Hartson. *Mammals of the Rocky Mountains.* Edmonton, AB: Lone Pine Publishing, 2000. A Lone Pine Field Guide for 91 species of animals found in the Rocky Mountains—a breeze to use. Each animal has details on physical description, behavior, habitat, food, denning, range, and young. Similar species are described to point out differences for identification.

Kershaw, Linda, Andy MacKinnon, and Jim Pojar. *Plants of the Rocky Mountains.* Edmonton, AB: Lone Pine Publishing, 1998. A Lone Pine Field Guide for eight types of flora found in the Rocky Mountains: trees, shrubs, wildflowers, aquatics, grasses, ferns, mosses, and lichens. Although the pictures are small, the detailed descriptions of appearance, season, and habitat help in identification. Notes

on each of the 1,300 species given include fun tidbits on the origin of names and Native American uses.

Kimball, Shannon Fitzpatrick, and Peter Lesica. *Wildflowers of Glacier National Park and Surrounding Areas.* Kalispell, MT: Trillium Press, 2005. One of the best regional flower guides. Flowers are categorized by color with big sharp photos allowing easy identification. Trees, ferns, and grasses are included, too.

Rockwell, David. *Glacier National Park: A Natural History Guide.* New York: Houghton Mifflin Company, 1995. A rather dense with detail but accurate description of Glacier Park's natural history not only on the big scale, but with personal narrative included, too. Rockwell covers geology, glaciers, flora, fauna, fires, and human impact on the ecosystem in the best in-depth natural history book available on the park.

Shaw, Richard J., and Danny On. *Plants of Waterton-Glacier National Parks and the Northern Rockies.* Missoula, MT: Mountain Press Publishing Co., 1979. The classic regional flower guide authored in part by the man for whom the Danny On Memorial Trail on Big Mountain is named.

Strickler, Dr. Dee. *Alpine Wildflowers, Forest Wildflowers,* and *Prairie Wildflowers.* Helena, MT: Falcon Press Publishing Co., 1990. Three books cover the flowers of different northern Rocky Mountain habitats. Descriptions and excellent photos make for easy identification.

Ulrich, Tom J. *Mammals of the Northern Rockies.* Missoula, MT: Mountain Publishing Company, 1990. Wildlife photographer Ulrich uses photos and descriptions to detail the life and habits of area mammals, from the little brown bat to the mountain goat. All the big megafauna are here—moose, bison, sheep, bear, wolf—as well as tiny pikas and mice.

OUTDOOR RECREATION

Arthur, Jean. *Montana Winter Trails: The Best Cross-Country Ski and Snowshoe Trails.* Guilford, CT: Globe Pequot Press, 2001. Trail descriptions include five detailed trips for Glacier and several more for Flathead Valley.

Duckworth, Carolyn, ed. *Hiker's Guide to Glacier National Park.* West Glacier, MT: Glacier Natural History Association, 1996. Covering Glacier only, not Waterton, the 110-page book describes popular trails. It's actually a reprint from a trail guide published in the 1970s.

Duckworth, Carolyn, ed. *Short Hikes and Strolls in Glacier National Park.* West Glacier, MT: Glacier Natural History Association, 1996. This short little 46-page book describes 16 favorite one- to four-mile walks in Glacier. Waterton is not included in this book.

Edwards, J. Gordon. *A Climber's Guide to Glacier Park.* Helena, MT: Falcon Press Publishing Co., 1995. The definitive guide to mountaineering in Glacier National Park. Edwards pioneered many of the routes up Glacier's peaks and is considered the park's patron saint of climbing. Routes cover technical climbs and off-trail scrambles. Includes climber safety info, too.

Good, Stormy R. *Day Hikes Around the Flathead* and *Nordic Dreams: Flathead Valley Nordic and Snowshoe Guide* Whitefish, MT: Flathead Guidebooks LLC, 2005. Two self-published books cover 85 day hikes and 33 cross-country ski and snowshoe trails. Both have maps, route descriptions, distances, and difficulty, with special emphasis on labeling trails as dog friendly or not. Available only through local bookstores and outdoor shops.

Molvar, Erik. *Best Easy Day Hikes in Glacier and Waterton Lakes.* Helena, MT: Falcon Press Publishing Co., 2001. A roundup of day hikes in both Glacier and Waterton. At half the size of his hiking guide book,

this is a shorter version focused only on day hikes with the emphasis on well-signed, less strenuous trails.

Molvar, Erik. *Hiking Glacier and Waterton Lakes National Parks*. Helena, MT: Falcon Press Publishing Co., 1996. The most definitive trail guide for Glacier and Waterton Parks. Molvar gives detailed trail descriptions, including maps and elevation charts, for all the popular trails inside the parks as well as less-traveled trails. Routes cover day hikes, overnights, and extended backpacking trips. Hiker safety, campsite details, and fishing information are also included.

Molvar, Erik. *Hiking Montana's Bob Marshall Wilderness*. Helena, MT: Falcon Press Publishing Co., 2001. A detailed trail guide covering the Great Bear, Bob Marshall, and Scapegoat wilderness areas. Trail descriptions include maps, elevation charts, and accurate information on how to find even the more difficult to locate trailheads.

Schneider, Russ. *Fishing Glacier Park*. Helena, MT: Falcon Press Publishing Co., 2002. The most definitive fishing guide to Glacier. Schneider explains what flies to use to catch certain fish, where you'll catch arctic grayling or westslope cutthroat trout, and where you'll get skunked.

Internet Resources

GLACIER PARK

Glacier National Park
www.nps.gov/glac
The official website for Glacier National Park. It provides information on park conditions, roads, campsites, trails, history, and more. Five webcams update every few minutes. Check in the In Depth section to access the online visitor center, which includes downloadable maps, publications, and backcountry permit applications as well as a Going-to-the-Sun Road status report updated daily.

Glacier Natural History Association
www.glacierassociation.org
The best resource for books, maps, posters, and cards on Glacier Park. A portion of the proceeds from book sales are donated back to the park.

Northern Rocky Mountain Research Center
www.nrmrc.usgs.gov
The research center works under the United States Geological Survey. The website contains current research in Glacier on grizzly bears, glaciers, weather, bighorn sheep, and amphibians.

The Glacier Fund
www.glacierfund.org
As an official nonprofit park partner, The Glacier Fund works with the National Park Foundation to raise money to assist with wildlife research, historic preservation, trails, and education to preserve Glacier's natural and cultural history. It supports what government funds cannot cover.

The Glacier Institute
www.glacierinstitute.org
An educational nonprofit park partner, The Glacier Institute presents programs for kids and adults in field settings taught by expert instructors. Field classes take place in Glacier as well as surrounding ecosystems.

Glacier National Park Associates
www.nps.gov/gla/partners/gnpa.htm
This volunteer nonprofit assists with historic preservation and trail work and is always looking for volunteers to help for a few days on projects.

National Park Service Reservation Center
http://reservations.nps.gov
For reservations in U.S. national parks, log on

to this website. Two campgrounds in Glacier— Fish Creek and St. Mary—take reservations from this service.

WATERTON PARK

Waterton Lakes National Park
www.pc.gc.ca/waterton
The official website for Waterton. It contains most of the basic park information on camping, hiking, and Parks Canada–operated services, but not the commercial services in Waterton Townsite.

Waterton Lakes National Park Information Guide
www.watertoninfo.ab.ca
Useful park information on boat tours, hiking, bicycling, dining, and lodging includes links for many of the commercial services in Waterton Townsite.

National Park Service Reservation Center
www.pccamping.ca
Log on to make reservations at Waterton's Townsite campground and other Canadian national parks.

Waterton Chamber of Commerce
www.watertonchamber.com
This website covers dining, lodging, recreation, visitor services, and camping for Waterton. Some services adjacent to the park are also included.

Waterton Park Information Services
www.watertonpark.com
This website details lodging, dining, services, and recreation, but also includes maps and a great history section.

FLATHEAD VALLEY

Flathead Valley Convention and Visitors Bureau
www.fcvb.org
The Flathead Valley's tourism board covers

info on Kalispell, Columbia Falls, Whitefish, Bigfork, Lakeside, Flathead Lake, and ski resorts. You'll find recreation, lodging, dining, and special events.

MONTANA TRAVEL

Glacier Country
www.glaciermt.com
The official state travel website for northwest Montana. You can find lodging, dining, and activity information here, and it's easy to navigate by activity or location.

Montana Travel
www.visitmt.com
The official travel website for Montana. You'll find access to the state's activities, lodging, dining, and recreation by location or activity.

Montana Department of Transportation
www.mdt.state.mt.us
This is the best website for travel advisories and road conditions for Montana. Be aware, however, that as of 2005 Glacier's interior roads are not yet included on the website, although the federal and state governments are negotiating how to include them.

Lewis and Clark
www.lewisandclark.state.mt.us
Montanans celebrate the bicentennial of Lewis and Clark in 2006. Not only does this website give a good chronicle of the pair's expedition in Montana and planned events around the state, but it also includes links to Montana historic sites, recreation, travel, lodging, dining, museums, and golf.

Flathead National Forest
www.fs.fed.us/r1/flathead
At the official website for Flathead National Forest, you'll find info on campgrounds, fishing, wilderness areas, cabin rentals, ski areas, trails, and other recreation. With some subjects, the website has yet to catch up to modern times with detailed information.

Montana Fish, Wildlife, and Parks
www.fwp.state.mt.us

Up-to-date fishing and hunting information, licenses, state park, and wildlife refuge details for Montana.

CANADIAN TRAVEL

Alberta Travel Guides
www.albertatravel.ca

Heavily funded by Alberta real estate agencies, the site does have some useful travel information if you can wade through the advertising.

Travel Alberta Canada
www.travelalberta.com

The province's official portal to Alberta resorts, parks, ski areas, festivals, events, cities, outdoor recreation, and touring. It's easy to navigate by location or activity to find what you want.

Alberta Travel and Tourism Guide
www.discoveralberta.com

You can access Alberta travel information here, but it all comes in the preformatted package of the WorldWeb network, which is not as easy to navigate or understand as the Travel Alberta website.

Alberta Transportation
www.tu.gov.ab.ca

Check here for postings of Alberta's road construction, advisories, and closures.

British Columbia Transportation
www.gov.bc.ca/tran

Road reports update travel information, closures, construction, and weather for British Columbia. Webcams will give you a firsthand look.

Akamina-Kishinena Provincial Park
www.gov.bc.ca/bcparks

Information on recreation, camping, and hiking in Akamina-Kishinena Provincial Park. Maps and a photo gallery, too.

Fishing Alberta
www.fishalberta.com

Although this is a television-sponsored website rather than an official government site, it is easier to navigate to find current license info, stocked waters, and regulations.

Index

HIKING

MAP SYMBOLS

▭	Expressway	🄲	Highlight	✗	Airfield	⚲	Golf Course
▭	Primary Road	○	City/Town	✗	Airport	🄿	Parking Area
▭	Secondary Road	◉	State Capital	▲	Mountain	▰	Archaeological Site
▭	Unpaved Road	⊛	National Capital	✛	Unique Natural Feature	⛪	Church
- - - -	Trail	★	Point of Interest			⛽	Gas Station
·········	Ferry	•	Accommodation	🌊	Waterfall	〰	Glacier
┼─┼─	Railroad	▼	Restaurant/Bar	▲	Park	▱	Mangrove
▭	Pedestrian Walkway	■	Other Location	🚩	Trailhead	▱	Reef
▥	Stairs	Λ	Campground	⛷	Skiing Area	▱	Swamp

CONVERSION TABLES

$$°C = (°F - 32) / 1.8$$
$$°F = (°C \times 1.8) + 32$$

1 inch = 2.54 centimeters (cm)
1 foot = .304 meters (m)
1 yard = 0.914 meters
1 mile = 1.6093 kilometers (km)
1 km = .6214 miles
1 fathom = 1.8288 m
1 chain = 20.1168 m
1 furlong = 201.168 m
1 acre = .4047 hectares
1 sq km = 100 hectares
1 sq mile = 2.59 square km
1 ounce = 28.35 grams
1 pound = .4536 kilograms
1 short ton = .90718 metric ton
1 short ton = 2000 pounds
1 long ton = 1.016 metric tons
1 long ton = 2240 pounds
1 metric ton = 1000 kilograms
1 quart = .94635 liters
1 US gallon = 3.7854 liters
1 Imperial gallon = 4.5459 liters
1 nautical mile = 1.852 km

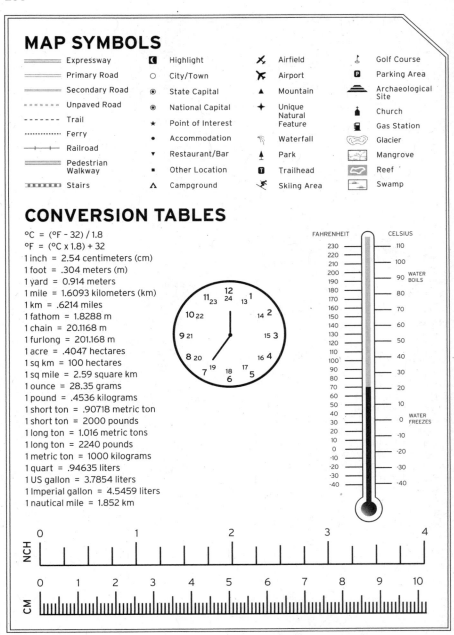

plugs
1st aide   flashlight   cameras
Pepper Spray   suits
                           hats
Bells

Walking Stix   compass
Back Pack   water bottle

Bug Spray   journal
Block · Sun Spray   little
                     tri pod
Layers   Binocular

Good Shoes   Socks

Plastic Bags
non smell towellttes
snacks cheese cracker granola
fruit trail mix

Wed 6 TSR
Hike St Marys Fall
Lunch Creek
Many Glacier
{ Two Sisters
{ Park Cafe ☆ Pie!

Thurs Many Glacier
Lake Hike
Chill
Make } Snow Goose Rest
reservation } St Marys

Fri Return Car
Train Home

Fri Train
Sat MT Pine Motel
mexican dinner
car

Sun look Glacier Hotel

Breakfast/Lunch Essex
Camas/North Fork Road
10:00 Hike Avalanche/Cedar
3:00 apgar village
5:00 Dinner North Pole

Mon Horses Hike
Binocular Sperry Glacier Chalet
Plastic Clothes Hike to Glacier
sunglasses Buy

Tues Hike down 6.5 mile
Belton Cabin
late afternoon Lake Boat Tour McDonald
Dinner Belton

www.moon.com

For helpful advice on planning a trip, visit www.moon.com for the **TRAVEL PLANNER** and get access to useful travel strategies and valuable information about great places to visit. When you travel with Moon, expect an experience that is uncommon and truly unique.

**MOON GLACIER
NATIONAL PARK**

Avalon Travel Publishing
1400 65th Street, Suite 250
Emeryville, CA 94608, USA
www.moon.com

Editor: Sabrina Young
Series Manager: Kathryn Ettinger
Acquisitions Editor: Rebecca K. Browning
Copy Editor: Deana Shields
Graphics Coordinator: Tabitha Lahr
Production Coordinators: Tabitha Lahr,
  Darren Alessi
Cover and Interior Designer: Gerilyn Attebery
Map Editor: Kat Smith
Cartographers: Kat Bennett, Christine Markiewicz
Cartography Manager: Mike Morgenfeld
Indexer: Rachel Kuhn

ISBN (10): 1-56691-950-9
ISBN (13): 978-1-56691-950-0
ISSN: 1557-6299

Printing History
1st Edition – April 2006
5 4 3 2

Text © 2006 by Becky Lomax.
Maps © 2006 by Avalon Travel Publishing, Inc.
All rights reserved.

Some photos and illustrations are used by permission
and are the property of the original copyright
owners.

Front cover photo: Crackee Lake, Glacier National
Park, © Shannon Nace/Lonely Planet Images
Title page photo: © Becky Lomax

Printed in Canada by Transcontinental

KEEPING CURRENT

If you have a favorite gem you'd like to see included in the next edition, or see anything
that needs updating, clarification, or correction, please drop us a line. Send your com-
ments via email to feedback@moon.com, or use the address above.